THE
BURDEN
OF BROWN

THE
BURDEN
OF BROWN
*Thirty Years
of School Desegregation*

RAYMOND WOLTERS

THE UNIVERSITY OF TENNESSEE PRESS

KNOXVILLE

PUBLICATION OF THIS BOOK
has been aided by a grant from the University of Delaware.

Library of Congress Cataloging in Publication Data

Wolters, Raymond, 1938–
    The burden of Brown.

    Bibliography: p.
    Includes index.
    1. Discrimination in education—Law and legislation—
United States. 2. School integration—United States—
Case studies. I. Title
KF4155.W64 1984   344.73′0798   83-21620
ISBN 0-87049-423-6   347.304798

To Mary

CONTENTS

Introduction   3

PART ONE   Washington: Showcase of Integration   9

PART TWO   Massive Resistance in Prince Edward County,
                Virginia   65

PART THREE   Beyond Freedom of Choice:
                Clarendon County, South Carolina   129

PART FOUR   The Bus Stops Here:
                New Castle County, Delaware   175

PART FIVE   Back in Topeka   253

Conclusion   273

Notes   291

Bibliographical Note   329

Acknowledgments   333

Index   335

TABLES

1   Enrollments by Race, Washington, D.C., Public
Schools, 1951–1981   16

2   Reading Scores, Washington, D.C., Public Schools,
1971–1974   54

3   Average Annual Salary of White and Black Teachers,
Virginia, 1940–1941 to 1949–1950   68

4   Index of Relative Status of Virginia's Black Schools   69

5   Reading and Math Scores, Prince Edward Public
Schools, 1972–1980   121

6   Test Results, Summerton Public Schools (1978) and
Clarendon Hall (1980)   171

7   Enrollments by Race, Wilmington Public Schools,
1954–1976   182

8   Comprehensive Tests of Basic Skills, Wilmington
Public Schools, Spring 1976   188

9   Enrollments by Race, Wilmington Public Schools,
1957   192

10   Enrollment by Race, P.S. du Pont High School,
1957–1977   194

11   Enrollment by Race, Wilmington High School,
1957–1977   196

12   Enrollments by Race, Kent and Sussex Counties,
1963–1964   203

13   Enrollment by Race, New Castle County "Desegregation Area" and Predecessor Components,
1971–1981   247

THE
BURDEN
OF BROWN

INTRODUCTION

Because it provided the impetus for a major change in American race relations, the Supreme Court's decision in *Brown v. Topeka Board of Education* (1954) is one of the most important events in the recent history of the United States. It is a landmark that separates Jim Crow America from modern America.[1] *Brown* prohibited the use of racial discrimination to separate the races in the public schools of Topeka, Kansas, but it was clear from the outset that the Court's decision eventually would affect public education throughout the United States. Similar cases from Delaware, South Carolina, and Virginia were consolidated with *Brown* on appeal, and a fifth case decided the same day held that public schools could no longer be segregated in Washington, D.C.

This book describes how things have worked out in the school districts where desegregation began. The experience of Topeka, ironically, has been less illuminating than that of the sister school districts. Compliance with the Supreme Court's order was readily achieved in the Kansas community, where blacks initially made up only 8.3 percent of the population. In the other districts, where blacks constituted between 25 and 90 percent of the students, there was protracted litigation as the communities struggled to comply with — or in some instances to evade — the Court's rulings. I have focused attention on the sister school districts because their experience illustrates how the law changed and how desegregation has been redefined.

In the 1950s desegregation meant eliminating a state-sanctioned policy of separating children solely on the basis of race. By the 1970s desegregation had come to mean racial balance. "We are under a Constitution," Chief Justice Charles Evans Hughes once remarked, "but the Constitution is what the judges say it is."[2] Nothing illustrates this point better than the fact that the Constitution, without being relevantly amended, first permitted racial discrimination in public schools to separate the races, then prohibited such

3

discrimination, and now sometimes requires discrimination in order to achieve racial balance.

In *Brown* the black plaintiffs persuaded the Supreme Court to repudiate an earlier decision, *Plessy v. Ferguson* (1896,) in which the Court had held that racial segregation did not violate the equal protection clause of the Fourteenth Amendment if the separate facilities were substantially equal.[3] The plaintiffs' principal argument was that official classification based on race placed the stamp of government approval on the doctrine of black inferiority. "That the Constitution is color-blind is our dedicated belief," read a key sentence in a brief submitted to the Court in behalf of the black plaintiffs.[4]

When questioned during the oral argument, attorneys for the National Association for the Advancement of Colored People (NAACP) repeatedly stated that they were "not asking for affirmative relief. . . . The only thing that we ask for is that the state-imposed racial segregation be taken off, and to leave the county school board . . . to assign children on any reasonable basis they want to assign them on." "What we want from this Court is the striking down of race." "Do not deny any child the right to go to the school of his choice on the grounds of race or color within the normal limits of your districting system. . . . do not assign them on the basis of race. . . . If you have some other basis . . . any other basis, we have no objection. But just do not put in race or color as a factor."[5]

As a secondary theme the NAACP maintained, on the basis of evidence drawn from the social sciences, that black children were psychologically injured if they attended segregated schools. Regardless of the condition of the separate facilities, the NAACP said, segregation had a belittling effect upon the blacks' self-esteem. Blacks who attended segregated schools allegedly developed a sense of inferiority that adversely affected their motivation and impaired their educational development. Lawyers for the plaintiffs also said that under segregation it was difficult for blacks to learn the social skills needed for easy interaction with whites, and they faulted the system for denying children the opportunity to develop mutually respectful racial attitudes.

The demand for color-blind application of the laws could have been satisfied if the Court had banned racial discrimination and had required that students be admitted to public schools on a nonracial basis. If black children were injured by lack of contact with whites, however, racial mingling seemed to be called for. The first remedy could be designated "desegregation," while the second, affirmative policy could be denominated "integration." Yet, in an unfortunate case of semantic confusion, the terms have been used synonymously since 1954.

The confusion is partly a result of an ambiguity in the Supreme Court's

Brown opinion. Segregation was found to deny equal protection of the laws since it amounted to official sanction for the invidious doctrine of black inferiority. But although the litigation involved state laws that required or permitted racial segregation, the Court equivocated when it came to the question of whether it was prohibiting separation that was not the result of official state policy. At one point in his opinion for the Court, Chief Justice Earl Warren wrote that the case concerned the "segregation of children in public schools *solely* on the basis of race"—thereby implying that it was no concern of the Constitution if the races failed to mingle because of nonracial factors such as choice or geographical residence. Elsewhere in the opinion, however, the chief justice boldly asserted, with no qualification concerning the origin or context of the separation, that "separate educational facilities are inherently unequal" and generate "a feeling of inferiority as to [the blacks'] status in the community that may affect their hearts and minds in a way unlikely ever to be undone."[6] The ringing rhetoric would be remembered long after most people had forgotten the factual setting of the case.

Some students of the Warren Court have subsequently expressed the wish that the chief justice had simply said that race is an inherently arbitrary classification—an official insult that tainted the education of black children. But the decision in *Brown* was justified on two separate but related grounds. The Court's major premise was that official segregation constituted a denial of equal protection, while its minor premise held that racial isolation damaged the confidence of black youths and distorted their self-image. Instead of merely overruling *Plessy,* the Court engaged in sociological theorizing that suggested that actual racial mixing was called for, not just an end to state-enforced segregation. Shortly after *Brown*, black psychologist Kenneth B. Clark observed that "it would be a mistake to assume that the content and spirit of the . . . decision apply only to the Southern states that have laws which require segregation. As I understand the decision, the United States Supreme Court has clearly stated that segregation itself damages the personality of human beings. The court did not limit itself to the statement that only legal segregation is detrimental to the human personality. It was explicit . . . in stating that various forms of racial segregation are damaging to the human spirit."[7]

The full ramifications of *Brown* were not apparent immediately. Until 1968, federal courts generally held that there was no violation of the Constitution if the races were separated by adventitious circumstances rather than by official classification. In a 1955 *Brown* opinion ordering the school districts to proceed toward desegregation "with all deliberate speed," the Supreme Court itself announced that "the fundamental principle" of *Brown* was that "racial discrimination in public education is unconstitutional."[8]

The idea that official racial classification was prohibited also seemed to be implied in *Bolling v. Sharpe,* decided with *Brown*, in which the Supreme Court forbade racial segregation in the public schools of the District of Columbia. Because the Fourteenth Amendment limits the power of the states, the equal protection clause does not apply to the federal government. In striking down segregation in the federal District, however, the Supreme Court held that racial classifications were so arbitrary and unfair as to amount to a denial of due process of the law. "'The Constitution of the United States, in its present form, forbids . . . discrimination by the General Government, or by the States, against any citizen because of his race.'"[9]

That *Brown* prohibited racial discrimination also seemed to be the message in a series of cryptic decisions in which the Court invalidated laws requiring segregation of parks, buses, restaurants, and the like. Throughout the land inferior federal courts affirmed that racial classifications were prohibited but that there was no violation of the Constitution if states uniformly administered programs that limited admission to schools on the basis of factors other than race—factors such as individual aptitude, geographical residence, or personal choice. The Constitution required only that each person be treated as an individual without regard to race. Stated most fluently, perhaps, by Circuit Judge John J. Parker in *Briggs v. Elliott* (1955), this point of view is frequently called the *Briggs* dictum:

> It is important that we point out exactly what the Supreme Court has decided and what it has not decided. . . . all that it has decided, is that a state may not deny to any person on account of race the right to attend any school that it maintains. This, under the decision of the Supreme Court, the state may not do directly or indirectly; but if the schools which it maintains are open to children of all races, no violation of the Constitution is involved even though the children of different races voluntarily attend different schools, as they attend different churches. Nothing in the Constitution or in the decision of the Supreme Court takes away from the people the freedom to choose the schools they attend. The Constitution, in other words, does not require integration. It merely forbids discrimination. It does not forbid such segregation as occurs as the result of voluntary action. It merely forbids the use of governmental power to enforce segregation. . . .[10]

Despite the reassurance of the *Briggs* dictum, for several years *Brown* was subjected to heated criticism, especially in the South. Segregationists warned that racial mixing would do more harm than good, and strict constructionists said it was wrong to have important social changes imposed by unelected judges. Yet the principle that the government should not discriminate among citizens on the basis of race was so appealing in the middle of the twentieth century that *Brown* won general acceptance. Most Americans opposed school assignments and other legal distinctions based on race. They thought it was unfair to enforce the separation of any group from the mainstream of society.

Responding to this sentiment, Congress in 1964 enacted a civil rights law that placed the legislature's stamp of approval on the emerging consensus. Section 407 authorized the attorney general to initiate school desegregation actions, and Section 401 defined desegregation as follows: "'Desegregation' means the assignment of students to public schools and within such schools without regard to their race, color, religion, or national origin, but 'desegregation' shall not mean the assignment of students to public schools in order to overcome racial imbalance." [11]

Yet the Civil Rights Act was hardly in place when the Supreme Court changed colors. In *Green v. New Kent County* (1968) the Court held that *Brown*, when illuminated by its underlying psychological rationale, required districts that had discriminated in the past to take affirmative action to achieve balanced racial enrollments. Rejecting the *Briggs* holding that racially neutral methods of assigning pupils constituted full compliance with *Brown*, the court held that school districts in the southern and border states must achieve as much racial mixing as was possible. Purporting to do no more than apply the holding of *Brown* to the case at hand, the Supreme Court accepted the view that the Constitution is color conscious rather than color blind. After *Green,* desegregation no longer meant assignment without regard to race; it meant assignment according to race to produce greater racial mixing. A constitutional provision that was thought to have prohibited racial assignments became the basis for requiring racial assignments. [12]

The judicial reinterpretation of desegregation affected both liberalism and conservatism, precipitated a crescendo of mounting criticism of "government by judiciary," and contributed to a major realignment in national politics. Sensing the possibility of achieving racial balance by judicial decree, many liberals endorsed the concept of government by an unelected judicial elite. At the same time, many parents of ordinary means found liberal social engineering so distasteful that they made an alliance with traditional vested interests. The liberals won most of the court cases, but parents resisted judicial reconstruction by moving to the suburbs, by retreating to private schools, and by becoming part of a new conservative coalition that now threatens to curb the federal courts.

In preparing this study I have found much that is discouraging about what has happened to public education and to the Constitution. In the *Brown* districts, education has suffered grievously from naively liberal court orders, from the influence of progressive education, and from the defiant and irresponsible behavior of some students. The Constitution has also suffered as judges have arrogated the right to make social policy. Segregation was anachronistic in the middle of the twentieth century, but in a democracy social reform should be undertaken by the people's elected representatives, not by unelected judges. I further believe the Supreme Court erred in policy as well as in prerogative when it moved from color blindness to color consciousness and began to impose remedies that require racial balance. My own point of view is so different from the prevailing wisdom that it seems advisable to state it candidly at the outset and then to present the evidence in detail and with a minimum of didactic intrusions.

PART ONE

WASHINGTON:
SHOWCASE OF INTEGRATION

I

In *Bolling v. Sharpe*, decided with *Brown* on 17 May 1954, the Supreme Court ruled that the 105,000 public school students of Washington, D.C., could no longer be separated on the basis of race. The equal protection clause of the Fourteenth Amendment applied only to states and their subdivisions and not to the federal District of Columbia, but the Court nevertheless asserted that "segregation in public education is not reasonably related to any proper governmental objective." Racial segregation in schools was said to be so arbitrary and unfair as to violate the guarantee of the Fifth Amendment that the federal government would not deprive citizens of liberty without due process of law. In view of its decision that the Fourteenth Amendment prohibited states from maintaining racially segregated public schools, the Court considered it "unthinkable that the same Constitution would impose a lesser duty on the Federal Government."[1]

Earlier in 1954 a study by the Fund for the Advancement of Education had found that "the Negro division of the Washington school system has remained inferior to the white." Teachers' salaries were the same in the black and white schools, and so were the standards of promotion, the length of the school year, the textbooks, and most courses of study. Expenditure per student, however, differed significantly; in the last year of segregation the District spent an average of $240.27 for the education of each white student and an average of only $186.17 for the instruction of each black student.[2]

Congressional regulations stipulated that school funds in the District should be allocated between the races according to the ratio of black and white students, as reported in the most recent census. This method of allocation prevented gross inequity but failed to take account of a major trend.

For twenty years there had been a noticeable exodus of whites to nearby suburbs in Maryland and Virginia, and many whites who remained in the District sent their children to private schools. At the same time, a growing number of black families, many with school-age children, moved into the District, and between 1930 and 1950 the proportion of black students in the public schools increased from 33 percent to 50 percent. Blacks were inevitably shortchanged by a method that apportioned money according to the racial balance that existed at the time of the last diennial census. In 1940, for example, 34 percent of the school-age residents of the District were black, and the black schools consequently were assigned that share of the total school budget. By 1947, however, black children made up 45 percent of the public school students.[3]

The overcrowding of black schools was aggravated when World War II interrupted school construction, while the great migration of blacks continued unabated. The scarcity of building materials in the immediate postwar period complicated the situation and left blacks with a critical shortage of classrooms while many white schools were underenrolled. Between 1941 and 1947 about 10 percent of the black students in the District were assigned to half-day schedules in either the morning or afternoon, and some were enrolled in a staggered triple shift.[4]

The District school board annually transferred a few schools from the white to the colored division, and when building resumed in 1947, black schools received 72 percent of the funds for new construction. The black schools in the nation's capital were more generously financed than public schools in most states. Nevertheless, as George D. Strayer of Columbia University demonstrated in 1949, in an exhaustive 980-page report, overcrowding had led to important disparities in the black and white schools.[5] In Washington, separate had not been equal.

In September of 1947 Marguerite Carr, the daughter of the president of the Browne Junior High School PTA, was one of 1,638 black pupils enrolled in Browne. The school had been built to accommodate approximately 900 students, and authorities had adjusted to the larger enrollment by devising a double shift. Pupils assigned to the morning session attended school from 8 A.M. until 12:30 P.M., and those in the afternoon session were in school from 12:45 to 5:15 P.M. But the nearby white junior high school, Eliot, operated on a single shift and had 150 unoccupied places. Several Browne parents, angered by this state of affairs, joined the Carrs in a class action suit to have their children admitted to Eliot. Although District school authorities managed to eliminate the double shift at Browne and all other black junior highs in February 1948, the black parents persisted in their contention that facilities at their school were substandard.[6]

In a 2-to-1 decision reported in February 1950, the Court of Appeals for the District of Columbia ruled against the black plaintiffs. The court's majority noted that the curricula and facilities in the black and white schools were equal in many respects and that the plaintiffs had not contended that there was any violation of the statutory provisions for appropriating educational funds. The court admitted that the black schools were seriously overcrowded but attributed this to a number of factors and noted that many white schools had implemented double shifts in the 1920s when the Caucasian population of the District had increased sharply. "So far as the facts and circumstances shown by this record are concerned," the court concluded, "it appears that the treatment accorded these Negro plaintiffs . . . would have been accorded them had they been white."[7]

Writing for the court's majority, Judge E. Barrett Prettyman denied that separation of the races by itself, apart from inequality of treatment, was forbidden by the Constitution. "Since the beginning of human history," Prettyman observed, "no circumstance has given rise to more difficult and delicate problems than has the coexistence of different races in the same area." Prettyman believed the problems were soluble only through experimentation and adjustment to current necessities, and he carefully documented his claim that the framers of the Constitution did not "foreclose legislative treatment of the problem in this country."[8]

The dissenting judge, Henry Edgerton, considered the pattern of inequality unjust and wrote a prophetic comment that the Supreme Court would later endorse. "School segregation is humiliating to Negroes," Edgerton asserted. "It 'brands the Negro with the mark of inferiority and asserts that he is not fit to associate with white people.'" Racial segregation fostered prejudice, hindered mutual acquaintance, and was so arbitrary that it "cannot reasonably be thought to serve a public purpose." The Constitution does not permit public officials to stigmatize citizens in this fashion, nor does it permit the courts to wait for Congress to act, said the judge.[9]

Judge Edgerton's dissent reinforced the position of black attorneys who wished to strike boldly at segregation itself rather than at the unequal facilities of separate institutions. One such attorney was James M. Nabrit, a law professor at Howard University and a graduate of Morehouse College and Northwestern University law school. When Nabrit filed pleadings in 1951 in behalf of twelve-year-old Spottswood Bolling, Jr., there was no claim that Bolling and the other blacks were attending schools unequal to those provided for whites. "Their plainly inferior facilities were entirely beside the point, as Nabrit framed the case. He based it entirely upon the fact of segregation itself. The burden of proof, he argued, was not upon the black plaintiffs but upon the District government to show that there was any reasonable basis for or public purpose in racial restrictions on school admission." In its *Bolling* decision, the Supreme Court agreed. Since it could find no compelling justification for segregation, the high court concluded that the District's black students had been deprived of liberty without due process of law.[10]

Young Bolling had no difficulty transferring from the previously all-black Spingarn High School, where he had enrolled in 1953, to the formerly white Eastern High School, where he matriculated in 1954. Even before the Supreme Court handed down its momentous decision, Superintendent Hobart M. Corning had made plans for desegregation, and on 25 May 1954, only eight days after the *Bolling* decision, the District's Board of Education adopted a desegregation policy. The press celebrated "massive compliance" when, on 13 September 1954, the Washington public schools opened with mixed classes and faculties throughout the District.

Under Superintendent Corning's plan for desegregation, geographic boundaries were traced around each school and the children who lived within the boundaries of each were assigned to that school. Elementary school districts were kept sufficiently compact so that most youngsters could walk to school. Yet, because of racial separation in housing patterns, the racial enrollment in most schools differed from the overall ratio in the District.

Integrationists would later find fault with the policy of neighborhood school assignments. In 1954, however, the word "desegregation" did not imply that black and white students should be balanced proportionately in each school and classroom. No such balance existed in Washington's schools, but members of the two races mixed together in various proportions at more than two-thirds of the District's schools. Washington was generally considered a model of desegregation that the rest of the nation might emulate. In 1955 the Supreme Court itself indicated that desegregating school districts should assign pupils to schools on the basis of their place of residence rather than on the basis of their race.[11]

II

Desegregation got off to a good start in Washington, although its first days were not without incident. There was a two-day student strike at McKinley High School, where whites complained about blacks' cursing and requesting the telephone numbers of white girls. "Integration Will Lead to Intermarriage," one placard proclaimed. A more serious situation developed at Anacostia High School, where 2,500 whites boycotted classes for four days in October 1954. School officials worked behind the scenes to quiet the rebellion, and the students returned to class after Superintendent Corning warned that they were jeopardizing their eligibility to participate in extracurricular activities.[12]

Beneath the general tranquility all was not well. Many of the problems that beset the District's desegregated schools were brought to general attention in 1956 when a congressional subcommittee, a majority of whose members were southerners, investigated the situation. Spokesmen for the NAACP warned that there was "a real danger" of "a scurrilous attack . . . on Negroes of Washington and the process of desegregation"; they characterized the inquiry as a "preconceived" sally by men who believed from the start that desegregation was a catastrophe. The Americans for Democratic Action similarly predicted that the committee would "scavenge a 'record' of failures and horror stories about desegregation."[13]

The investigators' motives may have been questionable, but testimony given by more than fifty Washington teachers and school administrators nevertheless pointed to grave problems. The investigators may have run advance checks to find witnesses who would confirm the case against desegregation, but, as even the liberal *New Republic* acknowledged, "the disturbing evidence that came out during the hearings is not made less disturbing merely because of the prejudice and ulterior motive of . . . Southerners."[14]

The black students' use of vulgar language bothered many whites. John Paul Collins, who had worked in the District's schools for thirty-four years and had been principal of Anacostia and Eastern high schools, declared that he "heard colored girls at the school use language that was far worse than I have ever heard, even in the Marine Corps." Eva Wells, the principal of Theodore Roosevelt High School, believed vulgar language was "the greatest cause" of fights at her school. She said that "so many remarks" had been made to Roosevelt's girl cheerleaders during the basketball season of 1954–55 that it had been necessary to switch to boy cheerleaders the next year.[15]

Nor was vulgarity confined to language. Arthur Storey, the principal at McFarland Junior High School, testified that in crowded corridors "boys would bump against girls" and "put their hands upon them," but discipline was difficult to administer because "a boy could say, 'I was pushed.'" White girls at Anacostia High School complained about "being touched by colored boys in a suggestive manner when passing . . . in the halls," and the situation at Wilson High School got to the point where the student newspaper, *The Easterner,* published an editorial under the title "Hands Off."[16]

Some whites expressed concern about venereal disease and pregnancies among students. The overall VD rate in the District was several times the national average, and blacks accounted for 98 percent of the 854 cases of gonorrhea reported among school children in 1955. Of the school girls reported as pregnant in the District, 90 percent were black, and 26 percent of all children born to blacks in the District in 1954 were illegitimate, as compared with only 4 percent among whites.[17] Marjory Nelson, a teacher at McFarland Junior High, spoke for many whites when she agreed that desegregation would have "a tendency to bring white girls down to that level." Several principals considered it advisable to discontinue dances and reduce other social events, despite the fact that black and white students tended to separate from one another in the cafeterias and in extracurricular activities.[18]

Some teachers said that fighting and petty theft had increased, although in retrospect these problems appear to have been relatively mild in comparison with the difficulties that would later accompany desegregation in some other school districts. Admitting that the decorum of students left something to be desired even before desegregation, Dorothy Denton, a teacher at Barnard Elementary School, said that behavior was "going from good, or medium-good, to bad, in my opinion." John Paul Collins said there had been "more thefts at Eastern [High School] in the last two years than I had known in all my thirty-odd years in the school system."[19]

When it came to disciplinary policies, many teachers believed they faced a difficult transition. Hugh Stewart Smith of Jefferson Junior High School said that before desegregation white teachers expected students to "do the right thing because it was the right thing to do." Most black teachers, on the other hand, were said to insist on "rigid discipline," for they had more experience dealing with "children who thought that you got what you wanted by fighting." Katherine Reid, a veteran white teacher at the Tyler School, admitted that she initially found it "very hard to make colored children do what I told them." One day when she was having trouble with a black girl, "one of the colored boys said, 'Miss Reid, why don't you stop talking to her and bat her over the head the way her last teacher did?'"[20]

Some teachers said their authority had been undermined. Katherine Fowler, who taught at McKinley High School, had an unpleasant experience after she scolded black students who were singing in the hall and disturbing others. The students said she was picking on them because of their race. An official of the NAACP discussed the matter with Fowler's principal, who warned the teacher to "be careful" in disciplining black students. A few weeks later Fowler came upon four black students riding noisily through the halls in a trash cart. "I started after them," she recalled, "and I am sure I did not take more than four steps before I remembered what had happened to me before, so I said: 'No, Katherine, you just let them go and let the principal of the school or somebody else . . . take care of it.' Of course . . . I felt that I was neglecting my duty. But I did not care to have that unpleasant situation again, so I neglected it."[21]

When citywide pupil achievement tests were given in 1955, the averages differed widely at schools that were either predominantly black or predominantly white. The average score for Washington's entire group of high school seniors was in the 45th percentile—5 percent under the national mean. But at Armstrong, Cardozo, Dunbar, and Spingarn high schools, where only 8 of the 5,019 seniors were white, the average score was in the nation's lowest 5 percent. By contrast, at Coolidge, Western, and Wilson high schools, where only 99 of the 3,129 seniors were black, the average score was in the nation's top 5 percent. One teacher expressed the view of many of her colleagues when she said she was "shocked at the low achievement of the Negro children who have been in the schools of Washington." In twenty-two predominantly white elementary schools the average I.Q. was 105, while the average in predominantly black schools was 87.

Walter E. Hager, the president of the District of Columbia Teachers' College, predicted that within ten years Washington's pupils would meet the national norms on standardized tests.[23] But others were not so sanguine. "It will become less of a problem every year, now that more attention is being given to educating the children who are below their grade level," said Irene C. Hypps, a black assistant superintendent. "But since the heart of the problem is the low economic level of many Negro families, the educational problem won't be solved until the economic problem is solved. . . . That will take a great many years."[24]

Whatever the cause of the low scores, classroom teachers clearly were confronted with serious problems associated with teaching students of varying abilities in the same class. Ruth Davis, a veteran teacher with 41 years' experience in the classroom, said it was difficult to teach when students of widely varying abilities were placed in the same classes. "It was hard on everyone concerned. It was hard on the boys and girls who needed the special help. It was hard on the ones who could have gone ahead. And it was very discouraging for the teacher who had no means of serving everyone." Helen Ingrick of the Emery School also found teaching "very difficult, because you had to have so many groups and so many age levels and so much preparation for the different range of abilities." Dorothy Denton of the Barnard School thought that her better students were suffering educationally because she had "to put so much time on discipline and on low ability that I haven't the time to give to the children who are able to go on."[59] After nine days of testimony, the congressional subcommittee concluded, "The evidence, taken as a whole, points to a definite impairment of educational opportunities for members of both white and Negro races as a result of integration, with little prospect of remedy in the future." The subcommittee recommended that the schools be formally resegregated, but its chairman, James C. Davis of Georgia, predicted that even if this were not done the departure of whites and the immigration of blacks would accomplish the same end—segregated schools.[26]

Why did so many white students depart from the public schools while blacks moved into the District? The change in the capital's racial composition had begun two decades before the schools were desegregated, and similar changes were occurring in cities throughout the nation, including some that never experienced massive integration. Nevertheless, it would be wrong to conclude that desegregation was not a major factor in the shift. After the *Bolling* decision, the rate of white withdrawal from the public schools tripled. Between 1949 and 1953 white enrollments had declined by about 4,000 students; between 1954 and 1958, white enrollments declined by almost 12,000 students. The District abandoned segregation, but white parents and students then abandoned the District (Table 1). The 500,000 blacks

TABLE I. Enrollments by Race,
Washington, D.C., Public Schools, 1951–1981

	Total Enrollment	Black Enrollment	White Enrollment	Percent Black	Percent White
1951	95,932	50,250	45,682	52.4	47.6
1952	99,860	54,180	45,680	54.3	45.7
1953	102,810	58,364	44,446	56.8	43.2
1954	104,330	63,403	40,927	60.8	39.2
1955	106,301	68,034	38,267	64.0	36.0
1956	107,312	72,954	34,358	68.0	32.0
1957	110,041	78,415	31,626	71.3	28.7
1958	113,030	83,733	29,297	74.1	25.9
1959	116,587	89,451	27,136	76.7	23.3
1960	121,448	96,751	24,697	79.7	20.3
1961	127,268	103,804	23,464	81.6	18.4
1962	132,900	110,759	22,141	83.3	16.7
1963	137,718	117,915	19,803	85.6	14.4
1964	141,396	123,906	17,490	87.6	12.4
1965	144,016	128,843	15,173	89.5	10.5
1966	146,644	133,275	13,369	90.9	9.1
1967	148,776	137,257	11,519	92.3	7.7
1968	149,063	139,512	9,551	93.6	6.4
1969	149,116	140,667	8,449	94.3	5.7
1970	145,762	138,207	7,555	94.8	5.2
1971	142,899	136,256	6,643	95.4	4.6
1972	140,000	133,651	6,349	95.5	4.5
1973	136,133	130,321	4,292	95.7	3.2
1974	131,758	125,854	4,324	95.5	3.3
1975	130,054	123,951	4,439	95.3	3.4
1976	125,908	119,814	4,406	95.2	3.5
1977	119,965	113,813	4,422	94.9	3.7
1978	113,050	106,977	4,216	94.6	3.7
1979	105,362	99,610	3,954	94.5	3.8
1980	99,225	93,746	3,611	94.5	3.6
1981	94,425	89,160	3,321	94.4	3.5

Source: District of Columbia Public Schools.
Note: Percentages do not add up to 100 after 1973 because Indians, Asians, and Hispanics are counted separately.

16

in the city included ten times as many school-age children as the 250,000 whites, Joseph Alsop noted in 1967. No such result "could conceivably have been produced in the normal course of events. It means, beyond question, that just about every white couple . . . has moved to the suburbs, at least as soon as it came time to send the children to school." Washington was on its way to becoming the nation's first predominantly black big-city school system.[27]

The flight from Washington's public schools was facilitated by the ready accessibility of predominantly white public schools in the nearby middle-class suburbs of Maryland and Virginia. Had Washington been surrounded by minimally developed rural areas, flight from the District would have been more difficult. Yet given the prevailing suspicion of those considered different,[28] substantial flight probably would have occurred even if suburban public schools had not been readily available. The white population of the nation's capital was composed overwhelmingly of middle-class professionals and civil servants whose family incomes were well above the national average. They could have sent their children to private schools if suburban schools had not been available.[29] In Washington, unlike many areas of the United States, there was no sizable number of working-class whites whose limited finances would have made it difficult for them to purchase homes in the suburbs or to send their children to private schools. The conditions necessary for stable integration of the public schools simply did not exist.

III

In retrospect, it is clear that desegregation in Washington was one phase in a chain of events that led finally to an almost all-black, resegregated public school system. This was not so evident in the late 1950s and early 1960s, however, and District officials mounted a spirited campaign to make desegregation a success. To head this effort they chose Carl F. Hansen, an experienced educator who combined administrative expertise with a deep and abiding commitment to desegregated education.

Hansen was forty-eight years old in 1954, bald, bespectacled, and unassuming. A native of Nebraska and a graduate of that state's university in Lincoln, Hansen had earned a doctorate in education at the University of Southern California and had taught high school English before becoming the principal of Omaha Technical High School. When desegregation began, he was associate superintendent of the D.C. school system, with special responsibility for the District's senior high schools.

At that time the student-teacher ratio was somewhat lower in the District's high schools than in its elementary schools, and some officials proposed to eliminate the disparity by reducing the number of high school teachers. Hansen vigorously opposed these proposals, and to strengthen his case he released a report containing test scores that indicated there was an enormous range in high school student performance on standardized tests.[30] Hansen's goal was to raise the achievement of poorer students while keeping able students from being held back by their slower schoolmates. To do this he advised grouping students with others of similar aptitude to reduce the range of ability in a typical classroom. But this could be done only if the District were to employ more high school teachers—teachers especially prepared to teach either slow learners or gifted children.

Hansen's report was brought to the attention of William Gerber, the chief counsel for the congressional investigating subcommittee. Gerber then invited Hansen to testify before the subcommittee, evidently because he assumed Hansen's concern with slow learners and ability grouping indicated opposition to desegregation. When Hansen appeared before the subcommittee, however, it was apparent that he and Gerber were working at cross-purposes.

Hansen knew that teachers found it difficult to teach classes in which there was an enormous range in ability, but he insisted that this was "an educational problem," not a racial one. He recalled that he had "the same experience when I was principal of a [predominantly white] high school in Omaha." Hansen emphasized that there was an enormous range of aptitude within each race and that some black pupils scored higher than most whites. He acknowledged that there were difficulties with desegregation, but he placed "the blame for that upon the system of segregation because under the dual school system that we had here there was insularity. . . ." Compulsory separation had established "an Iron Curtain between the two cultural systems," and this isolation had contributed significantly to the degradation of blacks. Hansen conceded that several teachers, "most of them people whom I knew and respected, [had] testified about scholastic retardation, delinquent behavior . . . , and the curtailment of normal social activities." Desegregation had not proceeded without incident, but Hansen was convinced that on balance "the integration program in this city has been a miracle of social adjustment."[31]

Hansen's surprising testimony irritated Gerber, who confessed that he had "a very severe headache [that] just seems to stay on and on." But Hansen's views pleased the Anti-Defamation League of B'nai B'rith, who invited the associate superintendent to write a pamphlet on desegregation in Washington. Hansen's thesis was summarized in his title, *Miracle of Social Adjustment*, and 90,000 copies of the account were distributed throughout the nation. The *Washington Post* praised the booklet as a "welcome antidote to the poison spread by the Davis subcommittee's venomous report."[32]

In the late 1950s and early 1960s Carl Hansen became one of the nation's most articulate advocates of desegregation. Ignoring threats to his life, he defied segregationists and traveled throughout the South speaking to various organizations. When Hobart Corning resigned in 1957, Hansen was the obvious and overwhelming choice to succeed him as superintendent of the District's public schools. For the next decade Hansen was the dominant figure in public education in the District of Columbia.

With 90 percent of high-school-aged Americans attending secondary school, Hansen thought it necessary to institute grouping by ability. The all-inclusive and democratic character of the high school was "a good thing," Hansen wrote, but it often led to "heterogeneous pupil programming, which is a bad thing."[33] In some instances academic subjects were watered down for the benefit of slow learners; on other occasions the pace was too fast for all but the brightest. As Hansen saw it, American students desperately needed systematic instruction at a pace appropriate to their abilities. The curriculum should be geared to the particular needs of diverse students—those below as well as those above the national average.

Where many observers sensed danger, Hansen saw the opportunity for progress. For years he had believed that ability grouping would be to the advantage of all students, but he knew that nothing as systematic as the program he had in mind would have been instituted "if we had continued under a segregated system." Hansen did not agree with those who said that "in desegregated schools the advanced student would be held back by the retarded student, the gifted by the less gifted, the white by the Negro." But he thought these "prophets of doom and gloom" could serve a useful purpose. Concern about desegregation provided the opportunity to make changes that were long overdue and should have been made solely for educational reasons.[34]

Beginning in the fall of 1956, each of Washington's high school students was placed in one of four separate tracks. A student's placement depended on motivation, past performance in the classroom, and scores on achievement and aptitude tests given by the district's Department of Pupil Appraisal. Students with IQs below 75—in the mentally retarded range—were grouped in a remedial or "basic" track, which also included pupils with IQs between 75 and 85 who were working three years below grade level. At the other end of the spectrum, high-performing students with IQs above 120 were placed in a special "honors" curriculum. Those with IQs between 75 and 120 were placed in either the "general" or the "college preparatory" track if they were performing near their grade level.[35]

Hansen emphasized that "more than an IQ score goes into placing a child in any one track"; special consideration was given to teachers' evaluations and the student's performance on achievement tests. He also noted that the 70 percent of students who were in neither the basic nor the honors curricula could choose either the general or the college preparatory track. Hansen confessed that he personally had little use for the general track, which allowed able students to "get by" with easy elective courses and without courses in mathematics and foreign language. "If I could be fully authoritarian," he declared, "I would require every capable pupil, college bound or not, to choose the college prep curriculum."[36]

There was some criticism of tracking when the system was introduced in 1956. "Why label students and put them in a narrow groove from which they might never escape?" some opponents asked.[37] Yet criticism was muted because the benefits of Hansen's program seemed beyond dispute. Washington's basic demographic pattern persisted in the late 1950s and early 1960s, with immigrants from the rural South swelling black enrollments by 6,000 students a year while the white exodus from the public schools continued. But the scholastic achievement of Washington's public school students, as measured by performance on nationally standardized examinations, improved significantly. "On three national high school achievement tests," *Time* reported in 1960, "Washington students have raised their position relative to the rest of the U.S. by 14 percentile points." During each of the five years after tracking began, Washington's high school students also improved their relative standing on the national SAT College Entrance Examinations — and this at a time when Washington sent a higher percentage of blacks to college than any big-city school system in the nation. The rise in academic standards, coinciding with an increase in the number of blacks enrolled, was testimony to "the capacity of the Negro pupil to respond to educational opportunity," Hansen declared.[38]

Carl Hansen, according to *Time,* had turned "the 'wreck' of Washington schools into a model that less beleaguered cities may envy." He had "confounded pessimists everywhere by raising academic standards higher than they had been under segregation." Writing in the *Saturday Review,* James Koerner reported that Hansen understandably enjoyed "the consistent support of all major groups concerned with the District's schools. . . . The tremendous progress in the Washington school system since the inception of his superintendency is proof that his ideas are effective."[39]

At the peak of his popularity Hansen moved forward with two programs that would later come under criticism. The first was the extension of tracking to include junior high and elementary school students, and the second was the establishment of a back-to-basics school called Amidon.

In the fall of 1959 the Board of Education implemented Hansen's recommendation that a three-track system of ability grouping be set up in the District's elementary and junior high schools. On the surface the plan represented simply an extension into the lower grades of the tracking program then in place in the senior schools. Beginning with the fourth grade, children with low IQs and a marked degree of retardation would be placed in the basic track. Students in the normal range on tests or classroom performance would be assigned to the general curriculum, and high-performing students with IQs above 120 would be steered into the honors track.

From the outset, the tracking of elementary and junior high students was controversial. Asserting that "the dunce of today is the brilliant student of tomorrow," school board president Walter N. Tobriner voiced the fear that the three-track plan "would stratify children well before their pattern of ability can be discerned even by experts." School board member Euphemia Haynes said Albert Einstein and Thomas A. Edison had shown little promise in the early grades. Their later development would not have occurred, Haynes suggested, without "the stimulus and the challenge of associating with brighter students." She feared that an initial premature assignment to a low or middle track might "stigmatize" a student and impede later development.[40]

Another controversy revolved around the curriculum that Hansen established at the Amidon School. This 26-room structure was completed in 1960 as part of an extensive redevelopment project in the southwest portion of the District. When construction was delayed on some of the apartment buildings that were to provide the school with much of its enrollment, Hansen discovered that there were 300 spaces available in the 800-student school. He then announced the kind of basic education program he had long envisaged, invited applications from interested parents, and 300 students from all over Washington were admitted on a first-come, first-served basis. This volunteer contingent complemented two groups that resided in the vicinity—one group of about 200 children of professionals and civil servants who lived in nearby townhouses and luxury apartments, and another group of about 300 youngsters from two military installations and a neighborhood public housing project where the average annual family income was $2,600. With a black enrollment of 70 percent in 1960, Amidon was one of the more racially balanced schools in a District where 86 percent of the students were black and where the enrollment in most schools tended to be predominantly of one race or the other.[41]

Amidon was more than an integrated school. It was, in Hansen's words, an experiment designed to test the theory that preadolescents need not "'an endless panel discussion' but 'firm grounding in the Three Rs.'" Beginning with the first grade, the curriculum at Amidon emphasized basic subjects—spelling, handwriting, arithmetic, and reading (taught by the phonic method). Grammar, normally taught in the sixth grade, was introduced in the third year along with French and Spanish. History and geography were taught individually and not grouped with other "social studies." There were no Halloween parties, no orchestra, no student government association, and field trips were held to a minimum. Most important of all, at Amidon students were grouped with others of similar academic achievement. Hansen insisted that some subjects were more important than others and that all students benefited if they were grouped so that they could be taught with others of comparable ability.[42]

Some critics began tilting lances at Amidon as soon as the plan was announced. John Parmenter, an assistant superintendent in Maryland's nearby Montgomery County, voiced an opinion shared by many progressives when he denounced Amidon as "a sop to all the reactionary forces afloat." Writing in the *New Republic* even before Amidon was opened, educationist Christopher Jencks argued that any success Amidon might enjoy would be due to the manner of selecting its students and teachers. "Students in the new school will almost certainly learn more," Jencks predicted. But this was because a disproportionate number would be recruited "from middle-class families who think good education important enough to bring their students to and from school. It will be no surprise when children from such families turn out to learn more than the progeny of more indifferent homes."[43]

By 1964 Amidon's reputation had grown almost to cult level, and the school regularly had a waiting list of hundreds. Some white parents transferred their children from expensive private schools at the first vacancy, and many youngsters were carpooled to and from the school from distant areas of the District. Writing in the *Saturday Evening Post,* Normand Poirier reported that "one little girl comes from nearby Maryland as a $318 a year tuition pupil. A doctor's son was hopefully enrolled on his first birthday, and an engineer's wife moving her family from Texas . . . wrote to a real estate firm that she wanted a home 'near the Amidon school, wherever that is.'"[44]

A social scientist might have set up a controlled experiment, with a second school staffed by progressive instructors and attended by students who voluntarily chose not to have a subject-centered curriculum. But this was not done, and progressive educators perceived the Amidon experiment as structured to accentuate the benefits of an orderly, systematic curriculum focused on basic subject matter. When an amazing 94 percent of the students at Amidon scored above the national norm in both reading and computation,[45] progressives were placed on the defensive. A growing number of parents were of the opinion that the Amidon concept should be implemented throughout the District.

Despite occasional criticism of Hansen's programs, until the mid-1960s most observers remained favorably disposed toward the superintendent. *Time* magazine expressed the consensus when it declared, in 1965, that

Hansen had "mixed innovation and firmness effectively on a big scale." With a student enrollment that was then 90 percent black, Washington's public schools had made "respectable progress in . . . turn[ing] out ever-brighter graduates from incoming students whose average cultural level drops as the proportion of underprivileged Negroes rises." The system was said to have demonstrated that, "given a reasonable chance, the Negro will learn and will achieve."[46]

I V

Hansen's supporters were in control of the District's Board of Education until the mid-1960s, but beneath the surface the deeper trend was turning away from basic education. One turning point came unexpectedly at a race riot following a high school football game in November 1962. For several years the *Washington Post* had sponsored a Thanksgiving contest between the champions of the local public and parochial leagues, which usually meant that one team and its supporters were predominantly black and the other predominantly white. The year 1962 was no exception. At the end of the game, in which a crowd of 50,000 spectators, three-fourths of them black, saw St. John's defeat Eastern, several thousand blacks "brandishing sticks and other assorted implements . . . raced across the field to have a go at the whites sitting together on the other side. . . . 'Get the whites. Get the whites,' they cried. . . . 'There's a white,' they'd yell and run over and beat him up. . . . One man was attending to his four-year-old daughter when a Negro tapped him over the head until he fell down. Other Negroes broke his daughter's ribs. . . . These 'scuffles' continued for two hours, during which time the police rather lost track of what was going on, partly because there was so much going on." During the melee 346 people were injured, all but 30 of them whites. There were 13 broken noses, 2 broken jaws, and 20 stabbings.[47]

The *Post* portrayed the incident as having little importance. Newsmen who witnessed the brawl (except for one who anonymously wrote the above description for the *New Republic*) did not report what they had seen. Instead, the *Post* quoted a deputy police chief's assertion that the turmoil was not racially motivated, although it conceded that others "felt the racial element was involved." On the sports page, columnist Bob Addie also made light of the riot. "It must be remembered that some of the college rallies are more violent," he stated. "For all of their tradition of dignity and learning Harvard students, for example, have been involved in dozens of battles with the police. You haven't lived until you've been in Harvard Square in Cambridge, Massachusetts, on the eve of a Yale game."[48]

While the local press and public spokesmen played down the racial character of the outbreak, one black leader laid the principal blame for the riot on members of his own race. Simeon Booker, the Washington representative of *Ebony* magazine, candidly stated that "the predominant number of offenders were Negro. . . . What I saw at the stadium easily could have duplicated what I saw covering the Little Rock school desegregation case, or the bus station mob during the Freedom Rides to Birmingham or the Emmett Till case in Mississippi. The difference, ironically, was that the predominant number of offenders were Negro. The explosion of hate stemmed mostly from my own people."[49]

Hansen believed the situation was serious and immediately set up a commission to investigate the question of violence in Washington's schools. The eleven-member commission included four blacks and was chaired by Shane McCarthy, a white businessman who had headed the National Youth Fitness Program for President Eisenhower. The commission's report, released after six weeks of probing, concluded that "conduct at athletic games—including the recent stadium contest—is symptomatic of the school conditions the committee discovered." "Not a single teacher to whom I have spoken in the past few weeks was surprised that the outbreak took place," McCarthy stated. "Why should we be?" asked one teacher. "We live with this brand of conduct every day in the schools." Numerous assaults were said to have occurred in the schools, most of which were never reported to police authorities.[50]

There was no consensus as to the cause of the trouble. Chuck Stone, the editor of the *Washington Afro-American,* said Hansen was "a man remarkably free from racial prejudice," but Stone thought some administrators did not share the superintendent's "intellectual and emotional commitment to an integrated school system." He thought the disorder was partly a response to their racial views. For his part, Hansen focused and expanded on McCarthy's assertion that the District's schools had been swamped by "the rapid growth in numbers of Negro pupils, many with low mental ratings." The major difficulty, in Hansen's view, stemmed from "the unusually large number of children from problem homes. In many cases, there is a total lack of supervision. If I could play God . . . I'd say to those parents: 'If you're going to work, both of you, then you have a legal as well as a moral responsibility to see to it that your children are given adult supervision after school hours when they come home.'"[51]

Hansen requested the authority to expel incorrigible pupils and to hire more male teachers. "Many of the youngsters don't have too much contact with adult males," he explained. "They are in a matriarchial kind of family situation where the female, the mother, runs the show. It's a good thing for children, as they grow up, to have some close contact, some relationship, with the male of the species. That's why I want more men teachers." Hansen also requested that the rules against corporal punishment of insolent pupils be rescinded, and he arranged to have police patrolmen put on "short beat" duty so they could be available if needed at one of the schools.[52]

McCarthy's commission placed some of the blame for the disorder on the disruptive black students, but it also criticized the track system. The basic track, the commission concluded, had become "the dumping ground for hundreds of Negro youth." These students allegedly became "discouraged at being tossed into a scrap heap, los[t] interest in schooling and bec[a]me dropouts, the members of a large grouping who form the 'social dynamite' to haunt our community."[53]

The commission's report "spotlighted the inadequacies of the public schools," the Jesuit journal *America* observed. After conceding that black leaders should "tackle this problem of rowdyism and juvenile delinquency," *Commonweal,* another Catholic journal, concluded that "the task of Washington's white population is no less demanding. Somehow it must find the courage to confront the fact of its irresponsible evasion of the problem of Negro rights and Negro progress."[54]

In blaming the Washington school system, at least partially, for the unruliness of some of its students, the commission reflected one of the major intellectual trends of the 1960s. At a time when millions of Americans doubted the wisdom of the government's policies in Vietnam, the authority of established institutions was called into question. Nowhere was this questioning more intense than in education, where disgruntled critics charged that America's schools were basically alienating, oppressive institutions. Charles E. Silberman, the author of *Crisis in the Classroom,* a most influential book, reported that schools were usually joyless institutions that overemphasized order and control. Most black youngsters started school "eager to learn," Silberman said, but "by the fourth or fifth grade they see school as an enemy to be hated and fought at every turn, and their teachers see them as 'alienated,' 'angry,' 'troublemakers.'" The blame for this, Silberman concluded, must be placed on the schools, for "it is in the school situation that the highly charged negative attitudes toward learning evolve." Critic John Holt suggested that bright and eager youngsters became hostile to education because they desperately needed to assert their autonomy and independence. "You know, kids really like to learn," Holt quoted one girl as saying. "We just don't like being pushed around." If left to themselves and not subjected to excessive pressures, children would develop their native curiosity and love of learning. Silberman favored the less structured "open" classroom that was then in fashion in England, while Holt saw the ideal school as "a great smorgasbord of intellectual, artistic, creative and athletic activities from which each child could take whatever he wanted, and as much as he wanted or as little.[55]

While progressives considered the formal classroom stultifying, radical critics insisted that the schools had not played the democratic, benevolent role that educators traditionally claimed for them. The conventional wisdom held that free public education prevented the hardening of class lines and offered everyone the opportunity to move ahead. Radicals insisted, to the contrary, that schools generally regimented and indoctrinated children and prepared them to take their places in an unjust, stratified social order. "The schools serve as sorting mechanisms," one sociologist observed, "insuring that the upper classes preserve their privileged positions and that the lower classes have little or no opportunity to reach them." The argument that individuals could improve their situations if they took advantage of public education, they insisted, camouflaged reality and was designed to make the lower orders content with their place in the social hierarchy.[56]

The progressive and radical educational views that were widely disseminated in the 1960s and 1970s differed on many key points, and to group these theorists without also emphasizing their differences is to oversimplify. Progressives stressed the importance of making children happier in school, while radicals feared that this would amount to little more than "a mechanism for the production of smiling, unaspiring lower classes."[57] Despite their differences, however, progressives and radicals shared common ground in focusing attention on the alleged shortcomings of America's public schools. Together they enjoyed enormous influence, and by the mid-1960s school administrators began to adjust to the new currents of opinion. Discipline and dress codes were relaxed; students were permitted to choose more elective courses; and a growing number of instructors came to appreciate the value of casual informality and nondirective teaching.

In Washington, Carl Hansen confessed that he was "impressed by the—let me put it in the most pleasant term—by the innovative aspects of [the critics'] approach to education. For them, the old ways won't do. Just simply to have a teacher to teach youngsters to read in a direct manner—that's not acceptable. They want change." Moreover, those with reputations for innovation were coming to occupy influential positions in the federal government. Hansen predictably cast a skeptical eye on radical and progressive criticism; "there's a definite motive," he claimed, "to disturb confidence in public education and in boards of education so that there can be an accumulation of controls in [the federal bureaucracy and judiciary] in Washington." Whatever the purpose of the progressive and radical critique, the superintendent had foreseen one of its results.[58]

The Washington schools were particularly vulnerable to criticism, for formal tracking had a disproportionate impact on blacks and whites. When tracking began in 1956, blacks made up 13 percent of those enrolled in the honors group, 28 percent of the college preparatory students, 70 percent of those enrolled in the general track, and 89 percent of those assigned to the basic curriculum. Although the various enrollments were not broken down by race during the 1960s, the proportion of blacks in the upper tracks increased as the overall black enrollment rose steadily.[59] There was, however, persuasive evidence that the children of well-to-do middle-class blacks were disproportionately enrolled in the upper tracks. Howard University professor Elias Blake prepared statistical tables that indicated a relationship between low placement in the track system and low family income. In one senior high school with a median family income of $10,374 a year, 92.2 percent of the students were assigned to the top two tracks. In another high school with a median family income of $3,872 a year, only 15.2 percent of the students were assigned to the top two tracks.[60]

The Reverend Walter Fauntroy of the Baptist Ministers Conference in Washington expressed the views of many critics of tracking when he charged that the system engendered "overconfidence . . . in a few, . . . in striking contrast to the damaging impact of lack of confidence, the feeling of inadequacy for many." David Glancy of the District's Southwest Neighborhood Association believed that tracking was "essentially a manifestation of class bigotry."[61]

Carl Hansen hastened to defend his system. Critics of tracking, he said, "would put the mentally retarded in the same classes as the average and above-average children." They mistakenly assumed "that the child who is far behind in reading can read the same materials . . . as the average or bright child." He dismissed as "uninformed" contentions that "if the slow are taught in the same classes as the bright, they will be inspired to emulate, to understand, and to cherish the bright, [while] the bright . . . will understand, cherish and learn from them." Hansen considered any system of individualized tutorials "unrealistic" for most students enrolled in Washington's public schools.[62]

Hansen feared that "brain power, the Nation's most important resource," would be "lost in the tide of equalitarianism." He warned that it was wishful thinking to suggest that the abolition of tracking would eliminate labeling. Without ability grouping the slow learners would fall behind and would receive daily reminders of the distance that separated them from better students. Unable to understand many class lessons and discussions, they would "withdraw or become unruly." Meanwhile, there was the danger that the brighter students, "left unchallenged and bored in classes with slow learners, [would] become lazy, indifferent, and rebellious." Without a college preparatory curriculum, many able teenagers would take "practically any subject they wanted, often bypassing the tough subjects so that enrollments in science, foreign languages, and higher mathematics [would] fall off seriously." Grouping for instruction, Hansen insisted, was "a question of educational methodology, and not of civil rights."[63]

Hansen was not without supporters in the 1960s. Although the *Washington Post* eventually became a major, persistent critic of what it called "the rut system," as late as 1962 it commended Washington's public schools for accelerating the pace of academic education. As ability grouping came under increasing censure later in the decade, middle-class residents (and especially teachers and white parents) rallied behind the beleaguered superintendent. The local affiliate of the National Educational Association asserted that democracy did not require "the same educational program" for all children, but only that "each child receive the education which is best suited to meet his needs."[64]

There had been widespread support for ability grouping in the late 1950s, when American educators were desperately trying to catch up with the Soviet Union. In 1959 school district officials unabashedly rejected "the fallacy that the most capable students take care of themselves." They proclaimed instead that "the brightest youngster in the school needs just as much special attention as the dullest."[65] Such statements were hardly conceivable a decade later, when the challenge of Sputnik no longer loomed large. Instead of the specter of Soviet science, there was the awful memory of racial violence—the Thanksgiving football tussle in the District and more ominous riots in other American cities. The primary task before educators was no longer to develop the intellects of the best and the brightest. It was to uplift those whose unruliness was said to stem from frustration.

In his own defense, Hansen frequently stressed the contrast between the declining socioeconomic status of Washington's student body and the respectable average standing on national examinations. "District performance on standardized tests exceeds expected levels of achievement," he declared. To do more, the schools would have had "to solve social problems" and "remake the families" of "the unusually large number of children from problem homes." Hansen warned that it would be a mistake to expect schools not only to educate but also to undertake major social reforms. "It is about time for people to realize that the school can't perform the function of the home and the church," he insisted.[66]

Many critics of the mid-1960s would not accept environmental explanations of the schools' failure to do more for slow learners. Some said there had been no significant improvement in academic performance and questioned the Washington test scores.[67] Others took a different tack. The well-known black psychologist Kenneth B. Clark insisted that students grouped in the lower tracks felt a sense of personal humiliation and unworthiness that rendered them ineducable and frustrated, ready to "react negatively and hostilely and aggressively to the educational process." Track-minded teachers, with their theories of cultural deprivation, were said to ensure the failure of disadvantaged students, for they assumed that slow students could not learn their lessons. If educators could teach the deaf and the blind, spokesmen for the Washington Congress of Racial Equality (CORE) asserted, surely they could educate "the so-called culturally deprived."[68] Doxey A. Wilkerson, dean of the School of Education at Howard University, summed up the critics' point of view when he wrote that "the school itself is the main cause of widespread academic failure among disadvantaged children."[69]

V

Carl Hansen and the tracking system had become anachronisms. But given the force of inertia, and the fact that the District's Board of Education was appointed by the judges of Washington's district court, both the superintendent and his program might have stayed in place a while longer had it not been for the persistent opposition of one of the most dramatic civil rights leaders of the era, Julius W. Hobson, Sr.

Born in Birmingham, Alabama, in 1922, Hobson had studied electrical engineering at Tuskegee Institute before volunteering for service as an army pilot during World War II. After flying thirty-five missions in Europe, he returned to study economics at Howard University and later worked as a statistician and economist at the Library of Congress and at the Social Security Administration. Married and the father of two children, Hobson was a self-styled Marxist who came to prominence as the leader of several demonstrations in the nation's capital. On one occasion he led a caravan of automobiles carrying cages of rats to Georgetown, insisting that the rich should share a problem they said was insoluble. On other occasions he picketed automobile dealers who refused to hire black salesmen and participated in "lay-ins" and "live-ins" at hospitals and apartment houses that served only whites. He demanded open housing, the desegregation of public accommodations, and the integration of retail sales staffs.[70]

Hobson's most important campaign focused on reforming public education in the District, a subject in which he first became interested during the 1950s, when he was president of the Slowe PTA and a member of the executive committee of the Washington branch of the NAACP. In these capacities he helped Ellis O. Knox of Howard University write a short book highlighting certain problems in the D.C. schools. In 1961 Hobson became president of the District branch of CORE, an organization whose direct-action programs were more to his liking than the relatively sedate tactics of the NAACP. In 1964, after quarreling with CORE's national leaders, Hobson and his closest associates formed a new organization called Associated Community Teams (ACT). Hobson called ACT "the organization of militants" who "went to sleep mad." Their agitation was as flamboyant as ever, but Hobson also began compiling a mass of statistics indicating that the schools were discriminating on the basis of race and class. Per-pupil expenditure in white and middle-class black neighborhoods clearly outdistanced that in poor black areas, and the great majority of white students were clustered in the area west of Rock Creek Park, which by 1965 had become "a verdant curtain" separating the races. Of the thirteen elementary schools west of the Park, twelve were more than 85 percent white. Elsewhere in the city, public school enrollments were fast becoming all black.[71]

Many liberals condemned the racially imbalanced pattern of congregation. Howard University psychologist Marvin Cline said that without integration there could be no quality education; black students would "fail to break the vicious cycle of negative self-images," and whites would consider themselves "as superior and Negro children as inferior." Desegregation, the Washington Urban League declared, was "merely the first step" toward achieving the desired end, while integration was "a situation in which heterogeneous groups can get to understand and respect each other."[72]

About a dozen of Washington's 135 schools had racially balanced enrollments, and Carl Hansen believed they were "better educational institutions than the schools that are all-Negro or all-white." Hansen and the Board of Education nevertheless opposed the Urban League's recommendation that pupils be bused for racial balance. To Hansen and the board it seemed pointless to speak of "integration" and "racial balance" in a school system that was already 90 percent black. Moreover, Hansen was "strongly in favor of the community-centered school." "Racial balance created by legislative or judicial fiat" would, he argued, destroy the "closeness among the pupils, the parents, and the teacher" that he considered indispensable for academic achievement. Hansen considered dispersion pedagogically unsound and probably unconstitutional because it called for color consciousness rather than color blindness on the part of the school system.[73]

Julius Hobson was ambivalent about integration. Friends who knew him well insisted that he was color blind, and during the late 1960s, when many blacks celebrated their ethnicity and abandoned earlier hopes for integration, Hobson continued to associate with whites. He left his wife, in fact, seeing first one white woman and then another, ignoring comments that he "talked black but dated white." As an economic determinist, however, Hobson believed the key to black progress was a more equitable distribution of basic economic resources. He considered it "extraordinary" that the

major civil rights organizations had "ignored for so long . . . the really significant [economic] questions," and he chastised the NAACP in particular
for failing to protest against "inequality in the distribution of public
resources."[74]

Hobson also condemned tracking as a "vicious injustice to thousands
of innocent children." His statistics demonstrated that if children were sorted
on the basis of performance on either achievement or aptitude tests, most
of the low-income pupils would be assigned to the lower tracks and most
of the high-income ones to the upper tracks. Hobson insisted, however,
that disadvantaged youths could not be classified correctly on the basis of
tests with norms based on the experience of middle-class students. It was,
he said, "a cunning and ingenious system of discrimination based on a new
kind of supremacy theory: cultural superiority"—a theory that rendered
many poor blacks ineducable because it "undermin[ed] the slum child's self-
respect."[75]

Hobson's criticism of tracking was endorsed by some members of Congress. Representative Roman Pucinski, chairman of a congressional subcommittee, noted that he had received numerous complaints from people
who considered "social and economic and intellectual and cultural discrimination . . . just as contemptible as racial discrimination." After holding
hearings on the subject, the subcommittee recommended that the track
system be abolished. It had "some sort of an intellectual or psychological
impact," Pucinski explained. "There does seem to be a kind of spirit of de-
jection. The track system does seem to add to intellectual segregation."[76]

Nothing came of the subcommittee's recommendation, however, for most
members of Congress thought it advisable to leave questions of pedagogy
to local boards of education. In Washington a majority of the judicially
appointed school board remained loyal to Carl Hansen and the tracking
program, although the unanimity of their support had been shaken by the
criticism. One member opposed tracking, and others believed that whatever educational merit the track system may have had, its utility had been
undermined by the widespread hostility it had engendered in the community. Nevertheless, after thoroughly discussing the question in 1966, the
board rejected a resolution to modify the track system, agreeing only to
commission an extensive review of the matter. By a vote of 5 to 4, the board
also extended Hansen's contract as superintendent for an additional three
years.[77]

Hobson received little support from the black community. Only 400 students joined a 1967 boycott he called to protest tracking. "The trouble with
Washington is that there are a lot of middle-class Negroes here, and they
are satisfied," said one protestor. Hobson acknowledged that "there is great
apathy in Washington," that many parents were "satisfied with Hansen."[78]

Hobson had stimulated debate, but he had not won many converts in Congress, on the Board of Education, or in black Washington. It was time to change tactics. Hobson's friend Patricia Saltonstall Rosemond suggested the new course. "I called Julius," recalled this scion of the Boston Saltonstalls, "and told him we should bring suit on the basis of economic differential treatment."[79]

The year 1966 was a propitious time to file a suit calling for the abolition of tracking and the equalization of school expenditures. Many informed observers no longer accepted the standard defense of ability grouping—that it enabled teachers to tailor their teaching materials and methods to meet the academic needs of diverse groups of pupils; they believed instead that grouping reinforced a sense of inferiority among slow learners while inflating a sense of superiority among those assigned to high groups. Moreover, although there was no consensus in the relevant literature, some studies indicated that ability grouping had a negligible positive effect on the academic achievement of high-group students and a significant detrimental effect on low-group students.

In the mid- and late 1960s there was also a growing demand for equalization of per-pupil expenditures. In every state except Hawaii a substantial portion of the funds for public education came from local property taxes—an arrangement that led to substantial disparities in the economic resources available for public education. Reformers lamented "the fundamental unfairness of a system where the fortunate few who live in wealthy suburbs gain a superior education with less tax effort by their parents." In a series of suits filed in the 1960s, the reformers asked the courts to redistribute revenues or otherwise eliminate disparities in school funding. The existing system, they said, invidiously discriminated on the basis of wealth and unconstitutionally denied equal protection of the law to residents of poor districts.[80]

Conservatives responded with several arguments. Above all, they defended local financing as necessary to local control of education. They also questioned whether differences in spending affected educational quality, and noted that many poor people did not live in districts with low property valuations. Most blacks, for example, resided in urban districts that spent more per pupil than the average in their states. These blacks stood to lose if expenditures were equalized.[81]

Studies of ability grouping proved inconclusive, and equalization litigation failed to pass muster when it came before the Supreme Court in 1973.[82] In the late 1960s, however, opposition to ability grouping and support for equalization were among the cardinal tenets of educational reformers. Hobson's friend Pat Saltonstall had a wide circle of friends, and before long Hobson, the man who once tried to relocate rats in Georgetown, had become a favorite of the chic liberal intelligentsia. He became particularly involved with lawyers and educators at the Center for Law and Education, an interdisciplinary institute established by Harvard University and the U.S. Office of Economic Opportunity. When Hobson's suit came to trial, his principal attorney was William Kunstler, a well-known radical who counted H. Rap Brown and the Chicago Seven among his other clients. Press reports indicated that prominent Harvard law professors assisted in preparing Hobson's complaint, and Stephen Michelson, a research associate at the Harvard center, later prepared a 146-page memorandum to supplement Hobson's allegations concerning the pattern of inequitable expenditure.[83]

Hobson's litigation was astutely prepared as two separate suits. One challenged school board policies relating to finance and ability grouping; the other questioned the constitutionality of Congress's giving the judges of the District court the authority to appoint the members of the local board of education. The constitutionality of the statute was ultimately upheld,[84] but since Hobson was suing the very judges who normally would have had jurisdiction in his case, the chief circuit judge appointed three appellate judges to hear the constitutional question and one of his brethren from the court of appeals to hear the challenge to the school board's policies. This unusual arrangement was necessary, for the reputation of justice depends on the appearance of objectivity on the bench. In this instance, however, procedural propriety redounded to Hobson's benefit, a consequence that his advisors must have forseen and that may have dictated the dual character of Hobson's suit. The chief judge of the circuit was David L. Bazelon, a jurist widely known for his liberal and egalitarian views. Bazelon had written so many liberal opinions, in fact, that J. Skelly Wright, a colleague on the court of appeals, once said that he and Bazelon were the two most liberal members of the entire federal judiciary.[85] When it came time to appoint a member of the court of appeals to hear Julius Hobson's challenge to ability grouping and unequal spending, David Bazelon gave the assignment to J. Skelly Wright.

Wright had spent most of his life in New Orleans before being elevated in 1962 to the federal appeals court in Washington. Born in 1911, he had graduated from Loyola University and taught English and history before becoming an assistant U.S. attorney and then a federal district judge. In this last capacity Wright had ordered the desegregation of buses, public accommodations, and schools in New Orleans. He was widely perceived as a liberal judicial activist who believed the Constitution required authorities to go beyond desegregation and to take affirmative steps toward integration.

On two occasions Wright had addressed questions similar to those presented in Hobson's litigation. In 1962 he had declared that it was "discrimi-

33

nation in its rawest form" for Louisiana to require black students "to pass muster under a pupil placement law." And in a 1965 speech at New York University, Wright insisted that disproportionately black schools branded blacks as inferior "in their own minds and in the public mind" and undermined the "ability to learn of Negro children." Equal educational opportunity was impossible in predominantly black schools, even if the racial imbalance was entirely adventitious and in no way the result of government policies. "Once substantial racial imbalance is shown," Wright stated, "no further proof of unequal educational opportunity is required."[86] Wright believed students should be grouped heterogeneously so they could learn from association with other children in the classroom. "Negro children," he explained, often lacked "exposure to the middle-class culture found in white but not in Negro schools" and suffered when denied "the stimulation and competition and association with children of other races and cultures." "No honest person would even suggest," Wright declared, "that the segregated slum school provides educational opportunity equal to that provided by the white suburban school." In his view, disproportionately black schools were inherently unequal, and the fact that racial imbalance resulted from assignments based on "geography, and not race, [did] not . . . make the schools less segregated or less inferior."[87]

Middle-class flight to suburbs and private schools admittedly created difficulties, but Wright insisted that "courts are not helpless to act." Racial balance could be attained if the judiciary mandated massive, integrated "educational parks" to which students would be bused from large metropolitan areas. Of course, any such mandate would "not find favor with the advocates of judicial restraint," Wright conceded, but he insisted that it was "necessary and proper" for the judiciary to play an "active role in shaping our society." It was "inconceivable" that judges would "sit idly by watching Negro children crowded into inferior slum schools while the whites flee to the suburbs to place their children in vastly superior predominantly white schools."[88]

Fearing that Wright would impose his own academic views at such a convenient opportunity, Carl Hansen and the Washington school board asked the judge to disqualify himself. They considered it improper for a judge to hear a case when he had already spoken "not only publicly, but spectacularly, vehemently, and precisely on the question at stake."[89] But Wright refused to disqualify himself—a decision that, ironically, created an unusual problem for Julius Hobson. Hobson had repeatedly insisted that his aim was the abolition of tracking and the equalization of spending, "quality education in Washington, not necessarily integrated education." On one occasion he even said that integration had been "a complete failure" and that it was "time . . . to make the schools good where they are."[90] Yet Judge Wright's integrationist views were so well known that Hobson's attorneys prepared a brief demanding a policy of dispersion similar to that suggested in Wright's speech at New York University, despite Hobson's personal rejection of the notion that disproportionately black schools were inevitably inferior. In conversations with the press, Hobson even dissociated himself from the briefs that had been filed in his behalf.[91]

The trial in the case of *Hobson v. Hansen* was lengthy, with both sides given considerable latitude in presenting their case. The court transcript ran to almost 8,000 pages and the defendants and plaintiff prepared 500 additional exhibits. Judge Wright's opinion ran to 119 closely printed, double-columned pages. The judge stated his central premises candidly in his first two "findings of fact."

> Racially and socially homogeneous schools damage the minds and spirit of all children who attend them—the Negro, the white, the poor and the affluent—and block the attainment of the broader goals of democratic education, whether the segregation occurs by law or by fact.
>
> The scholastic achievement of the disadvantaged child, Negro and white, is strongly related to the racial and socioeconomic composition of the student body of his school. A racially and socially integrated school environment increases the scholastic achievement of the disadvantaged child of whatever race.[92]

These findings, which reflected the conventional wisdom of integrationists in the mid-1960s, had been foreshadowed in the testimony and depositions of several prominent social scientists. Robert Coles, a Harvard psychiatrist, stated that black youths experienced "considerable turmoil" about the time they began school. This he attributed to the widespread belief that whites were better suited for academic work than blacks. This turmoil was "a nation-wide experience," but Coles was of the opinion that misgivings about schoolwork were intensified when a child attended a predominantly black school.[93]

Coles's view was seconded by Christopher Jencks, who would soon become a professor at Harvard's Graduate School of Education. Jencks told the court that "the Negro who goes to an all-Negro school is given the feeling that he is not able to participate in white insitutions, or to act as an equal to whites—or to be a full member of a society which he perceives as being a predominantly white society. And therefore, this gives him a sense of inferiority. And, by and large, people who feel they are inferior tend to . . . become inferior in their attainments."[94]

Further testimony came from James S. Coleman, a Johns Hopkins University sociologist who had just completed an impressive quantitative analysis that for a decade would be considered a major justification for integrating America's public schools. Coleman and his associates acknowledged that throughout the nation the academic performance of most blacks lagged far behind that of their white contemporaries. Some blacks performed better than most whites on standardized examinations, but the average black six-year-old was about one year behind the average white six-year-old, the average black twelve-year-old was scoring at about the same level as the average white ten-year-old, and the average black eighteen-year-old had scores comparable to those of whites at the age of fourteen or fifteen. Black children who attended predominantly white schools, however, scored slightly higher on achievement tests than blacks of similar background who attended predominantly black schools. Coleman and his associates concluded that the integrated environment was the key to improving the academic performance of disadvantaged blacks.[95]

Thus, when *Hobson v. Hansen* was decided in 1967, Judge Wright was not alone in believing that integration automatically improved the academic performance of lower-class blacks. Nonetheless, he was endorsing a controversial hypothesis that, given the knowledge available at the time, could best be said not to have been erroneous. Wright was also more daring than most of his judicial brethren in using this belief as the basis for a legal judgment that ability tracking and neighborhood assignments, as practiced in the public schools of Washington, unconstitutionally deprived black children of the equal protection of the laws. The essential problem with tracking, in Wright's opinion, was that assignments were influenced by aptitude tests in which middle-class whites set the standard. Such tests he considered culturally biased and "wholly inappropriate for making predictions about the academic potential of disadvantaged Negro children." Before tracking a student the authorities in Washington also considered academic grades and teachers' evaluations, but Wright thought these were inevitably biased by the teachers' familiarity with the unfair aptitude tests.

The system "simply must be abolished," he ordered, for instead of being grouped according to capacity to learn students were "in reality being classified according to their socio-economic or racial status, or—more precisely —according to environmental and psychological factors which have nothing to do with innate ability." Indeed, the separation along racial and socio-economic lines was so pronounced that Wright considered the system "wholly irrational and thus unconstitutionally discriminatory." "The real tragedy," he asserted, citing psychologist Kenneth Clark, was "the self-fulfilling prophecy"; all too often a teacher's low expectations induced low-track students to perform at substandard levels.[96]

In addition to ruling against tracking, Wright found that the District's neighborhood school policy was unconstitutionally discriminatory. The neighborhood schools were desegregated, but, because whites chose to live apart from blacks and the well-to-do kept their distance from the impoverished, students of different races and classes did not mix together in neighborhood schools. With citations to Robert Coles and James S. Coleman, Wright found that the "Negro student in a predominantly Negro school" received an "education inferior to the academic education he would receive in a school which is integrated or predominantly white." There could be no proper teaching, Wright insisted, without the "continuous actual experience of harmonious cooperation between members of various ethnic and religious groups." In a "society imprisoned by racial consciousness," schools should "produce attitudes of tolerance and mutual sharing that will continue in later life." Racism could be overcome "by the reciprocal racial exposure which school integration entails." "Negro and white children playing innocently together in the schoolyard" would establish the foundation for national redemption.[97]

All this was beyond the ken of traditional educators like Carl Hansen, who believed that the school's most important function was to teach students to read, write, and compute. Hansen was skeptical about some of the benefits alleged to flow from integration, and he disavowed any intention to move beyond desegregation to integration. He even said it would be "totalitarian" to assign students or teachers for the sake of racial mixing — an assertion that caused Wright to bristle with indignation. Although Wright absolved Hansen of any intent to discriminate on the basis of race, the judge pointedly condemned "the arbitrary quality of thoughtlessness," which could be just "as disastrous and unfair to private rights and the public interest as the perversity of a willful scheme."[98]

Having determined that tracking and neighborhood schools involved unconstitutional denials of due process and deprivations of equal educational opportunity, Wright proceeded to order integration. To prevent the few white students who resided east of Rock Creek Park from enrolling in predominantly white schools to the west, the judge prohibited an optional zone program that had allowed residents of some neighborhoods the opportunity to transfer to other schools. The court also required the school system to bus volunteering black children from overcrowded schools to the underenrolled schools west of the park. Another provision of the opinion called for the assignment of teachers on "a color-conscious basis" so that whites would be distributed more evenly through the schools of the District.[99]

These orders admittedly provided a more integrated education for only a small portion of pupils in a system where over 90 percent of the students and 80 percent of the teachers were black. However, since the Supreme Court had not yet ruled on the constitutionality of racial imbalance that resulted from residential separation, Wright stopped short of ordering consolidation with the suburban school districts in Maryland and Virginia. The most he could do was order the school authorities in Washington to prepare a plan that "anticipate[d] the possibility that integration may be accomplished through cooperation with school districts in the metropolitan suburbs.[100]

Most suburbanites, however, were opposed to any metropolitan plan for exchanging students. "I don't know how in the world we'd ever get a thing as emotionally charged as some school arrangement with the District into effect," commented James Stockard, president of the Arlington, Virginia, school board. "I see some merits to working out some possible arrangements, but I don't think it would ever be politically possible." One affluent suburb in Maryland, Bannockburn, did arrange to have about thirty black elementary students enroll in its predominantly white elementary school, but in 1971 the Washington Board of Education discontinued the program. The annual cost of $50,000 for busing and tuition seemed excessive, and some members of the board said it was an affront that the suburban parents had not sent any of their children to the city to school. In 1976 a new black superintendent of the District's schools unequivocally opposed busing black children to white suburbs. "I don't think it's necessary for black children to be with white children in order to achieve quality education," Vincent Reed declared. "I think we can achieve quality education in the District with the students we have right now."[101]

VI

The initial reactions to Judge Wright's opinion were mixed. Julius Hobson hailed the decision as "a sweeping victory." The *New York Times* considered the opinion "a monumental exercise in sociological jurisprudence." And Carl Hansen fumed that it was a milestone in judicial conceit. People were wrong to say "God is dead," Hansen wrote. "He is currently sitting on the Federal Bench in Washington, D.C. His name is J. Skelly Wright."[102]

The decision was a tremendous blow to Hansen. He still considered himself a champion of color blindness and equal opportunity, and his advocacy of basic education endeared him to those who thought progressive education had gone flabby. To many observers, however, the bespectacled superintendent was a symbol of a past era. The "miracle" of integration that had been hailed a decade before was proving to be short-lived, and the educational reforms Hansen had instituted, once cited as examples for others to emulate, were coming under attack. Now Judge Wright was siding with those who complained that Washington's schools had drifted out of the mainstream and that tracking relegated poor blacks to the educational junk heap.

Hansen was further dismayed when the Washington Board of Education refused to appeal Wright's decision. He promptly resigned as superintendent and pursued an appeal personally. Hansen acknowledged that public schools must not discriminate on the basis of race, but, citing numerous precedents, he maintained that there was no constitutional obligation to provide an integrated or racially balanced education for black students. The judiciary had already undertaken a massive task in prohibiting racially motivated educational policies, he argued, and should not intrude its judgment on policies that were not invidious but were merely said to be unresponsive to the needs of poor blacks. "No matter how well-intentioned [courts] may be," Hansen warned of "the dangers and stark impracticalities" that would develop if judges substituted their judgments for those of local school boards.[103]

Wright had addressed some of these points in his opinion. He regretted that the court had to enter "an area so alien to its expertise" and acknowledged that it would be "far better" if the problems of black education could "be resolved in the political arena by other branches of government." Unfortunately, American politics was dominated by interest groups that were well organized and politically influential. Since blacks were said to be neither, they usually gained little; this "voiceless and invisible minority" was not assured a "full and fair hearing through the ordinary political processes. . . . " Since the educational problems of black Washington could not be resolved through the regular political channels, it was necessary for the judiciary to accept its responsibility and "assist in the solution where constitutional rights hang in the balance." So it had been at the time of *Brown,* when "legislative response would have been a long time coming" had it not been for the prodding of the Warren Court. So it was also, Wright declared, with *Hobson v. Hansen.*[104]

By a vote of 4 to 3, the United States Court of Appeals upheld Judge Wright on virtually every point. Writing for the court's majority, Judge David Bazelon asserted that Wright's general comments about ability grouping and neighborhood schools were only "suggestions advanced for consideration by the Board [of Education]." "We are not to be taken as approving or disapproving [the] general philosophies" of either Skelly Wright or Carl Hansen, the court's majority asserted. "This court is concerned only with the provisions of the decree containing orders that something be done or stopped—and it is our view that these provisions do not improperly encroach on the Board's statutory discretion." Busing to the underenrolled schools west of the park seemed a reasonable way "to level out pupil density." Abolition of the track system did not prevent the board from developing an alternative method of ability grouping—although it is difficult to see what kind of a classification system Judge Wright would accept. And the elimination of optional zones and the color-conscious assignment of teachers broke no new legal ground. The three dissenters, including Judge Warren E. Burger, would have vacated Wright's decree on the ground that the judiciary should defer to the other branches of government in solving problems caused by adventitious de facto segregation.[105]

With the passage of time, critical evaluations of Wright's opinion became more trenchant. Integrationists complained that Wright's suggestions regarding the advisability of metropolitan consolidation were pitifully inadequate if blacks really had a constitutional right to education in integrated schools. Others questioned the judge's assumption that a busing program and the reassignment of teachers on a color-conscious basis would eliminate the disparities in per-pupil expenditure.[106]

Most of the criticism, however, came from the right. Conservative educators questioned the basic premise that Judge Wright had borrowed from James Coleman. They thought academic progress depended on the quality of teachers and the structure of the curriculum, not on interaction among students.[107] Conservative legal scholars also questioned the reasoning Wright had employed in condemning tracking and neighborhood schools. It was not simply that the judge had approached these questions obliquely, finding that the concept of "equal educational opportunity," in the light of James Coleman's sociology, required substantial integration. It was that Wright had developed a new test of constitutionality that enormously increased the scope of judicial review.

The equal protection clause does not prevent the government from classifying persons in categories that will be accorded differential treatment, provided that the classifications can be justified. The courts have regarded racial classifications suspiciously, however, and since World War II the Supreme Court has allowed such classification in only two instances where the government presented "compelling" reasons relating to a wartime emergency. In one of those instances the Court explained that "all legal restrictions which curtail the civil rights of a single racial group are immediately suspect." This did not mean that such restrictions were unconstitutional, but it did mean that they could be permitted only if they satisfied the most rigid scrutiny. To justify racial restrictions, the government had to present evidence so weighty as to be conclusive. The government has also been required to present strong justification for policies that restrict "fundamental rights" and for classifications based on "suspect traits" such as nationality or economic status.[108]

When dealing with classifications that do not single out individuals for differential treatment on the basis of suspect traits, the Supreme Court has applied a more relaxed standard of review. In these instances the standard of minimum rationality requires only that classifications not be arbitrary and that they be related to a legitimate purpose of government. In *Hobson v. Hansen,* however, Judge Wright held that policies that were neutral on their face but affected blacks or the poor disproportionately must satisfy the higher standard that was usually reserved for suspect classifications.

The most outspoken criticism of Judge Wright's opinion, surprisingly, came from liberal columnist Joseph Alsop. Writing in the *New Republic,* Alsop declared, "It is time to stop talking nonsense about Negro education. . . . Above all it is time to cease repeating, 'End *de facto* segregation!' as though this virtuous incantation were a magical spell." It was worse than misleading for Judge Wright "to put forward more desegregation as the solution for the ghetto school problems." Alsop predicted that the sort of "forcible homogenization" Wright recommended would leave the schools more "resegregated" than ever because it would stimulate flight and "increase the Negro percentage in the primary and elementary schools from 93 percent to 98 or 99 percent." [109] Alsop worried that the futile pursuit of integration deterred Americans from recognizing that "the problem of ghetto schools must be mainly solved inside the ghetto schools." Rather than stress the need for compensatory education of disadvantaged students, Judge Wright had emphasized the need for racial and socioeconomic mixing. Alsop lamented that the authors of the Civil Rights Commission's 1967 report, *Racial Isolation in the Public Schools,* had gone even further. After showing that there was no more mixing in America's schools than there had been in 1954, they had gone on to disparage attempts that had been made at compensatory education in black schools. Relying on "the extremely deficient Coleman report," they had concluded that racial mixing was more likely to raise black academic scores than Head Start, remedial reading, or other compensatory programs. In making the case for integration, Alsop concluded, the Civil Rights Commission had taken the "shocking though fashionable liberal educators' view once so bitterly but accurately summarized by Floyd McKissick, that if you 'put Negro with Negro you get stupidity.'" [110]

Judge Wright's orders would have been difficult to implement in the best of circumstances, and the situation in Washington was far from ideal. In 1968 board positions were the only elected offices in the District and consequently were seen as stepping-stones to more important posts if Washington should ever receive home rule. The Board of Education soon became mired in controversy.

The most prominent members of the first elected board represented divergent black constituencies. One was Julius Hobson, who spoke for poor blacks and stressed the need for equal educational spending. The other was Anita Allen, a black mother of four who worked at the U.S. Office of Education. She was especially concerned with maintaining academic quality in the public schools, and she drew her support from PTAs and from middle-class civic organizations. Having failed to develop strong ties with his lower-class constituency, Hobson left the board in 1969 after being defeated for reelection by Exie Mae Washington, a washer woman who had become a leader in the local antipoverty program. During the year that Hobson and Mrs. Allen served together, however, board meetings were marred by rowdy behavior by observers and the proceedings were often mired in time-consuming personal controversies.[111] The board also had to face the usual gamut of problems. Formulating a budget consumed a good deal of time; the problem of developing a new curriculum to replace the forbidden track system would touch off extended controversy; and there was the nagging problem of violence in the schools. A rash of daylight robberies and muggings occurred in 1969–70, and one assistant principal was killed by a student who had just robbed a school bank.

The board nevertheless tried to comply with Judge Wright's orders. Beginning in the fall of 1967 a few hundred students were voluntarily bused from overcrowded Anacostia to the white neighborhoods west of Rock Creek Park. Yet most black parents were cool to the program, and busing finally was phased out after only 150 youngsters took advantage of the option in 1975.[112]

Some new problems had developed in the meantime. The *Washington Post* noted a pronounced downward trend in test scores at the schools that were receiving children from Anacostia, and there were frequent comments on the problems caused by mixing students with "unequal academic preparation and different cultural values." The difficulties were especially severe at Deal Junior High in the upper northwest section of the District, where 400 black students were bused in to go to class with about 500 students from families that lived in the neighborhood. There were frequent scuffles and incidents of extortion. Mrs. Ronald Dellums, the wife of a black congressman from California and the mother of one of only two congressional children then enrolled in the District's public schools, reported that her son Eric never carried more than one dollar, for fear of theft. He was also afraid to use the school's bathrooms and came "charging home after school to use the rest room."[113]

Although Skelly Wright had excoriated the school system for not doing enough to promote integration, his own rulings actually put an end to policies that had permitted desegregation to hold at a few schools. Busing and the elimination of tracking speeded the exodus of whites. White enrollment dropped by 17 percent in 1968, and by 1973 the 4,292 white children remaining in Washington's public schools made up only 3.2 percent of the District's 136,133 public school students. A significant number of middle-income blacks were also departing. In the past these blacks had taken advantage of the now-prohibited optional zones to enroll in strong academic programs such as that at Western High School in Georgetown. Now they

42

began the trek to the suburbs. By the mid-1970s Washington's almost all-black public schools were losing 6,000 students a year, while black enrollments soared in the suburbs—reaching 33 percent of the total in Prince George's, Maryland, in 1975, and 43 percent in Alexandria, Virginia.

In the fall of 1967 800 new teachers were assigned to maximize racial balance, but this color-conscious policy did less to equalize per-pupil expenditures than Skelly Wright and Julius Hobson had anticipated. Because so few blacks volunteered to be bused west of the park, the neighborhood schools there remained underenrolled, and the underutilization of physical facilities contributed to higher costs per pupil. The financial picture was complicated because students with special problems were bused to the west from throughout the District and taught in small, expensive classes. Most of the extra expense west of the park, however, resulted from the presence there of a greater portion of tenured, long-term teachers who were protected from transfer by seniority rules. In Washington, as in most school districts, teachers' salaries increased according to length of service, and an unusually large number of white teachers in the west had seventeen years' experience and were at the top of the pay scale. Experienced black teachers similarly had gravitated toward upper-income black neighborhoods, leaving the new teachers to be assigned to lower-income black areas in the southeast and Anacostia. In 1971, when average teachers' pay west of the park was about 10 percent greater than in the rest of the city and average cost per pupil about 25 percent greater, Julius Hobson returned to Judge Wright's courtroom, demanding that the District be ordered to keep per-pupil expenditures for teachers within 5 percent of the average for all elementary schools in the District.[114]

The elected Board of Education was dumbfounded by Hobson's allegation that it had denied poor blacks equality of educational opportunity. The board, then headed by a black president and dominated by a black majority, professed to be as interested as Hobson in avoiding racial discrimination, and presented evidence, statistical and otherwise, against Hobson's claim.[120] But the court found their defense unpersuasive. Believing that poor blacks were disadvantaged by the differentials, Judge Wright again placed a heavy burden of proof upon the board and demanded compelling evidence that would satisfy strict judicial scrutiny. Admitting that the statistics at issue were "abstruse" and "complex," Wright nevertheless concluded that the discriminatory pattern of expenditure denied equal educational opportunity. He found that reading achievement scores were significantly higher in the elementary schools west of Rock Creek Park—2.4 grades higher than the average for the rest of the city—and that "these test scores reflect the results of the discrimination against the east of the Park children in per-pupil expenditure." Basing his remedy "upon straightforward moral and constitutional arithmetic," Wright ordered that expenditures for teachers' salaries in each elementary school not deviate by more than 5 percent from the average expense in the District. This could be accomplished either by distributing experienced teachers "uniformly among the schools in the system" or by giving an "offsetting benefit to those schools which are denied their fair complement of experienced teachers." "It is almost an affront to common sense," he concluded, "to say . . . that a pattern of spending so discriminatory on its face as the one which exists in the District reflects no discrimination in 'educational opportunity.'"[116]

To comply with the court's equalization order, the Board of Education transferred 306 classroom teachers in the fall of 1971. The original intention had been to shift a smaller number of high-salaried senior teachers, but when seniority rules prevented this, the board relied on computers to select transfers on the basis of salaries and seniority but without regard to academic specialties. This impersonal method enabled the board to avoid charges of favoritism, but the result was disruptive. Some schools were overstaffed with teachers whose specialties were in short supply elsewhere.[117] It soon became clear, moreover, that additional adjustments would be necessary to achieve equal expenditures. In the spring of 1972 the board transferred 100 more "special subject" teachers—teachers who taught art, music, and physical education at more than one school. In doing so the school system learned a lesson it never forgot: that equalization could be implemented by successive rounds of transferring teachers of special subjects, or by modifying the amount of time they spent at various schools, thereby avoiding the greater disruptions that attended the transfer of regular classroom teachers.[118]

Whatever "equal protection of the laws" meant abstractly, in the early 1970s in the District of Columbia it meant transferring enough special subject teachers annually, or more often if necessary, to equalize per-pupil expenditures. Believing that equalization had no relevance to the educational process and was simply a mathematical computation done to satisfy Judge Wright's definition of equality, the school system relocated as few classroom teachers as possible and settled on a rigid formula: "one child, one dollar." Schools with experienced, high-salaried classroom teachers had to make do with few or no special teachers, while schools with younger faculties had a surfeit of art, music and physical education.[119]

Julius Hobson never acknowledged the disappointing results of the equalization decree. He complained on occasion that, despite all the transfers, teacher costs at as many as 60 percent of the District's elementary schools had varied from the mean by more than the permissible 5 percent. He and his attorney requested fines and contempt citations, warning that if necessary they would "request that every board member and the top administrators be bound over to the custody of a U.S. marshall and placed in jail until compliance [with equalization] is achieved." [120] But a few months after Hobson's death in 1977, his former attorney joined with representatives of the school board in petitioning Judge Wright to set aside his equalization decree. Placing an ingratiating gloss on the facts, attorney Peter Rousselot discreetly curried favor with the court. The judge, Rousselot said, had "played a crucial role" in saving Washington's schools from "decades of neglect and discrimination," but there was a danger that the equalization decree would "in the future have whimsical and capricious effects." In 1978 Wright revised the order and substituted equality in class size as the test of whether the schools were offering equal educational opportunity. This presented no problem, for as far back as 1966 the average student-teacher ratios in predominantly black and white schools had varied by only 2 percent. [121]

The *Washington Post* characterized the settlement as a vote of confidence in the Board of Education and its superintendent. Perhaps by 1978 even Skelly Wright had come to realize there was little support for his version of educational reform. Some school administrators regarded Julius Hobson as a man acting alone without much public support, who never would have gained influence over the schools had he not found a soulmate on the federal bench. But in a series of important decisions in the 1970s, a divided Supreme Court had emphatically rejected Judge Wright's interpretation of equal protection. In the absence of intentional discrimination, disproportionate impact on poor blacks was not sufficient to require strict scrutiny, the high court ruled. Education admittedly played a "vital role in a free society," but the Court held that it was not among the fundamental rights entitled to special protection beyond the traditional standard of review. [122] With the constitutional ground cut from under him and lacking broad support in Washington, Judge Wright finally had no alternative but to revise his equalization decree.

VII

Judge Wright's decree abolishing the track system ultimately compelled a major reorganization of Washington's public school curriculum. For a while some teachers and principals continued to offer basic instruction in traditional subjects and to substitute informal ability grouping for the tracking that Wright had prohibited. The third-grade teachers at Shadd Elementary School, for example, said they could not teach effectively with classes of children reading from kindergarten to fourth-grade level, and their solution was to execute an end-run around the court order. One teacher took all the children reading at third-grade level; another took those reading at second-grade level; another taught those at first-grade level; and a fourth teacher took a very slow group of children reading below first-grade level. In 1970 the acting superintendent inadvertently acknowledged the persistence of ability grouping when he stated, amidst chuckles from his staff, "The track system has been eliminated, I hope." [123]

Beginning in 1967, however, school authorities in the District formally abandoned tracking based standardized examinations. The high schools discarded their aptitude tests, although admission to advanced courses was still restricted to those who had passed the prerequisite courses. In most elementary schools, slow learners were placed in the same classes with average and exceptional children. Not everyone was pleased with the result. One tearful mother told a reporter, "My daughter was doing well in her basic class last year. Now she comes home from school crying every day because she can't keep up with the other children. I just don't know what to do." Another mother wrote that her daughter had been "making good progress" in the basic track—"learning to read and everything. She was very happy at school. Now she's in a regular third grade class, and she comes home crying, telling me she can't understand the lessons. I just want to ask [Judge Wright] what he intends to do about my child. I don't care if my kids never sit beside a white kid, as long as they get a good education." [124]

Most educational reformers of the 1960s believed that heterogeneous classes would necessitate a welcome move toward individualized instruction. Since students could no longer be taught as a group, teachers had to develop independent study programs and tutorials that allowed youngsters to learn at their own pace. Increasingly, this new approach was also combined with a system of elective courses that allowed students to choose the subjects they would study on their own. The central administration called the program MIND—Meeting Individual Needs Daily. [125] Instructors were told to avoid the rigid authoritarianism of the teacher-centered drill-and-recitation classrooms and to substitute a problem-solving, student-centered curriculum that encouraged the child's natural curiosity and built upon his or her individual interests and experiences.

All schools did not implement the new curriculum simultaneously, and the pace and degree of implementation varied considerably, since individual teachers and principals retained some autonomy. A significant change occurred, however, the nature of which was exemplified by the changes at the Morgan School, an antiquated institution that drew its 700 students from a poor black neighborhood in southeast Washington.

In 1967 some parents at Morgan had protested when the administration proposed putting the school on double sessions to relieve overcrowding. Their cause was taken up by the Adams-Morgan Community Council, an organization of white liberals then searching for some means to establish an integrated community. The parents and the Community Council blocked the plan for double sessions, set up a small library, and eventually received authority to establish an experimental neighborhood school. Almost immediately liberal whites also began to work for revision of the Washington curriculum. Among them were Christopher Jencks, who had recently given court testimony supporting Julius Hobson, and the co-directors of the Institute for Policy Studies, Marcus Raskin and Arthur Waskow. They drafted a new curriculum and arranged for Antioch College of Yellow Springs, Ohio, to sponsor the project.[126]

To implement the new approach, the faculty at Morgan was reorganized to increase the number of adults working with the students. Instead of the usual complement of about twenty-eight teachers and three specialists, the school initially employed seventeen regular teachers; the remaining salaries were divided among a dozen interns from Antioch and fourteen adults from the neighborhood, who assisted in various ways and were called "community interns." The adults were organized into teams to work closely and individually with about one hundred children, who were organized in nongraded groups and who studied at their own pace.[127]

The national media gave Morgan much favorable publicity. The *New York Times* featured a story about "A Capital Success Story," and in 1968 Morgan received special praise from Harold Howe II, the U.S. commissioner of education. Generous grants followed, and from 1968 to 1971 Morgan was probably the most generously financed of the city's elementary schools; it ranked in the top fifth in spending from the regular budget and received more than $550,000 in supplementary federal grants. Money was available for expensive educational equipment, for student sightseeing trips, and for teachers to attend conferences and workshops. In 1971 Morgan employed twenty-eight neighborhood residents who worked as "classroom aides" and "parent stimulators" at salaries of between $5,500 and $6,500."[128]

Most of Morgan's experienced black teachers had come up through the Washington system, with its emphasis on teacher-centered authoritative classrooms. Efforts by the architects of the new curriculum to enlist these teachers' cooperation proved largely unsuccessful, and only three of the previous year's faculty remained at Morgan when the new program got underway in September, 1967. A few experienced teachers were recruited from elsewhere, but most of the teaching under the new program was done by young white teachers from Antioch. Some had served in the Peace Corps, but few had previous experience teaching in a black school. Many of the young teachers, according to project director Paul Lauter, "found it difficult to establish a comfortable relationship with the children, who were . . . used only to severely authoritarian discipline." Relations with adults in the community were also strained, especially after students began returning home in the middle of the day, informing their parents that the school did not require attendance at classes the students found boring. Many black adults expressed the view that "experiments of this sort were all right for suburban children, but *these* children . . . they knew them better; they needed control, discipline.[129]

Racial tensions also intruded at Morgan. Believing that the course of study should be relevant to the lives and interests of the students, the new teachers developed a "race pride" curriculum. Many black parents, however, looked askance at bearded white teachers, dressed in sandals and jeans and propagandizing for black power. The were "put off and a bit shocked by all the talk of the state of the black man in America, and indeed, by the use of the word 'black.' 'Negro' was usage advanced enough, and for many 'colored' was the norm."[130] The parents of the twenty white students enrolled in the school accepted courses on black history, but they questioned any more thoroughgoing rooting of the curriculum in the lives and experiences of black people. "If you organize a curriculum to teach Negro children to be proud of the fact that they are black, where does that leave my children?" one white mother asked. After a single year at Morgan nearly all the white children left, most for private schools; they had had to pay protection money to gain safe passage to and from school, and they were made to feel especially uncomfortable after the Washington riots of April 1968. Barbara Raskin, one of the white mothers, described her involvement with the school as being "like a bad love affair, a very passionate relationship which just didn't work out."[131]

The experiment at Morgan foundered and eventually was abandoned, largely because people from different backgrounds had proceeded with very different expectations. Black parents had been concerned about overcrowding, but most did not share the white progressives' concern for reforming the curriculum. The blacks' primary concern was that their children learn the three Rs. They practiced "a very traditional kind of discipline in their homes," Morgan principal Kenneth Haskins noted, and were suspicious and disapproving "of an educational philosophy that allows as much freedom for children as the one Antioch tries to instill."[132]

The black parents probably would have accepted the new methods if they had led to improved student performance, but Morgan could report little such progress. Reading scores improved at first but then quickly dropped to where they had been before—about two years below the national norms. When this became apparent, the parents reasserted control over the school. A new neighborhood board was elected, and the curriculum was redirected toward basics. "The black mamas triumphed," one D.C. school official stated, "and the reformers fled." The new board chairman, Robert Brown, castigated reformers who allegedly "saw a black community they could perform an experiment on. And when it was not working out, they withdrew and left the whole thing. . . ." Brown was convinced that most students from low-income black families "don't have the self-discipline that's necessary to go into a free form educational set up." Conventional textbooks were ordered instead of the comic books that for a season had supplanted basic readers. The young progressives who had called for freedom were replaced with more conventional teachers who stressed the need for guidance.[133]

A larger community project continued for a while east of the Anacostia River, and reformers enjoyed a brief resurgence when Barbara Sizemore became superintendent of schools in 1973. In 1970, however, a majority of the Board of Education believed that independent study did more to make students feel good than to improve their performance in basic subjects. They wanted to turn education back toward basics, and to this end they employed the prominent black psychologist Kenneth B. Clark to design a new curriculum for Washington's schools. When it came to the quality of education, Clark insisted that the teachers' expectations were as important as integration. He believed that too many teachers in the ghetto made excuses, saying that ghetto families provided such a bad home environment that it was impossible to educate most of the children. The teachers believed that the best that could be done was to salvage the few who showed some natural academic aptitude—something they might accomplish by concentrating their attention on the talented minority. Ability grouping and tracking, Clark said, had been adopted to benefit the "teachers' pets" and to protect them from the "troublemakers and nobodies."[134]

To Clark's chagrin, many teachers referred to one of his books, *Dark Ghetto*, when defending the track system. Tracking, they said, was a necessary adjustment to the "tangle of pathology" that Clark had described. Clark believed the educators had learned the wrong lesson from his book. They should have recognized instead the reality of the self-fulfilling prophecy. If teachers taught less to students whose cognitive abilities and language skills had been stunted in culturally deprived neighborhoods, then the students certainly would lag academically; the children would not learn because the teachers did not teach.[135] Clark emphatically rejected the usual explanations of the poor academic performance of black students. Explanations ranging from theories of cultural deprivation to allegations of genetic inferiority served only to excuse the failure of the ghetto schools. He insisted that teachers who believed in their students would do better than those who thought blacks had so many cards stacked against them that they could not measure up. "The students in Washington are normal human beings," Clark said. "If they are taught efficiently, they will learn."[136]

Clark recommended that each class include "individuals of different lev-

49

els of achievement," a grouping that would "enhance the student's self-image" and would "compel teaching in terms of individual needs." This call for heterogeneous classes was compatible with the progressive theory that children assigned to homogeneous lower-level groups sustained a loss of self-esteem, that they lost the benefits to be derived from interacting with brighter youngsters, and that they suffered when they were ignored by teachers or exposed to a diluted curriculum. The emphasis on personal instruction was also consistent with progressive views on the advantages of individualized pacing and familiar interaction with teachers.[137]

Yet in some respects Clark's plan was, as he later admitted, "very conservative." The emphasis was squarely on the basic subjects, especially mathematics and reading. Standardized tests were to be administered three times a year, and teachers were to be evaluated and rewarded for their success in improving their students' performance on the examinations. Moreover, during the first year of the program all other activity was to be suspended while teachers concentrated their energies on bringing every normal child up to grade level in reading and mathematics.[138]

Clark's suggestions for rewarding teachers were especially novel. He proposed to make promotions contingent upon the students' performance on standardized examinations. At the bottom of teachers' ranks would be the "resident teacher," the inexperienced beginner serving a probationary term of three to five years before becoming eligible for designation as a "staff teacher." After "staff teachers," roughly comparable to assistant professors in universities, would come "senior teachers," who would be the equivalent of associate professors and who would be paid on the same salary scale as assistant principals. A still higher step would be that of "master teacher," a rank comparable to that of full professor and one that was "reserved for truly distinguished, imaginative, creative, and consistently effective teachers." Master teachers would be paid on the salary scale of a school principal. Finally, there would be a small group of "distinguished teachers," whose pay would be at the level of assistant superintendents.[139]

This ranking plan would have made it possible to reward outstanding teachers without promoting them out of teaching. Nevertheless, the proposal was immediately condemned by the Washington Teachers' Union. Part of the union's objection was procedural. Union president William Simons complained bitterly that only one member of Clark's staff had spoken briefly with him before the plan was issued, although the union's collective bargaining agreement asserted that "teachers must participate at every phase and at every stage of staff and curriculum development." When a reporter asked if the union would oppose Clark's plan even if it was "good for the children," the union chief candidly replied, "Yes, if we're not involved. What is good for children is not going to be purchased at the price of dignity for adults. If we're going to be professional, we are going to be involved in what affects us." [140]

Beyond this procedural dispute lay the teachers' deep reservations about merit pay. Some noted the danger of favoritism when evaluating something as elusive as the quality of teaching. Others rejected Clark's premise that a teacher could be fairly judged on the basis of students' performance. "What do you do about the teacher who happens to have a group of students who do not get proper food at home or come from an environment that is not conducive to learning?" William Simons asked. Most teachers thought Clark's plan would penalize ghetto teachers and favor those who taught in middle-class neighborhoods because a teacher's influence would often be outweighed by what happened at home and elsewhere in the community. [141]

Brushing aside these objections, the Board of Education approved Clark's plan by a vote of 9 to 1. Board president Anita Allen praised the program as "a ray of hope for the school system," and many residents seemed to agree. Placing a half-page advertisement in the *Washington Post*, one group of 175 parents told the teachers, "Brothers and sisters, we've had it. We've supported you for pay raises. We've supported you for better teaching conditions. . . . Now it's time for YOU to listen to US. . . . We've had it seeing our children's education washed down the drain in a torrent of words. . . . As far as we're concerned, the Clark plan is IT. And we expect you to get with it." [142]

With the controversy swirling around Clark's plan, 1970 was hardly an auspicious time for a new superintendent to take office. Yet Carl Hansen's successor, William Manning, had been dismissed in 1969 after only one year of service, and the board did not wish to continue indefinitely with the competent but sedate acting superintendent, Benjamin Henley. The Washington schools needed a more dynamic leader, some said, and during the summer the board had appointed Hugh Scott, a handsome and eloquent thirty-seven-year-old school administrator from Detroit, as the first black superintendent of Washington's public schools. Scott had warmly endorsed Clark's concepts when he was interviewed for the position, and most board members hoped that he could break the deadlock that had developed with the teachers' union. [143]

Scott took office on October 1 and quickly concluded that Clark's plan could not be implemented over the opposition of the Washington Teachers' Union. "It makes no difference what type of plan you put in," Scott declared. "If you don't have the cooperation of the teachers, it's not going to work." Scott reaffirmed his support for the goals of Clark's plan but said it had been a mistake to thrust the program on the community without warning and extensive preparation. The program could not be put in place unless the teachers changed their attitudes, and most teachers were simply incredulous when Clark insisted, "It is the teacher's job to make up for the deficiencies in the home."[144]

Even if the teachers had supported Clark's plan, Scott doubted that the existing staff could have implemented the program. "Most teachers were not trained . . . to be reading technicians," Scott explained. There would have to be extensive retraining before they could contribute effectively to any mobilization program. Scott also considered it unduly optimistic to expect speedy progress in solving the "major problem of student retardation": it was misleading to minimize the deleterious effects of the culture of poverty, and "simplistic" to expect a dramatic improvement in academic scores if teachers viewed students from a different perspective.

Scott's evaluation was sensible, but it infuriated several members of the Board of Education. After all, they reasoned, Scott never would have been hired had he not pledged to support Clark's plan and voiced confidence that he could resolve the differences between the factions. Now it seemed he had gone over completely to the position of the teachers' union. Kenneth Clark was especially pointed in his criticism. The psychologist said his program was being "interred" and that parents were being "hoodwinked" by administrative "double-talk." Scott had "totally abandoned" the new program, Clark declared, and was "returning the schools to the usual pattern of inefficiency and retardation." "As long as this man is in this position, the plan is dead," Clark said. The schools would continue to be "instruments for producing illiterates."[145]

VII

The controversy over Clark's plan and the need to equalize expenditures consumed much time and left the board badly divided. One faction, headed by Anita Allen, remained loyal to Kenneth Clark and on the alert to criticize Hugh Scott. The other faction, headed by Charles Cassell, sided with Scott. Cassell joined with the teachers' union in calling for a moratorium on tests that measured blacks against white, middle-class standards. The tests were biased, said Cassell, and it was "racist" for Clark to propose that the city's schools teach standard English to black children who spoke a ghetto dialect. One of the major reasons for black academic retardation, Cassell thought, was that most middle-class teachers were instructing ghetto youths in what amounted to a foreign language—the Queen's English.[146]

With the board divided, the personal recriminations unpleasant, and the problems facing the school system complex and intractable, the superintendency at times seemed to offer few compensations. Scott's contract would expire in October 1973, and only six of the board's eleven members were willing to support a one-year renewal. In the fall of 1973, Scott accepted a position as professor of urban education at Howard University. The board then geared up to search for another superintendent—the fourth since Carl Hansen had resigned six years earlier. The majority faction specified that they wanted someone who was sensitive to the needs of ghetto youths, who knew how to move on Capitol Hill, and who could attract top managers to run a more decentralized system. After what had happened to William Manning, Benjamin Henley, and Hugh Scott, to say nothing of Carl Hansen, there were those who wondered "if anybody this side of an idiot would take the job." [147]

Barbara Sizemore, the person chosen as Scott's successor, had administered a $1.5 million grant for Chicago's Woodlawn Project and had been principal of a nongraded school where students discarded standard textbooks and shaped their own courses. This was hardly extensive preparation for administering a school system as large as Washington's, but Sizemore made such a favorable impression during her interview that a majority of the board discounted objections to her relatively limited administrative experience. One colleague who had known Sizemore in Chicago observed that the board had bought "a philosophy, a theory of education, not just somebody who can churn out a good budget." [148]

At the core of Sizemore's educational philosophy lay a commitment to decentralization and individualized teaching. She believed public school administrations were too hierarchical and elitist and that they should be reorganized to allow students, parents, and community members to participate in decision making. To this end she called for the physical decentralization of the school district into six regions and recommended the formation of pressure groups called PACTS—an acronym for *P*arents, *A*dministrators, *C*ommunity members, *T*eachers, and *S*tudents. Sizemore also believed that, because of the wide range of individual abilities, children should not be grouped according to age and grade. She favored open classrooms, organized in the manner then in fashion in some English schools, in which students could progress individually according to their interests and their mastery of various skills. Under this arrangement, she said, "a third or fourth grader [who] might be ready to study algebra . . . would be in the same class with a ninth or tenth grader." [149]

These views were in tune with the mainstream of educational reform in the early 1970s, but some of Sizemore's opinions on discipline and curriculum were exceptionally permissive. Discipline problems would not be solved, she said, unless teachers made their subjects more relevant to the students' lives. Most teachers, of course, recognized that children who were absorbed in learning something they found interesting were not likely to cause problems. But some said Sizemore was suggesting they should entertain pupils rather than teach them. *Washington Post* columnist William Raspberry noted that "an awful lot of teachers [had] come unglued" because of "Mrs. Sizemore's notion that punishments and exclusions aren't a very useful way to achieve classroom discipline."[150]

Sizemore's approach to the curriculum was consistent with her views on discipline. Since it was necessary to create courses that would hold the students' interest, Sizemore favored more courses on black history and the socioeconomic problems of the urban ghetto. Most parents endorsed this modification of standard social studies, but many had reservations about Sizemore's additional assertion that the "age-graded, monolingual, monocultural" program found in most public schools benefited only "affluent whites of European descent." It was necessary to design a distinctive curriculum for poor blacks, she insisted, but many wondered if Sizemore really had anything better to substitute for the traditional course of study.[151]

Many middle-class parents also became upset when Sizemore discontinued the use of the national tests that showed a steady decline in Washington's standing in mathematics and reading. Although Sizemore attributed the disappointing results to cultural bias in the tests, most teachers accepted the validity of the tests, at least insofar as they indicated trends in achievement. There was, however, no consensus when it came to accounting for the steady decline in scores (see Table 2). Many noted a strong link between socioeconomic status and test scores, attributing the decline to the flight of middle-class blacks whose places were being taken by disadvantaged immigrants. Several teachers, particularly the older ones who had taught in the system before Julius Hobson's lawsuit derailed tracking, said that the heterogeneous grouping of children was the biggest single cause of poor achievement.[152]

Whatever reservations parents and teachers may have harbored, the Board of Education thought Sizemore possessed special insight into how to teach disadvantaged black youths. Yet Sizemore's educational philosophy and programs were jeopardized when board members discovered that several ad-

TABLE 2. Reading Scores,
Washington, D.C., Public Schools, 1971–1974

Grade	Big City Norm	D.C. 1971	D.C. 1973	D.C. 1974
6	6.8	6.3	5.7	5.2
7	7.8	6.5	6.3	5.5
8	8.8	7.2	7.0	6.0
9	9.8	8.6	7.4	7.4

Source: William Raspberry, "Reading, Math, and 'Cultural Bias,'" *Washington Post,* 26 August 1974.

ministrative matters had not been handled properly: They said the annual report had not been filed on time, quarterly financial statements had not been prepared, a report on equalizing expenditures had not been done properly, many of the buildings had fallen into disrepair, school supplies had been mysteriously misplaced, and many teachers had been assigned too late to permit adequate planning for classes.[153]

Because of the factions on Washington's Board of Education, Sizemore's administration may have been doomed from the start. But Sizemore surrendered any chance she may have had by responding to criticism in a combative and tactless manner. In an interview with the press she admitted to major "philosophical differences" with board member Marion Barry, whose support had been indispensable in paving the way for her appointment. She heaped abuse on former board member Martha Swaim, a white, and said that black board member Virginia Morris was a dupe of the white elite. Then, in a speech that certainly reduced her effectiveness on Capitol Hill, Sizemore accused "the racist white power structure in Congress" of starving the schools financially—despite the fact that Sizemore's own figures showed that Washington's expenditure per pupil was on a par with that of the most affluent nearby suburban district and above the average for most big cities.[154]

By May 1975, seven of the board's eleven members had decided to drop Sizemore and prepared formal charges of administrative inefficiency. Sizemore then insisted on a formal hearing of the charges, a procedure guaranteed by her contract. The hearing began early in August and continued for three stormy weeks. It ended in a "mistrial" when Herman T. Benn, who was employed by the board as an administrative judge, ruled that there were irregularities in the way the board framed its charges against the superintendent. Sizemore's confrontation with the board was tumultuous. Even before the formal charges were heard, her supporters had packed board meetings, where they had hurled insults and physically threatened board members. Yet Sizemore would not disavow the intimidation. She knew the demonstrations would confirm the opposition of some board members, but she hoped the outbursts would help in rallying her supporters for the school board elections to be held in the fall of 1975. With six of the eleven seats up for election and two of her supporters occupying the remaining seats, Sizemore thought she could stay in office if enough new supporters were elected.[155]

It did not work out that way. "The great non-issue was the Sizemore affair," the *Washington Post* commented after the election; "to their credit, most of the incumbents and challengers concentrated their campaigns on the future rather than the disruptive past." One of Sizemore's principal critics was defeated, but other opponents were returned to office. Seven members of the board continued firm in their decision to oust the superintendent.[156]

The board proceeded with a second set of charges, and hearing officer Herbert O. Reid finally concluded that the evidence presented against Sizemore added up to a pattern of inefficiency sufficient to warrant removal from office. In October 1975, by a vote of 7 to 4, the board fired Sizemore and named Vincent Reed as acting superintendent.[157]

Sizemore considered herself a victim of racism. Four of the seven votes against her were cast by whites, she noted. The board had dismissed her, she said, because she wished to develop an innovative, multicultural curriculum that deemphasized European history and literature and prepared black students to "recognize social and economic injustice." With characteristic acerbity, she also said that Vincent Reed had been chosen to succeed her because the board considered him "a person [who] will not . . . challenge the system" but would "turn it over to white people to control."[158]

IX

Vincent Reed was forty-seven years old in 1975. Stout and sturdy, he had been a Golden Gloves boxing champion in St. Louis and had been named to the black college All-American football team in 1951 after an outstanding season as a linebacker for West Virginia State College. He began teaching at Jefferson Junior High in Washington in 1956 and had worked as a counselor and assistant principal before becoming associate superintendent of the District's schools. Known as "Vince" to his friends, he was easy to approach and was known as "a gregarious, hail fellow well met sort of guy." He was also a practical man who, at the beginning of his administration, clearly identified two goals: "We've got to stop telling people the system can't be managed," he said. "It can. And we've got to stop telling our children they can't learn because they're black, poor, or both. They can learn. We don't want them using racism as a crutch and an excuse."[159]

Reed's appointment represented something of a departure for the Board of Education. In the recent past the board had hired superintendents who were noted for their educational ideas and then judged them on the basis of their administrative skill. In naming Vincent Reed to head the school bureaucracy, the board indicated that above all it wanted a competent manager.

Reed did not disappoint them. In October 1975, just before Reed was appointed, 1,500 school employees complained of mistakes in their paychecks; a year later the number of complaints had been cut to just three.

Under Reed the delivery of books and supplies was also markedly better than in recent years.[160]

When it came to academic questions Reed tended toward cautious conservatism. He avoided taking a firm stand on ability grouping and aptitude tests—issues that had agitated Washington for more than a decade—and he kept most of Barbara Sizemore's decentralized administrative structure. At the same time Reed emphasized the importance of basic academic skills, favored special programs for gifted students as well as for slow learners, and saw nothing wrong with standardized achievement tests. When it came to teaching style, Reed's preferences were rather old-fashioned. He had reservations about the open classroom and chose an associate superintendent who said it was "a bunch of crap" for reformers to say, "'God made this child, and there should be a natural unfolding of his capabilities.'" "God may have made children," James T. Guines conceded, "but without the help of people they will never develop."[161]

Reed knew that, above all, something had to be done to raise academic standards in the District. If that were not accomplished, it would be impossible to stop the annual flight of middle-class black students. When standardized tests were administered in 1978, after a four-year hiatus, the results were hardly encouraging. The scores generally followed the income and educational level of neighborhoods, with most schools in low-income areas doing poorly despite extra federal aid, while those in affluent areas did better. On the average, Washington's sixth-grade public school students were one year behind the national mean in mathematics and 1.7 years behind in reading. By ninth grade, however, the average Washington public school student was three years below national norms in both reading and mathematics. Of course, these numbers did not reveal much about what a particular child might achieve, but many parents thought they suggested something about the level of instruction at the junior and senior high schools. "When the averages fall low enough," one distraught father wrote, "so does the teaching level. Even the most dedicated teacher finally has to gear her lessons to the bulk of the class."[162]

The plight and flight of the gifted were also suggested in the steady decline in the number of Washington public school students who qualified as semifinalists in the competition for National Merit Scholarships.[163] The decline of academic standards in the District's high schools was suggested as well by the low SAT scores of some of those chosen as valedictorians. One in the class of 1976 had scored only 320 in verbal aptitude and 280 in mathematical aptitude, placing that student in the bottom 39 percent of all students in the country and the bottom 13 percent of college-bound students in the verbal test; the math percentiles were 16th and 2nd, respectively. This performance was unusually low for a valedictorian even in Washington, but most other valedictorians that year had scores that were far from outstanding, averaging 540 on the mathematical part of the SAT test and 510 on the verbal, both about the 80th percentile nationwide. Many Washington students who went on to prominent colleges reported that they found themselves over their heads academically.[164]

Reed thought it imperative that the schools do more for students with exceptional ability. Since Judge Wright's decree banning the track system of ability grouping, Reed said, the D.C. schools had been "gearing most instruction at the middle of the class" and had been doing less for bright students. "We should add more advanced courses for those youngsters who are motivated to take them," he declared. "Maybe we have gone from one extreme [concentrating on the honors track] to the other. . . . We should be teaching all children, whether they be bright, extremely bright, or not so bright."[165] To assist gifted students, Reed endorsed plans to give Gordon High School a rigorously academic program that would draw students from throughout the District. Unlike some special schools, such as the Bronx School of Science in New York, Gordon would have no special entrance requirements. It would simply offer demanding scholastic work that would appeal only to students who were academically inclined.

Many citizens nevertheless feared that other schools would be neglected. "Why not institute a special academic program at every school?" they asked. This would have been difficult to manage under the terms of Judge Wright's 1967 decree, however, and some observers said that opponents feared that an academic program at Gordon would skim the black cream, thus causing academic programs at other schools to suffer. The school board was not enthusiastic about developing a rigorously academic high school, and Reed eventually abandoned the project.[166]

The opposition to a special academic curriculum at Gordon stemmed essentially from a deep-seated fear that the program would become a refuge for Washington's black elite. This sentiment was rooted in seventy-five years of experience with Dunbar High School, the academic institution that Washington's black elite had attended in the years before desegregation. Dunbar was located in an area of southeast Washington that had become increasingly unsavory over the years, yet it drew its students from throughout the District and was not a neighborhood school: "for years it had been the pattern that most youngsters who *lived* near Dunbar did not *go* to Dunbar." Dunbar did not base its admissions on test scores but relied on a sort of self-selection, abetted by its reputation for academic toughness.

This was sufficient to recruit a very high caliber of student. Surviving records indicate that the mean IQ of Dunbar students was slightly above the national average. Over an 85-year span, moreover, most of Dunbar's graduates went on to college. Financial limitations required most to attend low-cost nearby colleges, but an impressive minority achieved academic honors at prestigious schools like Harvard, Amherst, and Oberlin. Thomas Sowell has noted that "in their careers, as in their academic work, Dunbar graduates excelled. The first black general (Benjamin O. Davis), the first black federal judge (William H. Hastie), the first black Cabinet member (Robert C. Weaver), the discoverer of blood plasma (Charles Drew), and the first black Senator since Reconstruction (Edward W. Brooke) were all Dunbar graduates. During World War II, Dunbar graduates in the Army included . . . a substantial percentage of the total number of high-ranking black officers at that time." [167]

There were class-conscious and color-conscious cliques among the students, however, and local tradition insisted that Dunbar was a sanctuary for snobs who considered themselves "the lightest and the brightest." The high academic accomplishments of Dunbar's graduates were not forgotten, but many stories circulated about its elitism. "You'll hear tales of unconscionable caste discrimination," columnist William Raspberry reported, "charges that the only way dark-skinned Negroes could attend all-black Dunbar was if they happened to be the sons and daughters of the black middle class." [168]

Dunbar's legacy was ambivalent. There was the proud memory of impressive academic standards, but also the recollection of patronizing snobbery. [169] Consequently, those who wished to raise academic standards in the 1970s hesitated before issuing a call for an elite high school. Nevertheless, parents like *Washington Post*'s Raspberry finally decided there was nothing wrong with encouraging middle-class people to stay with the public schools. They doubted that the introduction of a first-rate scholastic program for gifted students would write off disadvantaged students "any more than they are written off right now." [179]

Fearing a backlash against elitism, the board decided against a special academic high school and instead focused on improving instruction in basic subjects. Joan Brown, the coordinator of a curriculum planning group, acknowledged that teaching top students was not the main priority of the D.C. school system. "What's needed is to take care of the broad base of skills first," she said, "because that's what many of our students are not getting." "We are not trying to do anything fancy," Vincent Reed told a congressional committee in 1977. "We want to teach our youngsters essential skills. We want them to read, to write, and to reason. . . . If the kids can read and write, that's an innovation because that's different from what we have now." [171]

Reed proceeded cautiously. Recalling the storm of criticism that had rained down on Kenneth Clark's plan for the schools, Reed believed that no program could be implemented over the opposition of the teachers. In public he always insisted that the number of incompetent teachers was small, and he was careful to consult the teachers' union while developing a plan of his own. The plan was christened CBC—Competency Based Curriculum —and was designed to minimize the damage weak teachers could do without casting aspersions on their ability. Between 1975 and 1978 the D.C. school system produced a stack of CBC curriculum books. Each subject was broken down into a series of specific components, and the teachers' manuals explained in unusual step-by-step detail how lessons should be taught. In some cases the plans were so detailed they even contained a script with the exact words for teachers to use in presenting new material. One administrator called CBC "the McDonald's approach to education." "That's nothing to be ashamed about," she said. "McDonald's isn't creative French cooking . . . [but] they don't leave anything to chance. The food is always OK no matter where the store is."[172]

Besides dividing each subject into step-by-step details, CBC allowed each student to move at an independent rate of speed. No student could begin a new topic before demonstrating mastery of the previous one by passing an examination. If need be, however, the student could take the examination repeatedly—as many times as was necessary to pass it. Under CBC, students could not fail a subject; the worst they could experience was slow progress.

CBC combined aspects of both traditional and progressive pedagogy. Its structured approach and emphasis on basic subjects tended toward the traditional; its provisions for individual pacing and the absence of competition with other students tended toward the progressive. But not everyone was satisfied with the compromise. Barbara Sizemore complained that Reed was an educational conservative; others considered CBC too liberal. Some teachers rejected official advice to the contrary and continued to teach the whole class together instead of managing several groups working on different levels. They said it was not enough for teachers to set tasks, grade papers, and offer occasional advice; most students could not master the complexities of English syntax or the quadratic equation if they were left to work on their own. "They tell us to individualize instruction," said Charles Riddick, a mathematics teacher at Francis Junior High. "'Individualize' is a nice word, but with 30 to 35 students that's all it is. You've got to do most things with a group.'"[173]

Vincent Reed generally received high marks for his work in restoring administrative order to Washington's public schools. Lawrence Feinberg, the *Washington Post*'s astute reporter on educational matters, noted early in 1977 that "the system's administrative problems . . . have been reduced substantially." William Raspberry agreed. "Slowly but surely," he wrote, "Reed is imposing order on what was a chaotic system." After only six months as acting superintendent, Reed was promoted to superintendent, and two and one-half years later the board reappointed him to a new three-year term. This represented a milestone, for no superintendent had fully completed a single term since Carl Hansen's resignation in 1967. In reappointing Reed the board officially commended him for making "a good start in turning around a school system that has been troubled for over a decade."[174]

It remained to be seen whether the CBC could reverse the declining academic performance of Washington's students. Most observers approved of the emphasis on basic skills, but many doubted the CBC would be the city's academic salvation. Late in 1978 the Board of Education had reappointed Reed by a vote of 10 to 0 with one abstention, but Calvin Lockridge, the abstaining board member, pointedly noted that no improvement in student performance had yet been recorded on standardized tests. Reed's major achievements were in management and public relations, Lockridge said. "When we look at the students' test scores . . . it brings us back to the question of what schools are for."[175]

Lockridge's pessimistic assessment was reinforced by a series of reports on the situation at Eastern High School—the school that young Spottswood Bolling had entered in 1954 after winning his landmark case before the Supreme Court. "Going to school at Washington's Eastern High used to be straight out of Andy Hardy," wrote Richard E. Prince, a black reporter. "Students launched campaigns to stop their peers from smoking on the football field; the talk was whether Eastern would beat Western on Friday night, or maybe whether the school newspaper would again be a prize-winner." After spending two weeks at the school in 1973, Prince reported that Eastern had changed radically "in attitudes about everything—dress and drugs, manners and morals." The daily absence rate hovered around 20 percent, and 300 of the 2,000 students quit school each year. Those who remained showed little interest in schoolwork, and there were serious disciplinary problems even in academic classes like algebra.[176]

A similar picture emerged in 1978 when reporter Juan Williams recorded his impressions after spending ten weeks at the school. The typical Eastern student read at the sixth or seventh grade level, and large numbers of "hall people," estimated at about 20 percent of those enrolled, regularly cut classes to hang out in the halls.[191] Many hall people had great ambitions —to become doctors, lawyers, engineers—but no realistic conception of how to fulfill their goals. According to government teacher William Broadax, many concluded "that they could do things and get away with things without sacrificing the time and energy to study. . . . Just demand a job. . . ."[177] Despite special efforts undertaken on behalf of able students, the atmosphere at Eastern High School was hardly conducive to learning. The school was, according to Williams, a place "where teenagers get together, plan parties, make connections to score a high, and pick up mates."[178]

In many respects Eastern High was a representative microcosm of the Washington public schools, where in 1979 two dozen shootings were reported along with a thousand burglaries, robberies, and assaults. By this time some schools in the city had areas—called "Fourteenth Street" in one school and "The Ghetto" in another—"where teachers and administrators don't walk. They have yielded those places to drug users, vagrants, and class-cutters to keep their disruptive influence from spreading throughout the school."[179] By the 1980s the Washington public schools had become a last resort for poor parents who could afford nothing else. Acting Superintendent James T. Guines, who replaced Vincent Reed when Reed became assistant secretary of education in the Reagan administration, explained that "most of the black middle class, the former backbone and beneficiary of the system, [had] dissociated itself from the school system as a source of instruction, although not as a source of income. In the wake of the abolishment of the track 'ability grouping' system, many middle-class black heads of households continue to work in the public school system as teachers and administrators and then use a substantial portion of their salaries to exercise their freedom of choice to enroll their children in expensive local parochial and private schools." On the twenty-fifth anniversary of *Brown,* James M. Nabrit, Spottswood Bolling's attorney in the landmark lawsuit, acknowledged that despite a multimillion dollar budget, the Washington public schools had drowned the courtroom victory in a sea of failure.[180]

With the aid of hindsight we can see that school desegregation in Washington was a transition between the eras of segregation and resegregation, between the time when the first blacks enrolled in mixed schools and the last whites moved out. Those who believe that blacks are congenitally inferior in reasoning power and imagination will conclude that the decline in academic standards was inevitable. Others will point to the disadvantages that a disproportionate number of blacks face in their homes and poverty-stricken communities. "You are not going to see massive changes for the better until you see massive changes in the environment," former superintendent Hugh Scott declared in 1975. "Children in the District of Columbia's public schools do poorly because so many of them come from impoverished homes, and they will continue to do poorly regardless of how the school system is reformed."[181]

Yet important consequences do not always issue from great, impersonal antecedents; personal predilections, prejudices, and choices can shape the course of events. Judge J. Skelly Wright established a standard of proof that made it impossible for Washington's school authorities to justify and continue pupil assignment policies that had worked reasonably well. To avoid "inflicting any further injury on the Negro," Judge Wright required that the school board be subjected to strict judicial scrutiny.[182] He might proclaim noble intentions, but he could not ignore the disappointing results.

Wright began with a strong personal commitment to integration and a particular distaste for people like Carl Hansen who were, Wright said, "affirmatively satisfied" with schools that were desegregated but racially imbalanced. Wright admitted that as a judge he possessed no special expertise in educational matters and that generally it would be better for questions of social policy to be resolved democratically in the political arena.[183] Yet he was so committed to integration and so captivated by the sociological theories then expounded by James S. Coleman that he could not let pass the opportunity to impose his views on Washington's schools. Instead of assisting school administrators in their efforts to upgrade public education in Washington, he identified them with the evil he was contending against, destroyed them, and in the name of the Constitution delivered the school system to excesses of disorder and academic experimentation. One cannot know that things might have been different if wiser people had made better choices. But if that possibility is admitted, then the story of public education in Washington since 1954 is an object lesson illustrating the perils of sentimental pedagogy and judicial arrogance.

MASSIVE RESISTANCE
IN PRINCE EDWARD COUNTY,
VIRGINIA

Washington was the first of the nation's school districts to implement
the mandate of *Brown*. It moved speedily to desegregate its public schools
in 1954 and conscientiously tried to comply with subsequent court orders.
The white citizens of Prince Edward County, Virginia, were not so oblig-
ing. For a decade they challenged the federal judiciary and refused to coun-
tenance even token desegregation. When their policy of massive resistance
could no longer be maintained, they refused to finance public schools in
1959 and established a private academy for white students. For four years
there was no formal education for blacks in the county, and when public
schools were finally reopened in 1964, their enrollment was almost all black.
Segregation was maintained by developing a new version of the dual school
system. This arrangement has been widely criticized, but there has been
no deterioration in the general quality of education in Prince Edward. The
schools established under the new regime are as good as or better than those
that existed in the county before *Brown*.

I

Prince Edward County is situated about sixty-five miles southwest of
Richmond in the rural region known as Southside. Technically, the name
"Southside" refers to that part of Virginia south of the James River, with
the exception of the easterly Tidewater region. But in 1950 Southside was
more than a geographical designation. It was the northern tip of the South's
black belt, an enormous region stretching for a thousand miles from Virginia through the Carolinas, Georgia, Alabama, and into Mississippi, Louisiana, and Texas. It included approximately 200 counties in which the black
percentage of the total population ranged upward from about 50 percent.

The white residents of the black belt traditionally possessed a deep and abiding concern for white supremacy. Prior to the 1950s this supremacy was maintained largely because the whites of the black belt had persuaded the nation that questions of local race relations should not be dealt with from outside the South. White southerners, particularly those who lived in the black belt and had first-hand acquaintance with large numbers of blacks, were thought to understand them as well as anybody and to be uplifting the black race. Nowhere else, it was claimed, had the masses of blacks progressed at such a rapid rate.

Throughout the region the races were segregated. They would mix in the world of work, but separation was invariably prescribed in social relations. Blacks in Prince Edward were employed in the local sawmill and various businesses, and they thought nothing of entering white-owned stores to make purchases. But blacks entered restaurants or approached drugstore counters only to get food to take out. Black youths attended separate schools that prior to the 1950s were not the equal of those provided for whites.

The prevailing pattern of race relations was most likely to be challenged in counties where blacks departed from some black-belt norms, developed a degree of economic independence, and cultivated leaders of their own choosing. Prince Edward County qualified in these respects. In the mid-nineteenth century the county boasted the largest population of free blacks in Virginia, and the agricultural census of 1950 indicated that there were almost as many black farm operators as white. Fewer than 20 percent of the farmers in the county were tenants. Bob Smith, a reporter who has written at length about Prince Edward, noted that "the Negro farmer of Prince Edward tended to be reasonably independent."[1] The 1950 census indicated that 55 percent of the county's 15,398 citizens were white, but 57 percent of the 3,462 students enrolled in the public schools were black.

For two generations blacks in Prince Edward had enjoyed considerable freedom in choosing their leaders. Their chief organization was the First Baptist Church of Farmville, the county seat and largest town. Located at the corner of Fourth and Main streets, First Baptist was housed in a large building that a white congregation had used before the Civil War. W.E.B. Du Bois reported that in 1897 the church was "much more than a religious organization." It was the black community's "chief organ of social and intellectual intercourse," "really the central clubhouse of the community."[2]

Presiding at First Baptist from 1949 to 1980 was the Reverend L. Francis Griffin, whose father had preceded him in the pulpit from 1927 to 1949. Born in 1917, the younger Griffin was a twenty-four-year-old handyman who had not yet graduated from high school when the Japanese bombed Pearl Harbor. He went into military service almost immediately and eventually joined the first black tank outfit (the 758th Tank Battalion). During the war he decided to become a minister, and after returning to the United States he quickly finished his last year of high school and enrolled at Shaw University in North Carolina. When the elder Griffin died in October 1949, the members of the congregation at First Baptist asked his son to take over the pulpit. Young Griffin accepted and then set himself to the additional task of organizing a local chapter of the NAACP. For Griffin the message of Jesus and that of the NAACP were complementary. He was convinced that American segregation was at odds with the Golden Rule of Christianity. In years past many a preacher at First Baptist, including the elder Griffin, had preached a gospel of Christian meekness, humility, and obedience. Under the Reverend L. Francis Griffin the religious impulse of black Prince Edward would be directed toward protest.[4]

Beginning in the 1930s, the NAACP made an attack on racial discrimination in education an important part of its campaign for the advancement of blacks. Financed by a grant from the Garland Fund, the association challenged the legality of flagrant racial discrimination in the public schools. The Supreme Court in several decisions had held that segregation did not deny equal protection of the laws unless the facilities provided for blacks were markedly inferior. In fact, however, the educational facilities provided blacks usually were far below standard, as was indicated in the disparity between black and white school expenditures recorded in 1930. In South Carolina the average annual expenditure for the education of white children was almost ten times the amount spent for black children. Mississippi was spending nine times as much for whites, and Alabama, Florida, Georgia, and Louisiana were spending more than three times as much.[5]

A demonstration that blacks received less than equal treatment in one school district did not necessarily prove unfairness in other districts. The NAACP nevertheless brought suits against school districts that disregarded the separate-but-equal principle. Successful cases focused public attention on the injustice of racial discrimination and encouraged other blacks to bring suits. There was also the hope, expressed in an internal memorandum to the NAACP, that equal expenditures "would make the cost of a dual school system so prohibitive as to speed the abolishment of segregated schools." It was hoped that successful suits demanding equalization might amount to an end run around segregation.[6]

The NAACP's equalization lawsuits prompted the South to undertake a massive campaign to upgrade its black schools. During the 1940s enormous progress was made toward eliminating racial differentials in salaries, and by 1950 Virginia's black teachers had achieved parity with their white counterparts (Table 3). In 1956, three years before the state abandoned its massive resistance to desegregation, Virginia's 6,204 black teachers were earning an average salary of $3,169, a sum that was $59 larger than the

TABLE 3. Average Annual Salary of White and Black Teachers
of Virginia, 1940–1941 to 1949–1950

School Term	Average Annual Salary				Percent Negro of White	
	Women		Men			
	White	Negro	White	Negro	Women	Men
1949–50	$2,160	$2,209	$2,719	$2,520	103.2	92.7
1948–49	$2,081	$2,124	$2,613	$2,434	102.1	97.2
1947–48	$1,927	$1,962	$2,515	$2,300	101.8	91.4
1946–47	$1,735	$1,724	$2,315	$2,040	99.4	88.1
1945–46	$1,486	$1,418	$1,987	$1,956	95.4	98.4
1944–45	$1,360	$1,264	$2,030	$1,661	92.9	81.8
1943–44	$1,254	$1,124	$1,877	$1,440	89.6	76.7
1942–43	$1,081	$910	$1,431	$1,071	84.2	74.8
1941–42	$857	$632	$1,400	$824	73.7	58.9
1940–41	$805	$553	$1,272	$726	68.7	57.1

Source: *Journal of Negro Education* 29 (Winter 1960): 19.

average earned by the 20,729 whites then teaching in the state's public schools.[7]

A similar trend could be observed with regard to equalization of facilities. In several counties the NAACP filed suits challenging the quality of the curricula, bus transportation, buildings, and equipment provided for blacks. Precedent-setting judgments followed, and by the mid-1950s the status of black schools approximated that of white schools. The *Washington Post* estimated that the NAACP's equalization drive in Virginia had produced $50 million in higher teacher salaries, new buses, and improved schools for blacks. Drawing on statistical information concerning the value of school properties, the per-pupil cost of educators' salaries, and the percentage of youngsters actually attending school, Doxey A. Wilkerson of Howard University developed an Index of Relative Status that marked the rapid progress toward equalizing Virginia's white and black schools (Table 4).[8]

The upgrading of black education proceeded at varying rates, and the record of Prince Edward was neither the best nor the worst among Virginia's 98 counties. In 1939 a substantial black high school building was erected and named for the county's most famous black native, Robert R. Moton, the man who had succeeded Booker T. Washington as principal of Tuskegee Institute. The existence of such a school represented real progress, and for some time Moton was one of only twelve black high schools in rural Virginia. Yet there were inadequacies from the start. Moton High School was built for a capacity of 180 students, but 167 enrolled the day it opened. The next year there were 219, and by 1950 student enrollment had increased to 477. Moton High soon became seriously overcrowded, and it never had a gymnasium, cafeteria, locker rooms, infirmary, or audi-

TABLE 4.   Index of Relative Status of Virginia's Black Schools

	1940–41	1947–48	1956–57	Increase 1941–1957
All Counties	63.1	75.9	89.6	42.2
All Cities	75.0	75.9	99.8	32.3
State	67.5	78.1	92.8	37.5

Source: *Journal of Negro Education* 29 (Winter 1960): 24.

torium with fixed seats, all of which were provided for whites in the county seat at Farmville High School.[9]

Little could be done about the overcrowding during and immediately after World War II, for construction materials were not available even if there had been funds. By 1948, however, the wartime shortages had eased, and the school board appropriated $17,000 for the construction of three temporary outbuildings. These economical stopgaps were made of wood, covered with tarpaper, and were quickly dubbed "the shacks." Each had a single wood stove, which made it necessary in winter for students who sat nearby to take off their coats while those who sat farther away bundled against the chill. The teachers had to pause occasionally to stoke the fires.[10]

Blacks naturally complained that second-rate structures seemed to betoken a belief that their education was unimportant. In the spring of 1950 a committee chaired by Griffin informed the board that a 63-acre site suitable for a new black high school was available just south of Farmville for $8,000, and a few months later the board began negotiations for the purchase of the property. In December 1950, the board also submitted a four-year building plan to the state Board of Education in Richmond. That year, the state legislature had appropriated $45 million for school construction — the so-called Battle Fund, named for Governor John S. Battle. Each county was invited to submit a list of its needs, and Prince Edward submitted a request for $1,125,000, $800,000 of which was earmarked for the construction of a new black high school. The state awarded $274,000 to Prince Edward, leaving the county with the responsibility for raising the additional money. Then, in the summer of 1951, the state's Literary Fund loaned Prince Edward an additional $600,000 (at only 2 percent interest) for the equalization of the county's school facilities. Construction of a new Moton High School proceeded swiftly, and the new school opened to about 500 students in the fall of 1953. Built at a cost of $850,000, the new Moton was assessed at a figure in excess of the combined value of all other public schools in Prince Edward County. It had an auditorium, gymnasium, cafeteria, "everything a modern high school should have." Its physical facilities were superior to those available to whites enrolled in the county's two other high schools, Farmville and Worsham.[11]

In the meantime, however, Prince Edward's impatient black students had gone on strike. Led by an intrepid sixteen-year-old junior named Barbara Johns, some 450 high school students marched out of their classes on 23 April 1951 and began to picket their schools with placards proclaiming "We Are Tired of Tar Paper Shacks—We Want a New School." The initial goal was not desegregation. "It never entered my mind at that time that this would turn out to be a school desegregation suit," Johns later said. "We didn't know of such things. We are thinking that the school would be improved, or at best, that we would get a new school." "We did not foresee the end results of our demonstrations such as the intervention of the NAACP, integration, etc." [12]

The students maintained that they had acted alone in organizing the strike at Moton. "We knew we had to do it ourselves," Barbara Johns wrote, "and that if we had asked for adult help before taking the first step we would have been turned down." Many influential whites nevertheless were convinced that the strike had been instigated by adults. A few minutes after the strike began, the Reverend Griffin arrived at the scene, and during the next few weeks Griffin and NAACP lawyers were observed meeting at the Ely Street home of Moton principal M. Boyd Jones. Jones advised against the strike in public, but Barbara Johns recalled that on one occasion the principal "whispered to me under his breath, 'Keep up the good work. I am behind you 100 percent but I must not publicly acknowledge this.'" [13]

When the Moton students got in touch with the NAACP, they discovered that the nation's most prominent black organization was changing its legal strategy. For years it had worked to equalize educational facilities and salaries. Its successes had made the South pay dearly for segregation, but by 1951 it was clear that most whites would sacrifice financially before they would abandon segregated schools. Equalization had been achieved in large measure, but integration seemed no closer. By eliminating the inequities associated with the dual system, the NAACP's campaign ironically seemed to have left segregation more firmly entrenched than ever. The essentials of the dual system had been preserved by reforming its most obvious defect.

During its first twenty-five years the NAACP had been dominated by leaders who distinguished between segregation and discrimination. Experience suggested that discrimination (inferior treatment based on race) usually accompanied segregation, but the leaders knew that segregation and discrimination did not always go together. Most agreed with W.E.B. Du Bois that "there should never be opposition to segregation pure and simple unless that segregation does involve discrimination." Blacks should fight against discrimination, "against the refusal of the South to spend the same amount of money on the black child as on the white child for its education. . . . But never in the world should our fight be against association with ourselves because by that very token we give up the whole argument that we are worth associating with." [14]

In the mid-1930s the leaders of the NAACP began to march to a different beat. After a heated dispute over the wisdom of supporting separate black institutions, Du Bois resigned in 1934, and Walter White, who became the chief executive in 1931, then appointed several influential officers who believed that integration and dispersion were the best ways to advance the status of blacks. White endorsed the equalization litigation of the 1930s and 1940s, but only because he thought equality was the most that courts would sanction at the time, and because he hoped the financial strain of upgrading black facilities would persuade whites to abandon segregation and integrate their schools. [15] When this hope proved erroneous, the NAACP's integrationist leaders reassessed their strategy. This reassessment was also prompted by the Supreme Court's 1950 decision in the case of *Sweatt v. Painter,* in which a black postman from Texas named Herman Sweatt had refused to accept admission to a hastily established all-black law school. Instead, Sweatt sought the aid of the NAACP and went to court for an order requiring his admission to the all-white law school at the University of Texas in Austin.

Thurgood Marshall, who handled Sweatt's case for the NAACP, feared that a frontal attack on segregation would not succeed. Consequently, he framed Sweatt's pleading to require only that Texas provide Sweatt with an equal law school or admit him to the state university law school in Austin. In an accompanying *amicus* brief filed by 187 law professors, however, it was argued that "separate legal education cannot be equal legal education." By assigning blacks to "a raw, new law school without alumni or prestige," Texas was said to have deprived them of the equal protection of the laws. [16]

When it rendered its decision in the Sweatt case, the Supreme Court avoided some of the broader issues posed by the case; focusing on the apparent inequality of the law school Texas provided for blacks, the Court decided for Sweatt. Chief Justice Fred Vinson noted for a unanimous court, "the University of Texas Law School possesse[d] to a far greater degree those qualities which are incapable of objective measurement but which make for greatness in a law school. Such qualities, to name but a few, include reputation of the faculty, experience of the administration, position and influence of the alumni, standing in the community, traditions and prestige." [17] The decision appeared to be a setback for integrationists, since it reaffirmed the constitutional validity of the "separate but equal" doctrine. Yet, by introducing intangible concepts such as "prestige" and "standing in the community," the Supreme Court suggested that no segregated black school could pass muster as truly equal. Commenting on the Court's rationale, the *New York Times* observed, "By the Supreme Court's yardstick there is not a single state-owned Negro school in the South that can measure up to similar white schools."[18]

Shortly after the Supreme Court announced its *Sweatt* decision, a conference of NAACP lawyers and officers decided that pleadings in all future education cases would be aimed at obtaining education on a nonsegregated basis and that no relief other than that would be acceptable. The NAACP would still take equalization cases, but only if the plaintiffs would argue that separate facilities were inherently unequal.[19] The two most prominent NAACP attorneys in Virginia explained the modified approach to the Moton students. On 25 April 1951, two days after the strike had begun, Oliver W. Hill and Spottswood W. Robinson drove to Farmville and said plainly that they would be interested in nothing short of a desegregation suit. The next night, at a mass meeting of about a thousand Moton students and parents, W. Lester Banks, the NAACP's chief executive in Virginia, declared that a new school would not mean equality even if it matched the white school "brick for brick, cement for cement."[20]

The NAACP was encouraged by the students' reaction. The young people "had not winced" when they were told that the NAACP would enter the case only if they were interested in suing for desegregation. Yet there was some question whether the black adults of Prince Edward would support such a suit. Willie Redd, a well-to-do black contractor who had close connections with the county's white leaders, rallied several black businessmen who believed that progress would be more likely without a frontal attack on segregation. And J.B. Pervall, a respected former principal of Moton High School, recalled that for years "all the parents had been begging for a new school, and all the people I talked with seemed to be leaning toward getting a new school." He told the students that "if they wanted to go in for a new school I would help them, but not integration." To one of the NAACP's lawyers Pervall said frankly, "I was under the impression that the students were striking for a new building. You are pulling a heavy load . . . coming down here to a country town like Farmville and trying to take it over on a non-segregated basis."[21]

The Reverend Griffin called a mass meeting to rally support for the protest, and student leader John Stokes later estimated that about 65 percent of the parents eventually supported the strike, whereas 10 percent were neutral, and 25 percent were opposed. It is hard to know whether the general support reflected an endorsement of the NAACP's goals or was simply an expression of pride and encouragement for the children of the community and of independence by land-owning black farmers. Barbara Johns later wrote that an account of the strike would not be complete if it failed to mention "the pride I had in the parents (and others) who supported us.

They were at first bewildered by it all—but, . . . [t]hey stood behind us— timidly at first but firmly."[22]

Some observers questioned whether the new school would have been built if there had been no student strike or desegregation suit. Authors Bob Smith and Richard Kluger, two perceptive students of the county, noted that the $274,000 awarded to Prince Edward under Virginia's Battle Fund fell short of the amount needed to build a new high school. An additional bond issue would have been necessary if the state's Literary Fund had not loaned another $600,000 during the summer of 1951. This loan came two months after the strike and was apparently influenced by a desire to under-cut the black position in the desegregation suit. "Efforts to build a new school, which had been languishing for years, now moved ahead at full speed," Kluger concluded. Longwood College dean C.G. Gordon Moss shared this view. Facing the threat of desegregation, he observed, "the rul-ing whites of the County . . . [found] the money they had previously said they were unable to find. They . . . were trying to 'buy the Negroes off' by giving them more than they had asked for in the way of physical facili-ties and thus hoped to stop the desegregation suit."[23]

Nevertheless, Prince Edward might have joined Virginia's march toward equalization even in the absence of the student strike and the desegrega-tion suit. Because the U.S. Supreme Court was demanding that public schools be desegregated if they were not equalized, segregationists really had no alternative to building a new black high school. Before the strike, the school board had begun negotiations for the purchase of a campus south of Farmville for the new black high school and had already filed an application for state assistance for its construction. Blacks such as Willie Redd and J.B. Pervall appear to have had sound reasons for believing that the school board would make good on its announced intention of build-ing a first-rate new school.

II

The whites of Prince Edward regretted that their county had been cho-sen for a test case on the law of segregation. Yet the NAACP had intervened, and the movement that had begun locally to focus attention on the need for a new school had become part of a campaign to eliminate racial segre-gation throughout the United States. The challenge had to be accepted, the *Farmville Herald* insisted, for segregation "was the outgrowth of les-sons and experiences in living together and until these have changed mate-rially the attempt to change the relationships will not inure to the benefit of either race."[24]

When a special three-judge U.S. district court convened to hear the Prince Edward case in February 1952, the defendant school board was represented by two well-regarded counselors. T. Justin Moore was a Phi Beta Kappa graduate of the University of Richmond who had gone to Harvard law school before becoming one of Virginia's best-known corporate lawyers. J. Lindsay Almond, the state's attorney general, had previously served as a judge and as a member of Congress. They insisted that there was "no foundation whatever for the fundamental theory on which this case is built—namely, that equal facilities and advantages cannot be provided regardless of the amount of money that is spent."[25]

In arguing the Prince Edward case, the NAACP insisted that "the original notion behind [Virginia's] school segregation laws was to impose upon Negroes disabilities." "The segregation laws . . . were intended to . . . limit the educational opportunities of the Negro," attorney Spotswood W. Robinson declared. Black youths educated apart from whites recognized that they had been stigmatized as unfit for participation in white society. Deep and corrosive feelings of inferiority often followed, so that the ambitions of many black students were thwarted and the development of their abilities was stifled.[26]

To establish the nature of the damages, the NAACP relied on the testimony of several social scientists whom the court referred to as "eminent educators, anthropologists, psychologists and psychiatrists." Isidor Chein was a psychologist who had taught at C.C.N.Y. for thirteen years before becoming director of research for a Zionist-oriented organization. He testified that 90 percent of the social scientists who had responded to one of his questionnaires believed that racial segregation had "detrimental psychological effects" on those who were segregated, "even if equal facilities were provided." M. Brewster Smith, a psychology professor from Vassar College, testified that the effects of segregation were "such as to make the Negro . . . more like the common, prejudiced conception of a Negro, as a stupid, illiterate, apathetic but happy-go-lucky person. . . . Children . . . who grow up knowing that they are despised by the people around them, are thought not as good as the people around them, are going to grow up with conceptions of themselves as being, in some way, not worthy." John Julian Brooks, the director of a private school in New York City, conceded that Virginia had made substantial progress toward equalizing its schools. Nevertheless, Brooks insisted, "the large teaching salaries, shining buses, [and] fine brick buildings, are poor compensation for humiliation, lack of self-respect, and a restricted curriculum."[27]

The NAACP's social scientists agreed that stigma and disgrace accompanied the segregation of black students, even if the separate facilities were equal to those provided for whites. By commanding that the races be educated in separate schools "the state is saying to the Negro that he should have no pride in his race," Isidor Chein asserted. Kenneth B. Clark, stated that through segregation Virginia "constantly and continuously" declared that blacks should "have no pride in race." [28]

In response, Attorney General Almond insisted that, given the sentiments prevailing when Virginia's public school system was established in 1870, the alternative to segregation was not integration but exclusion. Segregated schools were established "not as a badge of inferiority, not to place the Negro man or the Negro child in the position where he could never rise to take his place in a free society," but as the only arrangement that would make free public education possible. Eleven of the twenty-two blacks then serving in the state legislature had conceded the point when they voted against a proposal to prohibit racial segregation in the public schools. [29]

Almond's colleague, T. Justin Moore, also defended Prince Edward County. He conceded that the Farmville High School for whites was the best-equipped of the county's three secondary schools, but since construction was now under way on a new Moton High School, Moore assured the court that by September 1953 Prince Edward's black high school students would enjoy educational facilities superior to those provided for whites. [30] Moore then moved to a spirited critique of the NAACP's evidence. The real issue in the case, after all, was not whether the facilities at Moton High School were as good as those at Farmville High School, but whether segregation was intrinsically discriminatory and therefore illegal. Moore announced at the outset that he was "prepared to show by competent evidence" that the personal damage alleged to be inflicted by segregation was "purely speculative [and] not based on a sound scientific basis." [31]

Moore began by questioning the evidence of Chein's questionnaire. Although several thousand social scientists satisfied the requirements Chein had used in compiling the list of potential respondents, the questionnaire was actually submitted to only 850 men and women, of whom some 500 sent in replies; of these only 32 came from the South. Beyond the apparent sectional prejudice of Chein's sample, Moore suggested that the questions were slanted in such a way that the respondents' answers were preassured. "I say you might as well be asking people whether it is desirable for everybody to try to live according to the Sermon on the Mount as to ask them the kind of questions they had put to them," Moore informed the court. [32]

Next, noting that the NAACP's lawyers had placed "great stress on what they call the psychological issue," Moore and Almond were determined to establish that there was "quite a conflict of opinion among the experts on that matter." [33] In addition to John Nelson Buck, a clinical psychologist from Lynchburg, the state also called upon two well-regarded Virginia social scientists: Lindley Stiles, the head of the Department of Education at the University of Virginia, and William H. Kelly, a well-known child psychologist from Richmond. The star witness for the defense, however, was Henry E. Garrett, a former president of the American Psychological Association. Garrett had spent the previous twelve years as chairman of the Department of Pyschology at Columbia University, where he had taught for almost thirty years. A man of impressive, patrician bearing, Garrett scoffed at the NAACP's social science. He characterized Chein's questionnaire as a "blunderbuss" that lacked nuance and specificity "since it failed to explain what sort of segregation was referred to, whether it was practiced by law or custom, and in what way or ways it might be 'detrimental' to personality." "I am surprised he did not select his sample well enough to have gotten a hundred percent" response indicating that segregation had harmful effects, Garrett declared. The prominent psychologist said that if he were a gambler he would "wager that I could send a questionnaire and phrase it rightly and get almost any answer I wanted."[34]

Garrett rejected the NAACP's contention that separate education harmed blacks psychologically. Instead, he insisted that blacks could receive a quality education under segregation "provided you have equal facilities." In fact, "taking into account the temper of [Virginia's] people, its mores, and its customs and background," Garrett was of the opinion that "the Negro student at the high school level will get a better education in a separate school than he will in mixed schools." Garrett believed that "if the Negro child had equal facilities, his own teachers, his own friends, and a good feeling, he would be more likely to develop his own potentialities, his sense of duty, his sense of art, his sense of histrionics. . . . The Negroes might develop their schools up to the level where they would not [wish to] mix; and I would like to see it happen. I think it would be poetic justice."[35]

When it came to questions of law, Virginia's attorneys argued that the court should interpret the Fourteenth Amendment "in the light of what was really intended, and what was understood by Congress and by the legislatures at that time." In their view, the historical evidence demonstrated that neither the Congress that submitted nor the state legislatures that ratified the Fourteenth Amendment understood the equal protection clause to prohibit segregation in the public schools. The Thirty-ninth Congress that submitted the Fourteenth Amendment to the ratifying states also passed legislation providing for segregated schools in the District of Columbia. Congress endorsed the legitimacy of the District's segregated schools again in 1868, the year the Fourteenth Amendment became a part of the Constitution, and it had continued to do so thereafter. Moreover, only five states abandoned segregated schools after the passage of the Fourteenth. Twenty-three of the thirty-seven states either continued to operate segregated schools or, in the case of some reconstructed southern states, established segregated schools shortly after ratifying the Fourteenth Amendment.[36]

In addition to stressing that the Fourteenth Amendment had not been intended nor understood to outlaw school segregation, Virginia's lawyers noted that leading appellate courts and the U.S. Supreme Court had repeatedly ruled that segregation did not deny equal protection unless the separate facilities were inferior. Thus, if the Prince Edward case were decided on the basis of controlling precedents, the most the court should order was the equalization of high school facilities—something that would soon be accomplished in any event.[37]

Each member of the three-judge district court had ruled for the NAACP in previous school equalization suits. Nevertheless, as Richard Kluger has observed, all three were "lifelong Virginians deeply versed in federal and state law and not given to apostasy." Their verdict in the Prince Edward case was never in doubt. They unanimously found for the county.[38]

Segregation rested "neither upon prejudice, nor caprice, nor upon any other measureless foundation," the judges declared. For generations segregation had been "one of the ways of life in Virginia." It was a practice that had become "a part of the mores of her people." "In this milieu," the court concluded, "we cannot say that vast separation of white and colored children in the public schools is without substance in fact or reason." Referring to previous cases they considered controlling, the judges also noted that the Supreme Court and other appellate courts had already "rejected the proposition . . . that the required separation of the races is in law offensive to the National statutes and constitution."[39]

The controlling precedents were sufficient for disposition of the case, but the district court nevertheless addressed the NAACP's contention that segregation stigmatized the black as "unwanted" and implanted "a sense of inferiority." Expert witnesses had testified for the NAACP that separation "distorted the child's natural attitude, throttled his mental development, . . . and immeasurably abridged his educational opportunities." Testifying for the defense, however, witnesses whom the court characterized as "equally distinguished and qualified" emphatically asserted that, "given equivalent physical facilities, offerings and instruction, the Negro would receive in a separate school the same educational opportunity as he would obtain in the classrooms and on the campus of a mixed school."[40]

Each witness offered "cogent and appealing grounds for his conclusion," but the court was not willing to endorse any view. It concluded only that there was no incontrovertible evidence that segregation caused "hurt or harm to either race." Given the inconclusive character of the psychological evidence, the court was of the opinion that segregation should be considered a matter of legislative policy that the Commonwealth of Virginia should determine for itself. As for the admittedly inferior facilities at Moton High School, the court noted that an expressive new school for blacks would soon be opened and decided that an order to equalize was not necessary.[41]

The leaders of the NAACP had not expected to win in Virginia. They were interested primarily in building a record that would give the Supreme Court the opportunity to expand the rationale of its Texas law school opinion so as to strike down all school segregation. The wisdom of this strategy became apparent in May 1954, when the Supreme Court ruled on the NAACP's appeal of the Prince Edward case. In *Brown* the high court reversed the special district court and decided for the NAACP on every major point.

Writing for a unanimous Supreme Court, Chief Justice Earl Warren dismissed the historical evidence as "inconclusive." Referring to the Texas law school case, the chief justice then noted that the Supreme Court had previously taken into account "qualities which are incapable of objective measurement"—intangible considerations such as a student's "ability to study, to engage in discussions and exchange views with other students." Such considerations applied with added force to younger school children, Warren wrote. If they were separated from others of similar age and qualifications solely because of their race, they experienced "a feeling of inferiority as to their status in the community that may affect their hearts and minds in a way unlikely ever to be undone." "Whatever may have been the extent of psychological knowledge at the time of *Plessy v. Ferguson*," a new psychology was "amply supported by modern authority," the chief justice declared. "In the field of public education, the doctrine of 'separate but equal' has no place. Separate educational facilities are inherently unequal." Racial segregation was found to deprive children of equal educational opportunities "even though the physical facilities and other 'tangible' factors may be equal."[42]

The full ramifications of the *Brown* opinion would not be apparent for more than a decade, but most whites in Prince Edward immediately perceived trouble ahead. They could find solace only in the last paragraph of the momentous opinion. Acknowledging that "the great variety of local conditions" made it difficult to determine appropriate relief, the Court declined to issue a decree before hearing additional arguments. The Court had determined that blacks possessed a constitutional right to desegregated public education, but the enjoyment of that right would have to be delayed while the Court considered the practical difficulties in the way of implementation.[43]

Speaking for Prince Edward County when the high court met to consider its decree, attorneys Lindsay Almond and A. G. Robertson argued that the district court below had "much greater familiarity with local conditions" and consequently was in a better position "to determine a program for effective enforcement of the [*Brown*] decision." A period of gradual adjustment to the new interpretation would be necessary, they insisted, for successful desegregation depended on "an evolutionary change in the attitude of people in Virginia, both Negro and white."[44]

As things stood, a united majority of whites was said to be prepared to boycott desegregated public schools. "Much has been said of the emotional and psychological effects of segregation upon Negro children," Virginia's lawyers stated, but "no consideration has ever been given . . . to the effect of integration on white children." Referring to reading tests that had been given in 1954 to 31,000 eighth-grade students in Virginia, the lawyers noted that the average score of the top quarter of white students exceeded the average of the top quarter of black students by more than six years; in fact, the average score of the lowest quarter of whites exceeded the average of the highest 25 percent of blacks. Many white parents were said to fear that compulsory integration of students of the same age and grade would lead to lower academic standards. It simply was not practical "to mix everyone together and have one teacher instructing children whose levels of attainment are as diverse as the reading ages of 18 and 9," the lawyers declared. Almond stated that "the education of the white group must suffer . . . if the teaching level is pitched for the level of the median Negro child."[45]

Virginia's lawyers also cited statistics indicating that black students were ten times more likely than whites to have been born out of wedlock, and fourteen times as likely to contract venereal disease. The incidence of disease and illegitimacy was said to be "just a drop in the bucket compared to promiscuity," and the lawyers predicted that whites would withdraw from public schools before submitting to any plan that jeopardized the education or moral values of their children. They said *Brown* had raised "the spectre of impending educational chaos" and advised that "a substantial period for adjustment must be permitted before any sizeable number of white Virginians would accept desegregation."[46]

The NAACP accepted the need for remanding the Prince Edward case to the district court but warned that there would be interminable delays if the Supreme Court did not set a time limit for the implementation of *Brown*. In its formal presentations to the Court the NAACP ignored the allegations of black immorality, but in private correspondence executive secretary Roy Wilkins lamented that "Negro families and Negro school children have been the targets of unbridled slander from many sources." Oliver Hill conceded that illegitimacy and venereal disease were serious problems but argued that "the first step in eradicating this evil is the elimination of racial segregation—its breeding place."[47]

In its second *Brown* decision of 31 May 1955 (known as *Brown II*), the

Supreme Court remanded the Prince Edward case to the district court without mentioning a time limit. While reiterating "the fundamental principle that racial discrimination in public education is unconstitutional," the high court required only that Prince Edward make "a prompt and reasonable start toward . . . a racially non-discriminatory school system." Instead of immediately granting the relief requested by the victorious black plaintiffs, the Supreme Court instructed local authorities to desegregate "with all deliberate speed" and "as soon as practicable." The Court declared that "it should go without saying that the vitality of these constitutional principles cannot be allowed to yield simply because of disagreement with them." Yet the Court's postponement of relief was transparently a concession to anticipated disagreement and resistance.[48]

With the constitutional issue settled, the Prince Edward case was assigned to the resident district judge, Sterling Hutcheson. A lifelong resident of Virginia and a native of Mecklenburg, another of the rural black belt counties of Southside Virginia, Hutcheson recognized "the basis upon which the *Brown* case is founded . . . that segregation of white and colored children in public schools has a detrimental psychological effect upon the colored children." However, witnesses in his court were "unanimous in expressing the opinion" that Prince Edward would close its public schools if it was ordered to desegregate. The hardship visited on black students would be particularly severe, Judge Hutcheson noted, for white parents had more resources and had gone beyond blacks in making contingency plans for the private education of their children.[49]

In the second *Brown* opinion, the Supreme Court acknowledged that the district courts, because of familiarity with conditions in their areas, were in the best position to determine whether local authorities had begun to comply with *Brown*. Hutcheson believed compliance could be achieved in Prince Edward if the county was afforded "patience, time and a sympathetic understanding," but he feared that abrupt desegregation would stiffen the resistance of whites and delay a solution of the problems. Consequently, he found that the Prince Edward school board, by continuing to operate public schools (with the black schools now "concededly . . . equal if not superior to those available to children of the white race"), was doing "all that reasonably could be required of them in this period of transition."[50]

On appeal, the Fourth Circuit Court ruled that Hutcheson was "in error in not fixing a time for compliance." Instead of making "a prompt and reasonable start" toward desegregation, Prince Edward had manifested "an attitude of intransigence." "Deliberate speed," the pace ordered by the Supreme Court, was intended to permit adjustment to administrative difficulties but not to authorize indefinite delay pending a change in public opinion.[51]

Judge Hutcheson remained convinced that "much harm can be caused by ill-considered action." "An interrupted education of one year or even six months places a serious handicap upon a child," he observed. Nevertheless, the court of appeals had insisted upon a definite date for desegregation, and Hutcheson accordingly fixed September 1965, ten years after the date of the second *Brown* opinion, as the time for compliance. He explained that "crash programs" and "speedy action" were not applicable to the situation in Prince Edward. "Despite the great advances made in scientific and technological knowledge," he wrote, there was "no evidence that the modern human mind was any more adaptable to accepting new theories of social or moral reform than that of the Athenians of 500 B.C." Since the great Solon had absented himself for ten years to allow the people the opportunity to interpret, modify, and grow accustomed to his new laws, Hutcheson set a similar period to allow for adjustments to far-reaching changes in the customs of the people of Prince Edward County.[52]

The Fourth Circuit Court of Appeals was not persuaded by Hutcheson's historical analogy. Noting that the school board had taken no positive steps toward implementing desegregation, the appellate court reversed Hutcheson once again and ordered the public high schools of Prince Edward to admit students without regard to race for the term beginning in September 1959.[53] When that date arrived, however, there was no desegregation, for the whites of Prince Edward declined to levy taxes for mixed public schools and instead made arrangements for the private education of their children. Prince Edward ended public school segregation by closing its public schools.

III

From the outset the whites of Prince Edward insisted that they would abandon public education before they would integrate their schools. Yet they could not make definite plans until after the Supreme Court had laid down its program for ending segregation. On 31 May 1955, within hours of the order to proceed toward desegregation "with all deliberate speed," the county's Board of Supervisors convened and voted unanimously to appropriate for public education only the minimum amount needed to guarantee school debt amortization and to safeguard school property—$150,000. Instead of approving the remainder of a $685,000 school budget, the board decided to appropriate the necessary operating expenses on a monthly basis. "If one wished to oversimplify," Richmond editor James J. Kilpatrick observed, "it could be said that the court ruled at Noon that Negroes must be admitted to Prince Edward's public schools, to which the county replied, at 8 o'clock, there will be no public schools."[54]

That defiant opposition was widespread in the county was indicated again in May 1956, when 4,184 citizens of Prince Edward, more than had voted in any previous election, signed a statement affirming that they preferred "to abandon public schools and educate our children in some other way if that be necessary to preserve the separation of the races." If the schools were responsible for integrating blacks into the mainstream of modern culture, it was alleged, teachers would lose sight of the first priority—academic education.[55]

In *Brown* the Supreme Court had decided what the county could *not* do: it could not segregate public school students on the basis of race. The Court had not decided that counties were constitutionally required to operate public schools. Indeed, according to white Prince Edward, the judiciary would transgress the constitutional separation of powers if it prescribed how elected legislative bodies should spend tax money. Asserting that desegregated education would be "pernicious," the whites of Prince Edward proclaimed their resort to "that first American tenet of liberty:—that men should not be taxed against their will and without their consent for a purpose to which they are deeply and conscientiously opposed." For years this would be the bedrock of Prince Edward's legal position.[56]

Another showdown in the courts loomed in the future, but in the meantime it was necessary to make sure that teachers did not leave the county. On 7 June 1955, in response to a call from the PTA, almost 1,500 citizens assembled at Jarman Hall on the campus of Longwood College in Farmville, where they heard Maurice Large, a former chairman of the school board, propose the creation of a nonprofit foundation to raise funds to guarantee the salaries of the county's sixty-nine white teachers.[57] Some speakers expressed reservations about the proposal. James Bash, the principal of Farmville High School, asked several questions before candidly stating that he was "a public school man" and would refuse to work for a private corporation of this kind. Professor Foster B. Gresham of Longwood College suggested that an attempt be made to guarantee the salaries of all teachers—black as well as white—but his proposal was greeted with a chorus of negative comments and was ruled out of order. Dabney S. Lancaster, the president of Longwood College, spoke against abandoning public schools but also declared that integration would set education back half a century. "We'll fight it from the housetops, from the street corners, in every possible way," he said. "We are going to maintain our way of life."[58]

By a vote of 1,250 to 25, an overwhelming majority endorsed the proposal to charter a nonprofit foundation to be known as the Prince Edward School Foundation. J. Barrye Wall, the editor of the *Farmville Herald* and a principal proponent of the private foundation, candidly explained that an organization such as this would be indispensable for the long-term maintenance of education on a separate basis. Sacrifices would have to be made, and $46,375 was promised before the meeting was adjourned. By mid-July the foundation was a going concern that had collected $180,000 in pledges.[59]

Some in the large audience at Jarman Hall may have thought they were simply supporting their teachers. But those who listened carefully should have known they were doing two additional things that would shape the nature of education in Prince Edward County. "They were establishing an organization that could pay the white teachers privately, and they were making a distinction between these white teachers and the Negro teachers whose salaries thus were not guaranteed."[60]

Citizens of Prince Edward advanced a variety of arguments to support segregation. T.J. McIlwaine, who had been the county's superintendent of schools since 1918, said that standard tests showed that by fourth grade white students as a group were two and one-half years ahead of blacks in academic skills, and that the gap doubled by the time the children were in high school. It followed, he said, that "if we are ordered to carry out horizontal integration, that is, to combine white and Negro pupils according to their present grade, the teacher who now has an aptitude range of three years among white pupils in one classroom will find a range of five to six years in a mixed class."[61]

Blacks occasionally asserted that they were entitled to better themselves through association with whites, but whites feared their children would retrogress if they were exposed to a lower-class black lifestyle over a period of time. B. Blanton Hanbury, a Farmville businessman who became president of Prince Edward's private educational foundation, referred to his children as "six good reasons" why he opposed integration. Robert Taylor, a local contractor, declared in 1955 that he would rather have his children "miss a year or two of school than face the kind of bitterness and brawling that mixed schools will bring." Twenty-four years later he recalled, "We felt our primary duty was to provide for our children as best we could. Most blacks were so far behind our children academically and differed in mores and cultural attainment. There was nothing good that our children could gain from interaction in school with blacks."[62]

Whites in Prince Edward said there were only two ways to avoid a decline in educational and moral standards as schools staggered from crisis to crisis under the burden of a large influx of black children: whites could fight integration or they could run from it. Yet Prince Edward had been defeated in its courtroom fight, and most residents of the county lacked the wealth and mobility that enabled urban citizens to escape desegregation by moving to the suburbs. "We're a small rural county with little money," Robert Taylor explained. "Many families have lived here for 300 years and have no place else to go." He thought whites had no choice but to repair to separate private schools.[63]

After visiting Prince Edward on assignment for *Commentary* magazine, James Rorty reported that "the fear of racial intermixture is real to the point of pathology among poor white farmers and lower middle-class villagers. . . ." Nor was concern about miscegenation confined to these groups. *Farmville Herald* editor J. Barrye Wall tended to downplay racial arguments, preferring to focus on legal and constitutional questions. Yet Wall was an admiring student of several racist social scientists, whose views were published from time to time in the *Herald*. Readers were informed that "the long-term aim of the NAACP is intermarriage" and that "intimate race mixing of white and colored children in the classrooms" eventually would "sign the doom of the white race and the Negro race." Robert B. Crawford, a Farmville businessman who would play a leading role in the statewide effort to resist desegregation, similarly believed that "mixing children in school is the beginning of the end for both races. . . . It is inevitable that children who play together from the age of five will not stop at eighteen. There will be intermarriage." School superintendent T.J. McIlwaine declared succinctly, "Sexual promiscuity is what [whites] fear most."[64]

Two of Virginia's leading intellectuals also sounded the alarm. Henry E. Garrett, the former president of the American Psychological Association who had testified for Prince Edward in 1951 when the desegregation case was initially before the district court, had since become a professor at the University of Virginia. An authority on intelligence testing and racial differences, Garrett noted that 85 percent of American blacks regularly scored below the national average on standardized tests. Sympathetic humanitarians attributed the blacks' low scores to "invidious discrimination, oppression, prejudice, lack of incentives, and slum living." But Garrett was of the contrary opinion that blacks were genetically inferior to whites in reasoning power and imagination.[65]

Garrett believed many American liberals were so repelled by Adolph Hitler's misguided racial views that they had rejected a sane approach to inherent racial characteristics, focused attention on a minority of high-achieving blacks (who admittedly scored above average on mental tests), and attributed the relatively poor performance of the majority of blacks to a deficient environment. This was "wishful thinking of the most dangerous sort," according to Garrett. The fact is, he said, "the Negro brain is slightly smaller than the white (about 100 cc on the average) . . . less fissured and less complex than the white brain [with] reduced thickness in the frontal cortical brain layers. . . ." Egalitarians discounted the importance of hereditary characteristics, but Garrett traveled to Prince Edward and warned, "Unless the egalitarian dogma is discredited and abandoned, it will lead inevitably to social integration, intermarriage, amalgamation of white and Negro, and to a general deterioration in American standards of culture."[66]

A similar view was put forward by James Jackson Kilpatrick, the articulate editor of the *Richmond News Leader*. Kilpatrick maintained that "the Negro race, as a race, has failed to contribute significantly to the higher and nobler achievements of civilization as the West defines the term." For thousands of years the blacks of sub-Saharan Africa were "in effective possession of one of the richest continents on earth," but they developed "no more than the crudest smelting of iron and copper; . . . no written language, not even the poorest hieroglyphics; no poetry; no numerals; not even a calendar that has survived. Even so skilled a defender as Toynbee has to conclude, after a desperate flurry of coughs and sighs, that the black race is the only one of the primary races 'which has not made a creative contribution to any one of our twenty-one civilizations.'"[67] Kilpatrick inclined toward the view, as did many white Virginians, that black stagnation resulted from a deficient genetic pool that submerged an unusually small minority of intellect in an exceptionally large tide of mediocrity and backwardness. Some exceptional blacks admittedly had distinguished themselves, but these outstanding individuals had never been sufficiently numerous to uplift their race — not in Africa or Haiti, not in the black districts of the major American cities or anywhere else where blacks made up a majority of the population. Apologists attributed the blacks' failure to a lack of opportunities and to white oppression, but Kilpatrick regarded this as "the excuse, the crutch, the piteous and finally pathetic defense of Negrophiles unable or unwilling to face reality." Caucasians and Asians had repeatedly overcome the obstacles fate placed in their way, but blacks alone among the three primary races of man had never managed to develop an advanced civilization.[68]

Kilpatrick conceded, however, that modern social science had not developed methods to determine with precision the relative importance of heredity and environment. Environmentalism could be argued plausibly and provided "a fine topic for a sophomore's term paper." Yet in some ways the origin of the black's backwardness seemed "largely irrelevant." If the condition were intrinsic, Kilpatrick saw "nothing but disaster . . . in risking an accelerated intermingling of blood lines." If it were acquired, blacks still lagged far behind, and most southern whites were "determined" not to let their children be "guinea pigs for any man's social experiment."[69]

Elsewhere in Virginia, white moderates avoided talk of defiance and tried to appease the Supreme Court by accepting token integration. Most moderates hailed from the mountain counties of southwest Virginia or from the Shenandoah Valley, where blacks constituted less than 10 percent of the population. Some hailed from predominantly white suburbs near major cities like Norfolk, Richmond, and Washington. They conceded that most blacks trailed below grade average in their studies but thought it would be disastrous if public schools were closed. Striving for a solution, moderates believed local-option plans would make it possible for school districts to comply with *Brown* and yet avoid substantial integration.

The schools could be kept "99 percent segregated" if students were assigned according to scholastic aptitude, personality, and neighborhood residence, explained state senator Ted Dalton, a leading moderate from Radford, a small town in Appalachian Montgomery County (5 percent black). State senator Armistead Boothe, a leading moderate from the suburbs of Washington, similarly contended that desegregation did "not mean that a predominantly white school will have a large number of Negro pupils or that a predominantly Negro school will have a large number of white pupils." School officials in Richmond assured parents that there would be little racial mixing if students were assigned to schools in their neighborhoods. "For the past several years," they explained, "schools have been built in neighborhoods in which one race predominates, rather than near the border between a white and Negro residential area. Thus . . . many schools would continue the way they are now."[70]

Some confirmed opponents of desegregation initially sympathized with the moderates. In June 1954 J. Barrye Wall acknowledged that "in communities where there are few Negroes it is conceivable that some schools can be desegregated without harm to the students or to education." James J. Kilpatrick agreed and urged that local communities decide for themselves. He conceded that "many localities in the Southwest and the [Shenandoah] Valley, where Negro population is small, may wish to integrate their schools." But "the problem of integrating, say, 57 Negro students in Dickenson County with 6,460 white students in Dickenson County is one thing. The problem of integrating 1,500 white students and 1,800 Negro students in Prince Edward County is quite another." Kilpatrick thought "the feelings and wishes of the people of Dickenson County and of Prince Edward County should be equally respected."[71]

Upon further reflection, most segregationists opposed even a modicum of mixing. Once the dikes of segregation were let down to admit a few able black students, they feared white schools would be engulfed in a black flood. They also doubted that either the NAACP or the federal judiciary would accept any system under which a majority of blacks would be enrolled in different tracks or in disproportionately black schools. Roy Wilkins of the NAACP admitted as much in a 1959 speech in Portsmouth, Virginia. "Negro citizens cannot accept token integration as a satisfaction of the Supreme Court ruling," he said. "They can accept it only as a beginning, not as an end." They must recognize the "central fact that . . . this is a struggle to get a non-segregated education for two million Negro children."[72]

Some Virginians considered this "mixing just to be mixing." The *Richmond Times-Dispatch* warned, "the NAACP is not content with such integration as would take place along neighborhood lines. They wish to uproot white children from white schools, and uproot colored children from colored schools, in order to expedite race-mingling-by force." Lindsay Almond predicted that the NAACP would demand busing for racial balance—"a judicial order to transport Negro children to schools in white areas with the return trip loaded with white children to be forced into Negro schools."[73]

Nevertheless, in November 1955 a thirty-two-member commission of the Virginia legislature endorsed a moderate program that would have permitted local school districts to devise their own plans for assigning pupils to school, even if this led to mixing in some sections of Virginia. The Virginia Commission on Public Education acknowledged that public schools could not operate effectively without the support of taxpayers. It also warned that taxpayers in the black belt were likely to abandon public schools rather than accept integration. Yet, despite their reservations about desegregation, the members of the commission considered it impractical and unconstitutional to defy the Supreme Court. They were convinced, in any case, that there would be little mixing under local option, and to ensure that no student was subjected to unwelcome desegregation the commission proposed a system of tuition grants to aid children who wished to escape by attending private schools.[74]

Before tuition grants could be provided, it was necessary to amend Section 141 of the Virginia Constitution, which prohibited the use of state funds to aid private schools. To this end, the General Assembly called a popular referendum for 9 January 1956 on whether to hold a limited convention for this purpose. By a vote of 304,154 to 146,164 Virginia's voters endorsed the referendum. In Prince Edward County the vote was 2,835 to 350 in favor of the referendum. By the time the convention assembled in March to adopt the tuition grant amendment, however, Virginia was already moving toward what was called "massive resistance."

Leading the way was a group of Southside segregationists known as the Defenders of State Sovereignty and Individual Liberties. Incorporated in the fall of 1954, the Defenders maintained a state headquarters in Richmond, published a monthly newsletter, and eventually enrolled 12,000 members who affirmed their belief that "segregation of the races is a right of state government." J. Barrye Wall was among the principal founders of the organization, which took its name from the inscription on a Confederate monument that Wall passed on the way to his office at the *Farmville Herald*. The organization was active throughout the state and carefully nurtured an image of gentility that helped make it effective in Virginia. The Defenders resorted to a minimum of name-calling and disdained to distribute much of the literature prepared by the Citizens Councils and other groups.

In supporting the amendment of Section 141, many advocates of tuition grants gave assurances that each locality would be permitted to devise its own program for assigning students. In their Plan for Virginia, however, the Defenders called for laws that would prevent the use of state funds to support desegregated schools. Since the state supplied about 42 percent of the money used for local schools, they reasoned that communities would think twice before deciding to operate desegregated schools solely with local funds.

The Defenders found an influential ally in U.S. Senator Harry F. Byrd, the acknowledged leader of the dominant faction of Virginia's Democratic party. In a statement released before the constitutional convention, Byrd endorsed the amendment of Section 141 to permit tuition grants, but he carefully refrained from commenting on local option. After the referendum, Byrd threw his support behind the Defenders' proposal to deny state money to desegregated public schools. "Virginia stands as one of the foremost states," he said. "Let Virginia surrender to this illegal demand [desegregation] . . . and you'll find the ranks of the other Southern states broken." If Virginia could organize the southern states for massive resistance, Byrd thought that in time the rest of the country would realize that racial integration was not going to be accepted in the South.[75]

Most Democratic politicians followed Byrd's lead. Governor Thomas B. Stanley prepared a package of thirteen bills that would trigger resistance if any local school district decided to desegregate its public schools. In addition to proposing a state system of tuition grants, the legislation provided that, as a last resort, the governor could withhold state funds from desegregated public schools. The House enacted the governor's program, 59 to 39, but the legislative package barely passed the Senate, 21 to 17. The voting pattern was predictable, with legislators from the black belt supporting massive resistance, 31 to 2, while 25 of the 30 representatives from the white suburbs of Norfolk, Richmond, Roanoke, and Washington voted in opposition.[76]

The defiance of Virginia's segregationists was steeled by James J. Kilpatrick's editorials in the *Richmond News Leader*. From the moment of the first *Brown* decision, Kilpatrick regarded desegregation as "jurisprudence gone mad." He believed the Supreme Court had ignored eighty years of legal precedents and wilfully disregarded the original understanding of the Fourteenth Amendment. Since the justices had repudiated the Constitution and rewritten the fundamental law of the land "to suit their own gauzy concepts of sociology," Kilpatrick recommended that the South use every possible legal means to circumvent desegregation. "Let us pledge ourselves to litigate this thing for fifty years," he wrote. "If one remedial law is ruled invalid, then let us try another; and if the second is ruled invalid, then let us enact a third. . . . If it be said now that the South is flouting the law, let it be said to the high court, *You taught us how*."[77]

In an extraordinary series of editorials published in November 1955, Kilpatrick resurrected the Jeffersonian idea of interposition as a method by which the Court's "process of judicial legislation" might be ended. When a Federalist congress passed the Alien and Sedition Acts of 1798, in apparent disregard of states' rights and of the First Amendment's prohibition of laws that abridged freedom of speech, James Madison and Thomas Jefferson prepared protests known as the Virginia and Kentucky Resolves. Faced with a "deliberate, palpable and dangerous exercise" by the federal government of powers not granted to it, a state, asserted Jefferson and Madison, had the right to interpose its authority between the federal government and its own citizens. Just what interposition entailed was not specified clearly, however, for the offensive legislation expired on 3 March 1801, the day before Jefferson succeeded John Adams as president of the United States.

It was John C. Calhoun, writing in the 1820s and 1830s, who prescribed how states might resist unconstitutional federal encroachment without withdrawing from the Union. They could "interpose" or suspend the operation of a law considered unconstitutional pending resolution of the dispute according to the manner prescribed in Article V of the Constitution. In joining the Union, each state had conceded that the basic covenant might be amended by three-fourths of the states. Thus interposition by one state could prevail only if it was sustained by at least one-fourth of the sister states. Individual states possessed the right to set aside laws they considered unconstitutional, Calhoun asserted, but this right was to be checked and counterpoised by the power of three-fourths of the states acting in concert.

Kilpatrick thought the right to interpose could be inferred reliably from the nature of the Constitution and its system of checks and balances. By assuming the authority to amend through interpretation of the Constitution, the Supreme Court had upset the balance and had usurped powers that were reserved to not fewer than three-fourths of the states. According to the logic of Jefferson, Madison, and Calhoun, however, usurpations such as *Brown* could be checked and suspended pending appeal to the people of the states that had joined to form the federal Union.[78]

With Senator Byrd endorsing Kilpatrick's views, the Democratic organization quickly fell into line. In February 1956, Virginia's assembly adopted an interposition resolution asserting that, in the absence of an amendment to the Constitution, states retained the authority to operate racially segre-

89

gated schools, provided such schools were substantially equal. State senator Harry F. Byrd, Jr., predicted that "if people are firm enough and determined enough," the Supreme Court eventually would reverse the *Brown* decision.[79]

In Prince Edward County, *Farmville Herald* editor J. Barrye Wall similarly insisted that if southerners would "stand steady" and play "balance of power politics," they could see to it "that all future appointments to the Supreme Court are of men who will reverse the [*Brown*] decision." Standing on the doctrine of interposition and the "rights retained to the states under the Tenth Amendment," Wall insisted that Prince Edward should not desegregate its schools "unless or until the Constitution of the United States is amended." He thought northerners and blacks themselves eventually would suffer if federal courts continued to disregard states' rights. History might even prove that "the preservation of America's federal-state system, assuming it is preserved, can be credited to the staunchness of Southern defenders of States' Rights."[80]

The essential question, according to Wall, concerned the nature of the federal union. To prevent oppressive tyranny by a distant central government, the founding fathers had written into the Constitution explicit assurances that the states should retain authority over matters not delegated to the federal government. The Fourteenth Amendment admittedly guaranteed equal protection of the laws, but the Congress that had submitted the amendment, and the states that had ratified it, had not contemplated or understood that equal protection would require the abolition of segregated schools. If this had been the case, the Congress and ratifying states would have abolished segregation where it existed. Instead, one after the other, they established racially separate schools at the same time they endorsed the amendment. Much of the current controversy could have been avoided, Wall asserted, if advocates of desegregation had amended the Constitution "in an orderly manner—as prescribed in the document itself—instead of attempting in effect to amend the Constitution by judicial decisions . . . based on questionable sociological, historical, and legal evidence."[81]

Beyond this there lay another basic legal question: could an unelected judicial body require an elected legislative body, like Prince Edward's Board of Supervisors, to assess taxes for integrated schools? Referring to the American revolutionaries' principle that there should be no taxation without representation, Wall insisted that American citizens could not be compelled to support a cause that the majority conscientiously opposed. "The problem is larger than Prince Edward County, the principles are greater than education," he wrote. "We are standing up for what we believe to be the best interests of our people—and the people of the United States—the protection of the Constitution as we understand it and as the Supreme Court did until 1954."[82]

This is how things stood in the fall of 1957. The Supreme Court had ordered Prince Edward to desegregate its public schools and then remanded the case to U.S. district court, where the resident federal judge had declined to set a date for compliance. Prince Edward was still operating segregated public schools, and its taxpayers and Board of Supervisors said they would withhold appropriations for public education and find some other way to educate white children if their schools were desegregated. They believed that desegregation would lead to educational chaos and were influenced also by an eclectic but clearly articulated melange of constitutional principles and racist beliefs. For most whites in Prince Edward, "as soon as practicable" meant "never at all."[83]

In the meantime, Virginia's General Assembly had rejected a plan that probably would have led to token mixing of the races in some communities. Virginia's legislature instead challenged the Supreme Court and required unyielding segregation in all sections of the state.[84] Against this background the gubernatorial election of 1957 was held. State senator Ted Dalton, the Republican nominee, was a formidable candidate who had almost defeated the Byrd organization when he received a surprising 45 percent of the vote in the gubernatorial election of 1953. Dalton was not an integrationist, but he favored locally administered public assignment plans. By contrast, the Democratic candidate, Lindsay Almond, rejected the possibility of tokenism, arguing that it would be naïve to believe that the Supreme Court would approve any program which did not satisfy the NAACP. Asserting that his opposition to desegregation was "firm, unyielding, and unalterable," Almond supported the recently enacted legislation that authorized the governor to withhold state funds from public schools that were desegregated. He appeared to be an appropriate candidate for a party whose platform pledged it to "oppose with every facility at our command, and with every ounce of our energy, the attempt being made to mix the white and Negro races in our classrooms."[85]

Almond crushed Dalton in the general election by a 9-to-5 margin, receiving 63.5 percent of the vote. He rolled up his greatest margins in the black belt (receiving 73 percent of the vote in Prince Edward County), while Dalton's share of the vote was lower than it had been in 1953 in all sections of the state. According to James W. Ely, Jr., the election indicated that "the overwhelming majority of white Virginians, by perhaps as much as a three to one margin, supported a candidate who seemed to promise that the public school system would be closed before it would be integrated."[86]

Nine months after his inauguration, Governor Almond was put to the test when federal courts ordered that black students be admitted to public schools in Charlottesville, Norfolk, and Warren County. The desegregated schools were then closed after Almond withdrew their state funds, and

13,000 pupils found themselves with no classes to attend. In rural Warren County and the small city of Charlottesville, the great majority of white children were accommodated in private academies and makeshift classes, but several thousand white youths received no formal instruction in Norfolk, Virginia's largest city, where whites lacked the unity needed to provide alternative education.

At this juncture, in January 1959, the courts attempted to resolve the controversy. In *Harrison v. Day,* the Virginia Supreme Court of Appeals, although finding no constitutional objection to tuition grants and deploring the U.S. Supreme Court's "lack of judicial restraint" in *Brown,* ruled that Section 129 of Virginia's state constitution required the operation of public schools throughout the state. "That means," wrote Chief Justice John W. Eggleston for a 5-to-2 majority, "that the state must support such public free schools in the state as are necessary to an efficient system, including those in which pupils of both races are compelled to be enrolled and taught together, however unfortunate that situation may be." In a *per curiam* opinion released the same day, a three-judge federal district court in Norfolk held that Virginia's school-closing statute was unconstitutional. As long as the state maintained a public school system, the court ruled, "the closing of a public school or grade therein . . . violates the right of a citizen to equal protection of the laws. . . ."[87]

The next evening Governor Amond replied to the courts in a remarkable speech that raised the spirits of Southside whites and of states' righters everywhere. He declared that he would "not yield to that which I know to be wrong and will destroy every semblance of education for thousands of the children of Virginia." In ringing phrases he threw down the gauntlet

> to those of faint heart; to those whose purpose and design is to blend and amalgamate the white and Negro race and destroy the integrity of both races; . . . to those false prophets of a 'little or token integration'; to those in high place or elsewhere who advocate integration for your children and send their own to private or public segregated schools; . . . to those who would overthrow the customs, morals and traditions of a way of life which has endured in honor and decency for centuries and embrace a new moral code prepared by nine men in Washington whose moral concepts they know nothing about; to those who would substitute strife, bitterness, turmoil and chaos for the tranquility and happiness of an orderly society; to those who would destroy our way of life because of their pretended concern over what Soviet Russia might think of us. . . .[88]

Yet only one week later, in a surprising turnabout, Governor Almond returned to the General Assembly and proposed that Virginia abandon massive resistance. He knew of no way through "the dark maze of judicial aberration and constitutional exploitation." The only way to defeat integration, Almond believed, "was to close down every single, solitary [public] school in this state and keep them closed." This, the governor insisted, would be too high a price to pay to avoid token mixing.[89]

Two days after executing his about-face Governor Almond established a forty-member legislative commission on education. Known as the Perrow Commission, after its chairman, a moderate state senator from Lynchburg named Mosby G. Perrow, Jr., this body held hearings and finally recommended a "freedom-of-choice" plan that resembled the Virginia Commission's proposals of 1955. Forsaking massive resistance, the commission recommended that local communities develop their own pupil placement plans and further called upon the General Assembly to provide tuition grants without regard to desegregation, thus separating the grants from any formal connection with the racial controversy. Supported by a heterogeneous coalition of Republicans, moderates, and former resisters, Almond narrowly carried the proposals through the assembly, securing passage in the Senate by a margin of only 20 to 19. Virginia's era of complete segregation in the public schools came to an end in the spring of 1959, when twenty-one black students peacefully entered previously all-white schools in Norfolk and Arlington.[90]

In the final analysis, massive resistance collapsed because whites broke ranks. "United we might have stood for a generation," James J. Kilpatrick wrote to Senator Byrd. "Divided we are failing as surely as a cause can fail." In urban and suburban areas many whites saw no need for the sacrifices that would be required to maintain segregation. Some of the whites who broke from massive resistance believed in desegregation for reasons of principle, but others were moved by pragmatic calculations; they believed that courts would be satisfied if a few well-qualified black students were assigned to predominantly white schools. Reflecting this point of view, Lewis F. Powell, then the chairman of the Richmond school board and later an associate justice of the U.S. Supreme Court, promised in 1959 that "every proper effort will be made to minimize the extent of integration when it comes." Virginia had to choose between "some integration and the abandonment of our public school education," Powell explained. He asumed that Richmond's students would be assigned to neighborhood schools and predicted that "a majority of the elementary schools will have no more than a negligible percentage of integration for many years." When Lindsay Almond stepped down as governor in January 1962, fewer than 1 percent of Virginia's black students attended desegregated schools. Most whites were of the opinion that mixing could be kept to token levels.[91]

IV

While whites elsewhere in Virginia were opting for token integration, those in Prince Edward turned a deaf ear to what they considered the siren's song of moderation. When the Fourth Circuit Court of Appeals in May 1959 ordered Prince Edward to take "immediate steps" toward desegregating its public schools, the white citizens of the county responded by refusing to finance public education. On June 2, the Board of Supervisors cut property taxes from $3.40 per $100 of assessed value to $1.60, an amount sufficient to support the general county government but not enough to provide for public schools. The total budget was set at $210,654 instead of at the $982,000 that had been proposed when it was assumed that public education would continue. The county's taxpayers were urged to give the difference to private schools, and the Prince Edward School Foundation set about collecting almost $200,000 that had been pledged three years before.[92]

The time had come, the *Farmville Herald* declared, when the people of Prince Edward "must stand resolutely or supinely submit to intolerable conditions." They must "say with their dollars what they have so often said for the past five years." Elsewhere in Virginia whites had adopted a "policy of containment or freedom of choice," but the *Herald* considered this inappropriate in Prince Edward, where the nation would see "what happens when race mixing is ordered in a county where the Negro population outnumbers the white."[93]

During the summer of 1959 the whites of Prince Edward worked diligently to establish segregated private schools for their children. Sixty-seven teachers were employed, all but two of whom had taught previously in the county's public schools. A regular 180-day school year was established, several thousand books were collected for school libraries, and teachers' salaries, starting at $2,400, were the same as the previous year. By the end of the first academic year eight private schools, known collectively as the Prince Edward Academy, had received full accreditation from Virginia's State Department of Education.[94]

The speedy establishment of a countywide private school system was achieved through an extraordinary outpouring of zeal from the white community. On one rainy weekend volunteers laid cinder blocks to add four classrooms to the Sunday school of the Baptist church in Worsham, ten miles south of Farmville. On another weekend volunteers turned their attention to refurbishing the Sunday school at the Farmville Presbyterian Church. Together these two centers accommodated the county's high school students; other buildings were converted for the use of younger students. High school students volunteered to drive a fleet of seventeen used buses that a group known as Patrons had purchased from other school districts. A trucker purchased one bus personally, and two mechanics volunteered to keep the fleet in repair.

Civic organizations and citizens of every description cooperated in the effort. The local Junior Chamber of Commerce donated grass seed for a football field, and a contractor brought in his building crew to do the grading. Electrical workers volunteered to put up light poles for night games, while a supplier provided the big lights free of charge. At the makeshift school buildings, carpenters and plumbers worked in double shifts around the clock to install additional toilets, drinking fountains, and fire exits. Local merchants contributed electric drills and saws for shop classes and laboratory equipment for chemistry lessons. A supporter from Silver Springs, Florida, contributed 250 pounds of chalk. One teacher recalled having only about a week to make desk top attachments for six hundred folding chairs.

When the school year began in September 1959, almost all of the county's 1,400 white pupils were enrolled in the private Prince Edward Academy. There were problems, of course. Thin curtains were the only dividers between some classrooms, and the new schools had neither cafeterias nor study halls. Extracurricular activities were reduced, although the high school students still published a monthly newspaper and an annual yearbook and elected a student government and cheerleading squads. By and large, students seemed to accept their new environment; some said they preferred the new arrangement because of the 1:30 P.M. dismissal, made possible by the abolition of regular periods for lunch and study halls.[95]

From the outset the leaders of the Academy recognized that their venture was being watched with interest throughout the South. If Prince Edward made a success of its private schools, other black belt counties would be encouraged to follow suit. When the Academy students assembled at the State Theater on Main Street in September 1959, administrator Roy Pearson cautioned that their behavior should be above reproach. "If we have a successful year," he explained, "the hopes of hundreds of thousands will be kindled." Blanton Hanbury envisioned similar private schools as "the coming thing throughout the South" and predicted that the whole system of education would be improved if public schools faced competition from private academies. Others noted that the South had generally relied on private academies before 1870 and predicted that the trend would turn in that direction once again. Some day, they thought, the era of dominant public education would be recalled as a relatively brief interlude in the history of southern education.[96]

Throughout the 1960s and 1970s delegations of visitors traveled to Prince Edward from New Orleans, Atlanta, Baton Rouge, Nashville, and other points throughout the South. The county was no stranger to tourists, for it was studded with Civil War monuments, but most of the new visitors came not to mourn the Confederacy but to cheer Prince Edward's refusal to surrender to the Supreme Court. As white flight increased during the 1960s and 1970s, Prince Edward came to view itself as a symbol of states' rights and of defiant opposition to liberal social engineering. The county was "encouraged and admired privately by more people than any other county in the nation," an editorial in the *Farmville Herald* proclaimed.[97]

From the outset, officials of the Academy recognized that they must obtain permanent school facilities if their experiment in private education were to survive, and so money was raised to build a new high school on a hilltop near the outskirts of Farmville. When completed in September 1961, the handsome suburban-style campus included twenty-seven classrooms, a library, and facilities for shop courses and home economics. Appraised at $400,000, the actual cost was only $256,000 because of the volunteer labor, the donated materials, and the careful scrutiny of Harold Garrett, a local contractor who had previously built a score of schools. Almost all the furniture and laboratory equipment was used, but after two years of meeting in temporary quarters the academy's teachers and students were delighted to have a permanent school. In 1967 a companion grammar school was built at the foot of the hill, and in 1973 the high school added a 1,200-seat gymnasium and assembly room.[98]

The Academy buildings were sound, but the furniture and equipment would not have been tolerated in most public schools. As late as 1979, used student desks were still being purchased for the incredibly low price of fifty cents. Headmaster Robert Redd proudly asserted that students at the Academy could learn "just as much at a 50 cent desk as in one of those $25 'units' you find in the public schools." The Academy also lacked some facilities that were commonplace in public schools. Even in the 1980s it still had neither a cafeteria nor an auditorium with fixed seats.[99]

Most white parents believed the Academy offered their children a better education than they would have received in public schools. Sixty percent of the graduates of the first class continued their education in college, and by the late 1970s the figure had increased to 80 percent. This was an extraordinary record for a comprehensive high school that enrolled the great majority of whites in a rural county. Unlike some other private academies, which took pride in stressing basic academics to the exclusion of almost everything else, Prince Edward Academy offered shop, home economics, and secretarial studies and also developed a full program of extracurricular activities. The football team went undefeated in 1968, 1974 and 1979, and regularly attracted large crowds to its home games, where the Academy's marching band and high-stepping majorettes performed at half time. In the late 1970s the Pep Club, Honor Society, and Youth for Christ were all active on campus, and the debating team traveled through the South. During a period when much of public education in the South was in turmoil, Prince Edward Academy remained isolated from the conflict, an island of stability that reassuringly reminded parents of the schools they had known as youngsters.[100]

To a limited extent the Academy partook of the "back to basics" reaction against incidentals and irrelevancies that were thought to get in the way of academic education. In the early 1960s the school emphasized "no frills" education, with limited offerings in music, art, and physical education. Even after extracurricular activities were expanded, the Academy derived special satisfaction from its students' performance on standardized examinations. The students regularly scored above the national norms on the Science Research Associates (SRA) achievement tests, and average scores on the SAT increased by 5 percent during the 1970s, a time when the average national score was declining by about 9 percent. The percentage of Prince Edward students taking these tests far exceeded the national average, and some supporters of the Academy said that by stressing the basics in a controlled environment the school delivered twice the education for half the cost. During the 1970s, with an average annual enrollment of about ninety-five high school seniors, the Academy produced seven semifinalists who scored in the top one-half of 1 percent of those competing for National Merit Scholarships, and thirteen others who received letters of commendation for scoring in the top 5 percent. Five students from the Academy were Merit semifinalists in 1982.[101]

Headmaster Robert Redd attributed Prince Edward's academic success partly to its structured curriculum. The high school featured a three-track system, with the college preparatory curriculum, open to all who wished to enter, enrolling about 60 percent of the students—who were required to take prescribed courses in English, foreign language, history, mathematics, and science. The general curriculum, which allowed more electives, was chosen by 15 percent of the students, and 25 percent enrolled in the business curriculum. In the lower grades all students studied the same subjects, although classes were organized so as to permit some ability grouping within each grade.[102]

Ability grouping was more flexible at Prince Edward Academy than at many schools, but Redd's educational philosophy was similar to that of Washington superintendent Carl F. Hansen. "Hansen and I could have been great buddies," Redd declared. "We both know you have to have a basic structured situation for most children to learn. We both believe in ability grouping." The Academy used the phonic method for teaching reading in grades one through six, and Redd attributed the school's 97 percent average daily attendance and low dropout rate (about 2 percent) to early emphasis on reading. At some schools, he said, many students lose interest because they had not mastered the basics of reading.[103]

One crucial difference separated Redd's educational views from those of Hansen. "Hansen thinks blacks can achieve as much as whites if they are taught properly," Redd noted. "I doubt that." Referring to the scholarly studies of Henry E. Garrett and other social scientists whose work could be used to defend segregation, Redd insisted, "You can't solve an educational problem until you identify it. And most people won't admit that race is a problem. Most blacks simply do not have the ability to do quality school work. Some do, I admit. But only 10 to 15 percent of them score above the white median on most academic examinations. The rest are likely to become frustrated and disruptive. That's one reason why there are so many assaults and so much vandalism in schools with a sizeable enrollment of Negro students." Referring to a congressional report entitled *Violent Schools — Safe Schools,* Redd stated, "We felt back in 1951 that what is happening today would happen if the Supreme Court insisted on desegregation. . . . We felt we understood black people as well as anybody, because of our long interaction with them. We knew desegregation couldn't work because of the inherent temperamental and intellectual differences. Students of the different races couldn't mix effectively any more than oil and water — not even with the Federal Government acting as an emulsifying agent."[104]

Discipline, manners, and courtesy were an integral part of the program. "We insist on structure and discipline," Redd said. In twenty-one years only three students had been expelled[105] and vandalism and graffiti were almost unknown at the Academy. One student explained why. "It's our school. We pay for it. We respect it." School authorities also assigned work tours for minor infractions. Bo Prichard, a local newspaper reporter, observed that personal belongings must be locked to prevent theft at many schools, but at the Academy students routinely left their possessions piled outside on the walks while they went elsewhere on campus.[106]

During the 1960s and 1970s the turnover among teachers at the Academy was very low, although salaries lagged from $2,000 to $7,000 below the scale prevailing in nearby public schools. "About the only way we lose a teacher is by retirement or by her husband being transferred to another locality," Headmaster Redd stated. "The best teachers want to come here because we don't have many discipline problems." A foreign language teacher, one of only two instructors who have left the Academy in recent years to teach in a public school, observed that "Academy kids today are a lot like my classmates were in high school. They don't talk back and heap verbal abuse on teachers the way kids do in public schools."[107]

Most of those associated with the Academy were serenely satisfied with their school. They had done "what skeptics thought impossible," declared the *Farmville Herald*. They had "educated the children of the county in a manner acceptable to the majority of the people" and created "a formula by which the people of the rural South can live," said Roy B. Hargrove, a local doctor and a member of the board of directors.[108]

Many sympathizers outside the county agreed with this favorable assessment. "If every subdivision in the State of Virginia stood up as the people of Prince Edward have," declared former governor William M. Tuck, "our public schools would not be run today by emissaries and agents from Washington." The Prince Edward story was "a stirring chapter in the history of education in Virginia," said Mills E. Godwin, another former governor. "By doing what was right," added Jesse Helms, later U.S. senator from North Carolina, the citizens of Prince Edward had shown the rest of the country "what is wrong with the dangerously silly and fearfully destructive policies growing out of stifling federal control of public education." "The white parents of Prince Edward plunged energetically into the task of providing for the needs of their children," observed James J. Kilpatrick. "They worked; they sacrificed; they exhausted themselves. And to the monumental chagrin of their critics, they succeeded brilliantly."[109]

Although the Academy was successful in many respects, there were serious financial problems. Tuition initially was set at $280 for the high school and $255 for the elementary grades, and was increased gradually through the years until it reached $1,075 in 1980. This was a lot of money in a rural county like Prince Edward, and many parents were forced to scrimp, save, and apply for partial scholarships. To help families defray expenses, the school hired as many parents as possible — as bus drivers, secretaries, janitors, and groundskeepers. Many mothers went to work elsewhere and saved part of their income to cover tuition, a pattern of family financing that evoked some amusement in black Farmville. "We're going to win this one," said Clarence Penn, a black school administrator. "[Tuition] has . . . a lot of white daddies hurting and a lot of white mommies working." Parents with children enrolled at the Academy often refused to concede that paying tuition was a real hardship. "It's a question of where your priorities lie," one declared, adding that the family "could have a boat or some other luxuries, but we prefer to spend for what we consider a superior education for our children. Our priorities lie with our children."[110]

Some parents sacrificed much more than luxuries to meet tuition costs. To pay for four children who were attending the Academy in 1980, for example, Nathan Holman worked the night shift at the Post Office and then rushed home to grow soy beans and corn. His wife Nancy kept busy around the family farm — gardening, canning, making preserves, tending a baby, and earning extra money by grooming dogs in a backyard kennel. The younger Holman children went without shoes during the summer and helped in the garden. The oldest son was a crack shot who brought in venison during the winter and also bred rabbits in a hutch he kept behind the family's modest brick rancher. "We may be eating an awful lot of rabbit but we're going to make it," Mrs. Holman stated. She regretted that they would have to sell "the cow we raised for ourselves" in order to obtain tuition money for 1980, but she concluded on an optimistic note. "We have a calf on the way, so even that's not so bad." [111]

The financial burden of the Academy's patrons would have been lightened if they had received the tuition grants that were available until 1969 under Virginia's "freedom of choice" program. When the state abandoned massive resistance in 1959 the General Assembly and county governments were authorized to pay tuition grants for education in nonsectarian private schools. Except for the 1960–61 school year, however, federal courts forbade the payment of these funds to citizens of Prince Edward County. The litigation will be discussed below, but essentially the courts held that tuition grants in Prince Edward would make the state a party to an unconstitutional attempt to evade the mandate of *Brown*.

Although they refused to appropriate money for desegregated public schools, the county's whites insisted they were not against schools for blacks. It was integration, not education, that they opposed. Most whites professed a willingness to help blacks establish private schools, and in the spring of 1960 a few Farmville businessmen and professors from Hampden-Sydney and Longwood colleges discussed the possibility of reopening public schools for the county's black youths. The businessmen said the county had lost about half a million dollars in purchasing power when all but three of the county's seventy black teachers moved to positions elsewhere, and the colleges had some difficulty attracting and keeping professors who either feared unsettled conditions or opposed segregation.

Advocates of reopening the public schools were known as Bush Leaguers, a label that referred to meetings they held at an out-of-the-way country cabin in Cumberland County. Although the Bush Leaguers disavowed integration and insisted that their sole purpose was to make education available to blacks, they were viewed suspiciously in Prince Edward. Many residents thought it was disloyal to the Academy to be discussing the need for public schools in 1960. After the group's second meeting, mimeographed minutes were distributed by an informer, giving accurate information and quotations. Those whose comments indicated even tentative interest in reopening the public schools then felt "the bitter sting of rebuffs from townspeople who had been friends and neighbors." [112] "I have not lived in this town all my life to be an outcast at this late date," one man commented. Another resident of the county said, "Nobody can talk. In Farmville today they figure, 'You're either for us or against us.'" "We have to be all for the private schools," a businessman remarked. "Otherwise they say we're all against." The Bush League disbanded in June 1960, and with it passed "the only significant movement of dissent . . . that the county was to experience." [113]

Journalists focused attention on the activities of the Bush League, but in some ways this was misleading. Kennell Jackson, Jr., who graduated from Moton High in 1959 and has since become a history professor at Stanford University, came close to the truth when he observed that the whites were almost uniformly segregationists. "There did not exist a group of white moderates who could have stopped the school closure." Another observer commented in 1961, "Those whites not fully in sympathy with the private-school movement add up, at the moment, to about 5 percent of the community, and they do very little talking. Pressures are too strong for them to speak out." [114]

There were individual white dissenters, however, the most prominent of whom was Dr. C. G. Gordon Moss, a history professor and academic dean at Longwood College. Born only fifty miles away in Lynchburg, Dr. Moss had earned academic degrees at Yale and at Washington and Lee, had married a Farmville girl, and had taught American history at Longwood for twenty years. A popular teacher and dean, and a gentleman who was known for his courtly manners, Moss was highly regarded on campus. If the county's schools had been desegregated, Moss said, it would have been difficult "to find even a single Negro—certainly no more than a bare sprinkling—who would be able to persist in the white schools with the latter's higher standards and the difficult social situation for the Negro children." Initially as much a segregationist as an integrationist, Moss opposed interracial social mingling and shared many of the racial views prevalent in Southside Virginia. Nevertheless, he considered the school closings "unchristian" and could not see why "this mistreatment" was necessary. Elsewhere in Virginia, he observed, token desegregation seemed to be working tolerably well. [115]

During the early 1960s Moss was one of the few whites in the county who met regularly with the Reverend Griffin and other black leaders. These conferences eventually led to what Griffin called "an amazing transformation." Moss embraced integration, joined the Virginia Council on Human Relations, and even thought about joining the NAACP. The father of three children, one of whom was a boy still in school, Moss refused to send his son to the Academy. "I wouldn't let my son go to it for anything in the world," he stated, explaining why the youth had been sent to a prep school in Richmond "much against his personal wishes." "Maybe the [Academy] kids are doing all right in French and math and English—after all, they have the same teachers they had in the public schools—but they are learning principles that are far from what I would call a proper education. How, in a government class, can they teach democracy in such an undemocratic school?" [116]

For expressing such opinions, Moss came in for a good deal of criticism and some ridicule. Letters of complaint were sent to the governor and state superintendent of schools, and in Farmville the dean was called a "nigger lover" and "integrationist." "I get a right many black looks when I go downtown," Moss admitted. People who used to greet him warmly now turned away or spoke to him with restraint. The state Board of Education officially noted that Moss's activities had brought "considerable criticism" to Longwood College, and the president of the school told him that "should I open myself to renewed attack, he believed the state board of education would find it necessary to be relieved of so controversial a person as I seem to have become." [117] After Moss's predicament was called to national attention in the *Saturday Evening Post,* the dean enjoyed a degree of immunity. Neither the state board nor the segregationists of Prince Edward wished to be portrayed as enemies of free speech. The state board acknowledged the right of every American citizen to freedom of expression and conceded that "a person should [not] have to forgo this right in order to serve on the faculty of a Virginia institution of higher learning." [118] For the next two decades Moss would continue to challenge the orthodoxy of Prince Edward County.

In the meantime, there remained the problem of providing education for the black youths whose public schools had been closed. At a meeting sponsored by the National Council of Negro Women in Washington in January 1960, twenty-one organizations agreed to set up "activity centers" for out-of-school black children. Some blacks thought genuine education ought to be offered, but Griffin, who was named chairman of the project, carefully explained that the centers were not a private school and were intended primarily to keep the children busy. "We are operating activity centers to help maintain the morale of children," explained Dorothy Croner, the director of the centers. "The centers are not in any respect offered as a substitute for schools." [119]

The decision not to develop schools was largely tactical. The legal issues would be tested in court, but the NAACP saw in Prince Edward the opportunity to rally liberal opinion throughout the nation. In 1960 Arthur Flemming, the secretary of HEW, characterized the situation in Prince Edward as "indefensible, . . . a serious blight on the American educational scene." In 1961 a *New York Times* editorial referred to developments in the county as "fantastically discriminatory," and in 1963 *Time* magazine declared that Prince Edward's school closings were "the most infamous segregationist tactic in the U.S." If the black children had been educated in private schools, one observer noted, "consciences everywhere would be relieved and the chances of public schools' being reopened by social pressure would be sharply reduced." Consequently, the NAACP's official policy, as stated by executive secretary Roy Wilkins, was "not to encourage the setting up of separate makeshift schools for colored children displaced through school closings in order to avoid desegregation." The NAACP would do nothing to erase what the *New York Times* called "the image of bigotry created in Prince Edward County."[120]

The NAACP knew that a new legal strategy had to be devised to compel the county to reopen its schools, and it deliberated for a full year before returning to court. Nevertheless, most of those who chose to establish activity centers rather than schools expected that legal action would resolve the controversy without undue delay. They never dreamed public schools would remain closed until the fall of 1964. In 1960 the decision for activity centers seemed a shrewd tactic; by 1964, critics alleged, it involved a heartless and callous manipulation of the county's poor blacks.

The largest of the activity centers operated out of the basement Sunday school auditorium of Griffin's First Baptist Church in Farmville. Late in 1960 a reporter observed that it had "two blackboards, a couple of work tables, and a variety of books for its ninety-four 'pupils.'" The adult in charge was Helen Baker, a black Quaker from Baltimore. Mrs. Baker recognized that the center was organized around "basketball and handicraft programs and hobbies and all that," but when she saw the needs of the children she provided some instruction in reading and arithmetic. Generally, however, she accepted the overall strategy and spent most of her time teaching useful skills, sewing and knitting for the girls, woodworking for boys, and some creative crafts for both.[121]

During the first year of the school shutdown most of the centers were staffed by experienced teachers. Yet by 1961 all but three of the teachers had departed to take jobs elsewhere, and most centers were managed by local housewives and teenagers. Some of the centers were terribly overcrowded. One near the hamlet of Prospect served thirty-four children between the ages of five and ten who met in a deserted tenant farmer's shack with no plumbing and a tiny woodburning stove. Near the Loving Sisters of Charity Hall was another center frequently photographed by newsmen who wished to emphasize the difference between the centers and real schools. "It is . . . a two-by-four sized hut, which is so overcrowded it appears to be a health hazard and a fire-trap," wrote one reporter. "Twenty-nine youngsters of an enrollment of forty-one were jammed like sardines into the building." Elsewhere conditions were better; near Hampden-Sydney an experienced teacher named Julia Anderson worked with thirty-six children in a building that had the appearance of a colonial country schoolhouse, "clean and neat and utilitarian."[122]

Prior to the discontinuation of the activity program in 1962, approximately 600 black youths attended the centers annually, while another 400 to 500 arranged each year to obtain formal education outside the county. The first of these was a group of sixty-eight high school students who departed Farmville in September 1959, in a twenty-car motorcade headed for Kittrell College in North Carolina, a school that offered high school courses as well as college work. In 1962 the affiliates of the Negro Virginia Teachers' Association arranged homes-away-from-home where students from Prince Edward could live and take advantage of public education. The American Friends Service Committee also arranged away-from-home education for sixty-seven others—some in locations as far away as Iowa and Massachusetts. Other black youngsters managed to "bootleg" an education by moving in with friends or relatives elsewhere or by carpooling with blacks who worked in nearby counties.[123]

Some of the students who went away to school undoubtedly received as good an education as they would have received at home, but most blacks were not so fortunate. A survey made in 1963 indicated that 54.6 percent of the black students who had been enrolled when schools were closed in 1959 had received no formal schooling during the next four years; 44 percent had managed to obtain some formal training, but only 5.6 percent had been in school regularly since 1959.[124]

Faced with the blacks' decision to bear with activity centers, white Prince Edward sought to escape mounting criticism by organizing private schools for blacks. For a tuition charge of $240, which could be reimbursed through tuition grants from the state and county governments, an organization known as Southside Schools proposed "to set up good schools, get qualified teachers, and . . . to run these schools at least 180 days, which is a full school year." From the outset, however, Southside Schools labored under a double handicap. The project was organized by whites, and by whites who were prominent advocates of segregation. Dr. Roy B. Hargrove, who later became a member of the Academy's board of directors, was the president of Southside Schools, and J. Barrye Wall, Jr., was the agent officially registered with the state corporation commission in Richmond.[125]

In January 1960, Southside Schools sent letters to the parents of every black child in the county, but only one youngster applied for admission to the proposed schools. Some people suspected that the Southside segregationists had made their offer only after ascertaining that blacks would not accept private schooling. Others suggested that the offer was made with an eye toward defending Prince Edward against journalists who were said to be "doing their Ivy League worst to make it appear that the county has . . . scandalously trampled upon the poor colored children." Dr. Hargrove admitted that public opinion probably "would be better with the Negroes

in school" but insisted that "any Negroes who thought that we were proposing this just for propaganda could have called our bluff by applying
for the school."[126]

For the next few years segregationists would repeat that the Southside
offer was made in good faith. A constant refrain in the *Farmville Herald*
stated that the blacks simply had "not taken advantage of the opportunities which have been offered." No other group was interested in educating
the county's blacks, the Southside directors stated, so they had accepted
the obligation of providing schools. Writing with a characteristic blend of
paternalism and noblesse oblige, Colonel John Steck, managing editor of
the *Farmville Herald,* gave assurances that the plight of out-of-school blacks
would not be overlooked. "They will not be forgotten, nor forsaken to their
own people's dim, faint, undisciplined groping."[127]

Black leaders summoned persuasive arguments to discourage blacks from
accepting the segregationists' proposal. "The whole world is watching Prince
Edward," the NAACP's Oliver Hill declared during a rally in Farmville. If
blacks should permit segregation in this landmark county it would be more
difficult to achieve integration elsewhere. Speaking from the steps of the
county court house, Roy Wilkins urged blacks to sacrifice "a few years of
education in the name of freedom." In the end, Wilkins declared, "You can't
lose. You're bound to win. Just stay with us." Before leading a "Pilgrimage
of Prayer for Public Schools," Martin Luther King, Jr., expressed the hope
that the blacks of Prince Edward would not "sell their birthright of freedom for a mess of segregated pottage." Referring to the incorporators of
Southside Schools as "benighted individuals" who were "guilty of a crime
against humanity," Oliver Hill identified two considerations that lurked behind the proposed private schools: "either white schools are failing, need
bolstering, need money, or . . . the white people are afraid of the pitiless
spotlight of public opinion."[128]

Unlike whites attending segregated academies elsewhere in Virginia, the
whites of Prince Edward had not applied for tuition grants at the time the
Southside offer was tendered—evidently because they feared the courts
would rule the grants unconstitutional if given to whites in a county where
blacks had no schools. Many observers consequently suspected that the
Southside people wished to use tuition grants for black schools as a first
step toward securing similar assistance for the Academy. Since integrationists hoped the Academy would wither away from economic malnutrition,
they rejected the Southside proposal as hypocritical and self-serving.[129]

For their part, the rebuffed whites said the NAACP cared more for integration than for education. Segregationists regretted that there were no
schools for blacks, but their regrets were coupled with assertions that "they
brought it on themselves when they listened to those NAACP outsiders." If

the county's blacks had accepted assistance from their white neighbors instead of outside guidance for their "advancement," their children would have been attending good schools with qualified teachers. "Nothing has been gained and much has been lost in the cause of education," the *Farmville Herald* asserted ten years after the student strike at Moton High School. It was time for blacks to wake up, "think for themselves, and act for their own best interests." They should recognize that the NAACP had ulterior motives. Prince Edward had been used "as a pawn in a great game of national, possibly international politics." The NAACP was reaping "propaganda advantages nationwide." The county was "billed as a community of tyrants which has taken education from Negro children, and upon this fallacy has been built an appeal to the credulous for funds to aid the NAACP." [130]

By 1961 the two sides were locked in a stalemate, with each convinced it was dedicated to high principles. As the segregationists saw it, the basic question concerned whether the federal judiciary could compel a local legislative body to spend money for public schools. They believed they were standing up for the basic principles of the Magna Charta and the separation of powers. For its part, the NAACP insisted that the school closings were an unconstitutional attempt to evade a court order. The whites were fighting for the right of local communities to educate their children as they saw fit. The blacks stood for desegregation and public schools. Each recognized the honesty of the other's convictions, and neither was willing to budge until the questions were fully litigated.

In the meantime, the black youth of the county suffered grievously. Speaking on Chet Huntley's NBC television program in 1962, Dean Moss used the phrase "the crippled generation" in referring to the black students. Later he stated that the youngsters had been "so seriously handicapped they will never approach a life of richness they otherwise could have had." Expressing a similar point of view, one of the black students who had been fortunate enough to receive a good education wrote that many of his agemates had been "victimized in a . . . clash of abstract ideology." According to Kennell Jackson, the struggle left 2,000 black youths illiterate and had the effect of "reducing the kids to dust." [131]

Observations such as these found support in the research of Dr. Robert L. Green of Michigan State University. Financed by a $75,000 grant from the federal government, Green and a team of researchers surveyed the county in 1963 to determine the "effects of extended periods of nonschooling." Their work yielded some shocking information. Prince Edward's out-of-school students trailed behind youths from neighboring rural counties on reading and arithmetic tests, and since 1959 the percentage of illiterate school-age blacks in the county had increased from 3 to 22. The median IQ of the county students who had not attended school trailed 19 to 30 points (depending on the age group) behind that of students who had received some education (a group that averaged only 1.5 years of schooling during the four years of deprivation). The mean IQ of those without formal schooling averaged only 65—in the upper range of those considered mentally defective. The mean IQ of those with some education was approximately 80.[132]

As the extent of the educational calamity became more apparent, the Reverend Griffin circulated a petition in 1963 calling on President John F. Kennedy to devise a method for reopening the schools. The national NAACP also asked the federal government "to commit its full resources on behalf of the single most deprived group of children in the United States—the Negro children of Prince Edward County." The NAACP characterized the school closings as "a calloused act of entrenched bigotry" that had inflicted "incalculable harm on defenseless youngsters."[133]

During the summer of 1963 students from Hampton Institute and Virginia Union University began demonstrations in Farmville. Local blacks joined the protests; Griffin explained that they were "displeased about people saying they were satisfied. . . . They wanted to do this themselves to prove that they are not happy and complacent." "*Free public education is our inalienable right,*" one handmade sign proclaimed. "*Why take it out on innocent Negro children?*" another asked. "*We aren't dropouts. We are lockouts,*" declared a third. Sit-ins were organized at several lunch counters, hymns were sung outside segregated church services, and marches were held in the streets. The demonstrations were generally peaceful, and only thirty-three demonstrators were arrested that summer—ten for marching on Saturday (the rural marketing day and the only day of the week when demonstrations were prohibited in Farmville), and twenty-three others for violating an ancient statute that forbade interrupting or disturbing an assembly meeting for the worship of God.[134]

The demonstrations in Farmville were part of a larger protest movement that swept the nation and culminated when a quarter of a million people marched on Washington on 28 August 1963 and heard speeches by Martin Luther King, Jr., and other civil rights leaders. Even before the throng assembled in the nation's capital, President Kennedy had decided that something should be done to educate the blacks of Prince Edward. William J. vanden Heuvel, an assistant to Attorney General Robert F. Kennedy, then raised private funds and leased public schools from Prince Edward County.[135] There were similarities between vanden Heuvel's Prince Edward Free School Association and the program the incorporators of Southside Schools had devised in 1959. Each would provide blacks with private schools until the theoretical points at issue were resolved in court. In several important respects, however, the Free Schools differed from Southside Schools. Instead of using state tuition grants, the Free Schools raised their money from private philanthropy, with the Ford Foundation and the Field Foundation (headed by Adlai E. Stevenson) contributing one-third of the first year's $1 million budget. The six-member board of trustees was biracial, including three black college presidents as well as the white president of Washington and Lee, the dean of the University of Virginia Law School, and former governor Colgate W. Darden. The teaching staff was racially mixed, although predominantly black, and there were no racial restrictions on admission to the student body.[136]

Vanden Heuvel also reassured blacks when he persuaded Neil V. Sullivan to become the superintendent of the Free Schools. A forty-eight-year-old white educator from New Hampshire, Sullivan had been working as superintendent of schools in the suburban Long Island community of East Williston, New York. Although his school district was 99 percent white, Sullivan was known as an integrationist. He was on record as favoring busing, pairing, and the construction of large metropolitan educational parks to mix city blacks and suburban whites in racially balanced schools. In 1959 his school district had been among the first to send extra textbooks to the out-of-school blacks of Prince Edward.[137]

Sullivan had also pioneered in developing innovative teaching methods. East Williston was in the forefront of school districts in the use of educational television, audiovisual equipment, and other teaching machines. Sullivan also advocated the new math, independent study, and the inquiry method of teaching social and natural sciences. At East Williston he had set up a nongraded program which "freed students from uniform lockstep progression through twelve years of school and allowed each student to move along as quickly as his individual abilities dictated."[138]

Sullivan's racial and professional views were at odds with those prevailing in the rural South, and there were some who felt he would have been a more suitable choice for an urban area like Berkeley, California (where Sullivan would become superintendent of schools after leaving Prince Edward). Yet the trustees of the Free Schools thought Sullivan's experience with nongraded schooling would be particularly helpful in working with students who were trying to make up for lost years as quickly as possible. They knew that Prince Edward's black students could not be grouped according to age, since their educational experiences since 1959 had varied so greatly.[139]

Arriving in Prince Edward in August 1963, Sullivan threw himself into the work of organizing the Free Schools. With astonishing speed he assembled an integrated staff of about a hundred teachers, half from Virginia and the rest from all over the United States, including several recently returned from service abroad with the Peace Corps. The schools were then furnished with equipment donated by General Electric, Bell and Howell, and other corporations. In addition to scurrying across the nation to raise money, books, and teaching machines, Sullivan found time to write a 52-page teachers' manual explaining nongraded and team-teaching techniques. When students began classes in September they discovered that "the latest innovations and teaching procedures were being used in the Free Schools, and [Sullivan] was journeying to Richmond, to Roanoke and to cities all over the country to describe them." "We've probably the best equipped school system in the United States—bar none," he stated. "We have team teaching, teaching machines, and educational TV. . . . Our vocational education program probably is second to none in the South." [140]

The Free Schools took pleasure in noting that their students were integrated from the outset, with four whites enrolled along with 1,570 blacks when the 1963–64 school year began. Dean Moss's seventeen-year-old son Dickie returned to Farmville to enroll as a high school senior, thus ensuring that the first graduating class would be integrated. Fifteen-year-old Brenda Abernathy, whose family had lived in the county for only three months, was also enrolled in the high school. A shy girl, she was understandably confused by the cameras and newsmen who celebrated her contribution to changing race relations in the black belt. (When the opening school assembly was dismissed, the *New York Times* reported, "Brenda left the auditorium for an assigned homeroom with her right hand clasped firmly in the hand of a tall Negro girl. They were smiling.") Brenda's eight-year-old brother George was the subject of less attention at Mary E. Branch School 1, as was young Letitia Tew at Branch 2 grammar school. In 1964 the enrollment of whites doubled to eight with the addition of the four children of Mr. and Mrs. Walter C. Lewis. [141]

The black students' abysmally low scores on standardized examinations were the result of years of intellectual neglect, and many youngsters progressed rapidly once formal instruction was resumed. "The day-to-day progress of the children learning to read was almost breathtaking," Sullivan reported. At staff meetings teachers marveled at the fact that they were "actually able to 'see' learning occur among these children, as surely and as dramatically as the film of a time-lapse camera 'sees' growth occur in a plant." [142]

Expenditure per pupil at the Free Schools was about twice that at the Academy, and the salaries of the Free Schools teachers were set well above the usual level for Southside Virginia. The ratio of students to teachers (15 to 1) made it possible to offer small classes and individual tutoring, and money was available for many cultural activities and field trips. Expeditions were organized to visit Booker T. Washington's home plantation near Roanoke and Thomas Jefferson's estate, Monticello. To familiarize students with the history of Virginia, trips were arranged to Colonial Williamsburg, to Appomattox Court House, and to the state capitol in Richmond (where students also attended a symphony concert). There were trips to Washington, D.C., and to New York City, where the students were greeted by Mayor Robert F. Wagner, shown through the United Nations by Undersecretary Ralph Bunche, and entertained at the home of Mr. and Mrs. Jackie Robinson. These activities grew partly out of a desire to compensate for four years of intellectual neglect, but they were prompted also by Sullivan's belief that education involved expanding the students' horizons as well as instilling a knowledge of basic subjects. When long-distance travel was not possible, the superintendent arranged trips involving nothing more elaborate than visits to the local bank, the post office, and the fire station in Farmville.[143]

Critics would later complain that Sullivan was "way off into progressive education." Even Dean Moss regretfully acknowledged, "The Free Schools weren't interested in real education. They spent a lot of money on 'show-off programs'—taking students to various places and buying expensive machines. But it wasn't good basic education."[144] In 1964, however, the consensus was that superintendent Sullivan had done a remarkable job. Appointed only one month before classes began, he had rented school buildings, hired a faculty, and generally organized a private school system for approximately 1,600 students. His progressive teaching methods were in vogue at the time and seemed especially appropriate in view of the circumstances in Prince Edward County.

There were mixed reports on the community's response to the Free Schools teachers. Superintendent Sullivan wrote that local whites kept him at arm's length and showed no kindly interest in the Free Schools. They harassed him with late-night telephone calls, dumped garbage in his front yard, called him a "carpetbagger" and worse, and vandalized his Buick convertible. But while controversy swirled around the superintendent, other teachers managed to get along with the local community. One reported that the people she met were "warm and friendly, ingratiatingly polite and gentle mannered. If a casual question revealed you to be a stranger, there was no limit to the interest shown and the time taken to direct or explain." Another said she arrived in the county "expecting all sorts of strife and tension, and I have found instead a great restraint and an unfailing courtesy. These people are not gun-toting bums; they are gentlemen. They are, however, very stubborn gentlemen."[145]

V

While the public schools were closed in Prince Edward County, the courts moved slowly toward resolving the tangled issues of equity and constitutional law. In June 1960, at the end of the county's first year without public schools, a lawsuit was filed in the name of Leslie Francis Griffin, the thirteen-year-old son of the Reverend Griffin. In his behalf the NAACP contended that the Prince Edward program was a "deliberate, intentional, and calculated effort to circumvent" the mandate of *Brown*.[146]

Speaking for the county, attorney Collins Denny answered that *Brown* did not require the operation of public schools but merely prohibited discrimination if such schools were operated. J. Segar Gravatt, another attorney for the county, emphasized that education had not been abandoned in Prince Edward. The county had simply chosen to educate its children by offering every family the choice of a private school, with most of the expenses to be defrayed by public tuition grants. Prior to 1963 blacks rejected offers of private schooling, but Gravatt maintained that the Prince Edward system had "enlarged the liberty" of citizens by eliminating "the element of compulsion which results where parents may only choose between integrated public schools and private education at the parents' expense."[47]

Most blacks rejected this argument. They said there was no difference between segregated private schools and segregated public schools. Beyond this, they believed that Prince Edward Academy had forfeited its status as a purely private institution by accepting public tuition grants and tax credits. The school had initially refused tuition grants, but during its second year of operations caution was cast aside and tuition grants and tax credits in the amount of $318,000 were accepted at the Academy. As a result, for this one year only, parents were reimbursed for all but $15 of the tuition then charged. Blacks insisted that this arrangement would not hold up in court. "If you are collecting tax money and spending it for education," one NAACP official explained, "you can't discriminate this way."[148]

Oren Lewis, the federal judge presiding in the U.S. District Court for the Eastern District of Virginia, agreed with the NAACP on the economic questions. Tuition grants were not intrinsically unlawful, Judge Lewis held, but they became unconstitutional when used to perpetuate segregated schooling. The state grants were intended to provide students with freedom to choose between public and private schools, but in Prince Edward there was no choice since there were no public schools. Consequently, Judge Lewis ruled that as long as the county's public schools remained closed Prince Edward could not use public funds to maintain private, segregated schools.[149]

At first Judge Lewis declined to rule on the constitutionality of closing schools. In its brief the NAACP argued that the Virginia state constitution required the operation of public schools throughout the Commonwealth. Since state courts are responsible for interpreting state constitutions, Judge Lewis deferred decision until after the relevant questions of state law had been decided by state courts.[150]

In the state courts, white Prince Edward scored three victories, one in the Richmond circuit court and two in separate decisions from the Virginia Supreme Court of Appeals. Explaining that their duty was "to construe a Constitution, not to provide a remedy for a situation" that some people considered "shameful," the Virginia supreme court held that the constitution authorized counties to operate public schools, but that its language was discretionary; it did not require such operation. The court also stated that since the early days of the Commonwealth it had repeatedly noted that the exercise of the power of taxation is a legislative function. Consequently, it refused the NAACP's request for a writ to compel Prince Edward to appropriate funds for public schools. To do so, the court declared, "would mean that this court may substitute its discretion for that vested by law in the local legislative body. Clearly, under the division of powers embodied in our Bill of Rights, we may not do this."[151]

Defeated in the state courts, the NAACP fared better when the case returned to Judge Lewis's courtroom. Lewis noted that the Virginia supreme court could not pass upon federal questions, since that was the responsibility of federal courts. Basing his decision squarely upon the equal protection clause of the Fourteenth Amendment, Lewis held that "the public schools of Prince Edward County may not be closed to avoid [desegregation], while the Commonwealth of Virginia permits other public schools to remain open at the expense of the taxpayers." The children of the county enjoyed "federally protected rights," among them the right to "equality of opportunity . . . through access to non-segregated public schools."[152]

The Fourth Circuit Court of Appeals (with Judge J. Spencer Bell dissenting) reversed Judge Lewis's decision. In an opinion written by Judge Clement F. Haynesworth, the court held, "The negative application of the Fourteenth Amendment is too well settled for argument. . . . Schools that are operated must be made available to all citizens without regard to race, but what public schools a state provides is not the subject of constitutional command."[153] The whites of Prince Edward derived particular satisfaction from this decision, since the county's public schools had been closed in 1959 after this appellate court had ordered Prince Edward to abandon racially discriminatory practices in its schools. Now, four years later, the same court had found that unconstitutional discrimination had ceased when the public schools were closed. Prince Edward was found to be in compliance with the orders of the court "as fully as if [it] had continued to operate schools, but without discrimination."[154]

As Prince Edward presented the case, the fundamental question in the *Griffin* litigation was not whether schools were closed or children illiterate, but whether the federal judiciary could compel a local governing body to appropriate money for public schools. This was a states' rights lawyer's dream. Attorney J. Segar Gravatt considered it "the privilege of my lifetime to have worked so closely with the Board of Supervisors of Prince Edward County in our effort to resolve these issues." Suffering from emphysema, attorney Collins Denny begged his doctors to keep him alive long enough to plead the *Griffin* case before the Supreme Court (an extension they were unable to grant). Just before he died he requested that instead of flowers, donations in his memory be sent to the Free Schools as well as to Prince Edward Academy. He died with the consolation of knowing that the judges of the Virginia circuit court, the Virginia Supreme Court of Appeals, and the Fourth Circuit Court of Appeals found merit in the case he had made for Prince Edward County.[155]

Yet the only opinion that mattered was that of the U.S. Supreme Court, and most observers expected the high court to conclude that closing the schools was a clever way to avoid court-ordered desegregation. During the oral argument, when J. Segar Gravatt asserted that "education and the methods by which it is provided is a state matter—not a federal matter," Chief Justice Earl Warren interrupted to say that Prince Edward had given black children the "freedom to go through life without an education."[156] The decision of the Supreme Court was never really in doubt. On 25 May 1964, ten years after the *Brown* decision, the Court again found in favor of the NAACP.

Writing for the Court, Justice Hugo Black held that Prince Edward's public schools were closed and private schools established in their place "for one reason, and one reason only: to ensure . . . that white and colored children in Prince Edward County would not . . . go to the same school." As a result of this constitutionally impermissible purpose, the children of Prince Edward were treated differently from those elsewhere in the state. All other Virginia children could attend public schools, but in Prince Edward youngsters had to go to a private school or none at all. The Supreme Court unanimously concluded that Prince Edward had denied its citizens the equal protection guaranteed by the Fourteenth Amendment.[157]

When it came to framing a decree to remedy the violation, the unanimity of the Court disappeared. Writing for a seven-member majority, Justice Black concluded that the district court could require the Board of Supervisors to levy taxes to operate racially nondiscriminatory public schools. In a brief dissenting comment, Justices Tom Clark and John Marshall Harlan disagreed with the holding that the federal courts were empowered to order the reopening of public schools but otherwise joined in the Court's opinion.[158]

The northern press generally praised the Court's decision. Endorsing Justice Black's contention that there had been "entirely too much deliberation and not enough speed," the *Washington Post* featured an editorial cartoon by Herblock with a message inscribed on a school blackboard: "The time for 'deliberate speed' has run out." The *New York Times* wrote that the Supreme Court had spoken with "eminently warranted sharpness in rebuking Prince Edward County for its disgraceful record." Among the major liberal journals, only the *New Republic* expressed any reservations. While celebrating the Court's victory over Prince Edward's "resourceful, determined, peaceable, and . . . in its tragic way successful resistance," the *New Republic* noted that "some eyebrows were raised" by Justice Black's assertion that the federal courts could require local officials to levy school taxes.[159]

Many southerners predictably viewed the *Griffin* decision from a different perspective. "Never in the history of our nation has the Supreme Court intimated or held that it had the authority to compel a legislative body to levy taxes," said Southside congressman Watkins M. Abbitt. In *Griffin* the Court had "torn asunder the separation doctrine that has meant so much to America and with brazen power is arrogating unto itself legislative functions that the Constitution never conferred upon the Court." Making a similar point, the *Richmond Times-Dispatch* declared that "the manner in which the highest court in the land has arrogated to itself the 'right' to order a unit of local government to levy taxes . . . is alarming in the highest degree." In the guise of interpreting the Constitution, the Court had usurped a power that had been deliberately excluded from it. In the process it had established a dangerous precedent "and one that could rise to plague us in years to come."[160]

In *Griffin* the Supreme Court affirmed Judge Lewis's ban on tuition grants in Prince Edward "while public schools remained closed," but it denied the NAACP's request for a general order invalidating the payment of tuition grants to racially discriminatory private schools. "On the question of tuition grants," *Southern School News* reported, "the Supreme Court appeared to take the view that the grants, *per se,* are not unconstitutional. The court said Judge Lewis was right in enjoining the use of grants in Prince Edward as long as public schools there were closed. By implication, the court would approve tuition grants in Prince Edward, at least under some circumstances." In its brief and in oral arguments, the NAACP challenged the constitutionality of Virginia's tuition grant program and repeatedly requested an injunction against the use of state grants at any segregated school. Consequently, Virginia's governor Albertis S. Harrison attributed great significance to the Court's refusal to invalidate the state's tuition grants. "If the court wanted to say they were illegal, it had a wonderful opportunity to do so," Harrison stated.[161]

It was generally conceded that, even with the public schools reopened, there would be only token desegregation in Prince Edward County. The public schools in some Virginia counties had already become predominantly black, with most whites using tuition grants to defray the cost of private tuition, and the *New York Times* lamented that "no one can be sure how long it will require for a definitive ruling on [the] legality" of these arrangements. The *New Republic* foresaw that "the next step in the Prince Edward County litigation will be to test whether 'private' schools born and reared in such circumstances and supported by the state in this fashion are not in essence so public that they can also be required to desegregate."[162]

Additional litigation on tuition grants in Prince Edward began almost immediately. In another Griffin case, the NAACP argued that tuition grants were an unconstitutional means "by which Virginia sought to educate the overwhelming majority of its school-age children in racially segregated schools." In reply, the state argued that the tuition grants, which could be used in any nonsectarian school in the United States, evinced Virginia's racially neutral intention to give parents "a free choice concerning the character of the schools their children attend.[163]

In December 1964, the Fourth Circuit Court of Appeals decided in favor of the Griffins. In a unanimous opinion written by Chief Judge Simon E. Sobeloff, the court held that tuition grants would enable Prince Edward to accomplish "a remarkable feat, stultifying a decade of judicial effort to bring about compliance with *Brown. . . . .*" In the factual context of Prince Edward, the court held, tuition grants were "a transparent evasion of the Fourteenth Amendment." They were a device to maintain segregated public schools under the guise of private academies. Although individuals possessed a right to freedom of association, the Supreme Court in *Brown* was said to have determined that "white persons have no constitutional right to associate in publicly maintained facilities on a segregated basis." If whites wished to congregate separately, they would have to pay extra for the privilege.[164]

Surprisingly, only five months later another panel of judges of the Fourth Circuit Court upheld the constitutionality of freedom-of-choice plans in Richmond and Hopewell, Virginia. The Fourteenth Amendment did not prohibit segregation, the court found; rather, "the proscription is against discrimination." Everyone had a right to be free of discrimination because of his race, but there was nothing in the Constitution that proscribed a state program "which permits . . . voluntary association with others of his race."[165]

Thus, in every year except 1960–1961, Prince Edward was singled out as a county where parents were not eligible for tuition grants, although by then segregation academies had emerged in many areas of the state. "Why do [our] parents not receive the tuition grant when it is available in all other counties in Virginia?" asked the Prince Edward Academy *Reporter*. The answer, according to the school newspaper, was that the federal judiciary was using "financial pressure . . . to break the resistance and determination of a people dedicated to local control in the education of their children." [166] There was little that Prince Edward could do about the discrimination, however, for the Board of Supervisors and leaders of the state generally believed that it would not be expedient to present another test case from Prince Edward County. If the constitutionality of the state's tuition grant program was to be challenged again, most whites hoped the test case would come from some less notorious county.

Once more it was the Reverend Griffin who chose the terrain for legal battle. With the aid of the NAACP, he inaugurated still another lawsuit in 1964, this one on behalf of his daughter. The Griffins argued that Virginia's tuition grant law had been passed to avoid desegregation, and that the unconstitutional purpose of the law made the statute unconstitutional per se. By aiding whites who wished to flee desegregated public schools, the tuition grants were said to deny blacks their constitutional right to desegregated public education.

Rejecting this argument, a special three-judge district court found that Virginia's tuition grant law was not intrinsically invalid but enjoined payment of grants where they were the main support of segregated schools. "In the abstract tuition grants are not condemnable," the court ruled, but they became so if misdirected to provide most of the support for a segregated school, as in the case of Prince Edward Academy. [167] But the Griffins' partial setback proved to be only temporary. In 1969 judges Albert V. Bryan, John D. Butzner, Jr., and Walter E. Hoffman, the same district court panel that had previously decided that Virginia's tuition grants were not unconstitutional, set aside their earlier verdict in light of the Supreme Court's intervening affirmation of judgments arising out of litigation from Louisiana and South Carolina. In these cases the district judges held that tuition grants were invalid if they contributed in any measure, no matter how slight, to the continuance of segregated public education. Against this criterion, the Virginia tuition grant statue could not stand. [168]

In the meantime, public schools had reopened in Prince Edward County. In June of 1964, one month after the Supreme Court's decision in the first *Griffin* case, the Board of Supervisors appropriated $189,000 to operate public schools — an amount that was based on the assumption that enrollment would be limited to blacks. This assumption was correct, for only seven white students enrolled along with approximately 1,400 blacks. The state of Virginia contributed an additional $125,000, and the federal government chipped in with extra funds to upgrade programs, personnel, and teaching techniques.

The total expenditure per pupil at the reopened public schools was slightly larger than the amount appropriated at Prince Edward Academy.

Blacks nevertheless complained that the expenditure of approximately $350 per student was only half the amount spent at the Free Schools in 1963–64. In one of their legal briefs, Griffin and the NAACP argued that the "recalcitrant" Board of Supervisors should not be permitted to determine "the amount reasonably necessary for racially nondiscriminatory public schools." The *New York Times* characterized the public school appropriation as "the bare minimum the county could legally provide, and less than a quality education budget."[169]

The court, however, chose not to intervene, and the NAACP was mollified when the school board chose thirty-five of its sixty-eight-member faculty from among the ranks of former Free Schools teachers. To the surprise of nearly everyone, the board hired nine white teachers (two of whom had previously taught at the Free Schools), thus giving Prince Edward the first integrated public school faculty in recent Virginia history. However, blacks resented Bryant R. Harper, the new superintendent, who lived in an exclusively white neighborhood and attended a segregated church. The resentment became especially strong after Harper, in several public addresses, suggested that the county's black students were almost hopeless. Petitioning for Harper's removal, one thousand blacks expressed the fear that the superintendent would "transfer his own pessimism and lack of confidence to the teachers, and then the teachers [would] pass this lack of confidence on to the pupils with the inevitable result that the pupils will do less well than they otherwise could."[170]

A rising tide of black racial consciousness was manifested most clearly during the years from 1969 to 1972, the period of Ronald J. Perry's tenure as superintendent of schools. Perry's primary goal, according to Griffin, was to attract white students away from the Academy by "hiring an excessive number of white teachers, so that white students and their parents would feel comfortable and safe in coming to the public schools." Perry succeeded in increasing white enrollment to about one hundred students, but the pastor of First Baptist charged that the superintendent was "so obsessed with the idea of undermining the Academy" that educating children in the public schools became incidental.[171]

Perry emphatically denied these allegations. Charges that he had "loaded" the schools with white teachers were "completely untrue," he declared. Perry said he always recommended the best qualified teachers for employment regardless of race, and whites never made up more than 40 percent of his faculty. The real problem, according to Perry, was that "the primary aims of the black camp . . . have evolved from integration to black power," whereas the white board members sent their children to the Academy and also wanted the public schools to remain black. Whenever he recommended the employment of a white teacher, Perry said, he received "much abuse" and was given the "third degree," but he said no questions were asked concerning the employment of black employees. Perry thought this sort of racial discrimination would send the county's public schools "right down the drain."[172]

Griffin, usually characterized as an integrationist, insisted that integration was no cure-all but only "one in a series of steps toward freedom." It was the correct policy in the 1950s, but in the 1970s, the pastor said, a move toward nationalism was needed. Blacks had "a distinct culture — not an inferior culture or a subculture — but a separate ethos." They would never be brought up to national norms on standardized examinations unless schools were organized to give them a psychological boost by providing role models and courses on the history and culture of people of African ancestry. "Association with whites does have some beneficial effects," Griffin conceded. "But it has damaged blacks psychologically not to dominate their own institutions."[173]

Griffin's approach was echoed by the Reverend J. Samuel Williams, the only leader of the student strike of 1951 who continued to reside in Prince Edward during the 1980s. Like Griffin, Williams thought most of Prince Edward's public schoolteachers should be black. "I'm not saying all teachers there should be black," he stated, "but it is a predominantly black school." He questioned the propriety of employing white instructors who sent their own children to the Academy, and he thought the public school curriculum should stress black history and racial awareness.[174]

Negro attorney James E. Ghee also faulted the public schools for failing to do more to help blacks maintain a sense of ethnic identity. As a young teenager when the county's public schools were closed in 1959, Ghee had been sent to high school and college in Iowa City, where the American Friends Service Committee had placed him with a Japanese-American family. A Presbyterian group then financed a year at the American University of Beirut, Lebanon, before Ghee studied law at the University of Virginia. From 1973 to 1975 he was an Earl Warren Legal Fellow, working with the NAACP Legal Defense Fund in Richmond. He then returned to Farmville, where he practiced law, became involved in community activities, and was elected to the Board of Supervisors in 1979.

Despite his broad exposure to the American mainstream, Ghee had reservations about what had been accomplished in the name of integration. "Before you can integrate effectively, you must know yourself," he said. He opposed "assimilating to the degree that black Americans are just like white Americans." Through the mass media, blacks were constantly exposed to white culture, but Ghee feared that many had lost touch with their own unique traditions. He thought predominantly black schools should help black youths identify positively with their race. Otherwise, he said, blacks would be paralyzed by a lack of self-confidence and would be helpless before the white world. They should insist on equal rights but should also develop their unique Afro-American culture.[175]

In the spring of 1972 Superintendent Perry resigned. At a school board meeting punctuated by what the local newspaper called "insulting verbal exchanges," Perry denounced racial discrimination against whites and warned that Prince Edward would be "taking a step backwards" if it allowed black community groups to pass on the employment of new teachers. He agreed with Griffin on only one point: "that no true learning . . . can take place in an atmosphere of constant bickering."[176]

Perry's successor as superintendent was considerably more successful. James M. Anderson, Jr., a white, had been born in Farmville but had lived and taught in neighboring Buckingham County. He understood the situation in Prince Edward and yet was sufficiently removed not to have become involved in the county's controversies. After becoming superintendent he continued to reside in Buckingham but sent his three children to public schools in Prince Edward. Yet Anderson specifically disavowed his predecessor's interest in attracting more whites to the public schools. "That's really not my goal," he said. "I am not going to encourage anyone to do anything. I believe it should be up to the individual parent to determine where his own children should go to school."[177]

Anderson focused on improving the academic performance of the county's public school students—an area where there was considerable room for progress. Virginia required that achievement tests be given to students enrolled in the fourth, eighth, and eleventh grades, and when Anderson became superintendent of schools in 1972, Prince Edward's scores were among the lowest in the state. On SRA tests, where the national norm was 50 percent, the composite achievement percentiles for Prince Edward were 9 percent for grade eleven, 14 percent for grade eight, and 17 percent for grade four.[178]

Anderson attributed the low scores in part to the relaxed approach to teaching associated with the open classroom movement. Under his administration the pendulum swung away from individualized teaching and social promotion and toward grades, testing, and close monitoring of academic performance as students moved from one level to another.[179] Along with this went a precisely calibrated system of grouping by achievement. "If we have six classes in the fourth grade," curriculum director Vera Allen explained, "each class will be grouped rather homogeneously. One teacher will teach the highest group, as determined by tests and teachers' reports. Another will teach the next highest. And so on. And then there will be a special class for slow learners." "When you put the complete spectrum into a single classroom, you are giving the teacher a chaotic situation," Anderson stated.[180]

At the high school there was less need for ability grouping since students chose different courses according to their aptitudes and interests. Nevertheless, even there students were subtly grouped into three sections, and a special program was open only to the very best students. Superintendent Anderson and Mrs. Allen knew that ability grouping had been controversial in some school districts. They were familiar with the *Hobson* litigation in Washington, D.C. But as of 1980 there had been very few complaints in Prince Edward County. Even Griffin expressed no concern. "In both personality and in policies, the current school administration is the best we've had," he stated in 1979.[181]

During the 1970s the performance of Prince Edward's public school students improved measurably. Although SRA scores at the end of the decade were not spectacular, they were far better than the examinations given in 1972 (Table 5). After exposure to Anderson's traditional, back-to-basics curriculum, fourth graders in 1980 scored slightly above the national average in reading and mathematics (52nd and 59th percentile, respectively), and high school juniors raised their composite scores to the 28th percentile. Some whites noted that the decline in scores after the fourth grade was a common occurrence at predominantly black schools throughout Virginia and claimed that black youths matured physically at an early age but failed to develop mentally after puberty. Anderson emphasized, however, that Prince Edward's high school juniors of 1980 had been fourth-grade students when he became superintendent in 1972. Their performance had increased from the 17th percentile to the 28th, a progression that measured real improvement for students who had missed out on fundamental basic education in the early grades. Anderson predicted that the fourth graders of 1980 would maintain their respectable scores if the schools continued to stress the basics, to promote only on the basis of achievement, and to group students according to ability.[182]

After the steady progress recorded on the SRA achievement tests, the Prince Edward school system was not prepared for the poor scores its students made on the state's first high school minimum-competency examination. Believing that students should not be granted a high school diploma unless they could demonstrate a certain level of competence in reading and mathematics, Virginia's state Board of Education prepared a uniform examination. When the first results were reported in 1979, however, 49.7 percent of the students at Prince Edward County High School failed the examination. This record was far inferior to that of the Prince Edward Academy (where all but one student passed) and to that of neighboring Southside

TABLE 5. Reading and Math Scores,
Prince Edward Public Schools, 1972–1980

| | SRA Composite Average Percentile | | | | |
	1972	1974	1976	1978	1980
Grade 4	17	23	26	43	55
Grade 8	14	12	21	26	36
Grade 11	9	11	16	27	28

Source: *The Edwardian,* March 1980.

public high schools (where the percentage of students passing ranged from 71 to 85).[183]

Prince Edward's public school administrators offered various explanations for their students' poor performance on the minimum-competency examination. Yet they knew the academic reputation of their schools had been damaged, and changes were promptly made to assure better performance on later tests. Since many students had difficulty reading, English teachers added remedial programs and drilled students for retesting. Sample minimum-competency tests were used in classroom teaching, and parents were asked to review the questions to see if any were racially biased.[184]

The results of the remedial program were gratifying. When Prince Edward's students were retested six months later, 80 percent passed the minimum-competency examination—a record that compared favorably with that of other public schools in Southside Virginia and with predominantly black schools throughout the state. After noting that 42 percent of Virginia's black students (and 11 percent of the whites) had failed the examination, the *Washington Post* praised Prince Edward's achievement: "If a small, rural county can make such remarkable improvements, there is little reason for the school systems of Northern Virginia to remain content with the rather unimpressive scores that their students have achieved."[185]

The academic record at Prince Edward's public schools was not entirely satisfactory, but on balance standards improved during the 1970s. The experience in race and community relations also moved in a direction that most observers regarded favorably.

Although Anderson had initially disavowed the goal of recruiting white students, the number of whites enrolled in the county's public schools increased significantly in the 1970s. At the end of the decade approximately 23 percent of the 2,200 public school students were white. Unlike the trend in other sections of the nation, where whites departed from schools with large black enrollments, a growing number of whites were enrolling in Prince Edward's predominantly black public schools. Yet the majority of white children in the county still attended Prince Edward Academy, where enrollment stablilized at about 1,000 after peaking at 1,350 in the early 1970s. Many observers attributed the public schools' increased white enrollment to economic pressures. "Whites still feel the same way about us, but they don't want to pay the high tuition at Prince Edward Academy," Griffin stated. The truth, however, is more complicated than that.[186]

Even in the 1960s many professors at Longwood and Hampden-Sydney felt guilty about sending their children to the Academy. Some were northerners who had attended desegregated schools; others were southern liberals who favored integration. They nevertheless patronized the Academy, partly because of its higher academic standards and partly for fear of violating social conventions in the county. "You had to thumb your nose at the community to send a white child to the public schools then," Longwood professor Patton Lockwood recalled. Both colleges eased the financial burden by paying tuition for faculty children.[187]

The situation began to change in 1969 when Longwood opened the John P. Wynne Campus School, a grammar school that reflected the open classroom ambience then in vogue among progressive educators. Most significantly from the standpoint of race relations, Wynne's student body was carefully selected and biracial. The majority of the 200 students were children of professors at Longwood and Hampden-Sydney, but 10 to 15 percent of the student body were blacks from the county. This arrangement drew criticism from both integrationists and segregationists, but the Wynne school enabled liberals to avoid guilt feelings. "I felt it was wrong to send my daughter to the Academy," Professor Lockwood recalled, "but I was also afraid to subject her to inferior education in the public schools." Yet, since Wynne did not take students beyond the seventh grade, it was only a partial answer to the professors' dilemma. Therefore, in 1974 Lockwood and professor Gerald Graham organized a group of faculty members who met with Superintendent Anderson. The professors then decided to send their children as a group to the county high school.[188]

This decision changed the momentum in local race relations. Respectable college professors were patronizing the public schools, and before long the presidents of both Longwood and Hampden-Sydney enrolled their children. As a result, other whites learned they would not be ostracized if their children attended public schools, and many quickly availed themselves of free education. Some white students were also attracted by the superior facilities for vocational education at the county high school.

As might be expected, there were some tensions among white students enrolled in the public schools. Some of the professors' children kept their distance from the poor whites, whom they disparagingly called "the grits." Some academically talented whites wanted to attend the Academy and felt they had been abandoned by parents who did not appreciate the importance of education. Others with less intellectual aptitude did not wish to attend any school. They resented the college-bound students and spent as much time as possible hanging out in the smoking area behind the high school.[189]

But these tensions paled in comparison with interracial resentments at the county high school. "I hated it during my first year," said Kate Young, the white valedictorian of the class of 1979. "I wasn't used to a situation where students disliked you if you wouldn't pretend you're dumb." She joined the school band but was ignored by blacks except when she made a mistake. Robin Lockwood, a white girl who graduated fourth in the class of 1978, also mentioned a pervasive anti-academic attitude among students. Even in the gifted program, she said, students thought it was "cool" to pretend they did not care about schoolwork. Like Kate Young, Robin Lockwood was "really resented the first year. Curses greeted me when I walked down the aisle of the school bus." She tried out for the basketball team, "but the black girls froze me out." Other whites complained about the blacks' rampant use of obscene language and the ubiquitous presence of loud radios.[190]

Most whites, nevertheless, thought race relations improved as blacks became more accustomed to whites. By the late 1970s white students were no longer complaining that they received no recognition. A disproportionate share of the academic honors went to whites, and many left the school with fond memories. By the time she went to college, Robin Lockwood got along so well with blacks that she became the only white member of the Black Students Union at Virginia Tech. After completing her freshman year at Smith College, Kate Young was glad she had not attended a more sheltered high school. She thought her experiences in Prince Edward had prepared her to cope with a world that consists of diverse groups of people.[191]

Although whites generally avoided sports other than tennis and tended to cluster together in the cafeteria and at assemblies, there was no pervasive pattern of interracial avoidance at the county high school. Students mixed amicably in the hallways, and members of both races belonged to various school clubs. Blacks and whites both attended school dances but not house parties away from campus. Interracial fights occurred rarely.

The color line was recognized in one area, however. Black and white students were both strongly opposed to interracial dating, and high school principal Bill Townes could not recall ever seeing a mixed couple at a school function. Even Nancy Fawcett, a white school board member who was known for unstinting work on behalf of the public schools, confessed unabashedly that she would "have a problem" if her daughter dated a black boy. The color line was present in Prince Edward, but racial separation at the county high school was not as thorough and pronounced as at many integrated high schools elsewhere in the United States.[192]

Yet a current of racial rancor was always present. Students and teachers tried to ignore it, but on occasion the resentment came to the surface — as it did in 1979 when Eric Griffin denounced the white power structure while campaigning for a student office. The youngest of Griffin's children, Eric complained that whites dominated almost everything in America and had even begun to take over at the county high school. In a rousing speech to a school assembly he fretted that half the teachers were now white, and he said it was not right for the school to neglect black studies and to choose whites as valedictorian, homecoming queen, and editor of the student newspaper. Offended by Griffin's remarks, most whites walked out of the assembly, while blacks cheered and chanted, "Get out! Get out! We don't want you." Some teachers thought an interracial melee was in the making until Vader Colbert, the respected black captain of the football team, took the microphone and gave an extemporaneous speech in favor of integration. Several white students later said they were going to transfer to the Academy, and some refused to ride the public school buses for the remainder of the year.[193] Some observers questioned the significance of Griffin's speech. Superintendent Anderson noted that Griffin lost the election and later apologized for his remarks. The tempest subsided rather quickly, and the biggest controversy on campus the following year concerned disciplinary policies.[194]

In Farmville a few black activists also objected to ability grouping and to gearing the school curriculum to standardized tests. Attorney James E. Ghee favored structured education but complained that ability grouping harmed weak students. "I think slow students need a model," he said. "They don't get one if they are grouped in a class with other slow kids." He also questioned whether gifted students would be able to relate to other people if they were "separated off by themselves during their youth." Ghee's friend and pastor, the Reverend J. Samuel Williams, also raised questions about testing and tracking. Bright students could take care of themselves, he said, but grouping put slower students "on the track to welfare and unemployment and is part of a general system of institutional racism that turns blacks toward menial jobs." Amil Myshin and Leonard Brown, two lawyers who worked for the Virginia Legal Aid Society, raised additional objections to what they called "a record of discriminatory discipline." They said black students were "suspended for things whites wouldn't be suspended for" because whites were "super-sensitive about black troublemaking."[195]

Despite the problems, the 1970s witnessed a significant growth in community support for the public schools. More blacks were voting, although the percentage of blacks living in the county declined from 45 in 1950 to

38 in 1980, and whites who sent their children to public schools naturally joined with blacks in support of public education. As a result, public school facilities in Prince Edward were better than those in the neighboring counties, and the expenditure per pupil at the county's schools was half again as much as the amount spent at the private Academy. Many people did not think this was fair, but some integrationists were pleased to know that those who patronized the Academy were suffering financially. "For fifteen years I've been hoping the Academy would go bankrupt," professor Patton Lockwood stated. His only regret was that "so far their Spartan life seems to have been exhilarating to them." Griffin observed that there was "less hostility between blacks and whites than between the white liberals and the Academy crowd." [196]

The influence of the public school coalition became apparent in November 1979. For decades the local Board of Education had been appointed by the School Trustee Electoral Board. But advocates of public education were angered during the summer of 1979 when the judge of the local circuit court appointed two well-known partisans of the Academy to the Electoral Board. Parents of public school students responded by initiating a referendum providing that henceforth members of the school board should be appointed by the elected Board of Supervisors. The referendum passed easily, receiving a majority of the votes in each of the county's election districts. The same election saw the defeat of the white chairman of the Board of Supervisors, who had long been associated with the Academy, and the election of James Ghee (who had drafted the referendum) and of two other blacks. The 1979 election indicated that public schools enjoyed broad support in the county. [197]

It is hard to say who won the struggle in Prince Edward County. "It depends on how you look at it," Griffin stated. "If you're talking about integration, then it could be said that the whites won, because there's still a lot of segregation." Griffin nevertheless thought that the blacks had triumphed because public education had been preserved. "The South would have closed its public schools if we had not won our case in 1964," he said. "Prince Edward was a beacon. If the courts had permitted the schools to remain closed the rest of the South would have followed the example. I believe you could say the black people of Prince Edward saved the South's public schools. [198]

Griffin claimed too much. The whites of Prince Edward did not oppose the use of taxes to support education, but they extolled the parents' right to choose an appropriate school and they supported a system of tuition grants that could be used at any nonsectarian school, including those that practiced segregation. They said *Brown* did not require the operation of public schools but merely prohibited discrimination in government schools. In the *Griffin* litigation, the federal courts ruled otherwise. The courts required Prince Edward to operate nondiscriminatory public schools and made parents pay extra if they sent their children to segregated academies.

While whites had to dig into their pockets or submit to a kind of education many found disagreeable, the county's black youth lost several years of schooling. The extent of the resulting damage is difficult to calculate. Some observers concluded that a whole generation of black children were severely retarded by the lack of formal education. Yet when approximately four hundred of those who had been locked out met for a reunion in 1976, it was apparent that many had overcome their disadvantages; in their ranks were college professors and construction workers, accountants and social workers and a currency examiner. When asked to characterize the fate of those who had been locked out, James E. Ghee, who organized the reunion and had been in the ninth grade when the schools were closed in 1959, thought carefully and replied: "That's hard to say. Overall, I don't know." Most of those whom Ghee knew were doing well. "They own their homes. They are employed. Their wives are employed." But Ghee did not know what had become of many of his schoolmates.[199]

Southern moderates and the advocates of massive resistance both understood that desegregation would have varied effects in different areas. Moderates from Virginia's predominantly white districts recognized that desegregation would not disrupt education in areas where blacks made up only a small portion of the population. Segregationists from the black belt accurately perceived that once desegregation began their children would be engulfed by a black flood. A generation after *Brown,* racially balanced enrollments had been achieved primarily in rural school districts where many whites could not afford to move to suburbs or to enroll their children in private academies. In Prince Edward County, to be sure, more than half of the white children were still educated separately, but the portion of students attending segregated academies in other black belt counties was generally smaller, although rarely negligible. In the 1970s and 1980s the rural South became the most desegregated region in the country. Some observers questioned the morality of requiring a relatively poor segment of the national population to submit to a kind of schooling that was disagreeable to them and that others could avoid simply by living in other regions.[200]

Most whites in Prince Edward believed the Constitution had been vandalized by judges duly sworn to defend the nation's basic charter. Yet there was little commitment to states' rights outside the South, and without widespread popular backing the high court could not be overcome. After federal judges of the 1970s delivered broad edicts requiring busing to achieve racial balance, however, a political coalition emerged that centered largely on opposition to further integration. "The full impact of desegregation is just now hitting the North," J. Barrye Wall observed in 1979. "Now maybe something will get done. We were trying to save the United States Constitution. We got our asses kicked in court, but it doesn't matter. We had to fight for what we knew was right. The principles we fought for aren't settled. We lost in court—the South lost—but it's still not settled."[201] Even while acknowledging the setback, Wall was pleased with the results at Prince Edward Academy. Most others professed to be satisfied with the county's public schools. "The blacks lost five years of school, and they were hurt immensely by that," said former school board chairman Lester Andrews, "but now, they're probably getting a better education. The Academy was hard pressed to begin with, but whites have also ended up getting a better education than before. In a way, you could say we've got pretty much what we had before, only better."[202]

In the years since *Brown* the general liberalization of American racial attitudes has not been without effect in Prince Edward County. Segregationists no longer monopolize power and influence, and some whites profess that race is of no intrinsic importance. Integrationists expect this minority to grow, while segregationists presume that forced integration will finally educate northerners to their way of thinking. One cannot say how long the status quo will persist in Prince Edward, but as this is written the county's determined white people have largely nullified three decades of judicial effort to reconstruct their schools.

PART THREE

BEYOND FREEDOM OF CHOICE:
CLARENDON COUNTY,
SOUTH CAROLINA

White people in Summerton, South Carolina, were just as opposed to desegregation as whites in Prince Edward County, but Summerton was not required to desegregate until 1965. By then, the Prince Edward litigation had established that individual school districts could not refuse to operate public schools, although the courts still distinguished between desegregation (which was required) and integration (which was not). Public schools could not separate youngsters on the basis of race, but they were not yet required to assign students so as to achieve racially balanced enrollments.

Summerton desegregated under a freedom-of-choice plan, and by 1969 its previously all-white schools enrolled 28 black students along with 256 whites. Yet not a single white student enrolled with the 2,380 blacks who attended other public schools in the district. Desegregation had been achieved, but mixing remained at token levels in an area where there were approximately nine black students for every white.

Then the Supreme Court revised its interpretation of desegregation. In *Green v. New Kent County* (1968) the Court decided that southern school districts must assign students so as to achieve approximately proportional distribution of the races in each school.[1] In 1970, after the Fourth Circuit Court of Appeals applied this ruling to Summerton, almost all white students withdrew from the local public schools. Ten years later all but one of the 286 whites attending school in the community were enrolled in a private academy. Instead of achieving integration, the courts' requirement of racial balance had produced white flight and resegregated schools.

I

Summerton is a small town of 1,500 people, located in Clarendon County about sixty-five miles northwest of Charleston. Those who first settled in the community originally owned property on the banks of the Santee River. Mosquitoes were a problem when the weather was hot, and planters sent their families a few miles inland to spend the summers. There they were joined by other well-to-do refugees from the heat of Charleston. "The Summer Town" was the name first given to the settlement, and traces of the community's patrician origins are still visible. It is a town of nice homes, some with traditional Georgian architecture and white-columned porches.[2] In the nineteenth century, Summerton became more than a summer colony. A boom in cotton occurred after Eli Whitney built a machine that efficiently separated the seeds from the fiber of a cotton boll. With good soil, about 50 inches of rainfall each year, and an average annual temperature of 65 degrees, Summerton became a center of the antebellum cotton culture.

Summerton and Clarendon County were part of the black belt, surrounded by other counties whose populations were half black or more. In the 1950s almost three-quarters of the people living in Clarendon were black, and a disproportionately large share of the blacks lived in the southwestern part of the county near Summerton.

Clarendon County was relatively untouched by the industrial development that characterized much of South Carolina after World War II. It was, in fact, the only county in the state where no new plants were opened between 1974 and 1980. Sunbeam and Federal Mogul had moved to Clarendon before that, and there were a few lumber mills and the inevitable cotton gins. The most visible new industry of the 1960s and 1970s, however, was tourism. Clarendon was known as a haven for fishermen and hunters. The streams and marshland of the Santee River Basin were abundant with fish and fowl, and the forests were well stocked with deer. The county was also situated about midway between Miami and New York and was traversed by I-95, the major interstate highway along the Atlantic coast. Few rural counties could boast of as many lodges with familiar names like Sheraton, Ramada, Holiday Inn, and Howard Johnson, motels that provided employment for a few hundred workers. But farming continued to be the county's most important economic activity—cotton was still grown near Summerton and tobacco, soy beans, corn, and lumber were also important.

Although farming was the primary economic activity, mechanization sharply reduced Clarendon's need for agricultural labor. During the twenty years after *Brown,* the total number of farm operators in the country declined from 3,813 to 777, and the general population fell by more than 20 percent from 33,000 to 26,000. Between 1954 and 1974 the number of black farmers declined drastically, from 2,709 to 297, and the black proportion of Clarendon's population fell from 72 percent to 62 percent. "There's really nothing to hold farm workers here," explained Ralph Bell, a white landowner. "I would have thought the black population would have declined even more than it has." Henry Lawson, the black manager of a Gulf Oil station in Summerton, recalled that in the old days "there was a lot of small farming. A man could support a family by farming 25 or 30 acres and helping out with odd jobs on other farms." Then agricultural machinery took over, and "small farmers had to leave; there just weren't many jobs around here."[3]

In 1980 Clarendon County was officially designated as a distressed area. It had the lowest per-capita income and the lowest median family income of the forty-six counties in South Carolina. Its percentage of nonwhite population was the second highest in the state, and almost half of the housing in the county was classified as substandard. Billie Fleming of the NAACP calculated that Clarendon was one of the twenty-nine poorest counties in the United States.[4]

In the 1940s Clarendon's black schools were separate and unequal. In 1949 the annual expenditure for each white student was $179, but only $43 was spent for each black child. The situation was especially deplorable in Summerton. The white schools there were constructed of brick and stucco, while the black schools were wooden. There was one white teacher for twenty-eight children at the white elementary school, but at the black schools there were forty-seven children per teacher. The curriculum at all-white Summerton High School included academic courses in biology that were not available at the blacks' Scotts Branch High School. There were indoor toilets and drinking fountains at the white schools, but blacks had to use outhouses and galvanized buckets with dippers for drinking water. The white schools were equipped with lunchrooms and a gymatorium, but no such facilities were available in the black schools. Buses conveyed children to the white schools, but no provision was made for the transportation of black students.[5]

Whites in Clarendon offered various explanations for the disparities. The general poverty of the county had left all schools in difficult straits, and many whites thought their children were entitled to a disproportionate share of the scarce resources because whites paid most of the taxes. Beyond this, whites argued that black schools were at a disadvantage because black children often worked on the farms and their parents insisted on keeping them close to home in remote areas that were not reached by the county's power and water lines. Whites also said that teacher assignments and local appropriations were based on the number of students who actually attended classes. More was spent for white students than for blacks because daily white attendance was about 95 percent, whereas blacks attended school only 72 percent of the time. Whites also pointed out that state funds paid only for the teachers' salaries; people in the local communities were expected to build schools and provide for any amenities. Thus the brick buildings, indoor toilets, and drinking fountains at Summerton's white schools were provided by private funds, as were the maps, globes, charts, and musical instruments. Blacks, it was implied, had the freedom to do likewise but instead made few additions to their schools.[6]

Clarendon's explanation was not entirely without merit, although it called to mind the majestic equality of laws that make it illegal for the rich to steal bread and sleep under bridges. By 1948 some blacks wanted more than an excuse. They demanded equality, and bus transportation seemed a good place to begin. Clarendon's thirty-four school districts operated thirty buses to convey white children to and from school, but no such transportation was available for blacks. The younger black students generally could get to classes, since one- and two-teacher elementary schools were spread all over the countryside. But black parents had to provide transportation for children who wished to attend one of Clarendon's three black high schools.

The Reverend J.A. DeLaine knew all about the hardship caused by Clarendon's busing policy. Born in 1898 on a farm near Manning, the county seat, DeLaine as a youth walked ten miles to get to and from school. Eventually DeLaine attended Allen University in Columbia, where he received a degree in theology. During the Great Depression he returned to Clarendon, where he pastored at several small country churches and taught at a school in Silver, a crossroads settlement four miles north of Summerton. By then DeLaine had married a fellow teacher named Mattie Belton, who had also walked to school in nearby Orangeburg County and who wondered "if black children would ever get a chance to ride in a school bus." To make sure that their children did not suffer from the county's discriminatory busing policy, the DeLaines built their home right across the street from the Scotts Branch High School in Summerton.[7]

The DeLaines responded enthusiastically when an NAACP official suggested that the time had come to bring a court case against Clarendon's whites-only busing policy. Only one plaintiff was needed to begin such a suit, and at DeLaine's urging this step was taken in 1948 by Levi Pearson, a Clarendon farmer whose three children struggled each day to traverse the nine miles between their farm and the Scotts Branch High School. But Pearson's suit was thrown out of court when it was discovered that his farm was located outside the Summerton school district and that Pearson consequently lacked legal standing to request transportation to Scotts Branch High School.[8]

But the struggle for equality was not over. In 1949 DeLaine met with the NAACP's Thurgood Marshall, who explained that test cases were always uncertain if tied to a single plaintiff: "it was too easy to find some disqualifying ground, as they had with Levi Pearson, or to intimidate the plaintiff into dropping out." If DeLaine could find twenty reliable plaintiffs who would stay the course, Marshall and the NAACP were willing to bring a major test case. At Marshall's insistence, though, the second suit would ask for equal treatment from top to bottom: buses, buildings, teachers, and books—everything the same.[9]

After finding the twenty plaintiffs, DeLaine and Marshall returned to federal court with a petition alleging that Summerton's white public schools were "superior in plant, equipment, curricula, and in all other material respects to the schools set apart for Negro students." Thus began the case of *Briggs v. Elliott,* which eventually would be consolidated with similar cases and finally decided in the Supreme Court's *Brown* litigation. Heading the list of plaintiffs was Harry Briggs, whose children went to school in Summerton and who had worked at a Main Street garage for the previous fourteen years.[10]

Before the litigation was concluded, Briggs would lose his job and several other plaintiffs would be subjected to various sorts of economic pressure. In Clarendon the squeeze was used regularly. "To apply it to the Negro," one observer noted, "don't gin his cotton, don't renew his bank note, fire him from his job. This is reprisal for anyone who wants to 'stir up trouble' and sign a petition." Briggs's wife Liza lost her job at a local motel, as did plaintiff Maisie Solomon. John McDonald could not find financing for a tractor, Lee Richardson was denied credit at the local feed store, Thelma Bethune could not get credit to buy supplies, and William Ragin could not rent any land to grow cotton. Attorney S. Emory Rogers reflected the sentiments of many whites when he said he would not extend credit or rent land to a member of the NAACP. "Everybody in Summerton feels the same way. You would, too, if you had an organization that was trying to destroy everything you believed in. We would like, if they are not satisfied here, for them to go where their ideas are accepted."[11]

At the pretrial conference before *Briggs v. Elliott,* district judge J. Waties Waring noted that the NAACP's pleadings did not specifically challenge the practice of segregation. Under the existing "separate but equal" doctrine it would not be difficult to compel Summerton to equalize its black schools, Judge Waring observed, but he told an astonished Thurgood Marshall that the case really should be dismissed without prejudice. Then, Waring suggested, the NAACP could file a new suit, directly alleging that segregation itself was unconstitutional. The judge was a descendant of an old Charleston family and had never questioned the propriety of segregation before receiving his judicial appointment. On the bench, however, he issued judgments against peonage and the white primary and for black teachers who sought salaries equal to those paid whites.[12]

Waring's suggestion was favorably received at NAACP headquarters, for the organization had almost simultaneously decided that there could not be true equality as long as educational facilities were separate. When *Briggs v. Elliott* finally went to trial, the NAACP did not content itself with an allegation that Summerton's black schools were inferior and therefore unconstitutional. It argued that racial segregation of public school students, as required by the constitution and statutes of South Carolina, was itself a denial of the equal protection of the laws.[13] The NAACP presented several social scientists who said segregation damaged the personalities of black children. The most striking testimony in this regard came from psychologist Kenneth Clark, who showed black and white dolls to sixteen black children selected at random from Summerton's schools. Nine of the children, after having been asked which was the "nice one," selected the white doll. Only eleven said the black doll was the one that looked most like themselves. From this, Clark deduced that there was "confusion in the individuals. . . and conflicting self-images." He concluded that segregation had a detrimental effect on the personalities of black children.[14]

The doll tests received a great deal of publicity after Chief Justice Earl Warren cited Clark as an authority for the Supreme Court's finding that segregation thwarted the educational and mental development of black children and deprived them of some of the benefits they would have received in racially integrated schools. But Clark's was not the only evidence the NAACP presented in *Briggs v. Elliott;* several other social scientists also said that children who were educated in segregated schools were "definitely harmed in the development of their personalities." Summarizing this testimony, Thurgood Marshall asserted that "segregation brands the Negro with the mark of inferiority and asserts that he is not fit to associate with white people."[15]

The lawyers for Clarendon County considered the social scientists' testimony inconclusive and innocuous. Robert McCormick Figg of Charleston was content to establish that all but one of the NAACP's expert witnesses came from the North and had done no field research in states where segregation was practiced. He characterized their opinions as the result of general reading rather than practical experience. As for Kenneth Clark's doll test, once Figg discovered that Clark's testimony was "based on very few children, that there were no witnesses to the tests, and that this was his own test method and not a well-established one, I didn't press the matter. His numbers were small and unimposing."[16]

Figg and fellow counsel S. Emory Rogers might have confronted Clark directly if they had known the Supreme Court would later use the doll studies as a basis for its conclusion that separate schools are inherently unequal. Certainly Clark's testimony was vulnerable, as several commentators have noted. Author Richard Kluger, a celebrant of the *Brown* decision, has conceded that "sixteen children were not very many, to start with, and if even one or two of them had undergone atypical experiences or traumas in their young lives, the overall test results would have been thrown out of kilter." Edmond Cahn of New York University, another champion of the *Brown* decision, also noted that Clark's doll test did not purport to demonstrate "the effects of *school* segregation, which is what the court was being asked to enjoin. If it disclosed anything about the effects of segregation on the children, their experiences at school were not differentiated from other causes." Cahn thought there was a real danger in basing constitutional rights on social science evidence as flimsy as that presented by Kenneth Clark.[17]

The most damaging criticism came from Ernest van den Haag, an adjunct professor of social philosophy at New York University. Van den Haag thought Clark's research was not needed to establish "the common sense view that Negroes are humiliated and frustrated by segregation," but he questioned the implication that segregation was more humiliating than compulsory mixing with whites who resented the intrusion. He did not think that "being resented and shunned personally and concretely by their white schoolmates . . . would be less humiliating to Negro children than a general abstract knowledge that they are separately educated because of white prejudice."[18]

Moreover, van den Haag noted, Clark's research actually demonstrated that black children in segregated schools were less likely to prefer white dolls and more often thought favorably of the colored dolls. When testifying in the Clarendon case, Clark neglected to mention that he had previously shown dolls to hundreds of black children who were attending segregated schools in Arkansas and unsegregated schools in Massachusetts. The proportion of students who preferred the white dolls was actually higher in Massachusetts than in Arkansas. Thus, if the doll test was a valid means of indicating what sort of schooling enhanced black self-respect, the data tended to favor segregated schooling. "In short, if Professor Clark's tests do demonstrate damage to Negro children, then they demonstrate that the damage is *less* with segregation and *greater* with congregation." Van den Haag concluded that Clark had compromised himself professionally by deliberately misleading the courts. He had lent the prestige of social science to a pseudo-scientific exercise that was intended to advance a special pleading. "Clark told the Court that he was proving that 'segregation inflicts injuries upon the Negro,'" when the doll tests really proved the opposite, if they proved anything.[19]

Instead of criticizing the NAACP's social science, the attorneys for Clarendon County stressed that a vast body of legal precedent established that states could segregate students on the basis of race. Segregation was the normal practice prior to the Fourteenth Amendment, had been authorized in the District of Columbia by the Congress that had debated and submitted the amendment, and had been practiced by most of the states until such time as their respective legislatures decided to desegregate. After reviewing the record in 1927, the Supreme Court itself stated that the question of segregated schools had been "many times decided to be within the constitutional power of the state legislature to settle without intervention of the federal courts. . . ." The Constitution required only that segregated facilities be equal.[20]

When *Briggs v. Elliott* came to trial, lawyers Figg and Rogers conceded that the county's black schools were inferior and asked for time to remedy the situation. In 1950 South Carolina had begun a massive program to equalize educational facilities, and Figg predicted that complete equality could be achieved within a few years.[21] This prediction may have seemed extravagant but, thanks to the work of James F. Byrnes, it proved to be accurate. Byrnes was South Carolina's leading political figure of the twentieth century. He had been a congressman during World War I, a senator during the Great Depression, an associate justice of the Supreme Court, the unofficial "assistant president" to Franklin D. Roosevelt during World War II, and secretary of state during the critical postwar period. Upon returning to his native state to become governor in 1950, Byrnes determined that it was necessary to provide blacks and whites with substantially equal school facilities. "We should do it because it is right," Byrnes told the state legislature. "For me that is sufficient reason." Referring to the drift of social thought elsewhere in the nation, Byrnes then stated, "If any person wants an additional reason, I say it is wise."[22]

Acting on Governor Byrnes's recommendation, South Carolina sold $175 million worth of bonds and levied a sales tax of 3 percent, to be used only for public schools. Two-thirds of the state money was eventually used for black schools, although blacks made up only 43 percent of the students. More than 90 percent of the $900,000 appropriated for Summerton went to black schools.[23]

In 1951 Clarendon's thirty-four small school districts were consolidated into three larger districts, with the one near Summerton henceforth known as School District No. 1 of Clarendon County. The salaries of black and white teachers were equalized, and the one- and two-room country schoolhouses were replaced by two well-built consolidated schools, each on a ten-acre site. A new Scotts Branch School was opened with "concentric lighting, pale green blackboards, battleship linoleum on the floors, [and] expensive tile in the toilets. . . ." The general transformation astonished reporters who had visited the community only a few years before. The rundown hovels of black schools had been abandoned and sold at public auction; in their stead were modern schools that surpassed anything Summerton offered its white children.[24]

The three-judge district court in *Briggs v. Elliott* required the equalization of facilities, but since conditions had been improved so rapidly the court did not demand any actions beyond periodic progress reports. More importantly, the court, with Judge Waring dissenting, held that racial segregation in the public schools was not of itself a denial of the equal protection of the laws. Writing for the court, Judge John J. Parker noted that testimony about the effects of desegregation was conflicting. Some witnesses indicated that mixed schools would lead to better education and improved race relations, whereas others said that mixing was impractical in South Carolina and would exacerbate racial friction and tension. Parker and Judge George Bell Timmerman held that the court would exceed its proper authority if it tried to resolve this complex question by substituting its own judgment for that of the legislature. When they compared the social science evidence with the many legal precedents upholding segregation, the social science seemed to be of little consequence.

> When seventeen states and the Congress of the United States have for more than three quarters of a century required segregation of the races in the public schools, and when this has received the approval of the leading appellate courts of the country including the unanimous approval of the Supreme Court of the United States at a time when that court included Chief Justice Taft and Justices Stone, Holmes, and Brandeis, it is a late day to say that such segregation is violative of fundamental constitutional rights.[25]

On appeal before the Supreme Court, South Carolina's case was argued by one of the nation's most distinguished lawyers, John W. Davis. A former congressman, solicitor general, ambassador to England, and Democratic nominee for president, Davis had participated in more Supreme Court cases than any other lawyer in the twentieth century.

Davis insisted that neither the Congress that submitted the Fourteenth Amendment nor the ratifying states had understood that the amendment would require the abolition of segregated public schools. He said it was inconceivable that Congress would submit an amendment destroying the states' right to maintain segregated schools while at the same time establishing a system of segregated schools in the District of Columbia. A few of the ratifying states admittedly discontinued segregation after endorsing the amendment, but a far greater number continued to operate segregated schools. Eight of the Republican-controlled southern states that were then being reconstructed operated segregated schools after the Fourteenth Amendment was adopted—a fact that Davis regarded as of great significance. "If there was any place where the Fourteenth Amendment and its sponsors would have blown the bugle for mixed schools and asserted that the Fourteenth Amendment had settled the question, surely it would have been in those eight states under Reconstruction legislation, sympathetic to the party which was responsible for the submission of the Fourteenth Amendment."[26]

Davis insisted that it would not be proper for the Supreme Court to interpret the equal protection clause so as to give a construction directly opposed to the intention of the framers. If judges substituted their own views for the original intention, they became amenders of the Constitution, not interpreters. Fortunately, Davis noted, the Supreme Court itself had repeatedly acknowledged the importance of determining the intention of the framers. The very pole star of correct constitutional interpretation, he said, is to go first to the intention of the framers and ratifiers.[27]

Even if segregation were considered anew, Davis pointed out that the equal protection clause does not forbid all classifications. The Supreme Court had repeatedly held that different groups can be treated differently "provided there is a real and substantial, as distinguished from an arbitrary, basis for the classification." The NAACP's Thurgood Marshall conceded the point but argued that racial segregation falls within a group of unreasonable classifications that the equal protection clause calls into question.

Here a basic issue was crystallized. Referring to South Carolina's long experience with delicate problems of racial coexistence, Davis maintained that segregation is not manifestly unreasonable. History shows that race relations were properly the subject of experimentation and adjustment to local conditions. Marshall answered that laws that curtail the rights of a racial group are "immediately suspect" and should not be permitted without compelling evidence of their necessity. South Carolina had not proved that blacks and whites differ in intellectual aptitude and capacity. It had not demonstrated that segregation is necessary for the maintenance of an efficient system of public education. Clarendon had not presented a single witness "to show that [segregation] is reasonable—not one. Not a witness has been produced to show that [segregation] came about as a result of mature judgment."[28]

In *Brown* the Supreme Court did not mention the burden of proof in cases involving suspect classifications. Instead, it cited Kenneth Clark's doll studies and held that segregation is unconstitutional because it damages blacks psychologically. The *Briggs* case was then returned to the district court in South Carolina, with instructions that public schools in Summerton should be desegregated.[29]

Upon remand in 1955, judges John J. Parker, George Bell Timmerman, and Armistead Dobie (who had replaced the retired J. Waties Waring) issued a pilot ruling that would guide other courts and satisfy the Supreme Court for the next thirteen years. "It is important that we point out exactly what the Supreme Court has decided and what it has not decided," Parker wrote. Drawing on the language of the Supreme Court's second *Brown* opinion, Parker then ordered Summerton to proceed "with all deliberate speed" toward operating public schools "on a racially nondiscriminatory basis." In a passage that came to be known as the *Briggs* dictum, Judge Parker stated that the Supreme Court had "not decided that states must mix persons of different races in the schools. . . . What it has decided, and all that it has decided, is that a state may not deny any person on account of race the right to attend any school that it maintains." Under the *Brown* decision, public schools must be open to children of all races, but there would be no violation of the Constitution if children of different races voluntarily chose to attend different schools.[30]

In the *Briggs* dictum, Judge Parker offered an interpretation of *Brown* that differed sharply from that of the NAACP. The leaders of the NAACP insisted that the Supreme Court had considered its words carefully. The justices might have declared simply that the Fourteenth Amendment prohibits state-sponsored segregation. Instead, they stated that racial isolation harms black students psychologically. The Court had recognized "the educationally inhibitive effect of racial isolation," NAACP attorney Robert L. Carter noted. It had censured segregation "without defining how such segregation occurred." In resting its *Brown* opinion on psychological grounds, the Supreme Court did more than prohibit states from discriminating racially; it implied that states have an affirmative constitutional duty to provide integrated schools.[31]

The Supreme Court would not endorse Carter's exegesis until 1968. In the meantime the *Briggs* dictum was accepted as the correct interpretation of *Brown,* much to the relief of the white South. "The [Supreme] Court's action was not as drastic as it could have been," the *Columbia State* declared. It left open the possibility of "voluntary segregation," the *Charleston News and Courier* commented. A special committee of the South Carolina state legislature reassured white citizens "that the Court did not intend to force integration on an unwilling people. . . . [N]othing in the Constitution or the [*Brown*] decision . . . compels the state of South Carolina to deliberately mix the races in public schools."[32]

Desegregation finally came to Summerton in 1965 when five black students enrolled without incident at previously all-white schools. Long before then, the prime movers of the lawsuit had left Clarendon County. After losing their jobs, Harry Briggs and his wife had tried to earn a living on a farm just outside Summerton. When that proved difficult, they moved to New York, although they returned to Clarendon in the 1970s for their retirement.[33]

Unlike Harry Briggs, the Reverend J.A. DeLaine never returned to his native county. After instigating the litigation, DeLaine was continuously harassed. He was assessed damages of $2,700 when an all-white jury determined that his criticisms of a local black school principal were slanderous. Then catsup and eggs were smeared over the windows of DeLaine's home, and a load of trash was set on fire in a vacant lot next door. Things quieted down after DeLaine was transferred to a church in Lake City in nearby Florence County. But in 1955 DeLaine's church was burned and the pastor was told to leave town. An unsigned letter, scribbled in pencil, stated that "several hundred of us . . . have decided to give you ten days to leave Lake City. We have made plans to move you if it takes dynamite to do so. This is final."[34]

A few days later, several carloads of white men circled through DeLaine's neighborhood, shouting and firing gunshots into the air. While the cars were gone, DeLaine took out a rifle and ordered his wife to depart for safety in a neighbor's house. When the caravan returned, DeLaine fired into the cars, killing one man and wounding another. He then beat a hasty retreat to a local truck stop, where he got a ride out of state from a black truck driver. The African Methodist Episcopal bishop of New York gave DeLaine asylum, appointing him for brief stints at churches in Buffalo and New Rochelle and then for fifteen years at the Calvary Church in Brooklyn. South Carolina's pleas for extradition were rejected, and DeLaine lived the remainder of his life in exile. He derived some satisfaction from the knowledge that his work in Clarendon County was continued by a nephew, local NAACP leader Billie Fleming. To his regret, however, DeLaine never succeeded in his efforts to obtain the dropping of the criminal charges pending against him. He died in 1974.[35]

II

When the *Briggs* case was argued, Thurgood Marshall took the position "that the racial percentage one way or the other is unimportant." It did not matter whether a few black pupils went to classes with a majority of whites or whether a few whites attended predominantly black schools. Blacks were entitled to immediate relief from the psychological damage that segregation inflicted. In response to those who said it would take time for many communities to accept desegregation, Marshall replied that there was "no place for local option in our Constitution." Unpopular policies could be implemented if imposed firmly and without allowing a lapse of time to permit opposition to crystallize.[36]

Defense attorney Robert Figg said that the Clarendon case, probably more than any other case, demonstrated to the Supreme Court the need to grant time to meet the difficult problems that vary from state to state and from school district to school district. In Summerton integration meant "the assignment of white pupils, in the proportion of approximately one out of ten," and Figg and attorney S. Emory Rogers bluntly told the Court that whites would establish segregated private schools rather than send their children "to what are in reality Negro schools." The resulting damage to public education would be a serious matter, but Figg and Rogers said it was "nine times as serious [to the blacks] as it is to the white pupils and maybe more because [blacks] may not be as well able to take care of themselves. . . ."[37]

Among whites in Summerton there was no debate over the need to resist desegregation. At a meeting of 350 townspeople in 1955, a young landowner named W.B. Davis spoke strongly in favor of closing the public schools forthwith. Davis calculated that schools for white children could be operated for about $34,000 a year—about what whites paid in local school taxes. Closing public schools would draw criticism, since black parents would find it impossible to finance private schools for their children, but Davis and others said the blacks "would have brought the trouble on themselves."[38]

The county superintendent of schools, L.B. McCord, was especially outspoken in opposition to desegregation. "Here's the situation," he stated. "The Negro children have not had the educational advantages in the past that the whites have had. They haven't even taken advantage of the opportunities they have had." Since blacks as a group were "a retarded bunch," McCord thought compulsory mixing of students of the same age and grade would lower academic standards at the white schools.[39] McCord also thought that the liberty protected by the Fourteenth Amendment includes the parents' right to direct the education of their children. McCord said he wanted blacks "to get a fair break," and with equalization he thought this had been accomplished. Discrimination should not be confused with segregation, he said. "If we desegregate, neither race will receive any profit," McCord said. "Both races will be hurt."[40]

Nevertheless, local sentiment finally swung against abandoning the public schools. At the 1955 meeting town banker Charles N. Plowden, a large landowner and a former member of the General Assembly, argued that delay was the proper tactic. "If the Court orders us to integrate, we'll close," Plowden said. In the meantime he recommended that Summerton devise a method of voluntary segregation that would be acceptable to the courts. S. Emory Rogers also recommended delay. He said the South could gain twenty-five years of "segregation time" if it tested one method of resistance at a time. "One plan for the maintenance of segregation . . . would be tried," he explained. "When that is ruled out, another, then another, and another . . . until one is found that is acceptable." Closing the public schools was a "last resort," to be used only after the federal courts had ruled against every conceivable delaying tactic.[41]

Segregationist views, prevalent throughout white South Carolina, were reflected in the state's General Assembly, which built an intricate legal fortress against desegregation. In 1951 a special fifteen-member State School Committee was established to study and report on what could be done if the federal courts ruled against segregated schools. Popularly called the Gressette Committee for its chairman, state Senator L. Marion Gressette, the School Committee assumed a standby role and did little until the Supreme Court handed down the *Brown* decision in 1954. Then it swung into action and developed a plan to prevent the schools from being disrupted by what it called "outside forces and influences which have no knowledge of recent progress and no understanding of the problems of the present and future." Some laws were repealed, such as the one requiring compulsory school attendance; a number of others were enacted. One denied public funds to any school to which or from which pupils were transferred by any court. Another specified that school appropriations be made on a racially segregated basis. A third reinforced the local school boards' authority to handle requests for pupil transfers.[42]

Most white South Carolinians recognized that legislative defiance would provide only temporary relief, during which the state would try to rally public opinion throughout the nation. South Carolina legislators quickly spotted the phenomenon of resegregation in the North and West and concluded that most whites had reservations about mixing with large numbers of blacks. Although no prominent South Carolinian went as far as Georgia's Senator Richard B. Russell, who recommended that $1,500 be given to any black family that would settle in the North, Carolinians generally believed their viewpoint would gain popularity as blacks migrated and people in other regions had to face the difficulties of integration. "Released from the social restrictions of the segregation code, blacks are running wild in the North," the *Charleston News and Courier* reported. "If the people of New York, with their relatively low ratio of Negro to white population, find it so difficult to operate their schools and maintain law and order," Senator Strom Thurmond stated, "I cannot fathom how their political leaders can expect the people of the South to bow to their political demands that they accept an even more mammoth mess than their own people are willing to stomach."[43]

Because of his national prominence, it was especially important that James F. Byrnes made it his personal crusade "to let the people of other sections know that the attitude of the South is due not to racial prejudice but to the firm belief that the [Supreme] Court has arrogated to itself the power of a third legislature and if not curbed by the Congress, will destroy local government." As Byrnes saw it, in *Brown* the Supreme Court had disregarded its own previous decisions as well as the intention of the Fourteenth Amendment. In order to change a policy that the states and Congress had refused to alter, the Court had invaded the jurisdiction of the states and enacted judicial legislation which undermined the system of *federal* government. By concentrating power in Washington, the judiciary was building up a *central* government that ultimately would jeopardize freedom throughout the nation. Byrnes told a national audience, "Today this usurpation by the Court . . . hurts the South. Tomorrow, it may hurt *you.*"[44] Although he was a former justice of the Supreme Court, Byrnes called on Congress to save the Constitution from the Court and the Court from itself. "The Supreme Court must be curbed," he insisted, since it was undermining what Byrnes considered the twin pillars of American freedom: states' rights and the separation of executive, legislative, and judicial powers. Fortunately, the third article of the Constitution specifically authorized Congress to regulate the jurisdiction of the federal judiciary. "Congress should exercise that power," Byrnes insisted. It should strip the federal courts of jurisdiction over all matters having to do with education.[45]

Legislation to restrict the courts' jurisdiction over educational matters was introduced by South Carolina's senators Strom Thurmond and Olin D. Johnston, but it repeatedly failed to win passage through Congress. There simply were "not enough people in Washington concerned with the principles on which our Constitution was established," Thurmond lamented. Too many people failed to see that "the super-government they are building up . . . will become itself the greatest possible threat to the rights of the individual."[46]

Byrnes generally stressed legal and constitutional questions, but he freely admitted that "one cannot discuss this problem without admitting that, in the South, there is a fundamental objection to integration. White Southerners fear that the purpose of many of those advocating integration is to break down social barriers in the period of adolescence and ultimately bring about intermarriage of the races. Because they are opposed to this, they are opposed to abolishing segregation." Segregation was not based on "petty prejudice," Byrnes insisted, but on "an instinctive desire for the preservation of our race."[47]

Northern writers frequently implied that the spectre of racial amalgamation was a hobgoblin that demagogic politicians used to bamboozle their most ignorant followers but one that enlightened white Southerners recognized as a trumped-up thing having no real substance. Byrnes emphatically denied these insinuations. "Pride of race has been responsible for the grouping of people along ethnic lines throughout the world," he stated. Quoting Disraeli, he insisted that no one should "treat with indifference the principle of race. It is the key to history." Although Byrnes did not dwell on racial statistics pertaining to crime, illegitimacy, and venereal disease, he said parents should try to raise their children in an atmosphere reasonably free from moral dangers. When they were forced to give their children to school authorities for several hours each day, parents had the duty as well as the right to "control the schools their children attend." "The lives of our children must not be fashioned by some bureaucrat in Washington," he declared.[48]

Byrnes was not the only prominent South Carolinian to warn that integration might lead to a debasing assimilation. Herbert Ravenall Sass, a well-known Charleston author, also insisted that "integration of white and Negro children in the South's primary schools would open the gates to miscegenation and widespread racial amalgamation." In an article in the *Atlantic*, Sass maintained that integration rested on the premise that blacks and whites were essentially alike except for skin color. Integrated schools consequently would turn out "successive generations in whom, because they are imbued with this philosophy, the instinct of race preference would have been suppressed." Some people thought this would be a good thing, the happy solution to the race problem in America. But Sass maintained that one need look no farther than Latin America to see that the fusion of racial bloodlines led to second-class societies.[49]

Charleston editor Thomas R. Waring also warned that mixed mating would not be repugnant to generations brought up in schools that accepted the desirability of racial integration. Some observers placed more emphasis on environment than on heredity in explaining racial differences in health, marital standards, and intellectual development, but Waring thought "proof is lacking in so many phases of this controversy that we are forced to rely on everyday observations." Regardless of whether the differences are intrinsic or acquired, Waring cautioned, while white civilization is "rubbing off . . . onto the colored children, Negro culture will also rub off onto the whites."[50]

Rejecting the suggestion that blacks are racially inferior, Roy Wilkins of the NAACP insisted that statistics on black crime, disease, illegitimacy, and academic retardation were testimony to racial oppression. It was not fair to expect people who had been segregated and held to a substandard economic level "to be healthy, happy, thrifty, educated and responsible citizens." Arguments like those of Sass and Waring "blandly brushed aside the clear responsibility of the South itself for the present statistics on Negroes." Wilkins maintained that "the Waring thesis astounds and disgusts thoughtful people outside the South."[51]

Nevertheless, NAACP officials recognized that opposition to desegregation was intense in black belt counties like Clarendon. While visiting Summerton in 1955, Thurgood Marshall had a disquieting meeting with local whites who warned in no uncertain terms that the public schools would be closed before they would be desegregated. Banker Charles N. Plowden spoke with unvarnished candor. "I told them they can make us close the schools but they can't make us mix. I told them they've got more to lose than we have. We've got twelve white teachers; they've got sixty. They'd all be out of work. They've got twenty-seven bus drivers. They'd be out of work. There wouldn't be any school for their children but there would be for ours. I told them, 'You can go ahead and push us if you want to, and we'll close our schools!'"[52]

Shortly thereafter, the NAACP decided to leave the Summerton district alone. Roy Wilkins was quoted as saying, "if it were left to me to choose the place where we would try to integrate, Clarendon County would be the last place I'd pick. It doesn't matter from a practical standpoint if Clarendon is not integrated for 99 years."[53] Yet, while permitting the Clarendon case to remain dormant, the NAACP pushed forward to desegregate schools in South Carolina's oldest and most cosmopolitan city, Charleston.

When the Charleston case went to court in 1963, segregationists knew they could no longer rely on legal precedents and states' rights. They recognized that their case was lost unless they could prove that the 1954 *Brown* decision was based on incomplete and misleading evidence that would have been contested if the attorneys had known the case would be decided on sociological grounds. S. Emory Rogers declared that their only hope lay in "using the same psychological and sociological warfare that has been used so successfully against us."[54]

George S. Leonard, a Virginian who represented Prince Edward in the latter stages of that county's prolonged litigation, was a principal architect of Charleston's defense. On the basis of scientific evidence he considered more compelling than that introduced in the *Briggs* case, Leonard argued that innate differences in the races' aptitudes for education formed a rational basis for educating them separately. Classifications did not violate the equal protection clause, he said, unless they were arbitrary and capricious. The Supreme Court had decided that public school students could not be segregated "solely on the basis of race," but this did not prohibit classification on the basis of educational aptitude. Leonard proposed to answer a question that Thurgood Marshall had posed during the oral argument before the Supreme Court: "Why of all the multitudinous groups of people in this country," Marshall had asked, "[do] you have to single out Negroes and give them this treatment?"[55]

For several years students in Charleston had taken a series of reading and mathematics tests distributed by a reputable Iowa testing firm. Black students in the first grade scored about one year below the average for white children, and the gap widened progressively until whites were four years ahead in the higher grades. Because of the differences in average scores, Superintendent Thomas A. Carrere said, the quality of education "would disintegrate and we couldn't do anything" if the school district were forced to desegregate.[56]

NAACP lawyer Constance Baker Motley argued that the black curriculum was inferior in Charleston, that less money was spent for the education of blacks, and that black teachers were less qualified than whites. She noted that the school district spent $267 annually for each white pupil but only $169 for each black, and that white teachers were required to score at least 500 on the National Teacher Examination, whereas blacks were certified if they obtained a score of 425. It was no wonder that black pupils lagged academically. Their teachers were not as well prepared, and their schools were not as well financed.[57]

School board chairman Charles A. Brown discounted the importance of these points. He testified that there were no substantial differences in the curricula and said the financial disparity was due to a sharp decline in the number of white students attending public schools. Half the black high school teachers in Charleston had master's degrees, and 61 percent had eleven years or more of teaching experience. As for the National Teacher Examination, Brown said the school district could not find many black teachers who "measured up to the white standards." When asked why he did not assign white teachers to black classes, he replied that it was "against southern tradition" and "would cause chaos."[58]

Throughout the trial, attorney Leonard insisted that the differences in the areas tested were "inherent, not caused by the home or school environment of the students." Blacks and whites differ "in the relative size, proportion, and structure of the brain and neural system," Leonard maintained; consequently, the two races "differ sharply in the type of subject and type of teaching to which they respond most readily."[59] To support his case, Leonard called on several academic authorities. Psychologist Henry E. Garrett said that when conditions were equated "as well as they can be equated," blacks did not perform any better; on standard tests the difference between the children of black and white professionals was even greater than the difference between the children of black and white manual workers. Black students who attended desegregated schools trailed just as far behind their white counterparts as those who went to segregated schools. Moreover, Garrett said, the differences were greatest in "the realm of what you'd call abstract intelligence, that is, the ability to deal with numbers, pictures, diagrams, blueprints, words, things of that sort, those things which made European Civilization and never have made a civilization in Africa in five thousand years." Garrett predicted that most blacks who attended mixed schools would fall behind academically and then would become frustrated and disruptive. Since racial differences could not be obliterated by court decrees, he thought massive integration would ruin the public school system.[60]

Dr. Wesley Critz George, emeritus professor of anatomy at the University of North Carolina medical school, confirmed Garrett's opinion about the biological basis of racial differences. Blacks and whites had developed in geographically distinct regions over periods of time best measured in geological terms. As a result of this evolution, George said, the two races differed in the size, proportion, and structure of the brain and endocrine system. The average black brain weighed about 9 percent less than that of the average white, the cortex was about 14 percent thinner, and the prefrontal area of the white brain was larger. These hereditary characteristics influenced intelligence, George said, and their effects could not be overcome by desegregation.[61]

Dr. Ernest van den Haag then took the stand to explain how Kenneth Clark had slanted social science and misled the courts during the *Briggs* litigation. Referring to studies of integrated schools elsewhere in the United States, van den Haag also said prejudice was more likely to increase rather than decrease if the races were compelled to associate with one another. Mixing might lead to increased interracial friendship if it were voluntary and involved people of similar interests, he conceded, but this was all the more reason to permit freedom of choice. "Whether children are educated together or separately, it should be according to their own choice or the choice of their parents."[62]

There were substantial racial differences in the average scores compiled by black and white students in Charleston, but there was also an enormous range of academic aptitude within each race, with some blacks performing better than most whites. What was wrong with permitting superior black students to attend desegregated schools? van den Haag was asked. Why not do as Thurgood Marshall had suggested when the *Briggs* case was before the Supreme Court: "Put the dumb colored children in with the dumb white children, and put the smart colored children with the smart white children."[63]

Van den Haag acknowledged that this sort of desegregation would not undermine academic standards. If the black elite attended predominantly white schools, however, the black masses would be deprived of their natural leaders and would suffer feelings of rejection and inferiority. The elite would also suffer from "a conflict in terms of identification"; they would not know whether "to identify with their group of origin, or . . . with the group they now have joined."[64]

In the Charleston case, the segregationists in effect asked a district court to overrule the U.S. Supreme Court. This was something that Judge J. Robert Martin would not do. He permitted the introduction of a wide range of social science evidence and opinion that other courts could consider on appeal, but he held that under the doctrine of *stare decisis* an inferior court was not authorized to set aside the holding of a higher court. The Fourth Circuit Court of Appeals agreed with Judge Martin on this point, and by refusing to hear the case the Supreme Court avoided the question of whether its opinion in *Brown* was based on faulty social science.[65]

When eleven black students enrolled in predominantly white schools in Charleston in the fall of 1963, South Carolina became the last of the fifty states to desegregate its public schools. By then massive resistance had collapsed in Virginia, and federal troops had been sent to Mississippi. Many South Carolinians consequently believed that integration could no longer be prevented. Die-hard segregationists still wanted to close racially mixed public schools, but many others said it was time to face facts. South Carolina was enjoying a tremendous industrial boom, and it was feared that industry would not continue its migration to the state if public schools were closed. In the predominantly white Piedmont and in white suburbs of major cities, there were also many moderates who were convinced that desegregation would not involve much actual mixing of the races. Even in the black belt there were some whites who thought local school boards could assign pupils on the basis of nonracial characteristics such as personality and scholastic aptitude, and that only the better black students would be admitted to predominantly white schools. Desegregation was at hand, but in 1963 the *Columbia State* assured its readers that "large scale integration would appear still to be many years away."[66]

Responding to the changing temper of public opinion, Senator L. Marion Gressette's State School Committee modified its approach. Since 1954, the cornerstone of segregation had been Section 21–2 of the South Carolina Code, which cut off appropriations to integrated schools. By 1960, however, federal courts had knocked down similar laws in other states, and in 1961 the Gressette Committee persuaded the General Assembly to retreat to more defensible legal terrain. The words "for racially segregated schools only" were deleted from the appropriations acts, and local option became the state's chief defense against desegregation.

Black belt segregationists were bitterly disappointed. Florence attorney Richard G. Dusenbury observed that "no one can predict what a particular school board will do—particularly when great pressures are brought to bear on its members." Segregation could continue "if we keep our laws as they are," he said. Local option, on the other hand, would undermine statewide unity and would lead to racial mixing in some public schools. S. Emory Rogers continued to believe that abandoning public education was the only realistic alternative to segregation. Massive resistance had not failed in Virginia, he said. It had never been tried. Segregation could be preserved if whites remained united and interposed the authority of the state between the people and the federal government.[67]

To soften the impact of local option, in 1963 the General Assembly provided financial grants equal to the per-pupil cost of public education, which students could use at any school. The stipends were to be awarded without regard to race, and those who framed the program said its purpose was to improve public education by encouraging competition and giving students true freedom of choice. It was generally understood, however, that the system would make things easier for whites who did not wish to go to school with blacks.[68] Black belt leaders overwhelmingly favored the tuition grants program. Charles N. Plowden of Summerton stated that the tuition grants would give children of both races "full freedom of association." S.L. Gentry of the Citizens Councils called the program a "pioneering effort . . . to solve as far as possible a potentially troublesome problem." Senator Gressette declared in his reports, "South Carolina at all costs must prevent the development of its . . . schools into the lawless 'blackboard jungles' that integration has made in the District of Columbia."[69]

The tuition grants program was finally enacted by a vote of 78 to 28 in the South Carolina House of Representatives and 35 to 4 in the state Senate. The most vocal opponents came from the predominantly white Piedmont, where, for example, the PTA in Spartanburg (22 percent black) declared the program "would present an unneeded handout to well-to-do parents already able to send their children to private schools." J.W. Gaston, the chairman of the Spartanburg school board, predicted that the issue would become a bone of contention between the predominantly white upcountry and the black belt. State representative Harris P. Smith of Pickens (9 percent black) was one of the most outspoken opponents of the tuition grants plan. He said it "could not stand a court test and would be detrimental to the public school system." Another influential member of the House said that any act designed to circumvent desegregation would fail to pass the test in the federal courts.[70]

The NAACP and the U.S. Department of Justice promptly challenged the constitutionality of the tuition grants law, and in 1968 a three-judge district court struck down the program after finding that the record "clearly reveals that the purpose, motive and effect of the Act is to unconstitutionally circumvent the requirement that [public schools] not discriminate on the basis of race or color." The Supreme Court affirmed this judgment without offering any comment on the case.[71]

In 1964, ten years after the *Brown* decision, desegregation was under way in South Carolina. School District No. 20 in downtown Charleston had led the way in 1963, to be followed the next year by sixteen others, including the state's largest district in Greenville. The mixing was of the token variety, with the largest number of blacks attending school with whites occuring in Charleston, where eighty-four black pupils attended mostly white schools.[72] The desegregation was significant nonetheless, for it affected districts that together enrolled approximately one-third of the state's students. It also persuaded many leading citizens that time had run out on segregation. In 1965 token desegregation spread to almost all school districts in South Carolina, including Clarendon School District No. 1 (Summerton), the small country district that had been the site of the nation's first desegregation suit.

III

Desegregation came to Clarendon County in September 1965 when five black students enrolled at Summerton High School. By then, the plaintiffs in the original *Briggs* suit were too old for school, but one of the new black students, a girl named Rita McDonald, was a younger sister of one of the original plaintiffs. By 1969 the number of black students had increased to twenty-eight — approximately 12 percent of the students then enrolled in Summerton's predominantly white schools. The races tended to separate for social activities and there was no interracial dating, but the sports programs were integrated. Two black teachers were employed at the predominantly white schools, and three whites worked at the black schools.[73]

Most whites accepted desegregation as long as white influence continued to predominate in one elementary school and one high school. Unlike the 1950s when economic reprisals were directed at blacks who challenged the status quo, the parents of the desegregated black students of the 1960s were not subjected to economic duress. About 110 white students did transfer to a newly established, all-white private school, but 250 others remained in the desegregated public schools. The school board reported that the desegregated blacks generally kept up with the white children academically, and instructors such as Marian Barksdale, a music teacher, later stated that between 1965 and 1970 desegregation "worked just fine."[74]

The litigation that finally desegregated Summerton was begun in 1960 when fifteen black parents, some of whom had also been plaintiffs in the original *Briggs* case, brought a new suit on behalf of their forty-three minor children. The first-named plaintiff was fourteen-year-old Bobby Brunson, and the case became known as *Brunson v. Board of Trustees of School District No. 1.* The issues were essentially the same as those raised in *Briggs* a decade before.[75]

Brunson alleged that Summerton had "refused to take any steps to eliminate racial segregation in the school system." South Carolina's pupil placement laws permitted children to transfer from one school to another and provided that each appeal should be considered individually and not on the basis of race. Nevertheless, in Summerton, as elsewhere in South Carolina, the school board invariably denied blacks' applications for transfer, usually on the grounds that it was for the children's best interest to remain in the black schools. If the black applicants were weak students, the board would find that they would not do well in the more competitive white academic atmosphere. If the black applicants were strong students, authorities would find, usually on the basis of personality, that the students would be better off in the schools they had been attending. Transfer applications had been rejected so regularly throughout the state that Brunson and the other plaintiffs in Summerton did not bother to comply with the requirement that applications for transfer should be filed by the end of May. They alleged instead that pupil assignments in Summerton were still made on the basis of race.[76]

In August 1965, U.S. District Judge Charles E. Simons, Jr., ruled in favor of the black plaintiffs. He found that Summerton had made "no substantial effort to comply with the Supreme Court's ruling in the *Brown* decisions." The blacks admittedly failed to make timely applications for transfer to white schools, but if they had their requests "would have been denied." Summerton was operating its schools "in a discriminatory manner based exclusively upon the race of the students." This was precisely what *Brown* had condemned, and Judge Simons ordered Summerton to admit the black plaintiffs immediately to the white elementary and high schools. By the time this order was entered, however, only nine of the forty-three original plaintiffs remained of school age and only five of these still wished to attend the white schools.[77]

Summerton complied with Judge Simons's order, as well as with the court's additional requirement that in the future all transfers should be granted without regard to race. After 1965 no request for a transfer was denied for any reason at all. Under Summerton's freedom-of-choice plan, blacks eventually made up 12 percent of the students enrolled in the predominantly white schools, but not a single white student transferred to a black school, and the desegregated blacks amounted to fewer than 2 percent of all blacks attending school in the district.[78]

When *Brown* was decided, advocates of desegregation generally said that race and color were irrelevant to proper consideration of a person's worth. In his argument before the Supreme Court, Thurgood Marshall maintained that racial classifications were essentially irrational. "The only thing that we ask for is that the state-imposed racial segregation be taken off," he said. Students could then be assigned to school "on any reasonable basis."[79] *Brown* was widely understood to forbid the government from discriminating among citizens on the basis of race.

New ideas gained currency in the mid-1960s. To make amends for the segregation of the past, it was said, the government and private corporations should notice the black's race, not for the purpose of discriminating against him or her, but in order to give that person a special boost. In business and government this could be done through affirmative action and reverse discrimination; in education it could be accomplished by taking race into account when assigning students and teachers. If an insufficient number of students chose to transfer to racially mixed schools, the races could be compelled to congregate. "To get past racism," it was said, "we must first take account of race."[80]

This shift in thinking was reflected in an *amicus* brief that the U.S. Department of Justice prepared in 1966. According to U.S. attorney Terrell L. Glenn, the amount of racial mixing in Summerton failed to achieve the desegregation required by the Constitution. To satisfy the demands of the Fourteenth Amendment, a substantial number of minority students must attend desegregated schools, and their number should increase every year.[81]

Near this same time the Department of Health, Education, and Welfare decided that the 1964 Civil Rights Act required integration. This construction was an extraordinary feat, for the sponsors of the legislation in Congress repeatedly endorsed Senator Hubert H. Humphrey's assurance that "desegregation does not mean that there must be an intermingling of races. . . . It means only that they must not be prevented from intermingling or going to school together because of race or color."[82] When Senator Robert Byrd of West Virginia, an opponent of the proposed legislation, declared that he was still not convinced that the government would not "seek to achieve an objective of racial balance in the schools," Senator Humphrey offered additional assurances: "I want to set the troubled mind of the distinguished Senator at rest." "I am manager of the bill," Humphrey noted; therefore, his assurance that racial balance could not be required would be of "some importance" in any interpretation of the legislation. Humphrey also declared his willingness "to accept an amendment to clarify that point to make it more precise." To that end, Section 401(b) was added to the legislation. It stated: "'Desegregation' means the assignment of students to public schools and within such schools without regard to their race, color, religion, or national origin, but 'desegregation' shall not mean the assignment of students to public schools in order to overcome racial imbalance."[83]

By prohibiting racial discrimination in any program that received federal aid, the Civil Rights Act of 1964 gave HEW's Office of Education the power to stop federal money from going to any school district that was not desegregated. In formulating its 1966 guidelines for administration, however, the office disregarded the congressional declaration that "'desegregation' shall not mean the assignment of students to public schools in order to overcome racial imbalance." The office instead maintained that "desegregation" required racial assignments if greater "integration" would result: the meaning of desegregation was changed from a prohibition of racial discrimination for the purpose of separating the races to a requirement of racial discrimination to mix them.[84]

Traditionally the Office of Education had been one of the more cautious federal agencies, staffed by elderly educators who had spent most of their careers in state and local school systems, and who believed that local control was best for education in a country as large and diverse as the United States. In the mid-1960s this began to change, as the office employed younger bureaucrats who had participated in the civil rights movement, who were disillusioned by the slow pace of desegregation, and who generally believed, as one sympathetic observer put it, that "the use of governmental power to break up the remnants of the American caste system is the most pressing public issue of this generation." They proposed nothing less than a second Reconstruction, and they recognized that this could not be accomplished without challenging the nation's traditional commitment to local control of the schools.[85]

The decisive change occurred in 1966, when Harold Howe II became commissioner of education. A grandson of Samuel Chapman Armstrong, the Union army general who had founded Hampton Institute for Negroes in 1868, Howe grew up in Hampton as the son of the college's president, the Reverend Arthur Howe. Although himself educated at the elite Taft School and at Yale University, Harold Howe by the 1960s had developed the conviction that the nation's racial problem could be solved by integrated public schools. As commissioner of education he threw his support behind the efforts of officials who maintained that desegregation should be redefined so as to require integration. The 1966 guidelines for administering the Civil Rights Act held that freedom of choice did not satisfy the requirements of the Civil Rights Act unless it offered the prospect of substantial racial mixing. "The single most substantial indication as to whether a free-choice plan is actually working," the 1966 guidelines stated, "is the extent to which Negro or other minority group students have in fact transferred from segregated schools." A scale of normally expected progress was included; to satisfy the guidelines a freedom-of-choice plan was supposed to implement integration by geometric progression.[86]

Howe and the 1966 guidelines predictably came in for criticism in Congress, but Howe defended himself by saying that the guidelines merely sought to end the dual system that the Supreme Court had condemned in *Brown*.

Although conservatives in 1966 staged something of a comeback from the low point of influence they suffered after Lyndon B. Johnson's landslide victory over Barry Goldwater in the 1964 presidential election, liberals still dominated the crucial committees and Congress refused to repudiate the 1966 guidelines. Reflecting the consensus, the *New York Times* stated editorially that it was "not Federal arrogance but hardened local prejudice" that was responsible for the criticism of Howe.[87]

The initial results were mixed when the 1966 guidelines were challenged in federal courts. In the Fourth Circuit, which included the state of South Carolina, the court of appeals rejected the guidelines. In an opinion written by Chief Judge Clement F. Haynesworth, the court held that freedom of choice satisfied the requirements of the equal protection clause. Unless there was evidence of some sort of intimidation, there was no need for school authorities to assign students to achieve "a greater intermixture of the races." "If each pupil, each year, attends the school of his choice, the Constitution does not require that he be deprived of his choice. . . ."[88]

In the Fifth Circuit, which included most of the Deep South, the court of appeals rejected freedom of choice and declared that the 1966 guidelines were "required by the Constitution and . . . within the scope of the Civil Rights Act of 1964." In *U.S. v. Jefferson County Board of Education,* an opinion written by Judge John Minor Wisdom and later affirmed 8 to 4 by a panel of judges from the circuit, the court held that *Brown* imposed an "affirmative duty . . . to furnish a fully integrated education to Negroes as a class." The ruling applied, however, only to the states whose laws had required segregated schools when *Brown* was decided in 1954. The Supreme Court had ordered those states to "effectuate a transition to a racially nondiscriminatory school system," which Judge Wisdom understood to mean that the states must take "whatever corrective action is necessary to undo the harm [they] created and fostered." Lest there be any uncertainty about his meaning, the judge italicized his holding that "*the only adequate redress for a previously overt system-wide policy of segregation directed against Negroes as a collective entity is a system-wide policy of integration.*" When properly understood, *Brown* required more than the disestablishment of segregation; it also imposed "an absolute duty to integrate."[89]

In *Jefferson I* and *II* the Fifth Circuit Court of Appeals held that there could be no middle course with freedom of choice and no compulsion either way. Earlier decisions that distinguished between integration and desegregation were overruled with the remark that Judge Parker's dictum in *Briggs* was "inconsistent with *Brown*" and "should be laid to rest." Paraphrasing the 1966 Guidelines, Judge Wisdom declared that desegregation plans were to be judged according to the amount of racial mixing actually attained.[89]

Since the Constitution has come to mean whatever the judges say it means, Judge Wisdom's interpretation of equal protection was legally plausible. However, his additional effort to reconcile the mandatory integration of the 1966 guidelines with the Civil Rights Act of 1964 was pure sophistry. At the insistence of southerners like Senator Byrd, Congress had specifically stated that desegregation would not require racial balance. In a crafty but specious opinion, Judge Wisdom found that the prohibition against assigning students to overcome racial imbalance applied only to the states that did not have segregated schools in 1954—that the Civil Rights Act actually called for compulsory integration in the South.

A charitable way to account for this interpretation would be to endorse the comment of Professor Lino A. Graglia: "The court's reasoning is sufficiently illogical and obscure to defy explanation." In the mid-1960s sympathy for the civil rights movement touched the ermine of the bench. Judicial objectivity was swept along by the strong currents of popular sentiment for blacks and against the white South. "No army is stronger than an idea whose time has come," Judge Wisdom stated, and for the judges of the Fifth Circuit, as previously for the Office of Education, the time had come for compulsory integration. This was "commanded by *Brown,* the Constitution, the Past, the Present, and the wavy fore-image of the Future."[91]

The *Jefferson* court said it approached its decision "with humility" and with the recognition that "as far as possible federal courts must carry out congressional policy," but it then proceeded to defeat the very purpose of the Civil Rights Act. In 1964 Congress called for desegregation; the essence of the new law was the principle that racial discrimination was wrong. That was the "idea whose time had come," but the *Jefferson* court held that the Civil Rights Act and the Constitution required "color conscious[ness] to undo the effects of past discrimination." As Judge W. Harold Cox noted in a spirited dissent, "The English language simply could not be summoned to state any more clearly than does the very positive enactment of Congress, that these so-called 'guidelines' . . . are actually promulgated and being used in opposition to and in violation of this positive statute."[92]

In 1968 the Supreme Court settled the conflict between the Fourth Circuit (where freedom of choice was still the official policy) and the Fifth (where integration was compulsory). In *Green v. County School Board of New Kent County,* the high court unanimously sided with the Fifth Circuit and ordered southern school districts to eradicate the vestiges of segregation by assigning students so as to achieve substantial integration in each school. With this decision the era of desegregation came to an end. Purporting to do no more than apply the holding of *Brown* to the case at hand, the Supreme Court changed the constitutional mandate from a prohibition of segregation to a requirement that authorities employ racial discrimination to achieve a substantial amount of racial mixing.[93]

South Carolinians were particularly interested in *Green* because New Kent County was similar to Clarendon. Situated about halfway between Richmond and Williamsburg in Virginia, New Kent was a rural county with only two schools and 1,300 students, of whom 740 were black. Each of the schools was a combined elementary and high school, and prior to *Brown* the schools had been racially segregated, with blacks attending the George W. Watkins School in the western portion of the county and whites the New Kent School on the eastern side. Until 1965, Watkins continued to have an all-black student body, faculty, and staff, and New Kent remained all white. Then, to continue receiving federal money after passage of the 1964 Civil Rights Act, school authorities adopted a plan that gave students free transportation to whichever school they wished to attend. Thirty-five black students chose New Kent in 1965, 111 in 1966, and 115 in 1967, but no white student ever chose to attend Watkins. In 1967, one white teacher was employed at Watkins and one black at New Kent.[94]

Jack Greenberg, the NAACP's chief legal counsel, personally took charge of the New Kent litigation. He saw to it that the briefs and oral arguments focused on a crucial question: did a school board satisfy its obligations under *Brown* "simply by ceasing its illegal practices," or should it be required to take "affirmative steps to thoroughly dismantle the dual segregated system"? To clarify the issue, the black plaintiffs admitted that in New Kent "each child was given the unrestricted right to attend any school in the system." Elsewhere there might be various extraneous pressures to restrict freedom of choice, but in New Kent the choice was conceded to be completely free and unencumbered. Defense attorney Frederick T. Gray told the Supreme Court that "115 children of the colored race have elected to go to the white school, . . . and there is not a shred of evidence . . . that anyone has been, in any way, abused; that any parent has lost his job; that any pressure has been exerted."[95]

The NAACP urged the Supreme Court to invalidate free choice in principle, not simply in districts where the practice had been abused. The NAACP took care, however, to remind the Court that "in some areas of the South, Negro families with children attending previously all-white schools under free choice plans were targets of violence, threats of violence and economic reprisal. . . ." The NAACP maintained that the success of free choice "depended on the ability of Negroes to unshackle themselves from the psychological effects of imposed racial discriminations of the past, and to withstand the fear and intimidation of the present and future." Since segregation had "deep and long-term effects upon the Negroes," the NAACP said, it was not surprising that blacks "raised in that system and schooled in the ways of subservience . . . when gratuitously asked to 'make a choice,' chose

. . . that their children should remain in Negro schools." They did not have to be intimidated to know that most whites opposed desegregation.[96]

The Supreme Court was impressed by the NAACP's suggestion that southern blacks bore the marks of oppression and were not yet prepared to choose freely. Chief Justice Warren said the system in New Kent was "booby trapped" by "social and cultural influences and the prejudices that have existed for centuries there." Justice Marshall had to be reminded that the black plaintiffs had conceded that their choice was free and unrestricted. By putting "freedom of choice" in quotation marks in the opinion he drafted for the court, Justice Brennan implied that blacks who were just emerging from segregation could not make a truly free choice of schools.[97]

In *Green* the Supreme Court held that New Kent had not complied with the 1955 *Brown* order "to effectuate a transition to a racially nondiscriminatory school system." Since one school was still 100 percent black and the other 82 percent white, the Supreme Court concluded that New Kent had failed "to take whatever steps might be necessary to convert to a unitary system in which racial discrimination would be eliminated root and branch." The racially unbalanced pattern of enrollment was said to indicate that different schools were intended for students of a particular race. The schools were not racially segregated as they once had been, but they were still racially identifiable. "It was such dual systems," the court said, "that . . . *Brown I* held to be unconstitutional and . . . *Brown II* held must be abolished." The Supreme Court accordingly reversed the Fourth Circuit Court of Appeals and ordered New Kent to provide for more racial mixing.[98]

In some ways Justice Brennan's opinion was more subtle than Judge Wisdom's opinion in *Jefferson*. *Green* did not speak of integration. As Professor Graglia has noted, "a Constitutional requirement of racial discrimination to increase integration . . . would have been most difficult to justify as such. Instead of attempting such justification, the Court imposed the requirement—by what it actually did—while insisting that it was requiring only that all racial discrimination be eliminated. It was thus able to maintain the enormous advantage of seeming to combat racism, as in *Brown,* while in fact imposing a racist requirement." The rationale that integration was not constitutionally required for its own sake but was simply a remedy for the formal segregation of the past also seemed to mean that the requirement would be applied only in the South. "This served to minimize national attention . . . and to make the decision seem but another step taken by a patient Court to counteract still another attempt by the recalcitrant South to evade the requirement of *Brown.*"[99]

The essential question in *Green* concerned the precise point at which a school board had fulfilled its duty to provide equal protection of the laws.

New Kent maintained that it had satisfied its obligations by ceasing racial discrimination and offering free choice. It said that "desegregation" was different from "integration" and that under *Brown* the school districts were not required to take affirmative action to achieve a balanced racial enrollment in all schools; the availability of free choice was sufficient quite apart from the amount of mixing that resulted. The Supreme Court decided to the contrary that the school board must reorganize its program so that no school would be racially identifiable. It decided that *Jefferson,* not *Briggs,* was the correct interpretation of *Brown. Brown* did more than forbid state enforced racial separation. Affirmative action was necessary if substantial numbers of students did not mix when offered the opportunity to do so.

Southern school boards repeatedly warned that the ultimate outcome of racially balanced integration would be the opposite of what was intended. Rather than attend schools where a black majority would set the academic and moral standards, whites would transfer to private schools. If realities such as white flight were ignored, desegregation would lead to resegregation. The federal courts nevertheless demanded proportional mixing, regardless of the consequences. The fundamental question was not whether schools were operated without racial discrimination, one panel of judges from the Fifth Circuit acknowledged. "The ultimate inquiry is whether the board is fulfilling its duty to take *affirmative* steps, spelled out in *Jefferson* and fortified by *Green,* to find realistic measures that will transform its formerly *de jure* dual segregated school system into a 'unitary, nonracial system of public education.'" Another panel of judges declared that a point had been reached in the process of school desegregation "where it is not the spirit, but the bodies that count." "Good faith is not, and cannot be the standard. . . . [I]t comes down to figures. . . . If the result is satisfactory it is because of the numbers, not the effort or subjective motivation. If the result is unsatisfactory it is because of the numbers." In 1969 the Fourth Circuit Court of Appeals declared: "The famous *Briggs v. Elliott* dictum—adhered to by this court for many years—that the Constitution forbids segregation but does not require integration . . . is now dead."[100]

The Supreme Court never specifically required racial balance, but, despite repeated appeals for a ruling on the question, it also refused to set aside lower court orders that imposed proportional mixing. Dissenting circuit judges despairingly objected to the insistence on "racial balance, to the exclusion of all other considerations. . . ." They warned that, given the reality of white flight, the courts' orders had "the greatest possible potential for creation of all-black school systems. . . ."[101] This was not fright fantasy. It was an accurate prediction of what would happen in Clarendon School District No. 1 (Summerton).

Even before *Green* the black plaintiffs in the *Brunson* case had taken exception to Summerton's freedom-of-choice plan. In 1966 attorney Matthew Perry argued that free choice should not be permitted unless a substantial percentage of students enrolled in mixed schools. Urging the U.S. district court to impose the HEW guidelines, Perry said, "the single most substantial indication as to whether free choice . . . is actually working . . . is the extent to which Negro students . . . have in fact transferred from segregated schools."[102]

Judge Charles E. Simons thought freedom of choice was working well in Summerton and refused to order compliance with the 1966 guidelines. He said the Summerton school board had demonstrated its good faith by complying with all court orders and by granting the transfer of every black student who had requested assignment to a predominantly white school.[103] When attorney Perry returned to court after the Supreme Court's decision in *Green*, however, it was more difficult for Judge Simons to stand by free choice. Noting that blacks and whites were dispersed residentially throughout the district (although whites tended to cluster in parts of the town of Summerton), Perry maintained that more racial mixing could be achieved if students were assigned to schools on the basis of geographical attendance zones. Such a plan was now required by the Constitution, he argued, since the Supreme Court had decreed "that freedom of choice plans are constitutionally unacceptable where 'there are reasonably available other ways . . . promising speedier and more effective conversion to a unitary non-racial school system.'"[104]

Since whites constituted only 12 percent of the students in the district, the school board said it would be impossible to achieve significant racial integration. "In the final analysis there is no way to help the education of the Negro through the racial integration of pupils in a district where there are 253 white children and 2,176 Negro pupils. There are just not enough whites." The board also called the court's attention to a poll that indicated that all the white parents and 83 percent of the blacks wanted to continue with freedom of choice.[105]

Attorney Perry characterized the board's arguments as legally irrelevant. Many blacks admittedly preferred to continue with freedom of choice, but their preference was not grounds for dismissing the suit since it had not been shown that all blacks in the district felt the same way. As for the warning that whites would flee the public schools if integration was compelled, the Supreme Court had repeatedly insisted that the validity of constitutional principles "cannot be allowed to yield simply because of disagreement with them."[106]

Judge Simons agreed with the whites' assessment of the situation in Clarendon. He thought it probable that white children would flee from massive integration, with the result that "the public school system will have less racial integration than under the present freedom of choice plan." He agreed with the contention of school board attorney David W. Robinson that the Supreme Court had given two incompatible orders. It had ruled that a desegregation plan should be judged by its results and also that white flight should not be considered, since that would sacrifice constitutional principles because of popular opposition to them. Yet desegregation could not be achieved in Summerton unless white flight was taken into account. "If the court is to look at the 'end result' it should . . . weigh the evidence that there will be this exodus from the public schools," Simons wrote. Unfortunately, the law, according to Judge Simons, was out of touch with the facts. [107]

When the district court met to bring Summerton and twenty-one other South Carolina school districts into compliance with *Green,* Judge Simons was willing, perhaps even eager, to cede responsibility for what appeared to be an impossible situation. "It is true that the Courts may not abdicate in the field of education their responsibilities as the traditional guardian of constitutional rights," the judges stated. Nevertheless, the HEW guidelines were said to deserve "serious judicial deference" and "respectful consideration." The court then ordered the school boards to meet with officials from the Office of Education to develop satisfactory desegregation plans. If agreement could not be reached within thirty days, the parties were to submit their respective plans and the court would proceed "without further hearings to enter its decree, after due consideration of the proposed plan submitted by the defendant school district . . . and the plan submitted by the Office of Education." [108]

Summerton modified its free-choice plan after receiving the court's order. The Office of Education then sent two representatives to inspect school facilities, but these officials did not consult with members of the school board. Instead, they returned to Washington and prepared a plan to achieve substantial racial balance through geographic zoning and by assigning all eighth- and ninth-grade students to the same school. Under the HEW plan the proportion of whites in Summerton's schools would vary from a low of about 5 percent at St. Paul's Elementary to a high of about 17 percent at Scotts Branch Elementary. Whites at Summerton Elementary and High School would lose the majority status they had enjoyed under freedom of choice. [109]

Judge Simons saw no alternative to imposing the HEW plan. "It may be that the end result will affect adversely the education of the children of this district," he acknowledged. But "under the controlling decisions of the United States Supreme Court . . . the absolute requirement is to move *now* to a racially unitary system, apparently without regard to any adverse effect such move may have on the quality of the education to be provided in the public schools."[110]

Summerton could appeal, but Judge Simons knew this would be to no avail. The circuit courts of appeal, with the tacit approval of the Supreme Court, had interpreted *Green* to require substantial racial balance regardless of the consequences. The political process offered the only slight hope for overturning a decree that Simons had issued against his own better judgment. The judge pointedly noted "the efforts now being made in the Congress and by the [Nixon] administration to permit school boards wider discretion in assigning pupils." If legislation to that effect were enacted, Judge Simons indicated that he would promptly give "such relief as that legislation justifies." In the meantime, HEW's plan was imposed by order of the court.[111]

Simons was correct in predicting that Summerton's appeal would not succeed. The Fourth Circuit Court upheld the HEW plan in an abrupt one-sentence opinion, and the Supreme Court declined to review the case.[112] The verdict of the circuit court was not without interest, however, for several of the judges took advantage of the opportunity to file opinions expressing their individual views.

Judge J. Braxton Craven, joined by judges Albert V. Bryan and Clement F. Haynesworth, noted that it was "ironic and contrary to the spirit of *Brown*" that desegregation, as defined in *Green,* would probably lead to "a system with only 'black' schools." This sort of desegregation did not serve any useful purpose. The theory of equal educational opportunity held that the best situation for effective desegregation was one in which blacks made up about 30 percent of the total number of students. In such an environment blacks could escape the effects of being socialized in a lower-class black culture without suffering at the same time from psychological isolation. Judges Craven, Bryan, and Haynesworth regretted that the controlling interpretation made it impossible for them to approve a free-choice plan that could have provided this sort of optimal desegregation for at least some blacks in Summerton.[113]

In a separate concurring opinion Judge Simon E. Sobeloff, joined by Judge Harrison L. Winter, took exception to the theory of the "optimal mix." *Brown* had been concerned with equal educational opportunity, but its principal holding was that segregation was unconstitutional because it implied that blacks were "inferior and not to be associated with." The purpose of desegregation was to end this sort of "living insult." Yet the theory of equal educational opportunity suggested that whites were "a precious resource" and that black children would be improved by association with their betters. This theory might be camouflaged in terms of socioeconomic class and the necessity of creating a middle-class milieu, but it rested essentially on the generalization that, "educationally speaking, white pupils are somehow better or more desirable than black pupils."[114]

Sobeloff's critique of the optimal mix was telling but inconsistent, coming as it did from a judge who had previously taken the lead in prodding the Fourth Circuit Court to renounce *Briggs* and require racial balance.[115] Ironically, the most prominent contemporary advocate of the view that segregation should be banished as an insult but that proportional racial mixing should not be required was the president of the United States, Richard M. Nixon. In the 1968 campaign Nixon led the South to believe that as president he would prevent compulsory racially-balanced integration. Southern leaders knew it was late in the nation's history for a president to refuse to enforce a Supreme Court decision, but there were other ways for a president to make his influence felt. In a speech in North Carolina, Nixon declared that he personally favored freedom of choice, an objective that could still be obtained by appointing strict constructionists to the Supreme Court. As long as Richard Nixon was enforcing the law, many in Dixie thought, federal officials would not require of the South the sort of racial integration that did not exist elsewhere in the nation.[116]

After his election Nixon continued to court the South. Members of the White House staff were told to make no statements that would alienate Dixie (and one outspoken advocate of racial balance, Leon Panetta, was forced to resign). The Justice Department asked the federal courts to postpone balanced integration in Mississippi—the first time in a generation that the government had entered a major civil rights suit against the NAACP.

In 1969 President Nixon announced that he would nominate a southerner and a strict constructionist for a seat on the Supreme Court. To replace Associate Justice Abe Fortas the president sent forward the name of Clement F. Haynesworth, the chief judge of the Fourth Circuit Court and the author of the decision for freedom of choice that the Supreme Court had reversed in *Green*. Instead of openly repudiating HEW's 1966 guidelines, the administration chose to elevate a southern judge who only two years before had rejected the contention that freedom of choice did not satisfy the Constitution unless it led to substantial mixing of the races.[117]

By a vote of 55 to 45 the U.S. Senate refused to confirm Haynesworth's nomination, the first time a Supreme Court nomination had been rejected since 1930, when the Senate turned down John J. Parker, the author of the *Briggs* dictum. Haynesworth and Parker were distinguished judges, and neither rejection reflected credit on the Senate. In Haynesworth's case the opposition came from an alliance of special interests. The NAACP objected to the judge's record in desegregation cases; advocates of ethnic balance considered him an unsuitable choice for a seat that had been occupied since 1916 by a succession of Jewish judges; the American Federation of Labor took exception to Haynesworth's decision in a 1963 labor dispute; and ethical purists argued that he should have disqualified himself from hearing a case that involved a company that rented vending machines from another company in which Haynesworth owned stock.[118]

After Haynesworth's defeat, Nixon chose another southerner, Judge G. Harrold Carswell, whose nomination was also rejected after many senators concluded, with some reason, that Carswell was not a first-rate jurist and did not deserve a seat on the Supreme Court. An outraged Richard Nixon publicly charged that "when all the hypocrisy is stripped away, the real issue was [Haynesworth and Carswell's] philosophy of strict construction of the Constitution, a philosophy that I share—and the fact that they had the misfortune of being born in the South." "As long as the Senate is constituted the way it is," the president said, he would not nominate another southerner and let him be subjected to "regional discrimination." Many senators were infuriated, but the white South concluded that the president was doing his best to protect their interests.[119]

Having thus reinforced his support in the South, Nixon said no more about freedom of choice, and his administration moved vigorously to impose integration. In 1970 more than one hundred U.S. attorneys, federal marshals, and other civil rights enforcers were sent to the South to monitor integration, and the Department of Justice instituted a spate of suits against school districts that were clinging to free choice and resisting racial balance.[120] As a result of this vigorous legal offensive, more racial mixing was achieved during Nixon's first two years in the White House than ever before. HEW reported that the percentage of southern blacks enrolled in schools with a majority of whites more than doubled, from 18 percent in the fall of 1968 to 39 percent in the fall of 1970. At the same time the number of southern blacks attending all-black schools declined from 67 percent to 14 percent, and the number of blacks enrolled in the 80- to 100-percent black schools dropped from 79 percent to 39 percent. Meanwhile, the proportion of blacks attending all-black or predominantly black schools continued to increase outside the South. By 1970, HEW reported, the public schools of the South had become far more desegregated than those in other parts of the country.[121]

The Nixon administration claimed no credit for the mixing. After all, spokesmen explained, it was not the president or Congress but the Supreme Court that had required integration. The president was simply carrying out his obligation to enforce the law. "The highest court of the land has spoken," Nixon stated. "The unitary school system must replace the dual school system. . . . The law having been determined it is the responsibility of those in the federal government and particularly the responsibility of the President of the United States to uphold the law." [122]

Some observers grudgingly approved the Nixon administration's record on desegregation. "Having secured his Southern base," Rowland Evans and Robert D. Novak wrote, "Nixon in 1970 could act more responsibly on the school desegregation question than he had before." Writing in the *New Republic,* John Osborne admitted that the Nixon administration had a good record enforcing integration in the South—better than it was generally given credit for, and better in some respects than that of the preceding Democratic administration. The Nixon administration did not claim credit for the achievement, of course; virtue had been forced upon it. Nevertheless, the administration had "brought about more desegregation in the South . . . than anybody had reason to expect." The administration's official statements were spiked with reassuring southern comfort, but Nixon in fact had double-crossed his gullible supporters in Dixie. "However cynically the process of enforcement may be viewed and explained, . . . liberal critics of the Administration may as well face the fact that their image of the President . . . is outdated." [123]

Others had a different assessment. To say the administration imposed integration on the south because the courts required it was unsatisfactory, William F. Buckley wrote in the *National Review.* Nixon had a special talent for foreign policy, about which he was far more deeply concerned than racial issues. He feared that if he antagonized the integrationists, who dominated the media and congressional committees and who already disliked him personally, his ability to conduct foreign policy would be jeopardized. Nixon had to protect the national interest in a dangerous world, and once his southern base was secure he decided not to oppose integration. "The opinion-makers have said that we must have integrated schooling, that any slowdown in that program is nothing less than moral temporizing. So, Mr. Nixon has calculated, let's get on with it, and see what happens." Buckley also pointed to "the cynical-realistic" attitude, "confirmed by all past experience, that the desegregated schools will soon be resegregated again anyway, so what difference does it make?" [124]

In 1968 Richard Nixon carried South Carolina largely because many people thought his election would enable the state to maintain freedom of choice. "NIXON RAPS HEW ON SCHOOLS, FAVORS 'FREEDOM OF CHOICE,'" proclaimed one headline in the *Manning Times,* the leading newspaper of Clarendon County. By contrast, Democratic candidate Hubert H. Humphrey was said to promise "NO LET UP IN SCHOOL GUIDELINES." One year later the *Times* noted with dismay that past Democratic administrations, despite their rhetoric about integration, actually "did less in desegregating the schools . . . than the Nixon Administration is now doing." The compulsory integration plan that was imposed in Summerton in 1970 was devised by officials in Richard Nixon's Office of Education.[125]

IV

As Judge Simons had predicted, there was less racial mixing in Summerton under the plan for racially balanced integration than there had been under freedom of choice. In 1970 all but six of the district's white students withdrew from the public schools, with the overwhelming majority transferring to a Baptist parochial school that had been established in 1965. Since 1970 education in Summerton has been resegregated, with blacks enrolled in public schools and 99 percent of the whites attending private academies. In 1980 there was only one white student attending public school in Summerton.

In some respects the situation resembled that in Prince Edward County. White people in both areas thought academic standards would suffer as desegregation proceeded, and they shared a resentment of Washington bureaucrats who had come to reconstruct Dixie, not with the Union Army of yesteryear but with attaché cases filled with desegregation guidelines. They thought specious interpretation of the Constitution had been carried to the point of tyranny. In both communities there was widely felt a need to resist by setting up alternative private schools.

There were important differences nonetheless. One was timing. By the time Summerton faced desegregation in 1965, most whites considered token mixing inevitable rather than alarming. Under freedom of choice, 70 percent of the whites continued to send their children to the desegregated but predominantly white Summerton Elementary and High School. They were aware of the NAACP's demands for racially balanced integration, but, as one mother said, "we kept hoping to the bitter end that we could save one mostly-white public school."[126]

Yet, even before massive integration was imposed in 1970, approximately 110 of the 360 white students in the district had transferred to a local private academy. "We felt in our bones that complete integration was coming," one father recalled. He thought of the private academy as insurance against the day when desegregation went "beyond the point of admitting qualified Negroes into white schools." Others mentioned the Supreme Court's 1963 decision prohibiting prayer in the public schools, which they considered an attack on traditional values rather than an effort to maintain the constitutional ban against establishing a religion. "The people might have adjusted to one thing like desegregation, if they had to," one teacher stated. "But there were so many things the federal government began to insist on. We knew that desegregation was coming, of course. But the precipitating factor for establishing our private school was the court's school prayer decision." To this day many patrons of the private school maintain that the public schools' problems began with—and result from—the court's ban on prayer. [127]

With the assistance of the Calvary Baptist Church, the private academy— which is known as Clarendon Hall—built a handsome campus on eight acres of piney woods near I-95 in Summerton. Two substantial brick classroom buildings were erected in 1968 and 1970, and a gynmasium, cafeteria, and study hall were added in 1975. To meet the demand caused by a surge in the birth rate and the temporary presence of workers who were building the interstate highway, six more classrooms were added in 1972. By then enrollment had reached a peak of 425, which included almost all the white residents of the Summerton school district and others from as far away as the city of Sumter (sixteen miles to the north) and the town of Elloree (on the other side of Lake Marion).

The cost of Clarendon Hall came to only $215,000, a fraction of the amount taxpayers would have had to pay for twenty-two classrooms, a gymnasium, a cafeteria, a library, administrative offices, and lighted athletic fields. Savings were made at every step. A local farmer and an elementary teacher jointly drafted the architectural plans, and a sympathetic contractor took it from there. One of the three classroom buildings was put up with volunteer labor and donated materials. The only expensive feature on campus was the gymnasium, where $11,000 was spent for a hardwood basketball floor. A vinyl floor could have been installed for less money, but many parents wanted to go first class and promised to work on the interior free of charge. [128]

The patrons of the academy generally preferred a traditional academic program, although differing emphases were apparent from time to time. C. Ware Madden, the first headmaster, was a Baptist pastor who emphasized religious education. There were more Methodists than Baptists in Summerton, however, and also Presbyterians, Episcopalians, a few Roman Catholics, and one Jewish family. They all favored nondenominational Bible study, but many had reservations about evangelistic fundamentalism. Religion sometimes played no role at all in parents' motives. One parent supported the academy because there was "good reason to believe that integration would lead to low academic standards" and because she resented the way "nine old judges are telling us what to do." [129]

Some wanted the academy to be a preparatory school geared especially for those planning to attend college. In 1968 a more academically oriented headmaster was brought in from Florida, but he proved to be an unfortunate choice; it soon became apparent that he had a serious drinking problem. The reins were passed to Mrs. Edna F. Rowe, an elementary teacher and the daughter of S. Emory Rogers, the local attorney who had represented Summerton in the *Briggs* litigation. Under her leadership in the 1970s Clarendon Hall steered a middle course, combining nondenominational Bible study with secular academic instruction.[130]

During the 1970s about two-thirds of the high school students at Clarendon Hall were enrolled in the college preparatory curriculum requiring three years of mathematics, physical science, and history, and two years of foreign language. The remaining students worked for a basic diploma, obtained by completing a less structured program that included commercial classes and allowed students to study part-time at the public vocational school near Alcolu.

In the grammar school, classes were divided by ability. "The theory about grouping children heterogeneously so the slow learners can benefit from role models is just talk," headmistress Rowe stated. "We try to give the children a curriculum they can master and succeed in." English was required of all students each year, and religion was taught in grades one through eight and in the freshman and senior years of high school. Devotional services were held each morning and supplemented with special religious meetings.[131]

As a nondenominational but Baptist-affiliated Christian school, Clarendon Hall put more emphasis on religion than many of the secular academies that saw themselves as the only schools for whites in some rural counties, but less emphasis than many of the Bible-based schools that grew up in urban areas. White residents of the rural black belt identified with one another and were a sufficiently homogeneous group to work together for a common goal. In Summerton the children of the town's one Jewish family uncomplainingly took Bible courses, while their father served on Clarendon Hall's board of trustees and their mother taught history to a generation of young Christians. This sort of unity did not exist in many cities, where like-minded people usually met in their churches. Many urban academies consequently were sectarian and evangelical, denouncing evolution, prohibiting dancing, and requiring teachers to be born-again Christians. The urban academies were "the opposite of neighborhood schools," one observer reported. "Their clientele comes for miles, often in buses, and no neighborhood could produce the homogeneity of these schools."[132]

Yet the urban and rural Christian academies were similar in some respects. Patrons of both tended to view integrated public schools as tumultuous places with low academic standards, drugs, violence, and sexual promiscuity. Parents tried to recreate the sort of orderly middle-class schools they had known as youngsters. Alcohol and tobacco were strictly prohibited, dress codes were enforced, and attendance at athletic events was overflowing. At Clarendon Hall the authority of the student council was limited, but there was a large pep club, a safety patrol, and a glee club. In the 1970s the high school division, with only 75 boys enrolled in the seventh through the twelfth grades, somehow managed to field two football teams.[133]

The private school students made an impressive showing on Stanford Achievement Tests, where the average score of students at 73 members of the South Carolina Independent Schools Association was in the upper 24 percent of the national sample. At Clarendon Hall the scores were about one year above the national grade level in the second grade and three years above the norm for high school seniors.[134]

There were difficulties, of course. As the *Manning Times* noted in 1965, "The big problem is that most of the working people will not be able to send their children to the private schools." Clarendon Hall economized in the face of inflation and managed to hold tuition to $630 in 1980. White parents of modest means somehow managed to pay tuition for their children as well as taxes for the public schools, but it was a heavy burden only partly alleviated by scholarships. At Clarendon Hall the average salary for teachers in 1980 came to only $6,750, about half the amount paid in the district's public schools.[135]

Some critics complained that the academies did not impart a liberal philosophical outlook or the ability to interact with diverse groups. The emphasis on old-fashioned phonics and drill was said to pay dividends on standardized tests but to stifle the students' curiosity. Others noted that the private curricula were narrowly academic, with students given little opportunity to pursue art and music and with no facilities for remedial instruction.[136]

Some of the criticism was valid. At Clarendon Hall the average student IQ was 104, and applicants with scores below 90 were advised to go elsewhere. Music and art were available, but at no expense to the school. The veteran music teacher worked without salary coaching the glee club and preparing the spring operetta, in return for being permitted to teach private lessons during class time. The art teacher donated a few hours each week. Nevertheless, most patrons disregarded the more general criticism as elusive and theoretical, as revealing more about the critics than about the quality of education at Clarendon Hall.[137]

In one respect the academy movement fell short of its founders' original expectations. When the private schools were organized in the mid-1960s, Dr. T. Elliott Wannamaker, the first president of the association of independent schools, confidently predicted that almost all whites would flee to private academies as blacks pushed to enroll in previously white schools.

South Carolina's public school system was dead, he said. It was "just a matter of time before rigor mortis sets in."[138] This was an accurate description of what happened in Summerton and many other districts. In many places, and especially in the black belt, balanced integration was accompanied by massive white flight. But this did not happen everywhere, not even everywhere in Clarendon County. Almost half the white students in the neighboring Manning school district (50 percent black) continued to attend public schools after the courts imposed racially balanced integration. And in Clarendon's third school district near Turbeville (75 percent white), almost two-thirds of the white youths continued to attend public schools. A demographic law appeared to be at work in Clarendon County. The larger the percentage of white students, the less the white flight. Whites were more likely to remain in public schools if their numbers were large enough to ensure that they would not be isolated.[139]

Prior to 1978 financial limitations worked against dramatic improvement in the quality of Clarendon's public schools. About one-half of the money for public education came from the state in roughly equal per-pupil grants. Another 34 percent came from local property taxes, with the amount generally varying in proportion to the value of local property. Residents of the state's richest school district in Greenwood, where the assessed valuation per pupil was $7,611, found it much easier to raise money than those who lived in Summerton, whose $584 in assessed valuation per pupil in 1972 made it the poorest of the state's ninety-two school districts. Turbeville was the next-poorest district, and Manning placed 84th in terms of assessed valuation per pupil. To spend at levels equal to the richer districts in South Carolina, the school districts in Clarendon County would have had to impose exorbitant tax rates.[140]

The remaining 16 percent of school money in South Carolina came from the federal government. This was more than twice the national average for federal funds, and a disproportionately large share of the federal money was earmarked for districts with large concentrations of poor children. Since federal aid constituted a smaller source of revenue than local funds, it did not overcome the disparity that resulted from the variation in the value of local property. But it did reduce the inequalities substantially. The per-pupil expenditure in South Carolina's thirteen wealthiest districts ($570 in 1972) was only 11.8 percent greater than the amount spent in the twenty poorest districts ($503). There was even less variation if the school districts were grouped according to their racial composition.[141]

In the early 1970s some lawyers argued that the Fourteenth Amendment required the equalization of expenditures in public schools. Several courts agreed, and for a time it seemed that a new constitutional standard might be fashioned, one that required full state assumption of all educational costs.

In its watershed 5-to-4 *Rodriguez* decision of 1973, however, the Supreme Court held that it was for the legislatures, not the judiciary, to decide if public schools should no longer be financed by local property taxes.[142]

The subsequent action of the South Carolina legislature belied its reputation for hard-hearted frugality. Responding to a sense of fairness rather than to a court order, the General Assembly in 1977 established a foundation program which ensured that educational operating expenses would be roughly comparable throughout the state, "notwithstanding geographic differences and varying local economic factors." The Education Finance Act did not require completely equal spending, but by increasing the share of state money to 70 percent and by setting local contributions according to ability to pay, it put an end to a system that made poor districts tax themselves at exorbitant rates if they wished to spend at levels comparable to their richer neighbors. A minimum state-wide salary schedule for certified teachers was set at a level that raised salaries in Clarendon by an average of about 25 percent. A base student cost was set at $665, and provision was made for annual adjustment in the light of inflation, with the base figure reaching $913 in 1982.[143]

After passage of the Education Finance Act, the salaries of public school teachers in Clarendon County were competitive with salaries elsewhere in South Carolina. But, since the act did not cover the cost of building new schools, poor counties like Clarendon were still hard pressed when it came to new buildings. In 1980 the voters in Manning approved a referendum that provided $5.3 million for new construction, but the election was close and hotly contested, with 77 percent of the registered voters actually casting ballots and with partisans of the private academies generally favoring a less expensive plan for renovating existing buildings. Property taxes almost doubled after the referendum, a situation that led to grumbling even among some who had favored the proposal.[144]

In Summerton the thirty-year-old Scotts Branch High School had reached a state of dilapidation, and a referendum was expected. It would probably pass, since blacks made up the great majority of voters in the district, although many people wondered about the economic consequences. If the blacks voted themselves a larger share of the wealth, there was always the possibility that white businessmen and landowners would pull up stakes. Yet most whites were resigned and stoical, accepting without rancor the inevitability of additional taxes for schools their children would not attend. "We will face a bond issue here," said one man. "We're expecting it. I will oppose it. Physical facilities aren't what is needed to improve public education. But the blacks have the votes and will pass the bond issue. There's nothing we can do about it. You fight if you have a chance to win. But if there's no chance, you learn to live with defeat and make the best of it."[145]

Despite the likelihood of a new school and the generally improved financial situation, Summerton's public schools were in deep trouble. Some blacks took pride in having a school system of their own, the first in South Carolina to have a black superintendent and an all-black board of trustees. But Superintendent Alonzo P. Swinton emphasized that it was difficult for an all-black school to give students the experience and preparation needed for moving ahead in a mixed society. Henry Lawson, the chairman of the board of trustees, thought the disadvantage was that whites took no interest in the schools. "If the whites got involved we'd have a better PTA, a better relationship with each other, and more community concern," he said. "The white people of Summerton abandoned our public schools just when we needed them most."[146] The main problem in the public schools, Lawson said, was that "too many students cannot read and compute as well as they should."[147] On the 1978 Comprehensive Test of Basic Skills, approximately 90 percent of the public school students scored below the national average for their grade. In Summerton the average black high school sophomore was scoring at the level of fourth-grade students at Clarendon Hall (Table 6).

Some whites interpreted these scores as evidence of the folly of integration, but others had different views. The coordinator of the district's remedial programs thought much of the trouble stemmed from the cultural deprivation many students experienced at home. "So many parents just don't use language with their children," she said. To compensate for this the dis-

TABLE 6. Test Results, Summerton Public Schools (1978)
and Clarendon Hall (1980)

Summerton Public Schools (Comprehensive Test of Basic Skills)			Clarendon Hall (Stanford Achievement Test)		
	Mean Grade Equivalent			Mean Grade Equivalent	
Grade	Reading	Mathematics	Grade	Reading	Mathematics
2.7	1.8	2.0	1	2.3	2.8
3.7	2.4	3.2	2	3.9	3.3
4.7	2.9	3.3	3	5.4	4.4
5.7	3.4	3.5	4	5.8	5.9
6.7	4.0	4.5	5	6.0	6.2
7.7	5.4	5.4	6	8.7	8.9
8.7	5.0	5.2	7	9.2	9.0
9.7	5.0	5.2	8	10.9	10.1
10.7	5.7	5.4			
11.7	6.7	5.9			
12.7	7.0	6.0			

Source: Information provided by Doris Holladay, coordinator of Title One Programs, Summerton Public Schools and by Edna F. Rowe, Headmistress of Clarendon Hall. Clarendon Hall does not give achievement tests in grades 9 through 12. It gives the Iowa Silent Reading Test in grade 9, the PSAT and SAT in grade 11, and the CEEB Achievement Tests in grade 12. These are reported in percentiles, not grade levels.

trict developed a program to show parents how to make the home environment more supportive for education. The director of the district's programs for gifted and talented students hoped the parenting program would work but quickly added, "Nobody really knows why those children can't read. We have had lots of federal money in Summerton. We know where the slump in learning occurs—after about third grade. But we don't know how to teach them. It's all frustrating because I don't see any light at the end of the tunnel."[148]

Some teachers thought the situation might be improved if there were better discipline, especially in the junior high school. "The students there lack respect for all authority figures," one teacher stated. "The principal uses corporal punishment, but it doesn't have much effect."[149] One administrator thought the teachers were part of the problem. Many of the older teachers had been certified years before, with scores on the National Teacher Examination that qualified them for only a "C" certificate. In the 1980s higher scores were required for certification, and with its competitive new salary schedule Summerton had no difficulty attracting well-qualified applicants. The problem was that so few vacancies occurred. Student enrollment was declining each year, and a state law postponed the age of mandatory retirement to seventy. As a result, the older teachers stayed on at higher salaries. Often they were assisted by young college graduates who made higher scores on the examination but were hired as teachers' aides and paid $3 an hour. The administrator said that many veteran teachers were only marginally competent. "They can't teach what they don't know," she declared. "It's a pity we can't give more responsibility to the young aides, who are so much better trained than many of our experienced teachers."[150]

Billie Fleming of the NAACP thought consolidation would be the best way to improve the quality of education in Summerton. "Right now we have needless duplication," he said. "We can't afford that, not in the 29th poorest county in the United States." If Clarendon's three school districts were consolidated into one larger district, the county would qualify for more federal money and all schools would be racially mixed. "Left to itself," Fleming said, "Summerton cannot improve the quality of its public schools."[151]

Yet the idea of consolidation was not popular in Manning and Turbeville, partly because of traditional rivalries between the various sections of the county. But, as reporter Sally Smith has noted, on a deeper level the idea of consolidation was abhorrent to most school officials "for exactly the same reason the whites abandoned the Summerton schools in the first place—race and quality of education. In [Manning and Turbeville], where the schools have managed to hold on to some whites . . . no one wants to deal with Summerton's 2,000 mostly under-educated black students."[152]

Writing in the *Greenville News* in 1979, Smith characterized the Summerton public schools as "a mess," with dilapidated facilities, demoralized and incompetent teachers, and rampant discipline problems. School officials considered her account unsympathetic and unfairly derogatory. Superintendent Alonzo Swinton said, "The situation that exists here did not happen overnight. It was a long time in the making. It will take a long time to unmake it." Board chairman Henry Lawson agreed. "This is a poverty-stricken area," he explained. "It will take a long time to get the kids interested in school. It takes as long to get out of limbo as it took to get there. But we have good basic programs, and we're on the right track."[153]

In assessing the recent history of education in Summerton, one must face a fact that simply cannot be hidden. The attempt to integrate the schools was a failure. In Summerton, most whites could live with the sort of desegregation that occurred with freedom of choice, but they would not comply with court rulings that assigned their children to predominantly black schools. Whites saw no alternative but to retreat to private academies. And the separation was not confined to education. With the mechanization of agriculture, white landowners no longer needed black labor and tended to avoid contact with a race they thought was trying to pull white youths down to a lower cultural level. There had been a great deal of friendly interracial contact in the days before white supremacy was challenged. After *Brown* there was little racial conflict in Summerton, but black and white children grew up as strangers to one another. Life was more segregated than ever. When asked what blacks had accomplished in the generation since he filed his lawsuit, Harry Briggs stared at the field outside his window and answered, "Nothing."[154]

But that was not the whole story. Whites generally thought Clarendon Hall was as good as the old Summerton Elementary and High School, and blacks recognized that facilities in the public schools were much improved since the 1940s even if test scores continued to lag. In Summerton one encountered none of the worrisome concern often expressed by parents elsewhere—the fear that educational standards had declined as instruction was geared to a lower average in integrated classrooms. There was also general agreement among whites and blacks that Summerton was a better place to live now that public facilities had been desegregated. "Our petition was the first step toward knocking out the whole Jim Crow system," said Joseph Lemons, one of the original plaintiffs in the *Briggs* lawsuit. "I used to have to drink from a separate water fountain outside the courthouse in Manning. They wouldn't let me go inside. Things are better now."[155]

Whites in Summerton were not happy about paying extra to maintain a private academy, but they recognized that this hardship did not justify retaliation against local blacks. They hoped that citizens in other regions of the nation eventually would realize that Summerton had raised legitimate questions concerning the control of local schools and the role of the judiciary as an initiator of social change. They thought this might come to pass if the federal government pressed to enforce racially balanced integration in the North.

PART FOUR

THE BUS STOPS HERE:
NEW CASTLE COUNTY, DELAWARE

Within a few years after *Brown*, students throughout New Castle County, Delaware, attended racially mixed schools in their neighborhoods. Few problems were encountered in the suburbs and towns, where blacks made up only a small portion of the population. However, in the city of Wilmington, where blacks initially made up one-fourth of the students, academic and disciplinary standards declined so sharply that most middle- and upper-class parents transferred their children to private schools or moved to the suburbs—a trend that ultimately produced a new form of dual schools. By the mid-1970s, 90 percent of the public school students in Wilmington were nonwhite, while 90 percent of those elsewhere in the county were white.

To achieve proportional racial mixing in each public school, the judges of the federal district court redefined the meaning of desegregation and then imposed the most sweeping busing program ever required in the United States. Desegregation did not depend on whether race was used to prevent children from attending public schools in districts of their residence, the judges ruled; it depended on the number and percentage of black and white students enrolled in particular schools. In 1978 eleven previously independent school districts were consolidated, and black and white students were dispersed to create an 80-20 racial balance in each school throughout an area of 250 square miles. It was difficult to escape from county wide busing, but enough students withdrew from the public schools of the desegregation area to discredit the theory that metropolitan dispersion would ensure a stable racial balance. It remains to be seen whether white flight will proceed to the point where the second desegregation leads finally to a second resegregation.

I

Situated about halfway between New York City and Washington, fifty miles from Baltimore and twenty from Philadelphia, New Castle County is a predominantly suburban area. In 1970 only 80,000 of the county's 352,000 residents lived in Wilmington, the largest city, and the prevailing style of life was suburban—neighborhoods made up of houses and apartments clustered around nearby public schools.

In 1802 the E.I. du Pont de Nemours Company began manufacturing black powder along the Brandywine River, and Wilmington eventually became the hub of the nation's multibillion-dollar chemical industry. Immigrant workers made up a large part of the city's population when Du Pont was making gunpowder. In the years after World War I, however, Wilmington and New Castle County increasingly became the administrative and research center for the highly technical operations that led to cellophane, rayon, nylon, Duco paint, Lucite plastic, and other chemical products. In 1912 the Hercules and Atlas chemical companies broke away from Du Pont, but they kept their headquarters in New Castle County. A new social structure emerged, as the chemical companies employed thousands of middle- and upper-income managers, scientists, and technicians.[1]

In the twentieth century Delaware was best known as a good place to do business—a place where almost one-third of the companies listed on the New York Stock Exchange are incorporated. Yet Delaware had once been a slave state, and it remained a border state whose race relations involved a mixture of southern and northern customs, with the former prevailing downstate in Kent and Sussex counties and the latter more evident in northern New Castle County. The peculiarity of the situation was suggested by the fact that in 1950 the schools, restaurants, and theaters were segregated throughout the state while libraries, buses, and trains were not, and blacks voted as freely as whites.[2]

The initial plaintiff in the legal battle over desegregation in Delaware first came to public attention in 1944, when the Wilmington press reported that an abandoned one-year-old girl had been found in a white apartment house. The child was a lightly colored black and was adopted by Mr. and Mrs. Fred Bulah, a mulatto couple who lived ten miles west of Wilmington in the rural village of Hockessin. When Shirley Bulah reached school age, her mother enrolled her at Hockessin School No. 107, a one-room elementary school where two teachers taught forty-three black students. The school was two miles from the Bulahs' home, and no bus transportation was provided.

In 1950 Mrs. Bulah wrote to state officials, asking that Shirley be permitted to ride the white school bus that passed near her daughter's school on its way to the white Hockessin School No. 29. Officials refused on the grounds that busing was an integral part of public education and that the state constitution required that schools be segregated. Attorney General H. Albert Young explained that the state did not operate buses but instead furnished students with an allowance that could be transferred to private bus companies. The companies operated buses whenever there were enough students to make this feasible, but there were so few blacks in Hockessin that it was not profitable for any company to transport students to the black school.[3]

Mrs. Bulah asked Louis L. Redding, a black graduate of Brown University and the Harvard law school, for help. Redding said "he wouldn't help me get a Jim Crow bus to take my girl to any Jim Crow school," Mrs. Bulah recalled, "but if I was interested in sendin' her to an integrated school, why, then maybe he'd help."[4] Almost simultaneously, Redding accepted another case that presented a similar issue. In Claymont, a predominantly white suburb nine miles north of Wilmington, eight black teenagers were refused admission to the local high school. Like other black youths of high school age in northern New Castle County, they were assigned to all-black Howard High in downtown Wilmington. Ethel Belton, the mother of one of the teenage plaintiffs, stated that as a result her daughter lost thirty minutes a day that would have been available for study or piano practice if she had attended Claymont High. The matter of time and fatigue was not insignificant, Mrs. Belton said, but it was not the main reason for her lawsuit. "We are all born Americans," she said, "and when the state sets up separate schools for certain people of a separate color, then I and others are made to feel ashamed and embarrassed, because such separations humiliate us and make us feel that we are not as good Americans as other Americans."[5]

In keeping with the strategy of the NAACP, which financed the litigation and joined in preparing the briefs, lawyer Redding challenged the principle of "separate but equal." Segregated schools were inherently inferior, he argued, and thus in violation of the equal protection guaranteed by the Fourteenth Amendment. Redding knew, however, that the Supreme Court might not abandon a doctrine that had guided its jurisprudence for three-quarters of a century. Hence, while NAACP attorney Jack Greenberg stressed the psychological argument that separate could not be equal, Redding gathered information to the effect that the black facilities in Hockessin and Wilmington were inferior and thus in violation of the Supreme Court's accepted standard for measuring equal protection.

The judge in the case was Collins Seitz, the thirty-seven-year-old chancellor of Delaware, whose tribunal functioned as an equity court with original jurisdiction over a wide range of legal questions. Seitz personally believed that segregation created "a mental health problem in many Negro children with resulting impediment to their educational progress." He thought "separate but equal" should be rejected as an impossible contradiction of terms, but he also said it was up to the Supreme Court to make the repudiation. Since the high court had not done so, Seitz ruled against the plaintiffs on the question of segregation per se.[6]

Seitz nevertheless found for the black plaintiffs on the grounds that the facilities and educational opportunities offered at the black schools were inferior to those available to whites. In truth, the evidence was open to question. The black teachers at Howard were paid slightly more than white teachers in Claymont, and the black and white teachers in Hockessin were paid at the same rate. There were a few more students per teacher at black Howard than at white Claymont, but the situation was just the reverse in the black and white schools in Hockessin. The physical facilities at white Hockessin School 29 were superior, largely because the white PTA had supplemented state funds with private gifts. At the high school level neither school suffered in comparison with the other, but Seitz considered it significant that the suburban-style building in Claymont was situated on fourteen well-tended acres whereas Howard was limited to only three acres in the city of Wilmington. A ten-acre city park was located across the street from Howard, however, and George A. Johnson, the proud principal of the black school, would not concede that his school was inferior. Almost 40 percent of his teachers held masters' degrees, Johnson testified, and one-third of the graduates went on to college. He rejected the notion that black schools must be inferior schools.[7]

Because he said lower courts should defer to the Supreme Court, Seitz's opinion has been characterized as a model of judicial restraint. Nevertheless, while proclaiming that it was up to the Supreme Court to overturn its established doctrines, Seitz devised a standard that made it impossible for a black school to be considered equal to a white school. "Where the facilities or educational opportunities available to the Negro are, as to *any* substantial factor, inferior to those available to white children similarly situated, the Constitutional principle of 'separate but equal' is violated, even though the State may point to other factors as to which the Negro school is superior." This was admittedly "a harsh test," one that dismissed the need for any balancing of relative strengths before finding substantial inequality, but Seitz insisted that "a State which divides its citizens should pay the price."[8]

Seitz's opinion was beguiling; while asserting that he had no authority to overrule a superior court, the Delaware chancellor subtly ignored the established meaning of "separate but equal." Differences inevitably occur in any comparison of two schools, but Seitz did not concede that there was no constitutional violation unless on balance blacks were placed at a disadvantage because of their race.[9] According to the chancellor, a single material disadvantage could not be offset by compensating advantages. "I found it inexcusable that the State would lend its support to dividing its citizens this way," Seitz later stated. His opinion bristled with moral indignation.[10]

Seitz also refused to follow the example of courts that permitted segregating states to equalize inferior facilities. "When a plaintiff shows to the satisfaction of a court that there is an existing and continuing violation of the 'separate but equal' doctrine," Seitz wrote, "he is entitled to have made available to him the State facilities which have been shown to be superior."[11]

When desegregation began in the fall of 1952, Harvey E. Stahl, the superintendent of schools in Claymont, reported that everything went smoothly in his district. Dr. Leon V. Anderson, a black parent of children who transferred from Howard to Claymont, spoke for many blacks when he said, "The stigma is off of them. This business of being shunted here and there because of your color is gone." Beyond that, Dr. Anderson said, his children were "doing better work. The work is harder at Claymont than at Howard."[12]

In Hockessin, Mrs. Sarah Bulah also indicated that most things had worked out well. Shirley was making friends at school and had also improved her schoolwork. "She reads so much better," Mrs. Bulah said. Nor had Mrs. Bulah lost any of the white customers that patronized her fresh egg stand. In fact, she said, "a lot of whites congratulated me." When she attended a PTA meeting with another black mother, Mrs. Bulah reported, both women were received cordially. "I tell you, if they don't want us there they sure haven't showed it."[13]

There were some problems, however. Blacks thought one of the four white teachers at Hockessin School No. 29 was racially prejudiced. "Look at South America, where all the races and creeds have intermarried," this teacher said on one occasion. "What have they got? Lazy, unproductive, backward people." One black mother perceptively remarked, "The elementary school age is one in which youngsters are deeply impressed. They are having their characters molded. . . . They need to be encouraged at this age. They need a pat on the back when they do something well." She thought it would be better for black youngsters to have "Negro teachers who are likely to be sympathetic to them."[14] She had touched on one of the important but usually neglected aspects of a complex question.

Other objections were more mundane. Some black teachers feared their jobs would be jeopardized by desegregation and, according to Mrs. Bulah, one of them had retaliated by flunking Shirley during her last year at the black school. Another opponent of desegregation was the black pastor of the Chippey African Union Methodist Church in Hockessin, located next door to the black school. "I was for segregation," the Reverend Martin Luther Kilson stated. "These folks around here would rather have a colored teacher. They didn't want to be mixed up with no white folks. All we wanted was a bus for the colored. Redding and some members of the NAACP encouched this issue of segregation. I hated to see them tamper with that little old colored school."[15]

None of the other black parents joined Mrs. Bulah's lawsuit. In fact, far from being heroes in Hockessin, the Bulahs became the focus of the color consciousness that sometimes besets black communities. Mrs. Bulah later recalled that "some of the colored people were whispering that, just because Shirley is fair-complexioned we thought she was white, and that we were suing because we didn't want her to associate with colored children."[16]

II

In Wilmington, where blacks made up about 27 percent of the public school students, desegregation proceeded in stages, beginning with the grammar schools in 1954 and extending to the junior high schools in 1955 and the senior high schools in 1956.

Nothing was taken for granted. The state police were told that no matter what they personally thought of integration, "the most important thing is the preservation of law and order within the community." The National Conference of Christians and Jews sponsored special seminars on race relations, and the PTA made "door to door visits listening to parents, winning acceptance, and in some cases winning support." In keeping with an open enrollment policy that had been in effect for two decades, parents were allowed to transfer their children to other schools or classrooms—an option that undoubtedly helped to ease tensions.[17]

As a result of these policies, school superintendent Ward I. Miller reported that integration had "succeeded beyond our fondest hopes." Endorsing this conclusion, *New York Times* reporter Benjamin Fine wrote that "in less than three years a new way of life has taken hold in the city's schools." Although parents had the privilege of transferring their children to non-integrated classes, only twenty such requests were made in 1956–1957, in a school district that enrolled 13,000 students. Fine reported, "In the early grades [the children] accept integration without question. They do not know the meaning of the word, but they certainly practice it. They take turns swinging the jump rope. . . . During the resting period in kindergarten, the children stretched out on blankets on the floor. They lay side by side, regardless of color."[18]

Of course there were some problems, even in the heyday of desegregation. The average IQ of white pupils in Wilmington ranged from 105 to 108, while that for blacks ranged from 95 to 98. Differences in academic achievement were especially pronounced in the high schools, but even in first grade the average for blacks was behind the class average. Superintendent Miller nevertheless predicted that as a result of superior teaching in mixed schools "the educational difference will be narrowed, if not eliminated." [19]

The experience with extracurricular activities was more ambiguous. P.S. du Pont High School in Wilmington received much favorable publicity in 1957 when Michael Jenkins, one of only 61 blacks enrolled among 1,500 students, was elected president of the top student governing body. Yet social mixing at the high schools was limited. "White elementary school pupils invite Negroes to their homes for a glass of milk and cookies or to work on a school project," Benjamin Fine reported. "But there comes a time when this stops. Sometimes it is in the fifth or sixth grade. Or it might be in junior high school. By the time they get to senior high, the social separation appears decisive." As typical examples the principal of Wilmington High School cited one white girl who said she did not know a single black girl by name and a black student who admitted to knowing only a couple of white students. Probing the heart of the matter, one worried white father declared, "I don't want my boy to come away from school with a colored bride." [20]

Despite minor difficulties, desegregation seemed to go well. Most of the racial mixing occurred in Wilmington, the only school district in northern New Castle County where blacks made up more than 10 percent of the student body. For several years after 1954 the Wilmington public schools continued to be considered as good as any in Delaware. Bill Frank, the state's most prominent newspaper columnist, reflected the views of most informed observers when he wrote, "This is a fact. Where desegregation in Delaware has been given a fair trial . . . it has been successful in that it has not developed into any difficulty nor has it gone beyond any limit set by the educators." [21]

Many whites apparently thought otherwise, however, for with desegregation they began to leave Wilmington. At the same time a growing number of blacks moved into the city, many from the rural South. Total enrollment in the Wilmington public schools varied between 13,000 and 16,000 students, but the percentage of whites steadily decreased from 72.9 in 1954 to 9.7 in 1976 (Table 7).

Some of the white flight had nothing to do with desegregation. When they left the city, many whites were not consciously fleeing from blacks so much as choosing the advantages of suburbs or smaller towns — less con-

TABLE 7. Enrollments by Race,
Wilmington Public Schools, 1954–1976

Year	White		Black		Total
1954	9,702	(72.9)	3,593	(27.1)	13,295[a]
1955	N/A				
1956	N/A				
1957	8,508	(65.1)	4,565	(34.9)	13,073[b]
1958	8,252	(62.3)	4,994	(37.7)	13,246
1959	7,664	(58.3)	5,484	(41.7)	13,148
1960	7,194	(55.0)	5,889	(45.0)	13,083
1961	7,037	(54.6)	5,850	(45.4)	12,887
1962	6,627	(49.4)	6,774	(50.6)	13,401
1963	6,324	(45.5)	7,580	(54.5)	13,904
1964	6,373	(46.1)	7,444	(53.9)	13,817
1965	5,842	(39.9)	8,771	(60.1)	14,613
1966	5,568	(37.7)	9,213	(62.3)	14,781
1967	5,110	(33.9)	9,847	(65.4)	15,056[c]
1968	4,865	(30.3)	11,121	(69.2)	16,067
1969	3,677	(24.0)	11,561	(75.5)	15,320
1970	3,151	(20.7)	11,981	(78.9)	15,178
1971	2,860	(18.7)	12,229	(79.8)	15,327
1972	2,452	(16.2)	12,265	(81.1)	15,129
1973	2,064	(14.1)	12,141	(82.7)	14,688
1974	1,727	(12.0)	12,060	(83.6)	14,419
1975	1,360	(9.8)	11,733	(84.7)	13,852
1976	1,301	(9.7)	11,350	(84.8)	13,383

[a]State of Delaware, Department of Public Instruction, State Board of Education, *Annual Report* (1954–55), 171.
[b]State of Delaware, Department of Public Instruction, State Board of Education, Research & Publication, "September Enrollments (White and Nonwhite Pupils)" (1957–1977).
[c]Beginning in 1967 and thereafter, racial and ethnic enrollments include categories in addition to white and black. Thus, total is more than black and white enrollments reported.

gestion, newer homes, cleaner air, and more open space for children. Immigrant blacks, on the other hand, felt less comfortable in the suburbs than in Wilmington, where black churches and civic associations had long been established. It also cost less to live in the city, where many houses had been subdivided into apartments and subsidized public housing was available.

Ethnic and class considerations are difficult to separate, but both apparently contributed to white flight. Working-class whites often remained in Wilmington if they hailed from neighborhoods like Little Italy or Polish Browntown, where most white children were educated in inexpensive, predominantly white Catholic grammar schools. Some younger Polish and Italian families did move to the suburbs, but enough remained to maintain the character of their neighborhoods. Middle-class professionals, on the other hand, were more likely to depart for the suburbs when they sensed that educational standards were declining.[22]

The enrollment statistics presented in Table 7 indicate that in Wilmington the white migration proceeded steadily for two decades. Except during the late 1960s, there was no acceleration in the rate of white departures. Unlike the situation in the other *Brown* school districts like Prince Edward and Clarendon counties, in Wilmington there was no single point when enrollments tipped quickly from white to black, when black majorities suddenly enrolled at previously white schools. The black presence in Wilmington increased gradually over many years. Unlike the situation in Washington, where most whites were relatively well-to-do and could easily afford to move to the suburbs, in Wilmington there were many working-class white ethnics who found it difficult to relocate. In the end, though, the result was the same in all the school districts: resegregation.

In contrast to southerners, who routinely emphasized the importance of race, people in New Castle County generally maintained that race was of little consequence. Many of the teachers and administrators were from northern states, especially Pennsylvania and New Jersey, and were said to "go around pretending that race doesn't exist. . . ." The official position was that academic problems resulted from cultural deprivation and not from any inherent deficiency in the black's reasoning power or imagination. "The whole thing is simply a problem of class," one white teacher said. "Most of our Negro students are simply from poor families. They act pretty much the same as white lower-class children." A reporter for the *Wilmington Morning News* maintained that the problems were not caused "solely by Negroes and where they have been caused by Negroes it is not because of any peculiarity of race but because of the social and economic situations in which most Negro families have been forced to live."[23]

In an effort to retain academically talented students, the Wilmington schools moved toward further grouping of students by scholastic achievement. With desegregation there was no change in the range of ability, but there was a marked change in the frequency of distribution. Some students continued to do well in the traditional college preparatory curriculum, but a growing number needed to move at a slower pace. School officials consequently devised new programs for those with below- and above-average ability. "There are many more of the former than the latter," the *Wilmington Morning News* reported, "but special programs have been set up for each."[24] Especially in the late 1950s, school officials in Wilmington stressed the need for programs suited "to the needs of boys and girls with superior ability." According to one article in the teachers' *Staff Reporter,* the emphasis in education for several decades had been on programs for terminal high school students; "to a large extent, the group who expects to go on to higher education has been neglected." One of the major problems in American education, according to Superintendent Miller, was "an unwillingness to group pupils for instructional purposes in order that those with superior ability may progress in accordance with their capacities." To remedy this weakness the Wilmington schools inaugurated a system where, on the basis of tests, grades, and teachers' evaluations, principals were allowed to group pupils by subjects, "with the brilliant ones in math together, those in social studies together, and so on."[25]

After desegregation, however, and especially in the 1960s and 1970s, officials focused increasingly on the needs of disadvantaged students. As whites departed and blacks moved in, significant modifications were made in the educational program. Thomas W. Mulrooney, the director of child guidance, reported that a growing number of students came to school "unfed and clothed in rags." Many came from "unstable families and one-parent families with drinking mothers . . . who often fear to discipline their children." In 1965 Assistant Superintendent Muriel Crosby described the situation this way:

> These youngsters are accustomed to seeing a succession of men in the home, whose relations with the mother are transitory. *Such children lack the stability of normal family life which helps them feel important and wanted because it is centered in the welfare of the children.*
>
> The oldest children in the family are forced to assume the burdens of maturity too early in life. They handle the family food budget, shopping while mother is at work. They prepare whatever food is available for younger children. They often assume full responsibility for younger brothers and sisters. . . .
>
> For many disadvantaged children moral and spiritual perversion is the result of deprivation. Cramped and crowded living space denying any form of privacy introduces the child to adult sexual behavior before he is mature enough to comprehend the significance of it. He is often victimized by adults living in his home. This is particularly true of girls, who often become mothers when they are still little more than children. Illegitimacy is an accepted pattern of life, and marriage is of little consequence in sexual relationships.
>
> The source of family income frequently affects the values developed by the disadvantaged child. Many children are growing up in an environment in which, for several generations, the chief income is from public and private welfare agencies. A pattern is established wherein it is normal and acceptable to receive financial support without individual effort and initiative. This factor, together with an early awareness of the fact that racial discrimination often closes the door to opportunities for work, results in an attitude of defeatism and the acceptance of the *status quo.* It produces generations of children without hope and without the will to become individuals with a sense of dignity and worth.[26]

To cope with these problems, the Wilmington public schools became a pioneer in providing breakfasts and clothing and in employing social workers, psychologists, doctors, nurses, and psychiatrists. The old methods of teaching would "no longer suffice to deal effectively with the kind of problems now faced in our classrooms," Superintendent Miller reported. By the early 1960s Miller was convinced that the time had come "to cut the strings which tie us to traditions and habits established through the years." To make integration a success, several things had to be done in addition to teaching academic subjects:

1. We must inform ourselves concerning the problems these boys and girls face in their homes and neighborhoods.
2. We must be sympathetic with the defeats, frustrations and discouragements they meet.
3. We must really want to help them, not be affronted by their rebelliousness, shocked by their language, resentful of their lack of self-control.
4. We must avoid regarding every negative response as a personal insult, rather than an expression of rebellion against the total situation before these young people.[27]

Wilmington's first notable attempt to address the problems of culturally deprived children was a program entitled "Three Year Experimental Project on Schools in Changing Neighborhoods." Jointly sponsored by the Wilmington public schools and the National Conference of Christians and Jews, the project had two goals. One was to develop methods for teaching youngsters previously considered hopeless. The other was to improve family and community life. That the latter goal was beyond the reach of the schools was indicated when, three years after the inception of the program, it was reported that Wilmington led all American cities in the percentage of children born outside of marriage. Reports in the local press indicated, however, that the Experimental Project was more successful academically. It was said to have demonstrated that "it is possible to motivate and instruct the youngsters of low economic status who are turning many big city schools into 'blackboard jungles.'"[28]

The curriculum developed in the Experimental Project emphasized human relations and relevance. In history classes, Muriel Crosby explained, the teacher was not to confine the subject to academic content but was to stress the values and skills needed to understand and live successfully with others. A course of study on the westward movement might reach its climax when teachers and pupils would spend a full day acting out the role of pioneer families who had come together to churn butter, weave blankets, recite school lessons, and defend themselves against Indians. In this way students could learn the importance of cooperation, and teachers could reward students who performed well in group situations as well as those who did well on examinations.[29]

During the 1950s and early 1960s, when Ward Miller and Muriel Crosby were in charge of the Wilmington schools, the emphasis on innovative programs was kept in perspective. New programs were devised for a rapidly changing city, but traditional curricula were also maintained for academic students. The goal was to teach all the children of all the people. To do this it was necessary to develop distinctive programs for gifted, average, and disadvantaged students.

In 1963 Miller retired at the age of seventy, having completed seventeen years as superintendent of schools. During the next seventeen years, three white superintendents were succeeded by three blacks, and blacks also became a majority of the teaching staff and Board of Education. As the black presence increased, the academic emphasis moved even more toward designing new approaches to reach disadvantaged students. "The simple teaching methods of earlier days—long on repetition and repressive discipline—would no longer be adequate to meet the new situation," white superintendent Gene A. Geisert declared. Instead of requiring students to take academic courses in the traditional sequence, black superintendent Earl C. Jackson recommended individual attention in a less competitive atmosphere. The needs of Wilmington's predominantly black students of the 1970s differed markedly from those of its predominantly white students of the 1950s. "What we had in the past worked with the students who were taught then," P.S. du Pont High School Principal James Moore stated. In the 1970s, though, a large portion of the students were too far below grade level to understand traditional academic material. The time had come to develop more elective courses in subjects the students considered relevant and interesting.[30]

In the 1960s and 1970s Wilmington's schools experimented with many of the approaches dear to the hearts of educational reformers. Project Expansion gave high school students a heretofore unprecedented freedom to design their own courses of study. Project Open-Out was designed for hardcore dropouts, as was Project E.S.O., a street academy established with funds from the Du Pont Company. Increased emphasis was placed on vocational training, as venerable Howard High School was converted into the Howard Career Center. Early childhood education also flourished, with Head Start, Follow Through, and other programs subsidized by federal money. Ability grouping was phased out and replaced by mainstreaming—a program for teaching moderately retarded youths in regular classrooms.[31]

Beginning in 1968 several elementary schools in Wilmington also developed a progressive program of informal education in "open" classrooms. Financed by the National Follow Through Program and sponsored by Bank Street College in New York City, this program was for low-income children in kindergarten through fourth grade. It emphasized that a child's success in learning was "inseparable from his self-esteem," and that teachers should make the child "feel important as a person" and develop his "ability to work and play cooperatively with other children." Basic skills were important, but the teacher's role was "more that of a facilitator than a lecturer or director." Teachers were told that excessive requirements and direction would repress their students' natural inclinations and inborn "enthusiasm for learning." [32]

The new programs cost money, of course, but that was not a serious problem. Thanks to federal aid and a high tax rate, Wilmington's public schools were among the best funded in Delaware with the best-paid teachers in the state. By 1977 the average expenditure per pupil was in the vicinity of $2,900 in Wilmington, compared with an average of $1,850 in the rest of New Castle County. [33] In the end, though, the expensive new programs did not solve Wilmington's major educational problems. Middle-class flight to the suburbs continued as more emphasis was placed on teaching disadvantaged students. Meanwhile, the trend in academic achievement was steadily downward. By the mid-1970s Wilmington's public high school seniors, once the best in the state, were three and one-half years below national norms on standardized tests and four years behind students in the suburbs of New Castle County (Table 8). [34]

In retrospect, it would be easy to fault Wilmington's school officials for going too far in lowering academic standards. Yet their error, if it was an error, grew out of an earnest desire to teach disadvantaged students. The officials tried most of the approaches that were recommended at the time, and yet the students' academic performance declined significantly. Wilmington was caught in the grip of national demographic forces that were beyond the control of local officials. As middle-class whites departed for the suburbs, their places were taken by black migrants from the rural South and, in the 1970s, by a substantial number from Puerto Rico as well. In a relatively brief period Wilmington changed from a stable community of mostly middle-class families to a city with a substantial number of impoverished people.

By the late 1960s gang fights, muggings, and street crime were so common that local leaders funded an organization known as WYEAC—the Wilmington Youth Emergency Action Council—to work with the city's violence-prone black youths. The chief architect of the program was Edward J. (Ned) Butler, a liberal white ex-seminarian who worked for the Roman Catholic Office for Inner-City Development. Butler divided Wilmington's black youths into two groups, which he called "Classics" and "Trumpcats." The former were "school-oriented" and required no special help, since they were already on the road to good citizenship and upward mobility. The latter were alienated youths who had dropped out of school, often had police records, and were involved in gang activity. If their physical energy were not turned into socially acceptable channels, they would become like their older siblings, whom Butler called "Soul Brothers." Most

TABLE 8. Comprehensive Tests of Basic Skills,
Wilmington Public Schools, Spring 1976

National Norm	Wilmington Norm			
	Reading	Language	Math	Total Battery
Grade 1: 1.7	1.7	1.5	1.9	1.7
Grade 2: 2.7	2.3	2.6	2.7	2.5
Grade 3: 3.7	3.5	3.7	3.4	3.5
Grade 4: 4.7	4.1	4.3	4.0	4.0
Grade 5: 5.7	4.7	5.2	4.8	4.8
Grade 6: 6.7	5.1	5.4	5.3	5.2
Grade 7: 7.7	5.4	5.2	5.8	5.4
Grade 8: 8.7	6.3	5.9	6.4	6.2
Grade 9: 9.7	6.8	6.5	6.7	6.8
Grade 10: 10.7	7.8	7.8	7.4	7.8
Grade 11: 11.7	8.4	8.2	7.8	8.3
Grade 12: 12.7	9.1	9.1	8.4	9.0

Source: Annual Report, Wilmington Superintendent of Schools, 1975–76.

of the Soul Brothers were married, but "a majority had left their wives and generally 'hung in' with other women. Although most could claim a place called home, they were really highly-mobile in the physical sense so that no address that they might give actually represented more than an occasional bedding spot." They were led by people like George N. Brown, who was also known as "Soul Man." "Soul Man" Brown was employed as a laundry truck driver but had achieved prominence because "he exemplified those characteristics which were most highly prized by the membership—a flashy, fast style of life, engaging personality, a real mover with women, an excellent dancer and a leader who had proven his capacity to give and take punishment by establishing what in local circles passed for a 'respectable' police record and a street fighting reputation."[35]

After a member of the Mountain Dew Gang was killed in a gang battle in June 1966, Butler was able to implement some of his ideas. Enlisting the support of "Soul Man" Brown, Butler encouraged the Mountain Dew Gang to picket City Hall instead of seeking revenge against their rivals. In this way, Butler suggested, the gang members would be seen "in a new light . . . not merely as 'poor,' 'culturally deprived hoods and juvenile delinquents' but as active citizens concerned about their needs and willing to fight for them." By channeling the energies of the youths "in creative and positive directions," Butler hoped to prevent the festering of attitudes that would "possibly explode later."[36]

The response to the picketing was surprisingly favorable. The influential *Wilmington Evening Journal* editorially stated that the youths deserved a "'down payment' . . . to show that the community is really serious about its promise to do something." The local Catholic bishop provided a rent-free teen center that became known as B.J.'s Corner in honor of the slain gang member, B.J. Keller. Public officials also promised to consider additional demands for rent control, more playground equipment, and an end to checks to determine whether adult males were living with single welfare mothers.[37]

Butler's success in turning the Mountain Dew Gang toward social protest served as a model for other welfare agencies. The YMCA hired a former street youth named Charles (Chezzie) Miller to work with a group of young black toughs on the west side of town, and the Council of Churches and the Presbyterian Synod reached out to gang members elsewhere in Wilmington. Then, after racial disturbances in 1967, Ned Butler prepared grant proposals that secured more than $282,000 for WYEAC. "Soul Man" Brown was appointed project director, and ninety-two people were employed with impressive titles like program planner, economic developer, and legal aid specialist.[38]

WYEAC sponsored some worthwhile activities. There were picnics and dances, as well as a youth sports program and cultural events featuring prominent Afro-American musicians and dancers. Ninety percent of WYEAC's money, however, went to staff members who were involved in what is sometimes called "consciousness raising." Traveling in five smartly painted vans, WYEAC's staff commuted around the city speaking on behalf of racial pride and group unity. In their private conversations the staff referred to this activity as "soapboxing." Youth organizer Chezzie Miller explained that he was paid "to attend meetings, cruise around, talk to the guys to try to find out what's playing today. My job is not to tell the boys what to do, but to try to stimulate their ideas and help them to make their own decisions." George L. Johnson, the director of the Office of Economic Opportunity in Wilmington, explained that WYEAC was trying to make blacks recognize that they must "unite as blacks and move with a solid front" if they were to improve their position.[39]

Some citizens took exception to the fact that many WYEAC workers had police records. Of the ninety-two staff members, sixty-three had been arrested prior to working for WYEAC; the leaders were particularly conspicuous in this respect. At a time when beginning policemen received $5,600 a year, project director "Soul Man" Brown, who had already been arrested twelve times, received a salary of $9,932. Youth organizer Chezzie Miller, who received a salary of $7,748, had been arrested on thirty-two occasions. Critics said it was demoralizing for black children to see benefits given to black youths who had run into trouble with the law, especially when there were no similar rewards for those who behaved themselves.[40]

Some critics said that for the purpose of buying peace in the city, Wilmington's civic leaders had caved in before the demands of a group of young outlaws. But Edward J. Goett, the president of the Atlas Chemical Company, insisted that grants to WYEAC were "based solely on [its] value as a mechanism for dealing with the serious problems of alienated youth." To Goett it seemed more practical to work directly with alienated outlaw elements than with respectable blacks who were thought to have achieved their positions by betraying the black masses. Over the years Wilmington's chemical companies had benefited from research and experimentation, and the chemist-philanthropists of the 1960s hoped they would benefit again from what Goett characterized as a "social experiment."[41]

Things did not work out that way. WYEAC was one experiment that resulted in an explosion and a stink. The number of gang battles increased after WYEAC was established, with some evidently precipitated by the jealousy some gangs felt when a disproportionate share of the WYEAC funds went to only four of Wilmington's many youth gangs. More significantly, a dozen WYEAC workers were arrested in 1968 during the largest race riot in Delaware history when, in the wake of the assassination of Martin Luther King, 21 buildings were destroyed by fire, 40 people were injured, and 154 citizens arrested.[42] After the rioting, police uncovered arms caches at B.J.'s Corner, in WYEAC vans, and in the apartments of WYEAC employees. "This train of events climaxed in the 'Cherry Island Incident' of August 31, 1968, when police happened upon a group of six heavily armed black youths. Wearing bandoliers and sporting black berets, the group were engaged in target practice in the marshland east of the city along the Delaware River. Three wore badges that read 'I have already been drafted into the Liberation Army,' and four of the six were paid workers in WYEAC. They had driven out to the marsh in a WYEAC van." A search of their apartments yielded a small arsenal of rifles and 3,235 rounds of ammunition.[43]

As historian Carol Hoffecker has observed, "By comparison to the riots in Baltimore, Detroit, Washington and Newark, New Jersey, the Wilmington riot was a small, short-lived affair that did relatively little damage. But in the consciousness of the community, both black and white, it loomed large."[44] When Mayor John E. Babiarz asked for 1,000 National Guardsmen to ensure peace and order, Governor Charles L. Terry mobilized the entire state guard, 2,800 strong, and sent them to Wilmington, where soldiers remained on patrol for nine months.

Funding for WYEAC was cut off when the extent of the folly became known, but this venture in social reform was more than a sorry example of good intentions gone awry. By giving generous financial support to WYEAC, the federal government and local philanthropists had enhanced the status of a group of young ruffians—at the very time when the Wilmington public schools were neglecting their better students so they could devote more of their resources to programs designed to reach disadvantaged slow learners. Pearl G. Herlihy, the wife of former Wilmington mayor Thomas Herlihy, exaggerated Ned Butler's influence when she referred to the social worker as "The Man Who Corrupted Wilmington." But Mrs. Herlihy was on firm ground when she pointed out that mistaken policies had the effect of "consign[ing] black youth to the continued tyranny of the gang."[45]

When Wilmington initially desegregated its public schools in the 1950s, students were assigned to neighborhood schools unless they chose to go elsewhere. This arrangement gave students and their parents more free choice than was customary in many school districts, but it did not come in for special criticism because Wilmington had allowed students to transfer outside their neighborhoods ever since the 1930s. The overwhelming majority of students, in any case, chose to attend schools close to their homes. At the high school level, for example, most blacks enrolled at Howard because it was well regarded and was conveniently located in the midst of the city's largest black neighborhood. Some blacks did transfer to Wilmington High or to P.S. du Pont High School, and their numbers gradually increased in the 1950s and 1960s, but there was never more than a handful of whites who enrolled at Howard (Table 9).

The variance in racial ratios caused no legal problem, for in 1962 the federal district court had held that there was no affirmative constitutional duty to provide an integrated education. "Discrimination is forbidden but integration is not compelled," Judge Caleb M. Wright had ruled. The Supreme Court in *Brown,* Wright said,

> held only that a State may not deny any person on account of race the right to attend a public school. Chief Justice Warren, speaking for the court, said, "To separate them [Negroes] from others . . . *solely* because of their race generates a feeling of inferiority as to their status in the community that may affect their hearts and minds in a way unlikely ever to be undone." The clear implication of this statement is that if races are separated because of geographic or transportation considerations or other similar criteria, it is no concern of the Federal Constitution.[46]

There were disciplinary problems, however, as racial mixing increased in the wake of continuing white flight and black immigration. "It was almost as if there was something magic—or hellish—when the black enrollment reached 40 percent," recalled Jeanette McDonnal, the dean of girls at P.S. du Pont High School. "The black attitudes changed then, and the whites had reason to be frightened."[47] Beginning in the early 1960s there were frequent reports of petty extortion at P.S. du Pont as older black students demanded protection money from younger students of both races.

TABLE 9. Enrollments by Race, Wilmington Public Schools, 1957

School	White	Nonwhite
Bancroft	25	744
Bayard	685	154
Brown Vocational	420	62
Charles Drew	10	414
P.S. du Pont H. S.	1,447	72
Elbert	37	378
George Gray	605	364
Harlan	751	0
Highlands	329	5
Howard H. S.	0	498
Lore	735	193
Palmer	121	77
Pyle	57	203
Shortlidge	321	0
Stubbs	16	771
Warner	770	68
Washington	236	44
Williams	595	424
Wilmington H. S.	1,168	94
Number 19	180	0
Total	8,508	4,565

Source: Data from *Racial and Ethnic Reports,* Delaware Department of Public Instruction.

Graffitti appeared on the school's previously immaculate buildings, refuse littered the grounds, and windows were smashed. More serious trouble erupted after police picked up two black youths for questioning about some obscenities that had been painted on a building. "They didn't pick up any honkies," one black student declared, "so we were going to repay them. We were going to mess with somebody on their side." Spotting a white boy and girl after school that day, a group of blacks sprang to the attack. "There's some honkies. Let's go get them," the blacks cried. The white girl reported, "The girls came running across the street. They kicked me, hit me, pulled my hair and broke my brassiere. About a dozen of them. Some boys came over and started on my boy friend, who was trying to help me. All I got was a black eye, a stiff neck, and a sore head."[48]

More than one hundred white parents signed a petition asking for stronger discipline at "P.S." Spokeswoman Dorothy Worthy said her children were "getting an education all right—but not the right kind." Another parent said her son "ran home from school every day last spring, he was so scared." The parents criticized the courts which, they said, often released troublemakers without punishment and generally made it difficult for "our excellent policemen . . . to do the job they want to do."[49]

Faculty members at "P.S." also came in for their share of ill treatment. Most of the abuse was verbal, as insults were frequently uttered by students, but some of it was physical as well. One teacher was pushed down a flight of stairs and another warded off an assault by firing a stream of tear gas at a group of students. In 1968, sixty-seven of the eighty-five members of the faculty signed a petition protesting what they called "the continuous lack of administrative support of teachers in the resolution of disciplinary problems." The petition was organized when English teacher Bruce Laird staged a one-man strike to publicize the way the school's administration had handled an incident in his classroom. Several students had been walking in and out of the room, and Laird was threatened with bodily harm when he told one of the youths to stay out. When he reported the incident to the principal, he was told he could swear out a personal warrant if he wished, but the school would not take any action against the student. In 1975 the teachers at "P.S." demanded the immediate suspension of 200 students. "I've been teaching at this school for fifteen years and when I look at it now I could just weep," one teacher said.[50]

The violence at "P.S." was widely publicized in 1970 when Derek Johnson, an all-conference football player, was shot and killed outside the school cafeteria after he and a teammate had quarreled over a girl. The prevailing chaos was also evident in 1975, when black state senator Herman M. Holloway visited the school at the request of a constituent who said her daughter had been raped in one of the corridors. The principal was busy when Holloway and three companions arrived, so the four men stood in a hall and observed what Holloway considered a scene of complete disorder. "Disrespect for the faculty was evident. It was . . . a scene that belonged anywhere but in a high school." Holloway was discouraged by "the ultra sloppy dress of the students, the tremendous noise of the students gallivanting up and down the corridors, the absolute lack of discipline and even the timidity of the faculty members to attempt any control." When Holloway and his companions finally talked to the principal about the girl who said she was attacked, they were shocked to learn that the principal had no record of the incident, although police had visited the school to question the girl.[51]

Whites had steadily withdrawn from "P.S." even during the 1950s and early 1960s, when desegregation had been relatively trouble-free. After black enrollment reached the vicinity of 40 percent in the mid-1960s, however, the rate of white departures accelerated sharply. During the first decade of desegregation, the proportion of blacks at "P.S." had increased gradually from 4 percent to 33 percent, but during the next three years the school became a predominantly black institution, with a sizable portion of the students coming from public housing projects whose children had previously been sent to Howard High School (Table 10).

For years "P.S." had been considered the best of Delaware's public high

TABLE 10. Enrollment by Race,
P.S. du Pont High School, 1957–1977

	White		Nonwhite		Total
1957	1,447	(95.2)	72	(4.8)	1,519
1958	1,389	(93.5)	97	(6.5)	1,486
1959	1,376	(92.6)	92	(6.3)	1,468
1960	N/A		N/A		
1961	1,306	(90.7)	133	(9.2)	1,439
1962	1,259	(82.3)	271	(17.7)	1,530
1963	1,136	(74.7)	385	(25.3)	1,521
1964	1,141	(76.6)	349	(23.4)	1,490
1965	1,077	(74.2)	374	(25.8)	1,451
1966	999	(66.4)	505	(33.6)	1,504
1967	887	(58.7)	624	(41.3)	1,511
1968	698	(46.8)	794	(53.2)	1,492
1969	348	(37.8)	597	(63.2)	945
1970	229	(23.5)	745	(76.5)	974
1971	139	(13.6)	878	(86.2)	1,019
1972	80	(7.2)	1,033	(92.7)	1,117
1973	74	(6.4)	1,084	(93.6)	1,158
1974	75	(5.7)	1,231	(94.0)	1,310
1975	27	(1.9)	1,390	(97.7)	1,423
1976	26	(1.94)	1,305	(97.4)	1,340
1977	21	(1.96)	1,040	(97.4)	1,068

Source: Delaware Department of Public Instruction, *Racial and Ethnic Reports.*

schools. Situated on a knoll in a middle-class neighborhood, it was housed in a large, Depression-era imitation of a Georgian building. The facilities were excellent and included a Greek-style amphitheater and a cement football stadium where several championship teams had played. It was in academic work, however, that "P.S." really stood out. A disproportionately large share of Delaware's civic and business leaders had graduated from the school, and within the state there were some who hailed "P.S." as "the finest high school, public or private, east of the Mississippi River."[52]

That may have been stretching the point, but "P.S." certainly had a rich academic history and a long tradition. Many of the younger teachers were graduates of the school, a condition that contributed to conservatism regarding standards. "We had standards of dress and decorum," one teacher recalled. "Before the 1960s we really didn't know what discipline problems were, although at the time of course we thought we had some problems." A growing number of wealthy Jews from the Brandywine Hills neighborhood matriculated at "P.S." in the 1940s and 1950s, evidently because they did not feel welcome in the city's exclusive prep schools. The Jews never constituted a majority of the student body at "P.S.," but they earned an unusually large share of the academic honors. Some people thought of "P.S." as "a Jewish country club," but almost everyone conceded that the

Jewish students had, if anything, raised the school's already high academic standards.[53]

Most black students behaved themselves, but white parents were not prepared for the degree of antagonism and violence that some blacks brought to "P.S." Most of the white parents, especially the Jewish parents, had favored desegregation, but they would not expose their children to fear and declining academic standards. When white parents heard about chaos in the hallways, vulgar language, interracial skirmishes, and gang fighting among blacks, they transferred their children to private schools or moved to the predominantly white suburbs of Wilmington. "As the fear spread, the Jews just vanished," one teacher recalled. "They didn't even wait for the abolition of ability grouping and the other fads of the 1970s." The Gentiles followed close behind.[54]

Whites left Wilmington High School at a slightly slower rate than at "P.S.," but the pattern was similar at both schools (Table 11). Wilmington High was a comprehensive school with a respectable college preparatory course and an academically oriented principal, although a large portion of the Wilmington High students specialized in business education and secretarial studies. When the school was moved in 1960 from its downtown campus to modern buildings on the west side of town, it became particularly attractive to many of the Polish and Italian families who lived nearby. They often sent their younger children to parochial elementary schools and their teenaged sons to Salesianum School, a large Catholic high school for boys. The nearby Catholic academies for high school girls, Padua and Ursuline, were much smaller, and Ursuline offered a finishing school program for affluent young women. Most of the Catholic daughters of central and western Wilmington consequently were sent to Wilmington High, where they learned secretarial skills that would be of use someday in supplementing a family income. During the late 1950s and early 1960s, two-thirds of the whites attending Wilmington High were females.[55]

Rumors of violence and petty extortion at Wilmington High were doubtless exaggerated, as the *News Journal* newspapers maintained in their editorials, but there were enough incidents to fuel the fears of many parents. Readers of the newspapers learned that five Wilmington school girls, "armed with brass knuckles, scissors and a razor blade, among other things, were arrested to prevent a possible gang fight." They read that Wilmington High student Thomas Ward required fifteen stitches after being slashed on the left leg, and that student Dennis C. Hoyle had been stabbed in the back. In a particularly gruesome story, they were informed that two students had been charged with extorting money from fifteen-year-old William Ruggiero by threatening to cut off his fingers if he did not pay three dollars a day for the rest of the school year. In a letter to the editor, one student

TABLE 11. Enrollment by Race,
Wilmington High School, 1957–1977

	White		Nonwhite		Total
1957	1,168	(92.6)	94	(7.4)	1,262
1958	1,146	(86.8)	174	(13.2)	1,320
1959	1,091	(83.4)	217	(16.6)	1,308
1960	N/A		N/A		
1961	957	(80.8)	228	(19.2)	1,185
1962	1,029	(78.9)	274	(21.0)	1,303
1963	1,058	(75.7)	340	(24.3)	1,398
1964	1,029	(77.0)	307	(22.9)	1,336
1965	990	(67.0)	487	(33.0)	1,477
1966	953	(62.4)	573	(37.6)	1,526
1967	910	(60.1)	604	(39.9)	1,514
1968	769	(52.1)	706	(47.9)	1,475
1969	708	(41.9)	911	(54.0)	1,687
1970	634	(39.0)	993	(61.0)	1,627
1971	785	(42.2)	1,037	(55.7)	1,862
1972	705	(38.9)	1,054	(58.2)	1,812
1973	489	(24.9)	1,404	(71.4)	1,967
1974	389	(21.1)	1,313	(71.4)	1,839
1975	241	(12.6)	1,457	(76.2)	1,913
1976	206	(11.7)	1,411	(80.2)	1,760
1977	132	(9.6)	1,090	(79.2)	1,376

Source: Delaware Department of Public Instruction, *Racial and Ethnic Reports.*

told readers that white students had "to walk to school in groups so they will not be attacked by black gangs." School officials acknowledged that there was a crisis in discipline, with "fear and chaos [prevailing] in the halls of the secondary schools."[56]

A riot was touched off at Wilmington High School in September 1969 when police arrested several blacks for extorting money from other students. Several hundred black students left their classes to jeer the police, and fights erupted when additional students were arrested for profanity. The violence escalated again after some black students tried to liberate a policy paddy wagon. When the casualties were counted, twenty-five students, three teachers, and an unreported number of policemen had been injured.[57]

White flight accelerated after the Wilmington High riot of 1969, and by 1977 the school was 90 percent nonwhite. Interracial strife subsided as blacks became securely ascendant, but the general behavior of many students continued to shock observers. In 1973, for example, four state legislators and a *News Journal* reporter came away with unfavorable impressions after making unannounced visits to several city schools. Herman Holloway, Casimer Jonkiert, Amos McCluney, Marcello Rispoli, and Bill Frank represented the city's major ethnic groups—Negro, Polish, Irish, Italian, and Jewish. As a consequence, their observations were widely credited in Wilmington. At Burnett Middle School, where the curriculum stressed independent study and open classrooms, the visitors discovered a state of disorder that they characterized as "almost unbelievable." They described the girls' lavatory at Wilmington High as "dirtier than a pig pen" and complained that many pupils were sleeping at their desks while classes were in session. By the mid-1970s, as noted above, high school seniors in Wilmington were, on the average, performing at the level of eighth-grade students in the predominantly white suburbs of New Castle County. Helen Bayliss, the former principal of Harlan Elementary School in Wilmington, spoke for most informed citizens when she said it was "a real tragedy to see what education had come to." Public education in Wilmington had reached rock bottom.[58]

III

In 1978 Wilmington and New Castle County became the scene of the most sweeping busing program ever implemented in the United States. The program, ironically, grew out of a 1956 lawsuit in which blacks demanded that Delaware's two other counties, Kent and Sussex, be required to implement the sort of desegregation that New Castle put into place in 1954. Delaware is a small state, with only three counties, and it is only 110 miles long. It has two distinct regions, however, divided from one another by the manmade Chesapeake and Delaware Canal, which cuts across Delaware about twenty miles from its northern boundary and links the Delaware and Chesapeake bays. Northern Delaware is suburban and hilly. Southern Delaware is rural and flat and by tradition was as strongly in favor of segregation as the neighboring counties on the Eastern Shore of Maryland and Virginia.

Desegregation widened the gulf between the two Delawares. Wilmington and its suburbs implemented programs for nonracial school assignments immediately after the Supreme Court's first *Brown* opinion, but most communities in Kent and Sussex counties delayed desegregation for almost a decade. The official attitude of the local school boards in southern Delaware was not defiant. They did not follow the example of Virginia and South Carolina with resolutions of interposition or threats to close the public schools. They instead maintained that desegregation should be postponed "until a program of enlightenment effects a change in the attitude of the people." "Give us more time to educate our people," one school board requested. "Our people are not ready," declared another. Communities differed from one another in traditions and customs, it was said, and desegregation would take longer in some places than in others.[59]

The need for a gradual approach to desegregation was underlined by events that occurred in Milford in the fall of 1954. Situated on the boundary between Kent and Sussex counties and traversed by the picturesque Mispillion River, Milford was an attractive town of about 6,000 people, 20 percent of whom were black. Most white people in and near Milford, like those in country towns throughout the southern and border states, were not psychologically ready to accept desegregation. When school opened in September 1954, however, 10 black teenagers were enrolled along with about 675 whites at Milford High School. Desegregation in Milford did not result from a federal court order, for it was not until 1955 that the Supreme Court required school districts to proceed "with all deliberate speed" toward admitting students on a racially nondiscriminatory basis (*Brown II*). The decision for desegregation was made by the members of the local school board, who acted without consulting officials elsewhere in Delaware and without giving the people of Milford any indication of the impending desegregation. Most parents had not heard of the policy until their children returned from classes and said they now had black schoolmates.[60]

As soon as parents learned of the new policy, whites began a boycott of the public schools. By the third week in September 1954, two-thirds of the 1,500 white students in the Milford district were staying home, and sympathy strikes were occurring in other downstate school districts. More than a thousand parents signed a petition expressing their opposition to admitting blacks until the Supreme Court decided how and when desegregation should be established. The *Laurel State Register* said the boycotts would never have occurred "had it not been for the misguided thinking of a local board of education that the public need not be consulted even on so basic a decision as integration."[61]

A large wooden cross was set on fire across the street from the high school, and the integrating black students were threatened with bodily harm. Automobile caravans paraded through the town with homemade signs declaring "Our Schools Are Going to Pot" and "Get Them Out of Our Schools."[62] A telephone call to the Washington office of the National Association for the Advancement of White People brought to southern Delaware a thirty-four-year-old Floridian and former Marine Corps drummer by the name of Bryant W. Bowles.

Bowles was a drifting ne'er-do-well who would later be sent to prison in Texas for killing his brother-in-law. He possessed a talent for polemical invective, however, and his presence in southern Delaware undoubtedly inflamed public opinion against desegregation. Playing on a prevailing fear of internal subversion, Bowles maintained that the chief advocates of desegregation in Delaware were Jews of Russian extraction like Wilmington journalist Bill Frank and state attorney general H. Albert Young, whose family name had been Yanovich. They were "trying to shove the Negro down our throats," Bowles said, but "we're going to boot them out of the United States if we can."[63]

Bowles also took advantage of another prevailing fear, the great fear of miscegenation. One handbill featured a drawing of a black man kissing a white woman and asked, "Do you want your descendants to be Negroes?" Another declared that the Soviet Union was "laughing because she has a more deadly weapon than the atomic bomb. She knows our strength is in our white stock and that when she has mixed our blood with the Negro we are licked forever." Charles E. Boyce of Seaford spoke for many when he said it was naïve not to recognize that "the question of racial intermarriage is inevitably involved [in desegregation] and in the nature of things is bound to overshadow all other aspects of the problem."[64]

Public opinion in downstate Delaware was overwhelmingly against desegregation, with opposition expressed by all but 115 of the 10,052 people who voted in a series of unofficial referenda in fourteen downstate communities. Even many blacks were of the opinion that desegregation would heighten racial tension, jeopardize the jobs of black teachers, and deprive blacks of valuable community centers. A reporter who spent three days roaming about Kent and Sussex counties came to the conclusion that there would be bloodshed if integration was compelled. In certain parts of Sussex County, Thomas B. Malone observed, people were buying guns and storing ammunition and even engaging in target practice. In his columns for the *Wilmington Morning News,* Bill Frank conceded that the Milford Board of Education was "so far out in front" that it had lost contact with its local community. "Such 'leadership' is futile," Frank stated. The Milford board had gone about integration "stupidly, naively, and blindly." "The NAACP may say [Kent and Sussex counties] are ready for integration," Frank concluded. "It is wrong. And the Milford Board of Education . . . should have known that."[65]

With whites boycotting public schools and antiblack sentiment approaching the edge of violence, Governor J. Caleb Boggs decided that the basic need in Delaware was not for integration but for the preservation of order. He rejected the advice of integrationists, who wanted him to call out the National Guard to patrol the schools and protect black students, and of segregationists who demanded a denunciation of the way the Milford school board had mishandled the situation. Instead, Boggs played for time. He remained in his office, conferred with all parties, and urged everyone to remain calm. The governor personally accepted desegregation, but he was determined to prevent an incident from becoming an insurrection.[66]

The members of the Milford Board of Education resigned when Governor Boggs and the state Board of Education refused to give their full backing to the hasty desegregation. A new board was then elected and, after conferring with the governor and the state board, the ten black students were dropped from the rolls in Milford and sent to an all-black high school in Georgetown. At the same time Governor Boggs sought an advisory opinion from the Delaware State Supreme Court, which promptly held hearings on the situation and then, in February 1955, gave half a loaf to each side.[67] *Brown* was found to have nullified Delaware's segregation laws but not to require the immediate desegregation of public schools. The Supreme Court's opinion in *Brown* was "final," but it did not follow that black children had an immediate right to attend white schools. The Supreme Court had declared that blacks had a right to desegregated schooling but had deferred enforcing that right until it could hear additional arguments concerning practical problems. The "all deliberate speed" decision of *Brown II* was still some months in the future, and the Delaware judges thought it would be presumptuous to anticipate what the Supreme Court would require. "We can say only that when its decision is made, it may or may not accord immediate relief." In the meantime *Brown* did not require Milford to admit blacks forthwith to its high school. State regulations, however, did require local school boards to submit their plans to the state Board of Education. By acting unilaterally and in disregard of these regulations, the Milford board had exceeded its authority. As a consequence, the Delaware Supreme Court ruled, the admission of black students to Milford High School was "contrary to law."[68]

In the fall of 1954 the Delaware State Board of Education had asked local school boards to develop plans looking toward desegregation. One downstate community, Dover, came forward with a workable program in 1955. Others delayed for fear of "another Milford." It was at this point that blacks went to court once again. In a 1956 lawsuit, *Evans v. Buchanan,* a case that eventually became more famous in Delaware than *Brown,* they demanded immediate desegregation of seven school districts in Kent and Sussex counties. The first-named plaintiff was Brenda Evans, a nine-year-old schoolgirl from the town of Clayton. Her attorney was the ranking black member of Delaware's bar, the redoubtable Louis L. Redding.

The issue in *Evans v. Buchanan* was not desegregation, for in Delaware almost everyone accepted the validity of *Brown.* The basic question concerned where plans for desegregation should originate. The state Board of Education said that Delaware should follow the example of all other states, where the primary responsibility for desegregation rested with the local school boards.[69] Redding characterized this argument as "passing the buck," and for once the local school boards agreed. Given the state of public opinion, they said, it was not possible for individual communities to desegregate.[70]

There never was any doubt about where District Judge Paul Leahy stood on the question. During the trial he remarked that it was unconscionable for the state board to "sit back while the law isn't enforced." Declaring that the black's right to attend desegregated schools was "paramount" and that the state board had "general control and supervision" of all public schools, Judge Leahy ordered the state board to come up with a plan for statewide desegregation. In 1958 this decision was affirmed by the Third Circuit Court of Appeals.[71] In response to these court orders, Delaware developed a plan that provided for desegregation on a one-grade-a-year basis over a period of twelve years. The black plaintiffs objected to the plan,[72] but District Judge Caleb R. Layton, who inherited the case after Paul Leahy retired from the bench, approved Delaware's "stairstep" approach to desegregation.[73] However, on appeal, a divided panel of judges from the Third Circuit Court reversed Judge Layton. Rejecting the assumption that rapid desegregation would be disruptive, the court's majority observed that it was "common knowledge" that most blacks would "not seek integration even when offered the opportunity." Thus, the task imposed on Delaware was "not as difficult" as the state maintained.[74]

Even in downstate Delaware the feeling against desegregation was not as intransigent as that in the Deep South. Unlike the situation in Virginia and South Carolina, where the opposition was led by prominent public figures like Harry Byrd and James F. Byrnes, in Delaware the leading voice for segregation was that of an itinerant migrant from Florida. Bryant Bowles's chief assistants were the pastor of a small country church and a local dog warden. The most prominent public officials in Delaware, Governor J. Caleb Boggs and Senator John J. Williams, were convinced that desegregation was inevitable.

Williams, a downstate Republican who served in the U.S. Senate for twenty-four years, personally believed desegregation should have been left to the individual states. The Supreme Court had taken upon itself "too great a responsibility in determining so important a social question," he said. Nevertheless, the Court had spoken and, according to Williams, its decision was the law of the land. Unlike Strom Thurmond and James F. Byrnes of South Carolina, who insisted that states' rights could be protected if Congress restricted the jurisdiction of the federal judiciary, Williams maintained that decisions of the Supreme Court could be overruled only by constitutional amendment. With more than thirty states having abolished segregation by their own volition, Williams said it was "mathematically impossible" to obtain an amendment reversing *Brown*. It would be "sheer demagoguery," he said, "for any candidate for public office to campaign on the promise that if elected he can do something to nullify the Supreme Court decision."[75]

In 1961 the public schools in Kent and Sussex counties were desegregated under a freedom-of-choice plan that allowed students of both races to attend any school within their geographical district. As indicated in Table 12, this led to considerable amount of racial mixing, but some schools remained entirely black.

Unlike some educational leaders in other areas, who insisted that they had fulfilled their duty under *Brown* by allowing each student to attend the school of his choice, Delaware's state Board of Education was not satisfied with schools that were desegregated through freedom of choice. Nothing more was required by the federal court order, but Richard P. Gousha, who became state superintendent of schools in 1964, insisted that additional steps be taken to ensure that all students attended racially mixed schools in the district of their residence.[76]

Between 1964 and 1967 the state Board of Education affirmatively fostered integration by closing the remaining all-black schools. In the case of small elementary schools this was accomplished without much difficulty, but a problem arose with regard to phasing out the all-black William C. Jason High School in Sussex County. Since the facilities at Jason were, according to Superintendent Gousha, "far superior" to the facilities at the white high schools in Sussex County, many blacks understandably objected to having their children transferred to predominantly white schools with inferior equipment. Nevertheless, most local blacks eventually came around and supported the plan, even at the expense of giving up their major community center. The NAACP played a part in persuading them to accept the change, and they were also mollified by a plan to upgrade the Jason buildings and make them the heart of the Sussex County campus of the Delaware Technical and Community College.[77]

When Delaware's last all-black school was closed in 1967, students throughout the state, regardless of race, attended biracial schools in the districts of their residence. Most Delawareans thought desegregation had been achieved, and so did the federal Office of Civil Rights, which informed Superintendent Gousha in the spring of 1967 that Delaware had become the first southern or border state to have eradicated the dual system and to have come into full compliance with the Civil Rights Act of 1964.[78]

Later it would be said that federal assurances of compliance amounted to little if they were dated before the Supreme Court's *Green* decision of 1968. Louis Lucas, who would become the principal attorney for the black plaintiffs in the later stages of *Evans v. Buchanan,* argued that any certification granted before 1968 indicated only compliance with standards that accepted freedom of choice. Superintendent Gousha insisted, however, that officials in the Department of Justice and in HEW "knew we were going beyond [freedom of choice], and they were pleased that we were going be-

TABLE 12. Enrollments by Race,
Kent and Sussex Counties, 1963–1964

	White	Black
Kent County		
19 school buildings with black & white students	8,209	1,689
5 school buildings with only white students	326	–
7 school buildings with only black students	–	260
Totals	8,535	1,949
Sussex County		
11 school buildings with black and white students	3,871	213
9 school buildings with only white students	2,440	–
24 school buildings with only black students	–	2,685
Totals	6,311	2,898

Source: Delaware Department of Public Instruction, Annual Report (1963–1964), 60.

yond. . . . We had a working relationship with the Federal Government that they knew what we were doing, [and] they were in accord with it."[79] In the early 1960s freedom of choice was acceptable to the federal courts, but in Delaware the state Board of Education discovered that it was not providing biracial education in every racially mixed geographical district. The state board consequently took affirmative steps to phase out one-race schools and to make sure that all students from given areas attended the same schools. When this was done, they said, they had brought Delaware's schools into compliance with the Constitution and the civil rights laws.

Desegregation in downstate Delaware was not without minor difficulties, but on the whole the process went well. Surprisingly, in light of the experience elsewhere in Delaware and throughout much of the nation, the desegregation in Kent and Sussex counties was also quite stable. The desegregated schools there were not as highly regarded as their counterparts in suburban New Castle County, but there was no massive white flight and resegregation. Black enrollment increased by about 8 percent as white enrollment declined by 26 percent, but this resulted from a substantial difference in birth rates. Very few whites downstate responded to desegregation by pulling up stakes or sending their children to private schools.

The stability of desegregation was related to the social structure of the downstate white community. Kent and Sussex counties were predominantly rural, with only one city (Dover) boasting a population of more than 10,000, and only two other towns with as many as 5,000 people. There were no large, predominantly white suburbs in the region. Most of the whites were scattered over the countryside and found employment as farmers or laborers; they did not appear to place as much emphasis on academic education as the scientists, technicians, and business managers of New Castle County.

There were some professional and managerial families, of course, but the proportion of such people was much smaller than in Wilmington and its suburbs.

Delaware's desegregated schools of the 1960s were organized geographically. The students who lived in various districts were assigned, irrespective of race, to neighborhood schools. In Kent and Sussex counties this led to relatively balanced racial enrollments in the public schools. Conversely, in New Castle County, where racial separation was a striking aspect of the residential landscape, the schools reflected the racial imbalance of their neighborhoods.

With half of Delaware's black students enrolled in the Wilmington public schools, most Delawareans of course recognized that their schools were racially imbalanced. They nevertheless insisted that the state's public schools had been desegregated. Desegregation did not depend on the number or percentage of black and white children enrolled in particular schools, they said, but on whether there was any policy or concerted effort to use race as a means of preventing children from attending schools in their districts. Delawareans said race had ceased to be a method of assigning students, and they noted that in 1967 HEW had pointed to Delaware as the first border state that had "completely eradicated the dual system." [80] In the opinion of most citizens, blacks as well as whites, by 1968 desegregation in Delaware was a fait accompli.

IV

The Supreme Court extended the meaning of desegregation in 1968 when it converted *Brown*'s prohibition of racial discrimination into an affirmative duty to integrate. In *Green v. New Kent County* the high court held that racially neutral methods of assigning pupils did not constitute desegregation unless they led to relatively balanced mixing. Racial imbalance was said to make schools racially identifiable and to suggest that students of different races should attend different schools. Writing for the Court, Justice William Brennan said, "It was such dual systems that . . . *Brown I* held unconstitutional and . . . *Brown II* held must be abolished." In a fundamental way *Green* represented an important redefinition. As Justice William H. Rehnquist has noted,

> To require that a genuinely "dual" system be disestablished, in the sense that the assignment of a child to a particular school is not made to depend on his race, is one thing. To require that school boards affirmatively undertake to achieve racial mixing in schools where such mixing is not achieved in sufficient degree by neutrally drawn boundary lines is quite obviously something else. [81]

In Delaware the primary initiator of the lawsuit for metropolitan dispersion was a white mother who was deeply disturbed by what she considered the decline of Wilmington. A lifelong resident of the city, Marilyn Harwick was raised on 36th Street, almost within sight of P.S. du Pont High School, from which she graduated in 1948. After her marriage to R.D. Harwick, an engineer and hospital planner, she settled in a comfortable brick colonial house on 37th Street, where the couple raised a family of four children.

At first desegregation went well, as the Harwick children made interracial friendships in the predominantly white Harlan Elementary School. Then, between 1966 and 1970, the years when their oldest child was enrolled at P.S. du Pont, the black percentage of the high school student body increased from 33.6 to 76.5. Many of the black students came from public housing projects and, according to Mrs. Harwick, who observed the situation at first hand as a substitute teacher, some of them presented academic and disciplinary problems the likes of which "P.S." had never previously confronted. "There's no doubt about it," she recalled. "Academic standards were declining as the black enrollment increased. The other problem was discipline — not just minor infractions but serious matters. Many of the white teachers were intimidated by the black students."[82]

By 1970 the situation at "P.S." had deteriorated to the point where the Harwicks no longer considered the school suitable for their children. R.D. Harwick rented a house outside Wilmington, and the younger children attended suburban Mount Pleasant High School. "We felt guilty about abandoning the city," Marilyn Harwick said, "but we did it anyway. Our children have only one chance at education." Yet Mrs. Harwick continued to reside at the family's home in Wilmington. "My husband and I hate the suburbs," she explained. "We like the diversity of our neighborhood and of city life." Moreover, by the late 1960s property values in Wilmington had fallen so low that they could not get a fair price for their primary house.[83]

After the race riots of 1968, racial tension rose to the point where many wondered if Wilmington would become a predominantly black ghetto. The population of New Castle County soared between 1950 and 1970, from 218,879 to 352,318. But the total population of Wilmington declined from 110,356 to 80,386, and the number of blacks living in the city increased from 17,080 to 35,450.[84]

White residents developed a number of proposals to stop the spread of the ghetto. In an effort to discourage white flight, the Harwicks enlisted the aid of Mayor Harry Haskell and secured a city ordinance that forbade homeowners from displaying "For Sale" signs. They also persuaded the board of realtors and some corporations not to steer professional employees away from the city and into the suburbs. The Harwicks' efforts to place more public housing projects in the suburbs were less successful. So was their suggestion that an exclusively academic public high school be established in Wilmington—a proposal that school superintendent Gene Geisert rejected on the grounds that any such school would be "elitist."[85]

Unsuccessful in their effort to obtain a city school that would attract professional people, the Harwicks turned to the possibility of consolidating the Wilmington public schools with the predominantly white schools elsewhere in New Castle County. This had been one of the major recommendations of a team of New York University researchers who had studied the Wilmington schools in 1967. "To a significant degree integrated education has been achieved," the New Yorkers reported. "However, population changes and other demographic factors . . . have made it next to impossible to maintain proper racial balance in the schools." Reflecting a point of view that gained wide currency after the race riots of the late 1960s, one sociologist at the University of Delaware said the situation in Wilmington was so desperate that the only solution might be to "spread the problem—make it small enough to be manageable."[86]

Most black leaders were understandably suspicious of metropolitan consolidation. They thought the problem was white racism, not the ignorance and uncivilized behavior of many blacks. Beyond this, they wondered if dispersion was not intended to destroy a new power base blacks had secured in 1970 when they, for the first time, gained a majority on the Wilmington Board of Education. Community activist William "Hicks" Anderson thought it was "preposterous" and even racist to suggest that the school system in the state's largest city should be dismantled. "That hasn't happened anywhere else in the country," he maintained. Thomas K. Minter, the black superintendent of schools, was more favorably disposed toward desegregation but noted that dispersion would leave blacks "bereft of a board of education, bereft of an educational identity, [and without] a school board just as they have gained some degree of control over it."[87]

Noting that the Harwicks had transferred their own children to suburban public schools, some blacks thought the white couple were primarily interested in finding an inexpensive and trouble-free way to enable white children from the city to attend suburban schools. Marilyn Harwick conceded that throughout the 1970s and into the 1980s, most blacks in Wilmington were cool to the idea of metropolitan desegregation.[88]

By contrast, many of the Harwicks' white friends and acquaintances enthusiastically endorsed the idea of dispersion. Janet Greenwell, the president of the Wilmington PTA and a member of the Wilmington Board of Education, was a case in point. Having transferred a child to the private Friends School "because by then academic standards at P.S. du Pont had fallen so low," Greenwell shared many of the Harwicks' concerns. Like the

Harwicks, Greenwell and her husband had no desire to move to the suburbs, which they regarded as "sterile, monotonous, and boring." They had also lived through the cycle of desegregation and resegretation in Wilmington and "just could not understand why the leaders of the community allowed it to happen." They were ready to take action to reverse the trend. So was Phyllis Ploener, a Wilmington mother who had transferred her daughter from a public school to the private Tatnall School.[89]

Early in 1970 Phyllis Ploener and Marilyn Harwick asked Gerald Kandler, Irving Morris, and Joseph Rosenthal, three lawyers known in Delaware for their work on behalf of the American Civil Liberties Union (ACLU), if there was "something the courts could do to improve the quality of our children's education." Keenly interested in civil rights, Kandler, Morris, and Rosenthal recognized that the growing concentration of blacks in the city of Wilmington was inconsistent with the Supreme Court's evolving definition of segregation. The lawyers nevertheless told Harwick and Ploener that for tactical reasons it would be desirable to have black plaintiffs so that a petition for dispersion could proceed under an open court order from *Evans v. Buchanan*, the 1956 lawsuit that had speeded desegregation in Kent and Sussex counties. The plaintiffs would then enjoy the advantage of portraying Delaware as a recalcitrant southern state willfully maintaining its traditional system of racial segregation.[90]

Irving Morris then got in touch with Louis L. Redding. He knew the grand old man of Delaware civil rights was too old to play a leading role in the protracted litigation that was impending, but no other lawyer could more effectively enable the plaintiffs to appear to combat racism while in fact pleading that students be assigned on the basis of race. If Redding joined in the case, dispersion could seem just another remedy a patient judiciary must impose on an obdurate state. The initiators of the litigation also hoped that Redding would help them locate black plaintiffs, which was "no easy task," Marilyn Harwick recalled.[91]

These hopes were not misplaced. Shortly after being contacted, Redding visited the home of Jeanne Q. Lewis, who had been a secretary in his law office during the 1950s. Mrs. Lewis had since become a schoolteacher and was married to Clifton Lewis, the head football coach at Howard High School. Their oldest child had graduated from P.S. du Pont High School before enrolling at Princeton, but their younger two children had been sent to private schools, for the Lewises believed that academic standards were declining as more blacks from the housing projects enrolled in the Wilmington public schools. Like the white initiators of the lawsuit, the Lewises had no desire to move to the suburbs.[92]

The Lewises did not comment on the legal issues raised by *Brown* and *Green*, but they were distressed by the fact that most students in Wilmington were black while most pupils in the rest of New Castle County were white. They especially wanted their son Tony "to get out and meet other people." Otherwise "fear and suspicion" would grow up about white people, whom he would have to work with some day. Coach Lewis expressed concern that his son might become a black militant if he did not have the opportunity to make white friends. Beyond this, the Lewises believed that their children would benefit from academic competition with suburban youths. Mrs. Lewis said that schools that enrolled predominantly black students could not "provide the competition, the variety of course offerings, that you would get in a school where you have more highly motivated children."[93]

Lillian Richardson, a third black plaintiff, was separated from her husband and the mother of eight children who had attended the Wilmington public schools. Far removed from the Lewises in socioeconomic standing, she shared their belief that public education in Wilmington was inadequate "because, No. 1, of the racial composition which is predominantly black." A fourth plaintiff, Wilber C. Carr, was a graduate of Wilberforce and Columbia and had taught in the public schools since 1953. Before a divorce, Carr had lived in the suburbs and at various times his children were enrolled in both the suburban and Wilmington public schools. In his opinion, neither situation was desirable for blacks. In the predominantly white suburbs, he said, the teachers often ignored black students, who also suffered from feeling "socially unwelcome" and from failing to see black students and teachers in positions of leadership. Things were not satisfactory in the predominantly black Wilmington schools, however, for there, standards had fallen to the point where students were not challenged academically.[94]

In their original petition for the plaintiffs, Redding and Morris presented statistics to show that the public schools in Wilmington "are in many instances almost entirely composed of black pupils, whereas the public schools in districts in suburban New Castle County, with few exceptions, are almost entirely composed of white pupils." Because of this enrollment pattern, Redding and Morris said Delaware had failed to establish the sort of desegregated schools that *Brown* and *Green* required. They knew, however, that there was nothing illegal if people chose to live in districts that were inhabited primarily by members of their race. To obtain legal redress it would be necessary to demonstrate, or at least contend, that racial imbalance in Delaware was the result of unconstitutional state action. It could be argued plausibly that blacks would benefit if they were dispersed so as to constitute about 20 percent of the enrollment at each school. But the Fourteenth Amendment did not avowedly enact the sociology of James S. Coleman. A legal rationalization for dispersion would have to be devised.[95]

Constructing the legal argument would not be easy. In *Green v. New Kent County* the Supreme Court had required racial balance in a small rural district, and in *Swann v. Charlotte-Mecklenburg* (1971) the Court had approved busing as a method for achieving balance in a unified metropolitan district. Yet neither case addressed a key question at issue in Delaware — the matter of racial imbalance among independent school districts. When the Delaware plaintiffs filed their petition in 1971, there was no established constitutional obligation to achieve racial balance across district lines. The *Briggs* dictum had been set aside in terms of intradistrict mixing, but it was still good law between districts: "The Constitution . . . does not require integration. It merely forbids discrimination."[96]

In the years since 1954 blacks had concentrated in Wilmington as whites had gravitated toward the surrounding suburban and rural areas. The same pattern was evident in most American cities, however, and informed observers thought racially discriminatory state actions contributed only minimally to the trend. Commenting on the situation in Richmond, Virginia, the Fourth Circuit Court of Appeals declared, in language that also applied to Wilmington:

> The root causes of the concentration of blacks in the inner cities of America are simply not known. . . . What little action, if any, the [suburban officials] may seem to have taken to keep blacks out is slight indeed compared to the myriad reasons, economic, political and social, for the concentration of blacks . . . and does not support the conclusion that it has been invidious state action which has resulted in the racial composition of the . . . school districts.[97]

The need to demonstrate that the racial disparity in school enrollments was the result of discriminatory state action was only the first of several legal difficulties the plaintiffs faced. Beyond this lay the necessity of grappling with such concepts as white flight, discriminatory intent, and incremental segregative effect, at a time when appellate courts were in the process of revising the law. None of the plaintiffs had the financial resources to pay for the sort of legal battle that was impending, and Redding and Morris doubted that they had sufficient expertise to deal with such difficult questions in an area where the law was especially abstruse and where judicial standards were evolving and changing.

After making inquiries about civil rights lawyers, Morris chose Louis R. Lucas, a young attorney who had previously worked in the Civil Rights Division of the U.S. Department of Justice. Born in New Orleans and educated at Tulane University, Lucas was a southern liberal who was deeply committed to integration and who had argued for metropolitan dispersion in lawsuits involving Detroit, Dayton, Columbus, and other cities. He had not won every case and some of his early victories were later modified or overturned on appeal, but Lucas had developed a reputation as a modern David who would slay the redneck Goliaths. He knew the desegregation cases intimately, had assembled a team of academic witnesses who were willing to testify anywhere, and was adept at playing on the sympathies of judges who were looking for an opportunity to impose social reform.

Lucas was willing to take command of the Delaware desegregation case for little more than expenses, but even these were hard to come by. Fearing that black adults would lose control over the Wilmington Board of Education and that black children would gain nothing from being bused all over the county, the local NAACP initially refused to have anything to do with the lawsuit. The national office of the organization was no more forthcoming. Jack Greenberg, the director of the NAACP's Legal Defense Fund, had cooperated with Louis Redding and Irving Morris in earlier phases of the Delaware desegregation litigation, but he was convinced that their new petition was "a loser for certain."[98]

Rebuffed by the NAACP, Morris approached Victor F. Battaglia, a friend who was then serving as city solicitor in Wilmington. Although Battaglia had attended Catholic schools in the city, Morris knew that the solicitor shared many of the concerns that had prompted Marilyn Harwick to initiate the new lawsuit. Like Harwick, Battaglia had lived through the cycle of desegregation and resegregation. He was born in 1933 in an almost all-white, predominantly Italian neighborhood in West Center City. By the time he was ten years old the neighborhood was well integrated, and by the time he graduated from high school it was all black. Battaglia feared that unless something was done to turn things around, all of Wilmington would soon follow the same course.[99]

Working through Battaglia, Morris then got in touch with the mayor of Wilmington, Harry Haskell. Haskell knew that property values in the city had plummeted to the point where, despite the highest real estate tax rates in Delaware, bankruptcy had been avoided only by imposing a tax that required all residents and those suburbanites who worked in the city to render 1.5 percent of their wages to Wilmington. Mayor Haskell recognized that metropolitan consolidation would probably lead to a single school tax throughout northern New Castle County, and he calculated that Wilmington would benefit tangibly if suburban tax rates were increased by 20 percent while Wilmington's rate declined by 36 percent (as happened after the federal courts required dispersion in 1978). In the 1960s and 1970s, property values had soared in suburban New Castle County, where parents could send their children to well-regarded public schools. If Wilmington's troublesome black youths were dispersed while whites entered the city as exchange students, the suburbs would lose their advantage and the stage would be set for a renaissance of property values in Wilmington.[100]

With these considerations in mind, the Haskell administration urged the Wilmington Board of Education to finance the plaintiffs' court costs. The four blacks on the board, like most blacks in Wilmington, had misgivings about metropolitan desegregation, but the three whites were in favor— two of them having participated in some of the parlor discussions where Marilyn Harwick had first broached the subject. If the support of even one black board member could be secured, the lawsuit could begin in earnest.

Finding the essential black vote was no easy matter, for the board postponed a decision and discussed the question extensively for six months. Hermania Garrett, the daughter of a local minister and the director of a day nursery, took particular exception to the economic argument for desegregation. The suit had nothing to do with improving the education of black children, she said. It was simply a clever way to reduce tax rates in Wilmington. Robert Mitchell, who worked for Du Pont, agreed with Garrett and also stressed that blacks would suffer if they lost control of their only real base of political patronage and power. He questioned whether the white liberals had the best interests of black children at heart and said he did not want his children to attend schools that were less than 30 percent black. The two other black board members—Lloyd Casson, an Episcopal priest, and Roy Wagstaff, who worked for Hercules (a chemical company)—shared these misgivings but were also committed to integration and thought metropolitan consolidation would be good for Wilmington. "It was hard going to get their support," recalled white board member Janet Greenwell. "They gave it very reluctantly." In June 1972, by a vote of 5 to 2, the Wilmington Board of Education finally decided to finance the lawsuit. By 1980 the board had paid legal fees of $380,109.[101]

In explaining its decision to intervene in the litigation, the board of education naturally stressed educational concerns and made no mention of economics. According to the board, there were two major reasons why "racially disproportionate schools are by their very nature inferior." In the "affective domain," predominantly black schools failed to inculcate the social skills that were necessary for easy interaction with middle-class whites, while predominantly white schools were said to instill a superiority complex that made it difficult for their graduates to appreciate the important cultural contributions of blacks.

The board also suggested that Wilmington's black students would do better academically if they were freed from the negative influences of their neighborhoods and taught in predominantly middle-class schools. Referring to James S. Coleman's famous study *Equality of Educational Opportunity,* Superintendent Thomas K. Minter asserted that "it has been shown that in those classrooms where there is a broad mixture of students, the majority students continue to perform as they did before while minority students tend to improve on their past performance, thus narrowing the gap between the two." [102]

The bedrock of the plaintiffs' complaint was that they were dissatisfied with the blackness of Wilmington, but their legal argument stressed that the state was significantly responsible for the demographic imbalance in New Castle County. They faulted the state not just for what it had done but also for failing to take affirmative action to eradicate an array of traditional southern "customs, usages, policies and practices." Delaware had not insisted that public housing be dispersed throughout the suburbs and, prior to passage of open housing legislation in 1968, it had not prohibited racial discrimination in the sale or rental of private housing. It never publicly repudiated the 1936 Federal Housing Administration mortgage underwriting manual, which advocated racially homogeneous neighborhoods. It also paid part of the cost of busing students to private schools, thereby augmenting the racial imbalance between Wilmington and the suburbs. All this, according to the plaintiffs, had the effect of perpetuating the segregation of the days when Delaware had sanctioned racially restrictive deeds, prohibited interracial marriages, and generally practiced racial discrimination. [103]

The plaintiffs recognized that the same could be said of many other states, but they maintained that the Delaware state legislature had committed one additional "flagrant act" which stood out as "the ugly pinnacle of State action which perpetuated racial segregation in the public schools." In the Educational Advancement Act of 1968 the legislature gave the state Board of Education for one year the authority to reorganize and consolidate school districts without holding a referendum in each district, a practice that had been required by a longstanding Delaware law. The legislation also provided that districts consolidated during that year should have enrollments of between 1,900 and 12,000 students. "As a result of this act, the number of districts was reduced from 49 to 26, continuing the policy of consolidation begun in 1919, when there were 450 school districts in Delaware." Three of the newly consolidated districts were in northern Delaware, but most of the consolidation in 1969 occurred downstate. [104]

Because the Wilmington public schools already enrolled more than 12,000 pupils, they were prevented from joining with other districts during the year of grace—as were two large suburban districts, Newark and Alfred I. du Pont. The plaintiffs complained that the Educational Advancement Act "was designed to perpetuate and has in fact perpetuated [a] racially discriminatory dual school system." It had "as its natural, probable and foreseeable consequence, the drawing of school district lines so as to circumscribe the overwhelmingly black Wilmington area into an identifiable black school district." It was "purposely taken to lock in the . . . 'threat' represented by black children and their parents." It "re-established the state-mandated pattern of segregated schools in New Castle County." [105]

The plaintiffs' argument was that Delaware, as a southern state, had an affirmative duty to dismantle the racial separation it had required prior to *Brown*. It was not enough that black and white children now attended school together if they lived in the same area. That satisfied the *Briggs* interpretation, but it did not meet the requirement set forth in *Green*. "This case arises in a State having a long history of maintaining two sets of schools," the plaintiffs observed. Since the question of desegregation was last before the district court in 1962, the *Briggs* dictum had been laid to rest, and the Supreme Court had established that southern states must take affirmative action to eradicate the last vestiges of segregation. [106]

However sincere the plaintiffs' contention, their evidence was far from incontrovertible. The FHA policies alluded to were terminated in 1949, and racially restricted covenants and marital prohibitions had not been enforced in New Castle County for a generation. The national Congress did not outlaw racial discrimination in the sale and rental of private housing until 1968, the same year that Delaware enacted an open housing law. The allegation that subsidies for private school transportation contributed to racial imbalance was purely speculative. Evidence presented at the trial indicated that in 1967, prior to any such subsidy, there were 11,257 suburban residents and 7,693 Wilmington residents attending nonpublic schools. By 1973, there were 10,009 suburban residents and 6,526 Wilmington residents attending private schools. Whatever assistance the subsidy might have offered to children who were attending private schools, it did not aggravate racial imbalance by siphoning students out of the public schools. As for the suburbanites' rejection of public housing, this was a nationwide phenomenon and one that, according to no less an authority than the U.S. Supreme Court, was influenced by nonracial considerations such as preference for open space and unwillingness to allow real estate to be used for nontaxable purposes. [107]

With regard to the Educational Advancement Act, the sponsors of the measure in the state legislature maintained that it was intended to facilitate the consolidation of small, rural districts that had too few students to operate a high school. Prior to 1967, when the last all-black schools were closed in Delaware, educators had focused their attention on desegregation. With that problem seemingly behind them, they turned in 1968 to the issue of consolidation to enhance educational quality and efficiency. "We took it for granted that Delaware's schools were integrated, and we were trying only to improve the quality of education . . . in the poorer, smaller districts, most of them rural," recalled Clarice Heckert, the chairman of the House Education Committee. Hearings on the Educational Advancement Act were held throughout Delaware, and "at no time was integration or racial composition discussed or any figures having to do with race called to our attention. . . . It was taken for granted that integration of the schools had been completed."[108]

The Educational Advancement Act did not change the boundaries of the Wilmington public schools, which had been coterminous with the city of Wilmington since 1905. Nor did it prevent Wilmington from coalescing with other school districts. It simply exempted Wilmington (and two other school districts) from the temporary interval when this could be done without a referendum. The 12,000-student limitation (which also applied for only one year) was included in the education act because Wilmington had traditionally been the largest school district in a small state, and because in the mid-1960s there was much talk about the importance of community involvement in the public schools.[109]

In 1968 no one of prominence in Delaware wanted to merge any of the larger school districts. The Wilmington Board of Education had not endorsed the 1967 New York University recommendation for metropolitan consolidation, nor had any black organization in Delaware. All of Wilmington's representatives in the state legislature, including four blacks, voted for the Educational Advancement Act. Without their support the measure would have failed of passage, for it survived a crippling amendment by only a single vote. Opposition to the measure was centered in southern Delaware, where many people feared a loss of local control and opposed consolidation with traditional rivals.[110]

A divided federal district court nevertheless held that "to a significant extent . . . the net outmigration of white population and increase of city black population in the last two decades, resulted . . . from assistance, encouragement, and authorization by government policies." The court's majority conceded in a footnote that private fears and prejudices had contributed to the white flight, but they essentially endorsed the plaintiffs' argument. "Since *Brown* governmental authorities have contributed to the racial isolation of city from suburbs. . . . [They] have elected to place their 'power, property, and prestige' behind the white exodus from Wilmington . . . [G]overnmental authorities are responsible to a significant degree for the increasing disparity . . . between Wilmington and its suburbs. . . ."[111]

The district court did not, however, find a racially discriminatory purpose. Conceding that the focus of the Educational Advancement Act had been on "small, weak, ineffective school districts" and that all Wilmington legislators, black and white, had voted for the measure, the court found that "the record does not demonstrate that a significant purpose of the Educational Advancement Act was to foster or perpetuate discrimination through school reorganization." The court nevertheless concluded that the act had a discriminatory effect and that this effect was a constitutional violation that could be remedied only by requiring mandatory busing for racial balance throughout the public schools of northern New Castle County. [112]

Many people were stunned by the court's decision, thinking that the public schools in New Castle County had been desegregated promptly after receipt of the Supreme Court's order in *Brown*. There was, to be sure, a disproportionate concentration of blacks in Wilmington, but this was not the result of discriminatory state action but of economic and demographic forces and of private housing choices. Breaking sharply from this view of Delaware's recent history, the district court found that the formerly segregated schools had never been completely dismantled but had been perpetuated by the Educational Advancement Act and the other contested "customs, usages, policies and practices." The court's findings were based on such a strained reading of the historical record that they cannot be accounted for except on the basis of the judges' earnest desire to solve a pressing social problem. Coming in the wake of the Wilmington race riots, the decision in *Evans v. Buchanan* was intended to turn back the tide of urban blight and black violence.

Since the plaintiffs in *Evans v. Buchanan* had challenged the constitutionality of a state law, a three-judge district court was required to hear the case. This gave rise to perhaps the key development in the litigation — the appointment of John J. Gibbons to the panel of judges. Because of his strong convictions and forceful personality, and because of his superior position as a circuit court judge, Gibbons dominated the local district court. A graduate of St. Benedict's prep, Holy Cross College, and the Harvard law school, Gibbons had no close personal familiarity with public schools. Yet as a native of Newark, New Jersey, he had seen how black immigration and white flight could transform a thriving city into a bleak ghetto. In 1968 he had also served on a special state commission investigating the Newark race riots. That experience, according to one of his associates, "sensitized the judge to the social, economic and educational problems troubling urban areas." Gibbons's friends knew him as an outspoken, socially conscious liberal. So did lawyers for the defense. After reading Gibbons's earlier opinions in civil rights cases, they knew he was likely to decide against them. "Gibbons had it in his mind all along that racial imbalance was a condition that the State had an affirmative constitutional obligation to change," one lawyer maintained. [113]

Joining Gibbons on the bench were Caleb R. Layton and Caleb M. Wright, Jr., two federal district judges who were natives of southern Delaware. A graduate of Phillips Andover Academy, Princeton University, and the University of Pennsylvania law school, Layton recognized that *Brown* had been superseded by *Green,* but he thought the plaintiffs' contentions in *Evans v. Buchanan* were "unsupported by real credible evidence." He thought there was "no definitive explanation for the huge tide of black immigration into the nation's cities, and the white flight therefrom" and that the plaintiffs' argument to the contrary "fell flat."[114]

The third judge, Caleb Wright, was a graduate of the University of Delaware and the Yale law school. When the Delaware desegregation case was last before the district court in 1962, Wright had rejected Louis Redding's argument that school districts should be gerrymandered to promote racial mixing. In *Brown* the Supreme Court's interpretation of the equal protection clause held only that blacks and whites could not be separated *solely* because of race, Wright explained. "If races are separated because of geographic or transportation considerations or other similar criteria, it is no concern of the Federal Constitution." Desegregation law had evolved since 1962 — some would say it had been inverted — and court watchers had observed a progressively liberal drift in Wright's opinions. From the outset it was clear that Wright would be the swing vote on the three-judge panel. Much of what was said in court was directed at Caleb Wright.[115]

In the court's first opinion, in 1974, judges Layton and Wright held that Wilmington had failed to eradicate the last vestiges of racial segregation in its schools. The basis for this finding was that five schools in predominantly black neighborhoods had black enrollments of at least 91 percent during the period from 1956 to 1973. Since the black portion of the total school enrollment did not reach 90 percent until the 1970s, the court concluded that Wilmington's optional transfer program had fostered the sort of intradistrict racial imbalance that *Green* had proscribed. The remedy for that sort of constitutional violation did not satisfy the plaintiffs, however, for it required only that the few remaining white students be spread more evenly through the overwhelmingly black public schools of Wilmington. Judges Layton and Wright initially deferred decision on whether the Educational Advancement Act and the customs of Delaware were responsible for the racial imbalance that existed in New Castle County.[116]

In a strongly worded dissent, Judge Gibbons maintained that racial balance should not be limited to the city of Wilmington. He though it was of crucial significance that Delaware was a southern state that had formally segregated its students at the time of *Brown.* The southern states, he wrote, "reacted to *Brown II* by assuming that some formally neutral pupil placement arrangement . . . would satisfy the Supreme Court's mandate." Nevertheless, in *Green* it was established that "the mere removal of the legal requirement, or even the formal adoption of racially neutral criteria, is insufficient compliance with the fourteenth amendment. States like Delaware have the affirmative duty to establish a unitary school system in which all vestiges of the formerly legally required racial segregation have been eliminated root and branch." It did not matter whether the Educational Advancement Act and other state policies were intended to promote a pattern of racially imbalanced congregation. "The presence or absence of a benign legislative motive is not relevant to our inquiry." "The test is effect not motivation." "If the effect of the provision fixing the boundaries of Wilmington is to prevent desegregation of white schools outside the city and black schools within, we need look no further." [117]

After considering the case for several months, Caleb Wright broke with Caleb Layton and joined John Gibbons in a second opinion that required metropolitan consolidation in northern New Castle County. Because of the persistence of racially imbalanced public schools in Wilmington after 1954, and because of the state's subsequent failure to take affirmative action against the remaining vestiges of segregation, Wright decided that Delaware had failed to provide "racial integration in the proper sense of the word." [118]

A problem was presented, however, by the Supreme Court's decision in *Milliken v. Bradley,* a Detroit desegregation case that was decided two weeks after Layton and Wright had released their initial opinion but before Wright endorsed Gibbons's point of view. In *Milliken* the Supreme Court had censured the lower federal judges for requiring a metropolitan plan simply because a plan that was limited to Detroit "would not produce the racial balance which they perceived as desirable." Racial balance was not required as such but only as a remedy for unconstitutional actions, and dispersion should not be required of separate school districts unless there had been interdistrict racial discrimination. "The mere fact of different racial composition in contiguous districts does not itself imply or constitute a violation of the Equal Protection Clause." The Supreme Court also indicated that the Constitution did not require more of the South than of other regions, and it cautioned that judicial remedies for unconstitutional racial discrimination should do no more than "restore the victims of discriminatory conduct to the position they would have occupied in the absence of such conduct." [119]

If the principles of *Milliken* had been applied in Delaware, nothing like racial balance would have been achieved throughout New Castle County. Judge Wright had belatedly joined Judge Gibbons in believing it was wrong to have predominantly black city schools surrounded by predominantly white suburban schools, but this morality could not properly be imposed unless Wilmington could be distinguished from Detroit.

In one respect this was easy to do. To get a 75 percent white majority in Detroit, blacks had to be dispersed through three counties and fifty-four school districts with a total enrollment of 780,000 students. In Wilmington, by contrast, an 80–20 white majority could be achieved by busing only the 80,000 students who lived in that portion of New Castle County that lay to the north of the Chesapeake and Delaware Canal. Yet the size of the different regions was not supposed to be of legal importance. As Judge Layton observed in a dissenting opinion, "*Milliken* is not a rule of size; it is a rule of law." [120]

The prospects for dispersion were further dimmed because judges Gibbons, Wright, and Layton, like the trial judge in Detroit, found no unconstitutional racial discrimination in any of the suburban school districts. The only hope for a metropolitan remedy seemed to hinge on the finding that the state of Delaware had been significantly responsible for the pattern of racial separation. The problem with this was that the Supreme Court, in *Milliken,* had ruled against metropolitan dispersion in an area where the district court had found the state of Michigan guilty of purposeful acts that created or aggravated segregation in the Detroit schools. In Delaware, by contrast, judges Gibbons and Wright had not found the state guilty of intentional discrimination and had based their finding on the effect of state laws. [121]

The lawyers for the suburban school districts and for the State Department of Public Instruction naturally took hope from the Supreme Court's ruling in *Milliken.* If *Brown* and *Green* were watersheds, *Milliken* seemed to mark the water's edge. It said that the purpose of desegregation was to correct the racial separation that had resulted from official discrimination and that dispersion could be required only in districts that had been found guilty of constitutional violations. Since in Delaware, as in Michigan, the suburban school districts had not been found guilty, it seemed that the remedy must be limited to the center city school district that had been found at fault. "There is in this case no inter-district violation which the Supreme Court held to be the *sine qua non* of inter-district relief," a lawyer for Delaware maintained. If the decision of judges Gibbons and Wright were not reversed, the federal judiciary would "condone the proposition that the people of Delaware live under a different Constitution than those of Michigan." [122]

The case for Delaware was initially handled by Alfred Avins, a constitutional specialist who was organizing a new law school in Delaware. Avins was an indefatigable worker and the author of several law review articles on the history of the Fourteenth Amendment. He was as well versed on the legalities of desegregation as anyone in Delaware, but he was so busy with his fledgling law school that he did not have time for a protracted lawsuit. Moreover, as a newcomer to Delaware he had not established the political connections that would entitle him to be chief counsel in a case where legal fees would ultimately amount to hundreds of thousands of dollars.

In 1973 William Prickett replaced Avins as chief counsel for the defense. Prickett was a Harvard law graduate and an experienced trial lawyer who was familiar with Delaware Governor Russell Peterson. He had not worked with civil rights cases before but was fortunate to have the assistance of a hard-working young graduate of the University of Virginia law school, Mason E. Turner, Jr. On appeal, Philip B. Kurland also joined the defense team. A professor of constitutional law at the University of Chicago, Kurland was an articulate advocate of judicial restraint and was widely recognized as one of the nation's leading authorities on the legalities of desegregation. It was thought that he would be paticularly helpful in arguing before the Supreme Court, which now included four Nixon-appointed justices who supposedly favored strict construction and who were known to admire Kurland.

The Supreme Court gave the defense still more reason for hope when it emphasized, in *Washington v. Davis* (1976), that policies must be intended to discriminate, as well as have a racially disproportionate impact, before there could be a finding of unconstitutional racial discrimination. Although *Washington* involved police department personnel tests, the Supreme Court stressed that in school desegregation cases the lower federal courts should not impose remedies unless there had been a prior finding of intentional racial discrimination. Writing for the Court, Justice Byron White said that in its school cases, the Supreme Court had

> adhered to the basic equal protection principle that the invidious quality of a state law claimed to be racially discriminatory must ultimately be traced to a racially discriminatory purpose. That there are both predominantly black and predominantly white schools in a community is not alone violative of the equal protection clause. The essential element of *de jure* segregation is "a current condition of segregation resulting from intentional state action." "The differentiating factor between *de jure* segregation and so-called *de facto* segregation is *purpose or intent* to segregate."[123]

The Supreme Court's ruling in *Washington v. Davis* seemed to be especially relevant to Delaware, where the district court had not found the state guilty of intentional racial discrimination. Judge Gibbons had insisted from the outset that "the test is effect not motivation" and that "the presence or absence of a benign legislative motive is not relevant to our inquiry." Judge Wright maintained that policies that had "a pronounced racial effect" could be justified only if they could withstand especially searching judicial scrutiny.[124]

Caleb Wright's standard of proof was strikingly similar to the one developed in *Hobson v. Hansen* by circuit judge J. Skelly Wright. Like Skelly Wright of Washington, Caleb Wright of Delaware maintained that classifications that appeared to be racially neutral were actually racially suspect if they affected blacks disproportionately. Such classifications could not pass muster if the state merely demonstrated that they were not arbitrary and were related to a legitimate purpose of government. This minimum standard of rationality was all that was required to justify nonracial classifications, but, according to Caleb Wright, if a state had practiced racial discrimination before *Brown* it had to supply "a particularly strong justification" for policies that were neutral on their face but affected blacks disproportionately.[125]

Wright's opinion was so labored that it bordered on the obscure. Buried in the lumpy texture of his prose, however, was a holding that intent to discriminate need not be demonstrated because Wilmington's schools had been racially imbalanced throughout the 1950s and 1960s. Like Judge Gibbons before him, Judge Wright concluded that, at least in the southern and border states, policies that have a disproportionate racial impact can withstand constitutional challenge only if there was compelling evidence to establish their necessity.

Lawyers for Delaware recognized that the most that can be adduced for any educational policy is a preponderance of the evidence, but they took solace from a recent decision of the Supreme Court, *San Antonio School District v. Rodriguez* (1973). By the narrowest of margins—5 to 4—the high court had held that racially neutral policies in this Texas school district should not be subjected to searching judicial inquiry. In the absence of fresh intentional discrimination, the Supreme Court had ruled, disproportionate impact was not sufficient to warrant strict judicial scrutiny.[126]

The defendants received still more cause for optimism when the Supreme Court handed down its decision in *Dayton v. Brinkman* (1977). In *Dayton* the Court reaffirmed *Washington*'s holding that racial imbalance was not unconstitutional unless there was "a showing that this condition resulted from intentionally segregative actions on the part of the [school] Board." Even if intentional infractions were found, the Supreme Court cautioned the lower federal courts not to impose "a remedy which . . . is entirely out of proportion to the constitutional violation." A basic principle of equity was to restore victims to the position they would have enjoyed in the absence of illegal action. In school segregation cases this meant that the district court should

> determine how much *incremental segregative effect* these violations had on the racial distribution of the . . . school population as presently constituted,

when that distribution is compared to what it would have been in the absence of such constitutional violations. The remedy must be designed to redress that difference, and only if there has been a systemwide impact may there be a systemwide remedy.[127]

The Supreme Court's decisions in *Milliken, Washington, Rodriguez,* and *Dayton* imbued defense counsel with the belief that there was a "substantial probability" of their winning on appeal. One of the lawyers compared the Delaware desegregation case to a dinosaur, since every day the case seemed more and more to be an overweight relic from another era. *Green* had spoken of the need for "root and branch" eradication of the last vestiges of segregation. *Swann* had instructed federal judges to "make every effort to achieve the greatest possible degree of actual desegregation." But those opinions were handed down in 1968 and 1971, when the Supreme Court was zealously promoting racial balance as the best alternative to racial strife. By 1976, when the Delaware case was going up on appeal, sentiment was swinging in another direction. The Warren Court had passed into history. The Supreme Court now had five new judges, and it was thought that they would find a way to overturn Judge Caleb Wright's opinion.[128]

Yet the predictions that Delaware's court-ordered dispersion would eventually be reversed failed to take account of an important practical consideration. The pivotal *Rodriguez* and *Milliken* decisions were reached by bare majorities of 5 to 4, while the vote in *Washington* was 7 to 2 and that in *Dayton* was 7 to 0. There was one concurring opinion in *Milliken* and *Washington,* and two concurrences and an abstention in *Dayton.* This was a far cry from the unanimity that the Warren Court manifested in *Brown* and *Green.* In a dissenting opinion, Justice William O. Douglas characterized *Milliken* as a "dramatic retreat." Justice Thurgood Marshall went even further. He characterized the Court's rejection of metropolitan mixing as an "emasculation of our constitutional guarantee of equal protection of the laws" and a "solemn mockery" of *Brown.*[129]

Divided decisions of the Supreme Court are theoretically entitled to the assent that should greet all decisions of the nation's highest tribunal. In fact, however, if lower federal judges conscientiously believe a divided Supreme Court opinion is mistaken, they may try to stare down their superiors. The Supreme Court can hear only a fraction of the appeals it receives, and if the Court takes an appeal on an issue on which it is sharply divided there is the chance that one of the justices will change his mind or retire or be absent from the deliberations. The majority opinion at the time of the appeal could then become a minority view when the case is decided. Of course, this sort of brinksmanship exacts a cost in intellectual honesty, but if the lower federal judges are primarily concerned with the results in the litigation before them, as seems to have been the case with Caleb Wright and John Gibbons, they will pay the price. Wright characterized *Milliken* as a "plurality opinion," and Gibbons refused to concede that officials in a northern state like Michigan came under "the same legal obligation as State authorities came under in Delaware." [130]

Making the best argument he could for Delaware, Philip B. Kurland reminded Wright and Gibbons that in the 1950s several southern judges had disregarded their oaths and sought to evade *Brown*. "In 1974," Kurland said, "the Supreme Court handed down another landmark case, *Milliken v. Bradley*, and once again there are those who find the decision abhorrent, and some will seek to evade the decision by artifice and subterfuge. But once again it is incumbent on all of us to obey the law of the land, as stated by the Supreme Court, whether we like the decision or not." [131]

The lawyers for Delaware were so confident of their chances on appeal that they took their case directly to the Supreme Court in 1975—after the high court's rulings in *Rodriguez* and *Milliken* but before it had spoken in *Washington* and *Dayton*. This unusual step was taken on the advice of attorney Kurland, who noted that the U.S. Code authorized (although it did not require) a direct appeal in cases decided by a three-judge district court. [132]

Delaware was mistaken to appeal directly to the Supreme Court. That Court, for reasons known only to itself, refused a hearing and then upheld the decision of the district court in a one-word opinion, "affirmed." Consequently, the state never received an appellate review of its contention that Judges Gibbons and Wright had misstated the facts as a prelude to imposing their version of correct social policy. As Justice William Rehnquist noted in a dissent joined by Justice Lewis Powell and Chief Justice Warren Burger, the summary affirmation left the important questions in the Delaware desegregation case "totally beclouded." [133]

A panel of seven judges of the Third Circuit Court of Appeals was also troubled. Writing for a four-member majority in 1977, Judge Ruggiero Aldisert concluded that, because of the Supreme Court's ruling, the Third Circuit Court was now barred from reviewing the facts in the Delaware desegregation case. The majority conceded that a district court was "not at liberty to issue orders merely because it believes they will produce a result which the court finds desirable." They observed, "The existence of a constitutional violation does not authorize a court to seek to bring about conditions that never would have existed even if there had been no constitutional violation." They acknowledged that "the remedy for a constitutional violation may not be designed to eliminate arguably undesirable states of affairs caused by purely private conduct." But the Supreme Court had already affirmed the decision of the three-judge district court in *Evans v. Buchanan.* The majority of the Third Circuit Court therefore decided that the affirmation must stand.[134]

The three dissenting circuit judges would have remanded the Delaware case for consideration in light of the Supreme Court's holding in *Dayton v. Brinkman.* They noted that judges Gibbons and Wright "never attempted to ascertain what the racial composition of the schools of northern New Castle County would be but for the constitutional violations which [they] identified." Yet even the dissenters conceded that the majority had a point. In this case, because of the unusual direct appeal to the Supreme Court, it was "the province of the Supreme Court and not of the Court of Appeals" to insist that judges Gibbons and Wright enforce the mandates of *Rodriguez, Milliken, Washington,* and *Dayton.*[135]

Many Delawareans thought the Supreme Court eventually would review the case and bring the decision in *Evans v. Buchanan* into line with the Court's recent rulings on "intentional discrimination" and "incremental segregative effect." Yet this never happened. Four justices of the Court must support a petition for review, and on two occasions Delaware fell one vote short. In the first instance, in 1977, justices Lewis Powell and William Rehnquist and Chief Justice Warren Burger voted to remand the Delaware desegregation case for further consideration in light of the Court's decision in *Dayton.* In 1980 the state's lawyers found in Potter Stewart a fourth justice who thought their case merited review. In the meantime, however, they lost the support of Chief Justice Burger and thus continued to come up one vote short.[136]

Coming up one vote short had become a habit for Delaware. The State lost in the District Court, 2 to 1. It lost before the Third Circuit Court of Appeals, 4 to 3. And now it had twice failed by one vote in its petition for review by the Supreme Court.

To make the situation even more galling, Chief Justice Burger wrote that he thought the case merited review, "but only when a full Court is available to consider the important issues presented by the petition." Justices Thurgood Marshall and John Paul Stevens had not participated in the Delaware case when Burger had voted to remand in 1977. It was thought that Marshall had abstained because for years he had been a lawyer for the NAACP, which had sponsored the *Evans v. Buchanan* case in the 1950s and early 1960s. Justice Stevens, who in 1975 had become the newest member of the Court, had abstained because he had formerly practiced law with Philip B. Kurland, the constitutional expert whom Delaware had hired to work on its appeal. In 1980, with the Supreme Court obviously divided on the constitutionality of metropolitan dispersion, Justice Marshall decided not to abstain. If Chief Justice Burger had provided the crucial fourth vote for review, the case probably would have ended in a 4-to-4 deadlock, and when the Court is evenly split the decision of the lower federal court is affirmed without comment. The chief justice was said to consider it "a total waste of time" to have a full-scale review of a case that was headed for a deadlock. [137]

There was irony here. Delaware had hired Philip B. Kurland to help with its appeal because he was known to have the respect of several members of the Supreme Court. After Kurland took the Delaware case, his former law partner from Chicago was appointed to the Supreme Court and conscientiously declined to sit on the case. In the end Delaware failed to obtain a full appellate review because one of its lawyers was too well-connected.

Saved from a full review by jurisdictional nuances of the federal appeals system and by intricate shifts in judicial alignments, judges Gibbons and Wright were free to work their will in Delaware. They proceeded, as Justice Rehnquist has written, to impose a remedy "more Draconian than any ever approved by this [Supreme] Court." Eleven independent, locally elected school boards in northern New Castle County were dissolved, with their places taken by a single court-appointed school board. "Within this judicial school district, which comprise[d] in excess of 60% of all the public school students in the State of Delaware, every single student [was] reassigned away from his or her local school for a period of no less than three years and for as long as nine years. The plan [was] designed to accomplish a racial balance in each and every school, in every grade, in all of the former eleven districts, mirroring the racial balance of the total area involved." [138]

Before imposing this plan, the district court held three weeks of hearings to consider the best means of achieving desegregation. According to Judge Gibbons, the most seriously litigated issue at these hearings was whether students from Newark should be included in the dispersion. [139] Situated about fifteen miles southwest of Wilmington, Newark was a college town, the home of the University of Delaware. It had been a small, independent entity for more than two centuries, and during the 1950s and 1960s it had grown rapidly to become the second largest city in Delaware, with a population of about 25,000. Newark developed suburbs of its own, and by the time of the remedy hearings in 1976–77 the Newark School District, which included students from both the city and its suburbs, was the largest school district in Delaware, with an enrollment of 17,000 students. The Newark public schools were generally well regarded, although per-pupil expenditure was only two-thirds the amount then spent in Wilmington. There was no allegation that Newark had discriminated racially in the years since *Brown*, but 95 percent of its students were white.

Newark maintained that its schools should not be consolidated with those of Wilmington. Newark was not a suburb of Wilmington, and the bus ride between the two cities could amount to as much as an hour each way through heavy traffic on a high-speed turnpike, a situation that Newark said was dangerous. If the court's objective was to achieve racial balance throughout the county, Newark would have to be included. But attorney John P. Sinclair insisted that any constitutional violations could be cured without Newark. If Newark were excluded from the impending reorganization, 75 percent of the students in northern New Castle County would still be white. If Newark were included, the proportion of whites would increase by only 5 percentage points.[140]

The plaintiffs *and* the suburbs of Wilmington thought these statistics were crucial. If blacks made up only 5 percent of the student enrollment in Newark but 25 percent elsewhere in northern New Castle County, there was the danger that many whites would move to Newark. If that should happen, the white majority in the desegregation area would not remain at 75 percent. If Newark were permitted to remain as "a uniquely white island in New Castle County," lawyers for the Mount Pleasant School District maintained, there would be an "incentive for so-called 'white flight'" to Newark. The remainder of northern New Castle County would then be left with "a percentage of black students which approaches the 'tipping point'" where white flight would accelerate sharply.[141]

Judges Gibbons and Wright were impressed by this line of argument. They acknowledged that "the mere existence of racial disparity in the enrollments of neighboring districts is not a constitutional violation," but they also believed that "the stability of any desegregation plan is enhanced by the inclusion of . . . higher white populations." For that reason, they decided, the desegregation area must include all of New Castle County except the Appoquinimink School District. Appoquinimink was excluded because it was even farther from Wilmington than Newark, because it was small (with a total enrollment of only 2,500 students), and because 30 percent of its students were black. "Since its inclusion would . . . be of very little impact on the existence of predominantly white or black schools in other areas of the country," judges Gibbons and Wright decided, "Appoquinimink need not be included."[142]

A second major point at issue during the remedy hearings concerned the possibility of developing a voluntary plan that would satisfy the court. The state and all the suburban districts would have preferred this to the sort of court-ordered, racially balanced mixing that was impending. Thus, in 1976, the state legislature provided that students could transfer from schools where their race was in the majority to schools where their race was in the minority. Under this provision, some 2,000 blacks from Wilmington (and from the predominantly black De La Warr School District just south of Wilmington) transferred to predominantly white schools. Only three white students, however, chose to transfer to predominantly black schools.[143]

With approximately 15 percent of the black students in northern New Castle County voluntarily enrolled in predominantly white schools, Delaware maintained that its transfer program had achieved at least as much racial mixing as would have occurred in the absence of the policies the plaintiffs had censured. In these circumstances, the state said, there was no need for the district court to impose a plan of its own. If the majority-to-minority transfer program were not enough, the state was prepared to enact a program that the press dubbed "reverse volunteerism." It provided that students from mainly black districts would be assigned to predominantly white schools in the suburbs unless they expressed a wish to remain in their home districts.[144]

Judges Wright and Gibbons noted that voluntary arrangements were not likely to lead to balanced racial mixing, but the possibility of a voluntary plan was not finally rejected until 1978. By then the rulings of judges Gibbons and Wright had been affirmed, the special three-judge district court had been dissolved, and the Delaware desegregation case was assigned to a resident district judge, Murray M. Schwartz.

Born in Ephrata, Pennsylvania, and a graduate of the University of Pennsylvania law school, Schwartz had once been a law clerk for Judge Caleb Wright. Appointed to the federal bench by President Nixon in 1974, Schwartz was a hard-working, conscientious judge whose opinions on the Delaware desegregation case were thorough and well-informed. By the time he received the case, the most important decisions had already been made. As Schwartz explained, "Because the inter-district extent of the violation and the inter-district scope of the remedy have previously been confirmed in this case," the remaining judicial task was severely limited. His job was "to implement a remedy, the parameters of which have already been established. . . ."[145]

Judge Schwartz then laid to rest the state's hope of developing a voluntary plan. He thought it was abhorrent for Delaware even to have suggested "reverse volunteerism," which would place the responsibility for correcting segregation on "those who have been wronged." Noting that only three white students had transferred to predominantly black schools, in contrast with the 2,000 blacks who choose to attend predominantly white schools, Schwartz also decided that the majority-to-minority transfer program imposed a "disproportionate burden" on blacks. The judge said that "ordinary fair play" required that the constitutional violations be corrected without unduly inconveniencing blacks. He then proceeded to require that all of Wilmington's students attend predominantly white schools and that they be bused to the suburbs for nine of the twelve basic grades! Meanwhile, students from the suburbs were required to attend school in Wilmington for three consecutive years. [146]

Like Judges Gibbons and Wright before him, Judge Schwartz quoted the standard maxims of equity law. He dutifully mentioned the Supreme Court's insistence that "the nature of the desegregation remedy is to be determined by the nature and scope of the constitutional violation." "The decree must indeed be remedial," Schwartz wrote, designed as nearly as possible "to restore the victims of discriminatory conduct to the position they would have occupied in the absence of such conduct."[147] Then he proceeded to require racial balance in every grade, something that no one honestly believed would have occurred in the absence of the alleged constitutional violations.

Judges Gibbons, Wright, and Schwartz had no intention of restoring blacks to the position they would have occupied in the absence of unconstitutional discrimination. They meant to remake the public schools of New Castle County after the fashion of the sociology in vogue among integrationists of the late 1960s and early 1970s. That sociology held that blacks would benefit academically and socially, and whites would not suffer, if blacks were dispersed throughout metropolitan regions so that all students attended racially balanced, predominantly white schools.

Yet the sociological evidence in support of liberal jurisprudence was far from conclusive. After reviewing 120 studies of the relation of school racial composition and the achievements, attitudes, and behavior of students, Nancy St. John, a committed integrationist, reported that there was no reliable evidence that compulsory racial mixing significantly improved the attitudes or the performance of black students.[148] Summarizing a large body of literature on the topic, Christopher Jencks, another integrationist, concluded that the measurable effects of desegregation were small and uncertain. By 1978 even James S. Coleman, who once had been the most prominent proponent of the optimum-mix theory, had renounced his belief that blacks would gain academically if they attended integrated classrooms.[149]

Thus the district judges in Delaware disavowed the liberal sociological rationale for dispersion. "Our duty here is not to impose quality education," they declared. "There has been much discussion . . . upon the topic of whether black children learn better in desegregated classrooms. Our holding does not rest upon these considerations. . . ."[150] Caleb Wright, John Gibbons, and Murray Schwartz justified their decision on the grounds that dispersion was required to restore the victims of official racial discrimination to the position they would have occupied but for violations of the Constitution. It goes without saying that they made no mention of the economic considerations that originally prompted the lawsuit. In few other instances, one would hope, has the law been manipulated so disingenuously to achieve a result the judges considered socially and economically desirable.

V

It remained to be seen how metropolitan desegregation would work out. If the academic performance of black youths improved to the point where they could find good jobs in northern New Castle County, sociological jurisprudence would have defused the social dynamite that threatened to destroy Delaware. There was, however, another possibility. If the schools had to grapple with complex conditions that went beyond the schools, the architects of dispersion might fail to solve the social problem and instead lower the quality of public education.

Geographic and demographic considerations encouraged advocates of proportional mixing to believe that a stable racial balance could be achieved in northern Delaware. To the east lay the waters of the Delaware River. To the south lay Kent and Sussex counties, where the public schools already enrolled a larger proportion of blacks than the newly created New Castle County School District. In the rural countryside of Maryland and Pennsylvania, which lay to the west and north, there were not enough schools to absorb large numbers of fleeing whites. White flight and resegregation, the nemeses of desegregation in many areas, also seemed unlikely because, as the judges of the district court noted, an 80–20 white majority could be achieved with only one-tenth as many students as were included in the proposed Detroit desegregation plan. Given the manageable size of the busing area, the preponderance of whites, and the absence of other predominantly white public schools nearby, northern Delaware seemed to be the sort of area the U.S. Civil Rights Commission had in mind when it asserted that metropolitan desegregation would be "quite stable. . . because there is simply 'no place to flee.'"[151]

The prospects for successful desegregation were enhanced by the support of the influential *News Journal* newspapers. Noting that 90 percent of Wilmington's public school students had been black and 90 percent of those in the rest of the county had been white, the editors stated that "simply on that record, none of us has any right to be surprised by the decision of the federal court." To those who grumbled about "judicial intrusion," the editors answered, "Enough. There is no longer any argument about liability nor remedy in this case." The judges had required "racial balance for the sake of constitutional compliance" and only after state officials had "looked the other way as the Wilmington school system turned black and socio-economically disadvantaged."[152]

Delaware's leading religious organizations also helped to legitimize court-ordered desegregation. The Delmarva Ecumenical Agency, an organization of fifteen denominations in Delaware, Maryland, and Virginia, expressed the hope that "Wilmington and New Castle County can be an example to the nation of orderly compliance with the law." The National Conference of Christians and Jews organized human relations programs to ease the process of desegregation. And an Interfaith Task Force sponsored religious rallies and ecumenical services intended to sooth the community and ensure peaceful implementation. The Reverend F. David Weber, a suburban Methodist minister, was especially active in organizing religious activity. "The issue is not busing," he insisted. "The issue is desegregation, ending a wrong. We stand squarely in favor of desegregation."[153]

The Du Pont Company desired peace and order above all, and also stood to benefit tangibly from an annual reduction in taxes on its property in Wilmington. For these reasons, and also because many executives already sent their children to private schools, the company did not view the impending reorganization of the public schools with alarm. It joined with other major corporations to finance an organization called SANE, which was headed by an executive on loan from Du Pont. SANE then hired a Philadelphia public relations firm, distributed newsletters, and encouraged everyone to remain calm in the face of dispersion. The message of Delaware's corporate elite was summed up in SANE's slogan: "Help keep the peace, so kids can learn in peace." With Du Pont and the other major corporations in favor of peaceful implementation, middle-management personnel who patronized the suburban public schools were reluctant to jeopardize their careers by speaking out against busing.[154]

Pierre S. du Pont IV, the governor of Delaware, also did his part to achieve effective implementation. Governor du Pont thought there was "no constitutional foundation for the sweeping pupil reassignment plans that the federal courts have foisted upon city and county alike." Yet he recognized that states could not set aside federal court orders. After six years in Congress, and repeated votes for antibusing legislation that failed of passage, du Pont also knew that the national legislature was not ready to take action against court-ordered busing. Du Pont consequently did his best to see that busing was implemented peacefully. As he explained in his 1978 State of the State speech, "I and most of us in Delaware disagree with [the court order], but we nevertheless have a constitutional responsibility to obey it . . . without rancor, without antagonism, and without violence."[155]

The court order required the schools to implement a number of programs that were intended to lift black students to the educational level they supposedly would have achieved if they had been attending racially balanced classes. Ninety-eight teachers were employed as human relations specialists, and 470 others were paid to attend four-week summer workshops at the University of Delaware. These workshops dealt with various aspects of race relations and were based on the premise that training was the key to successful school desegregation. Acting Dean Billy E. Ross explained that middle-class teachers needed to improve their ability to resolve conflicts with disruptive students whose values differed from their own. One session recommended "empathetic listening" as a means for effecting "behavior modification." Others dealt with "values clarification," "action planning," and "consultation skills." All the workshops stressed the need for combating racial stereotypes and for preserving respect for the racial and ethnic backgrounds of black students. Some dealt specifically with the need for what Judge Schwartz called "affirmative reading and communication skills programs" to ensure that black children would not be resegregated in low-level classes. Still others addressed the judge's call for "non-arbitrary and nondiscriminatory discipline" and for counseling black students to enroll in advanced academic courses. [156]

Critics later said the special programs in human relations and affirmative action played into the hands of academic quacks who had no use for discipline, ability grouping, or academic competition. "With the willing cooperation of activist federal courts," they said, "those same people who brought us 'progressive education'" had launched an insidious campaign to gear public education to "the lowest common denominator." When desegregation began, however, the special programs had the effect of encouraging the upbeat notion that good will and constructive action would ensure success. One teacher reported that, after completing a four-week workshop, she was "confident that I could act as a facilitator to help others meet the educational problems resulting from desegregation." Another said she had developed "a much more positive attitude toward the desegregated classroom and more faith in my ability to cope with the changes it will occasion." [157]

The planning was generally considered a success in September 1978, when the public schools of northern New Castle County were desegregated without serious incident. Disorder had accompanied busing in Boston, Louisville, and other cities, but in Wilmington the nation's most sweeping experiment in court-ordered racial dispersion was peacefully implemented. Speaking on NBC-TV, correspondent Robert Hager summed up the prevailing view: "[Desegregation] went smoothly. . . . For 21 years Wilmington's white suburbanites had fought against busing in the Court, but now it was a reality and all was going well." [158]

The peaceful implementation of metropolitan desegregation was achieved despite wide opposition. Eighty-nine percent of the suburban parents responding to a University of Delaware poll in 1978 were opposed to busing.

The great majority of suburbanites (84 percent) agreed that it was "a good idea to have people of different races going to school together and living in the same neighborhoods." They favored desegregation when it occurred naturally and had uncomplainingly sent their children to neighborhood schools that enrolled children of all races. With busing to distant communities, however, many parents worried about the safety of their children and the lessening of their influence as parents. "A majority of suburbanites also saw academic harm in the future and accepted the statement that white achievement test scores would drop as a result of desegregation." [159]

In Wilmington, on the other hand, 48 percent of the parents favored busing, and 52 percent thought dispersion would "provide a better education for most black students." Only 9 percent of the Wilmingtonians were strongly in favor of busing, however, and a majority agreed with the suburbanites that the reorganization would be costly, would increase disciplinary problems, and would reduce participation in after-school activities. "If the samples were weighted to reflect the true proportions of suburban and city parents in the desegregation area," Jeffrey A. Raffel noted, "then we would find only about 15 per cent of the parents . . . in favor of busing and over 80 per cent opposed in 1978. In fact, using this weighting procedure, only about 3 per cent of the area's population would be strongly in favor of busing." [160]

In New Castle County the leading voice of opposition to forced busing was that of the Positive Action Committee (PAC), an organization that differed in important respects from groups that had opposed desegregation in the South in the 1950s. PAC professed to favor desegregation, and most of its 11,000 dues-paying members sent their children to racially mixed schools in the suburbs. They resented allegations that they were bigots and said they opposed metropolitan dispersion because it was a waste of time and money and because it created more problems than it solved.

The president and chief spokesman for PAC was James A. Venema, a suburban father who owned a small sign manufacturing business. Venema thought that in the process of interpreting the Fourteenth Amendment federal judges had usurped powers that belonged to the legislatures and had made a mockery of the concept that government should not discriminate among its citizens on the basis of race. He was outraged "to think that in 1976, when we are supposedly celebrating our 200th year of independence from tyranny, we have become the victims of a [judicial] tyranny more insidious and more dangerous than that which was visited upon our forefathers." He was convinced that the people of New Castle County were being ruled not by the enduring principles of the founding fathers but by the transitory personal notions of liberals who temporarily occupied seats on the federal bench. If forced busing should be implemented "with nary a whimper," he said, "it would show that the American people will knuckle to anything, and there'll be nothing left for us but more oppressive schemes."[161]

Venema and the PAC knew that federal court orders took precedence over state legislative actions, but they thought the people's elected representatives could still be an effective "line of defense against federal power running crazy." Interposition was no longer possible, but PAC advised state officials to resort to a form of nonviolent, passive resistance that would force the federal government to implement its own program. "Put the onus on Judge Murray Schwartz," Venema recommended. "Let the courts pull the trigger." "The thing I'd like to see . . . is to have everybody say to hell with it and have them bring in the olive drab buses and the olive drab troops and run the whole damn state."[162]

PAC clearly differed from the "make it work" groups who tried to implement the court's program peacefully and effectively. In one important respect, however, PAC contributed significantly to the peaceful acceptance of dispersion. PAC meetings had attracted as many as 850 people, but the leaders of the organization recognized that demonstrations could get out of hand, and when desegregation began in 1978 they held no mass meetings and staged no antibusing rallies. "Our goal certainly wasn't to achieve implementation, peaceful or otherwise," said Venema. But PAC was committed to nonviolence and recognized that demonstrations had not stopped busing elsewhere. Because PAC influenced people who were beyond the reach of the major corporations and churches, it deserved a share of the credit for the lack of violence. "By channeling the tremendous feelings of private frustration into relatively conventional political activity," one observer noted, PAC "effectively preempted the ground from more extreme individuals and groups and thus contributed to a relatively tranquil desegregation process."[163]

From its beginning in 1975, PAC stressed politics as the key to ending forced busing. The organization focused initially on state elections, but with 80 percent of the Delaware electorate opposed to dispersion almost all politicians outside Wilmington tried to please the PAC. In suburban districts the rival candidates usually differed, if at all, not on the merits of busing but on whether state officials should defy the judiciary or attempt to make the best of a mistaken court order. In these circumstances the value of a PAC endorsement was open to question.[164]

It was doubtful, moreover, whether the state could do anything. Since federal court orders took precedence, many members of the legislature believed, as state senator David Elliott put it, "that the General Assembly really is powerless to act in a significant manner on this segregation issue." There was the additional consideration that until 1980 Delaware was appealing to higher courts on the grounds that it had not been found guilty of intentional segregation but only of failing to take affirmative action to ensure racial balance. Any action by the general assembly that purposely interfered with court-ordered dispersion would undermine the chance for success on appeal.[165]

The impotence of the General Assembly led some observers to conclude that PAC was wasting its time "putting a lot of pressure on people who can't do anything for them." Even some opponents of dispersion said it was "deceptive and phony" to suggest that anything could be done to stop busing. PAC leaders nevertheless insisted that Congress could "regulate excesses in the courts just as it regulates excesses of the presidency." Under Article III, Section 2, of the U.S. Constitution, they maintained, Congress "can stop Federal courts from ordering forced busing by simply removing federal court jurisdiction in so-called 'school desegregation' cases." After 1978 this became the standard refrain of the antibusing movement.[166]

In persuading Congress to call a halt to forced busing, busing opponents first had to win the support of Delaware's two senators and its single congressman. This was easily accomplished. Given the prevalence of antibusing sentiment in the state, it was generally recognized that no candidate for Congress could succeed without opposing the dispersion. This axiom of Delaware politics was illustrated when Wilmington mayor Tom Maloney ran for the U.S. Senate in 1976. As mayor of Wilmington, Maloney had welcomed court-ordered busing as clearly beneficial to the city in terms of education and property values. As a candidate for the Senate, he declaimed against "our national nightmare of forced busing"—a policy that "simultaneously fails to improve the performance of our students, increases the hostility between our adults, and is opposed by the large majorities of our citizens of both races."[167]

Maloney failed in his bid for the Senate, but the victor in that race, William V. Roth, was even more outspoken in opposition to busing. The sure way to put an end to what Roth called "tyranny by judicial fiat" was to pass a constitutional amendment prohibiting government from making distinctions on account of race. It would take a long time to secure such an amendment, however, and in the meantime Roth endorsed PAC's call for transferring jurisdiction over education from the federal judiciary to the state courts. The balance of power in America had "gotten all out of whack," Roth maintained, and it was time for Congress "to restore the checks and balances within the federal government and between it and our state and local governments."[168]

Tom Evans, a moderate Republican who became Delaware's only member of the House of Representatives when "Pete" du Pont became governor, not surprisingly endorsed the views of Roth and the PAC. Civil rights activists were shocked, however, when these positions were also endorsed by Joseph R. Biden, the liberal Democratic senator from Delaware. Like Roth and Evans, Biden thought the only certain way to curb judicial action was to amend the Constitution. This was "a difficult, time-consuming process," though, and in the meantime Biden insisted that "legislative measures must be taken to provide relief to communities already disrupted by busing or the threat of busing." He joined with other Delawareans to sponsor legislation to restrict the jurisdiction of the federal courts. Then Biden and Roth drafted legislation that codified language the Supreme Court had used in two important decisions of 1976 and 1977. From *Washington v. Davis* came the notion that intent to discriminate must be proved before busing was ordered. From *Dayton v. Brinkman* came a section to prevent sweeping busing orders, stating that courts can order only as much racial integration as a constitutional violation itself prevented.[169]

Roth and Biden's proposal failed of passage and was denounced as racist by spokesmen for the NAACP, but the Delaware Democrat predicted that "within a few years the great body of opinion within the civil-rights movement will agree with me." Given the wide popular opposition to busing, Biden thought it inevitable that the policy eventually would be abandoned. In the meantime, he warned, the civil rights movement would come to a dead halt. Busing was "counterproductive . . . because it undermines the basic support . . . that we need in order to pass major civil rights legislation." "When you lose the support of the great middle class," Biden said, "no social policy in this country will move."[170]

With Delaware's congressional delegation committed to the proposition that Congress could remove federal jurisdiction over education by a simple majority vote, PAC leaders joined with like-minded people in other states to establish a national antibusing lobby, the National Association for Neighborhood Schools (NANS). The activities of William D. D'Onofrio were particularly important. A self-employed tax accountant and insurance agent who in 1978 had succeeded James Venema as president of PAC, D'Onofrio agreed with his predecessor's philosophy but differed in style and tactics. Because he was tall and slender, dressed impeccably, and spoke in a rich baritone, "as if Archie Bunker had borrowed Johnny Carson's tailor and Walter Cronkite's voice," Venema excelled in attracting local media coverage. D'Onofrio, on the other hand, was a semiprofessional baseball manager who emphasized the importance of what he called "political hardball." Given the liberal biases of most reporters, D'Onofrio thought it was "spitting in the wind" for busing opponents to seek media attention; all they gained was slanted coverage that made them look bad. He even questioned the wisdom of court cases challenging the constitutionality of required racial balance. Things might change if one or two strict constructionists were appointed to the Supreme Court, but D'Onofrio doubted that a divided Court could control liberal judges who were defiantly ensconced in the lower ranks of the federal judiciary.[171]

D'Onofrio's technique for grass-roots organizing was straightforward. When a local community was faced with the prospect of dispersion for racial balance, speakers from NANS would join with local leaders in holding meetings at which the injustice and folly of busing were related and repeated until members of the community brought effective pressure on their local congressmen. D'Onofrio was convinced that ultimately the battle against forced busing would have to be won in the political arena. Judicial arrogance and usurpation would not end until a majority of both houses of Congress realized that to continue in office they must exercise their authority to stop forced busing by restricting the jurisdiction of the federal courts.[172]

The sociological rationale for dispersion has been described above; with desegregation, it was thought, students and parents would develop more positive attitudes toward persons of other races. If inner-city youths were dispersed, their values could also be reshaped in predominantly middle-class schools. Freed during the school day from the influence of their neighborhoods, but still grouped with enough blacks so as not to be a helpless minority, inner-city blacks would simultaneously avoid the perils of lower-class socialization and psychological isolation. Black academic achievement was expected to improve in schools with an optimum 80–20 racial mix.

Although the evidence is not incontrovertible, Delaware's experience with metropolitan desegregation lends some credence to this theory. "I didn't know what I was missing until I [was bused to the suburbs]," said one black high school senior. "After two years I realized I had been cheated out of an education [at P.S. du Pont High School in Wilmington]. I was terrible in math. I abhorred algebra and geometry." Another black student said that in Wilmington "all the teachers were grouchy for some reason. All of them. My teachers were all black, but all of them seemed like they'd rather be somewhere else." In the suburbs, by contrast, the teachers were said to "explain more [and] take time to make you understand." The suburban schools were also more orderly, this student noted. "Everything is done by the bell . . . and when the bell rings the teachers and administrators expect you to be in class." In contrast, at Howard High School in Wilmington "kids walked around and went to class when they felt like it."[173]

Test scores released after the first year of busing seemed to corroborate the favorable impressions about academic learning in desegregated schools. In the fall of 1978 Delaware's students had scored close to the national average on the California Achievement Tests (CAT), but by the spring of 1979 their scores had improved dramatically, with the various grades ranging from 9 to 14 percentage points above the national average. "To see that kind of learning achievement in a school year complicated by the massive reorganization . . . is heartening," an editorial in the *Wilmington Morning News* declared.[174]

The encouraging test results of 1979 were repeated during the second and third years of forced busing. In 1980 the *Sunday News Journal* reported, "The results of the California Achievement Tests . . . show that Delaware students, on the average, did better than about 60 percent of students nationally. That's a quantum jump from the fall of 1978. . . . Then, Delawareans' scores hovered right around the national average of 50 percent." In 1981 test scores rose for the third straight year. By then, the class averages ranged from 6 to 20 percentage points above the national average.[175] The school district initially refused to release a racial breakdown, but many people assumed that the academic performance of inner-city blacks had improved spectacularly after they were exposed to better teachers in the suburbs and freed from the rampant disorder of their neighborhood schools.

This interpretation was challenged by Robert L. Green, a Michigan State University social scientist who had testified for the plaintiffs in *Evans v. Buchanan* and who later received $668,000 from the Rockefeller Foundation to study how achievement and attitudes had changed in New Castle County. Green confirmed earlier reports that academic achievement had improved since 1978. When busing began, he reported, "the students in the district scored four months above the national norm, on the average. In 1979 they scored eight months above the norm, and in 1980 the students were a full year above the national average." After tracking the progress of a nonrandom sample of 578 students, however, Green also reported that the gap between black and white elementary students, as measured by the CAT tests, had almost doubled between 1978 and 1981. Black students had done better than would have been predicted on the basis of their previous performance. But whites had registered "more than twice the expected gains." Green did not analyze the factors responsible for these results but said white scores may have increased "because most white parents . . . expected disaster . . . [and said] to their children, 'You have to work even harder to keep your achievement up.'"[176]

School administrators were reluctant to provide an overall racial breakdown on test scores since, as state superintendent William B. Keene explained, they feared it would reinforce racist suspicions. The district court nevertheless ordered the schools to prepare a racial breakdown, on the grounds that this would enable the schools to evaluate the effectiveness of their programs. When released in 1982, the results indicated that black and Hispanic students scored an average of 15 points lower than whites on the CAT tests, while Asian students scored slightly higher than Caucasians. The blacks scored close to the national averages in the first, second, and third grades but fell below the norms in the remaining grades tested. These results were similar to those reported in other studies throughout the country, but integrationists were again jolted to learn that the differential in racial averages apparently increased during the first years of court-ordered busing. In 1976, when only 9.7 percent of the students in Wilmington were white and only 6 percent of the students in the suburbs were black, first-grade students in Wilmington scored 15.4 percent lower than first graders in the suburbs. Five years later, the sixth-grade students from Wilmington (whose numbers remained fairly stable) were scoring 26 percent lower than the average for their white classmates (whose numbers had declined by more than 40 percent in the interval).[177]

In the meantime, parents of both races and all social classes thought the quality of the public schools had declined appreciably with metropolitan dispersion. There were some variations, with the negative perception of school quality more prevalent among whites than blacks. Yet Robert Green reported that the negative attitudes prevailed "across the board for all parents, regardless of race, social status or other measured variables." Racial tensions were also heightened as middle-class suburbanites mixed with disadvantaged blacks from the inner city. "The racial attitudes of both black and white parents became slightly less positive from 1978 to 1979 after the first year of desegregation, with no change from 1979 to 1980," Green reported. The same trend was evident in the racial attitudes of students, with "the [negative] impact of desegregation on white students' attitudes . . . greater than the impact on black students' attitudes."[178]

The prevalence of negative attitudes was confirmed by a 1979 poll conducted by the College of Urban Affairs at the University of Delaware. Before the dispersion, 52 percent of the parents in Wilmington had expected desegregation to improve the quality of education for blacks, but after the first year of busing only 38 percent still felt that way. During that time the number of Wilmington parents opposed to busing increased from 42 percent to 53 percent, with only 40 percent in favor. Sentiment in the suburbs remained strongly against busing, with those opposed declining only slightly from 89 percent to 88 percent. The proportion of suburban parents who thought desegregation had lowered the quality of education for whites increased slightly from 54 percent in 1977 to 57 percent in 1979, while the number who rated their school districts as "good" or "excellent" declined from 79 percent to 37 percent. In the words of the pollsters, "one could say that in the eyes of many suburbanites [busing] has meant a leveling down of educational quality. . . . Suburban parents . . . remain convinced that busing is detrimental to the education of white children. In 1977 and 1978 a majority predicted that desegregation would harm white achievement. In 1979 a majority of suburbanites believed that the prediction came true."[179]

The contrast between the improving CAT scores and the perception of declining public schools suggests that most parents considered the tests a poor index of the quality of education. Some of this may have been due to prejudice, since many people were convinced from the outset that busing was an unsound policy. Some of it also grew out of skepticism on the part of those who know how test scores can be manipulated.

With the onset of busing, the types and methods of testing were changed. Prior to 1978 Delaware state tests had been given in New Castle County, but with busing the consolidated school district changed to the CAT test, a standardized examination that had allowed students to record dramatic improvement when it was introduced in Cleveland and other cities.[180] The suspicion that the CAT tests were being used as propaganda was reinforced when it became known that high school students took exactly the same test each year. Elementary students took different examinations as they progressed through their grades, but the same test was given at each grade level every year. In other words, fourth-grade students took a different test than they had taken the year before, but the fourth-grade teacher administered exactly the same examination that she had given the previous year.[181]

Desegregation had been under way for only half a year when newspaper accounts pointed to racial imbalance in individual classrooms. One story in the *Wilmington Morning News,* for example, described a third-grade homeroom in Wilmington where fifteen of the twenty-two children were whites who had been bused in from the suburbs. Shortly after the first bell, these pupils and other third graders were regrouped according to ability for mathematics, and more than two-thirds of the students in the slowest math class were black. Proponents of the arrangement said that racially balanced individual classrooms would leave the brighter students bored and the slower children uncomprehending, but integrationists maintained that ability grouping violated the court order and gave "institutional approval to the idea that blacks have inferior academic abilities."[182]

Responding to allegations of resegregation, the New Castle County school board called for a study of the extent to which individual classes were racially imbalanced. When completed, this report indicated that one-quarter of the schools in the district had some classes in which black students outnumbered whites, and 13 percent of the classes in the district had a black enrollment in excess of 40 percent.[183] Some of the imbalanced classes were small, and others were in studies where relatively few blacks had completed the necessary prerequisites (e.g., calculus and advanced foreign languages). Still others were remedial classes (where blacks were over-represented throughout the United States). School administrators were nevertheless alarmed at the extent of the imbalance. It seemed ridiculous to have imbalanced classes after having gone to all the trouble and expense of busing.

To avoid another lawsuit the New Castle County School District decided that in elementary school most slow learners should no longer be taught in special classes. Wherever possible they were to be grouped heterogeneously with other students. The school district also took steps to increase the number of blacks who enrolled in honors courses. "We had a meeting with Superintendent Biggs," one high school counselor recalled. "He was afraid Paul Dimond [an attorney for the black plaintiff class] would go back to Murray Schwartz's courtroom and get an order requiring that all racially imbalanced classes be abolished." To avoid this, the counselors were told to go through their files and to identify and then steer the best black students into honors classes, even if they had been making only C grades. The school district officially denied the existence of racial quotas, but by 1980 the informal guidance program had been replaced by requirements that instructional groupings should not vary by more than 10 percentage points from the overall racial ratio. If the school population ratio were 80–20, then individual classes "could be 90–10 or 70–30, or any range in between."[184]

Many parents feared that a shift away from ability grouping would jeopardize the quality of education. One father warned that "public education in New Castle County cannot possibly bear the burden of "insuring the best education' for our children while . . . being the vehicle for so-called 'social change.'" Another characterized busing as "a multi-million dollar scheme to lower the quality of education." When integrationists spoke of "equalizing opportunity," their opponents huffed about "leveling down or 'education by the lowest common denominator.'" When school administrators spoke of teaching the "whole child," conservatives called for more emphasis on academic subjects of traditional content.[185]

Despite the equivocal data, the *Wilmington Morning News* correctly observed that it was "on the educational front . . . that the best record was established."[186] In other major areas, especially discipline, busing was associated with a marked retrogression. Some people said this was due to misunderstanding and a general failure of communication. Others attributed most of the problems to the misbehavior of blacks. There was evidence to support both points of view.

Since schools in Wilmington could accommodate only one-fourth of the students in the desegregation area, Judge Schwartz decided that residents of the city should be bused to the suburbs for nine of the twelve basic grades. Thus from the outset there was the danger that blacks would feel unwelcome as a minority intruding in predominantly white schools. This malaise was aggravated when they became the butts of epithets and racial jokes.

The word "nigger" was heard in the hallways, and occasionally the antipathy went beyond verbal insult. There was a cross-burning at Casimir Pulaski Elementary School, and the letters KKK were painted on the Wilmer E. Shue Middle School.[187]

White supremacy was maintained in most mundane matters. At Claymont High School, for example, whites rejected the suggestion that black transfer students from P.S. du Pont High School (whose colors had been blue and gray) should be recognized by changing the colors of the school yearbook from the traditional purple and gold to purple and gray. At Brandywine High School the student council took exception to suggestions that there should be black and white Christmas queens and that speakers from both races should address the spring commencement. A black girl who had been a cheerleader at Wilmington High recalled, "Almost everything was stacked against us" at Dickinson High School, a suburban school.[188]

These instances were symptomatic of a larger pattern. Despite busing for racial balance, most high school students avoided interracial contact. Although there was some mixing in the elementary grades, a pattern of self-segregation began in junior high school, and by the time the students reached adolescence there was virtually no mixing outside classes, sports, and drug dealing. "BUSING IS LOSING THE RACE TO RESEGREGATION," one newspaper headline announced. Reporter Steve Goldberg noted that "despite the massive effort to bring the races together, students and even teachers segregated themselves at lunch, in the hallways and in the classrooms if they were given the opportunity." The Reverend David L. Himmler, a spokesman for the Human Rights Advisory Council, a group that sent volunteers to observe the situation in fifty-one schools, reported that "while desegregation has taken place, integration . . . has not taken place."[189]

A much-publicized instance of self-segregation occurred in the spring of 1979, when blacks complained that they had been excluded from planning for social activities and then organized a dinner-dance that turned out to be a district-wide black senior prom. Integrationists were deeply concerned about this manifestation of racial separation, and the school district decreed that blacks must be included in future planning. The practice of holding separate dances nevertheless continued into the 1980s. "I'm a little ambivalent about the whole thing," said a black mother who was also chairman of the Delaware Advisory Committee to the U.S. Commission on Civil Rights. She finally allowed her daughter to attend the separate dance because "children do miss their friends" and blacks had been "scattered . . . all over hell's half acre."[190]

Some blacks were outspoken in maintaining that dispersion had damaged black social life. Jea P. Street, a social worker at the Hilltop Lutheran Community Center, recalled that when he attended Wilmington High in the 1960s, "I didn't have any talent for basketball, but I went to all the games because the social life was the best I've known." With dispersion, there was less participation in school activities, and Street maintained that blacks had been "systematically deprived of fun." "I don't like to oppose change or modern times," Street continued, "but as far as I can see we need schools that are in close touch with their communities. If the communities are predominantly black, the schools should be predominantly black. That's fine with me. Some of the most successful people I know went to predominantly-black schools." Street acknowledged that "anti-busing white people will love to hear a black person say this. They hate busing because they don't like blacks. I see how much damage dispersion has done to the black community."[191]

Lillian Richardson, one of the plaintiffs in *Evans v. Buchanan,* continued to believe that busing would improve educational opportunities for blacks but conceded that this was a minority view in the black community. "I haven't talked to one black person that believes in busing," she said. "Most blacks don't see quality education as the issue. They just know they don't want their children bused."[192]

While blacks complained about white dominance and insensitivity, whites took exception to black misbehavior. Violence occurred infrequently but was a matter of concern to parents, who noted with dismay that although blacks originally made up only 20 percent of the school population, they were reported at fault in more than half the instances of violence and in more than two-thirds of the interracial assaults. Most of the clashes were minor fights, although some students suffered serious injuries ranging from knife wounds to a broken jaw. There were a number of sexual assaults, mostly involving boys who grabbed a quick feel while passing girls in the hallway. One young bus driver was raped and robbed after completing her route in Wilmington, however, and two blacks were sent to Family Court after they allegedly forced a black schoolmate to participate in oral sex in the basement of the Central Middle School in Newark. A similar case involving two black boys and a white girl at William Penn High School was not investigated promptly because school officials delayed before filing a police report. The girl was said to be antiblack, and the results of a belated lie detector test were inconclusive. Nevertheless, news of the incident circulated in the community and contributed to what one reporter called "an undercurrent of tension" and "a public perception that police and school authorities have adopted a fortress mentality, minimizing or simply covering up serious incidents." Two black students at suburban Brandywine High school were sent to prison after raping girls on the campus of the University of Delaware.[193]

Reports of endemic theft were as influential in shaping a negative public impression as were the occasional instances of physical abuse. In the city of Newark the number of criminal complaints from the public schools increased from about ten per year to 165 in 1978–79, while throughout the county there was a fourfold increase in the number of thefts reported at the schools. Nothing like this had happened before, and it was widely assumed that black students were responsible. "We'd arrest guys for stealing twenty jackets at a time," police major John Lingo recalled. "Twenty lockers would be cleaned out, and girl friends would conceal the stolen goods when they boarded the buses back to Wilmington. Some youths were coming to school primarily to steal merchandise that could be sold in the city." Laboratory equipment was pilfered, a form of theft that was difficult to detect because suburban schools had not previously kept a careful inventory of their supplies. At Christiana High School even the brass plates behind the door knobs were stolen and fenced.[194]

Thefts declined in frequency as students and teachers learned to leave their valuables at home or to keep them securely locked. Nevertheless, vandalism and disorder persisted. At Newark High School stalls in the lavatories were ripped from the walls and auditorium seats were kicked to pieces. False fire alarms were common, and during class time many black students roamed through the halls. "From the appearance of things in the hallways, you'd think our school had become all black," one teacher said. Between classes and during lunch periods the students from Wilmington congregated in separate groups, often to gamble, and teachers said the noise level was "simply deafening."[195] Others were astonished by the frequency of cutting classes and the casualness with which students openly smoked marijuana. "You could see it. You could smell it in the halls. One day we even filmed it," said Sergeant Alex Von Koch, a police officer who was stationed at Newark High School. At Von Koch's invitation Pat Downs of WHYY-TV set up cameras near the football field and across the street from the main entrance. During an hour and a half of filming eight students were observed dealing drugs, and 140 others were counted leaving the school to go elsewhere in town. Parents understandably came to believe that standards had deteriorated. When thinking back to their own school days, they recalled lavatories that were smoky but intact, "and the smoke was R. J. Reynolds, not Columbian."[196]

Teachers especially were troubled by the pettiness of much of the misbehavior. In some schools they could not walk the halls without being called twelve-letter names, journalist Gary Govert reported. Instructor Dan Defoe quit teaching after being sassed by students who refused to clear the halls and go to their classes. Teacher Gladys Sharnoff encountered defiance when she came upon students who had stolen balloons and aluminum foil needed for a physics experiment. "Their attitude was, 'If you didn't lock it up in your desk, it's your fault. And if you didn't see us take it, you should shut up because you've got no proof.'"[197]

Many parents recalled the legendary female teachers of yesteryear who could tongue lash adolescent giants into humble submission. But that was possible only because the teachers were supported by the power structure and because students, despite occasional recalcitrance, really wanted to attend school and knew they would be expelled if they did not shape up. Anna Hayes Owens, a McKean High School teacher with seventeen years' experience in the classroom, knew those days were gone, but she did not quit teaching until she heard Superintendent Caroll W. Biggs describe how well desegregation was going. Biggs reminded her of "a general behind the lines who doesn't really know what is happening to the soldiers on the front line." She offered the following description of conditions at her suburban school.

> The problems involving discipline are so acute in many classes that the teacher's role is changing to that of a policeman but with none of the safeguards. The problems of vandalism, violence, drug abuse and thievery seem to get worse each year. Cheating and copying have become endemic diseases. Graffiti appear on the walls, desks, and books. Litter piles up—a daily burden for overworked janitors. Too many students are absent or late for class. Noise in many classrooms has to be experienced to be believed. There is constant gossiping, bickering, intermingled with threats and obscenities.[198]

Court-ordered busing brought about a clash of cultures, and on occasion it was the blacks who took exception to improper white behavior. Black students did not hug and kiss in public, and sometimes they complained when whites did so. When blacks took exception, however, they touched a raw nerve among whites who felt that blacks had intimidated school authorities and were having almost everything their way. In November 1979, Christiana High School was closed for a week to allow an easing of tensions that erupted after black girls assaulted a white girl who told them to mind their own business when they complained about her kissing her boyfriend in the hallway. Whites then organized a protest with impromptu signs. "*Why can't people who are repeatedly causing trouble be expelled?*" they asked. "*They are infringing on the rights of others who want to learn.*" The school administration was accused of covering up

THE BURDEN OF *Brown*

problems and taking too much from repeat offenders. Similar protests occurred at Wilmington High School in 1981 and at Concord High School
in 1982.[199]

Busing opponents had predicted that in the name of equal education,
standards would be lowered "to allow more hell-raising in the classroom."
They had warned that teachers who meted out punishments "on other than
a strict 'racial balance'" would be "disciplined by being called racists." After
experiencing desegregation at first hand, they felt that these predictions
were coming true. A University of Delaware professor whose daughter attended Newark High School lamented, "One element that is missing from
the desegregation plan is the will to maintain academic standards and standards of behavior that are generally accepted in Western society. . . . There
is a great deal of fear among teachers and administrators that they will be
guilty of—or accused of—discrimination. This leads to a lowering of academic and behavior standards."[200]

Despite the reluctance to punish transgressions, black students in the
desegregated New Castle County school district were suspended twice as
often as whites, a ratio that was about the same as the national average.
The overall proportion of students suspended in New Castle County, however (8.7 percent), was double the national average (4.2 percent). Whereas
6 percent of the nation's black students and 3 percent of the whites were
suspended from school at least once each year, in New Castle County after
busing the figures were 14 percent and 7 percent, respectively. There was,
moreover, a great surge in the number of both blacks and whites who were
suspended after compulsory integration began. In 1975–76, the last year
before voluntary busing, 1,637 black students and 4,555 whites had been
suspended, a total of 6,292 (counting repeat offenders) of the 79,039 students then enrolled in the public schools. By 1978–79, the first year of court-
ordered busing, the number of students had declined to 63,558, but the
number of suspensions had increased to 10,906 (5,442 whites, 5,291 blacks,
162 Hispanics, and 9 Asians). Before desegregation, about 25 percent of
the suspensions were given to blacks; after desegregation blacks received
50 percent of the suspensions.[201]

Blacks said they were being treated unfairly, and federal judge Murray M.
Schwartz virtually ordered school authorities to commission an independent study of possible discrimination. Yet the ensuing study by Charles M.
Achilles and a biracial team of educational researchers from the University
of Tennessee found no evidence of racial bias. White students were disciplined as frequently as blacks for truancy, cutting classes, and using drugs,
but the overall black suspension rate was greater because blacks were disproportionately punished for theft, fighting, and defiance. "Defiance" was
not precisely defined but often involved the use of vulgar street language

when a student was told to stop talking, turn down the volume on his portable radio, leave the halls, or go to class. Many teachers considered profanity "as offensive . . . as some epithets are to Blacks," the researchers reported. However middle class the teachers might be, the researchers thought "very, very few" were racially prejudiced. They also noted that blacks made up 56 percent of those found guilty of fighting and assault and that during the second and third years of desegregation blacks made up 75 percent of those who were expelled after hearings that left "little room for error or bias."[202]

Teachers and community workers had various explanations for the disproportionate incidence of misbehavior among blacks. Bruce Laird, who was the only white member of the Union Baptist Church in Wilmington and who taught English for twenty-five years at P.S. du Pont before being transferred to Claymont High, observed that the younger generation of blacks came from a world that differed markedly from that of their parents and grandparents. The older generations had been raised within the orbit of their churches, but many young blacks were being socialized in a secular and matriarchal welfare community. "You wouldn't have this increase in theft and defiance and promiscuity if the churches still exercised influence over black youths," Laird said. "Girls in the welfare culture don't obey anyone. They learn to give orders, not take them." Many boys who had a bad attitude toward school had grown up with a minimum of parental supervision and had learned to get what they wanted at home by fighting. Lisa Bullock, who worked on a federally funded study of discipline problems, observed that even students who came from intact families sometimes brought defiant attitudes to school. "Parents used to tell their children to do whatever the teacher said, but now they tell them to do what they want. Teachers can no longer assume that students will be obedient." Olivia E. West, a black grandmother, complained that "instead of telling them to go and learn," some parents put a chip on their children's shoulder when they left for school.[203] "Don't take nothing from nobody," they advised. "Stand up for your rights."

One of the more ambitious efforts to reach hostile and alienated youths was the federally financed Student Special Concerns Program headed by Gloria Grantham, a black educational psychologist. By developing "innovative and affective classroom management skills" to replace the "power-based discipline" of yesteryear, Grantham said teachers could reform youths who were not disposed to behave properly. Teachers must recognize that many students would resist adult authority rather than lose face with their peers; if teachers were to succeed, words like "manners" and "respect" had to be defined and discussed, and students had to agree that certain punishments were appropriate if they broke the rules. Grantham recommended that teachers encourage "active student involvement" and move away from "repressive measures based on arbitrary authority."[204]

While these methods of reaching alienated youths were being developed, Grantham made it inconvenient for teachers to send unruly children to the principal's office. At her pilot project at the Darley Road Elementary School students could not be referred for traditional discipline unless the teacher prepared a written description and also listed witnesses to the incident. "We are piling on the paperwork to discourage teachers from suspending unruly children," Grantham's assistant explained. "We prefer other disciplinary policies. We want teachers to take the time to discuss the rules with the children. We think that if the children understand the rules and the reasons for the rules they will be more likely to obey."[205]

Most teachers remained skeptical. They doubted that such approaches to classroom management would be any more successful in reforming alienated youths than WYEAC had been in the 1960s. One instructor, Donna J. Lilly, expressed a prevalent view when she predicted that students would continue to misbehave as long as they thought adults would step in, "bail them out," and protect them from "suffer[ing] the consequences of their actions and lack of effort."[206]

Rather than cope with cultural conflict and a breakdown of discipline, thousands of parents removed their children from the public schools (Table 13). During the decade after the *Evans v. Buchanan* lawsuit was reopened, white enrollment in the public schools of the northern New Castle County desegregation area declined from 70,173 to 35,674, while enrollment in the county's private schools increased from 17,235 to 21,598. Of the 103 public schools that had been open in the year before busing, only sixty-eight remained in operation four years later. Meanwhile, the number of private schools increased from forty-four to seventy-eight—most of which were filled to capacity, many with waiting lists. Although some new schools were opened, most of the growth in private enrollments was due to increased matriculation in established Catholic schools that had been underenrolled on the eve of desegregation. Senator Joseph R. Biden recalled that as a practicing Catholic he had been

> out in our parish raising money trying to keep the [parochial] school open—everybody was leaving. [Then] busing comes along, and all of a sudden [students] are standing in line—literally standing in line. . . . I would argue that the reason there is not more flight now is that there is no place to fly to. Those who could move to Pennsylvania have done it, and that was a big move. And those who could get into the [private] schools have gotten in. Nobody else can make it, and there is no place else to go.[207]

Statistics pertaining to student enrollments should be interpreted cautiously; there are factors other than desegregation that influence the situ-

TABLE 13. Enrollment by Race,
New Castle County "Desegregation Area"
and Predecessor Components, 1971–1981

Year	White	% White Change	Black	Other	% Non-White	Total
1971	70,173		15,623	557	18.7	86,353
1972	68,827	– 1.9	15,782	887	19.4	85,496
1973	66,912	– 2.8	15,708	1,184	20.2	83,804
1974	64,679	– 3.3	15,804	1,351	21.0	81,834
1975	61,769	– 4.5	15,148	1,561	21.3	78,478
1976	57,019	– 7.7	15,271	1,571	22.8	73,861
1977	52,998	– 7.1	15,309	1,646	24.2	69,953
1978	47,008	– 11.3	14,891	1,659	26.0	63,558
1979	42,306	– 10.0	14,547	1,606	27.6	58,459
1980	39,980	– 7.8	14,317	1,849	29.3	55,146
1981	35,764	– 8.3	14,103	1,926	30.1	51,793

Sources: State of Delaware, Department of Public Instruction, Racial and Ethnic Reports.

tion. Advocates of metropolitan desegregation generally minimized the importance of white flight by attributing much of the decrease in public school enrollments to a declining white birth rate and to a general migration of families away from the Middle Atlantic region—phenomena generally thought to be unrelated to forced busing.[208]

Critics of the court's plan, on the other hand, portrayed the 50 percent decline in New Castle's white public school enrollment (especially when compared with the 25 percent increase in private enrollments) as striking testimony to the fact that resourceful parents can evade the best-laid plans of sociological jurisprudence. These critics noted that a 1976 state study that took account of birth rates and mobility patterns but did not consider the possible impact of desegregation had projected an annual decline of only 3 to 4 percent. They also recalled the 1960s, when the population of New Castle County increased by 25 percent and Delaware ranked second only to Florida as the fastest-growing state east of the Mississippi River. Since the white populations of Kent and Sussex counties continued to increase in the 1970s, while New Castle's white population decreased by 1.1 percent, critics again pointed to the schools. "The heart of the busing story," according to one observer, was not that some families moved away and others sent their children to private schools; it was that "people do not move into communities where there is forced busing." School district officials attributed half the enrollment decline to a drop in the white birth rate and the other half to rejection of the desegregated schools.[209]

The reasons for the flight were as diverse as the individual families. "You can say I'm chicken and that I'm running away, but I don't want to get involved in the whole thing," said a textile research specialist at Du Pont. A teacher who had taught in inner-city schools was convinced that her children's education would suffer under busing. A Chinese father was upset when his son described the disruptive behavior and disrespectful attitudes of several of his black classmates. A Railway Express worker complained that the federal judges had misinterpreted the Constitution. A black father wrote, "Assignment of students on the basis of the color of their skin is an American and South African indignity to which no children should be subjected." Antibusing leader William D. D'Onofrio characterized the flight from public schools as a principled rejection of what the judges had done in the name of the Constitution. "You simply cannot do to Americans what the courts have done on this issue. That is all there is to it."[210]

Many middle-class parents had purchased homes in the suburbs because they feared the pull of downward mobility. They thought drug addiction, early pregnancy, and low achievement were endemic in Wilmington, and they were adamantly opposed to having their children associate with lower-class blacks. A university professor said that under busing his daughter "would have a 30 to 45 minute drive into a neighborhood where I wouldn't want to spend the day." A suburban mother recalled that "once the school nurse telephoned and said my daughter was sick and I was afraid to go down to Wilmington and pick her up. I had to call my husband and have him leave the office and get her from school. I was that afraid." Another mother, a native Delawarean whose son had been enrolled in the same elementary school she had once attended, said she "love[d] this little state, but I'll be darned if I'll stay around to pay for the busing. I won't fight. I'll just move out." Many suburbanites felt cheated of something they had worked hard to obtain. "Oh, believe me, there is resentment here," one of them declared.[211]

The resentment was evident in October 1980, when more than 50,000 residents voted 10 to 1 against a referendum that would have increased the local school property tax by 20 percent. The school board maintained that the additional money was needed to meet the high cost of energy, spiraling inflation, and increasing salary and fringe benefits. Without the extra funds, one board member had said, "we're going to see . . . what happened in Cleveland and Philadelphia, where the public education system goes down the tube."[212]

These arguments were to no avail with voters who were unhappy with busing, angry at U.S. district judge Murray M. Schwartz, and distrustful of those who said desegregation was going well. So many people went to the polls that there were long lines and waits of up to two hours; there were not even enough printed ballots to accommodate the unusually large turnout. With 46,740 votes against the tax increase (and only 4,851 in favor), it was clear that many people had cast their ballots against court-ordered busing. "This is the first time the people in the county have had an opportunity to voice their opinion on the question," one school board member explained, "and I think it shows their negativism to the desegregated school system."[213]

Although resentment of busing was a major factor in the defeat of the referendum, the roots of the school district's financial difficulty were complex and tangled. Suburban school property taxes had been increased by 20 percent in 1978 to cover additional expenses related to desegregation — expenses for busing, for human relations specialists, and for developing a uniform curriculum. As a result, the annual expenditure per pupil in the desegregated school district was about $700 more than the national average and about $500 more than the amount provided elsewhere in Delaware.[214]

Shortly after desegregation began, however, suburban teachers went on strike, demanding that their salaries be increased to the level of the predominantly black Wilmington teachers, who were earning from $500 to $4,978 more than their suburban counterparts with similar credentials. The strikers demanded that the disparity be eliminated immediately, but the school board said it could only afford to equalize salaries over three years. In the end the dispute was settled by a complex financial package that froze the highest salaries so that "leveling up" could be achieved in half that time.[215]

Although the school board could not afford to increase the suburban salaries so rapidly, the strikers' demand for "equal pay for equal work" struck a responsive chord, and the board feared white flight would accelerate if the schools were closed for a long strike. The board also ignored recommendations that it could save $1 million each year by closing underenrolled neighborhood schools. Parents protested so vigorously whenever that possibility was mentioned that the superintendent feared the savings would be offset by a new and increased withdrawal pattern from the public schools.[216]

Governor du Pont correctly characterized the referendum vote as a rejection of lax financial management, but it would be a mistake to underestimate the prevalent resentment of busing. In 1981 Judge Murray M. Schwartz, who had transferred his own children to private schools, conceded that support for public schools had declined to the point where public education was in jeopardy. "You are at the crossroads," he told a group of school officials and lawyers. "If you do not have public support for your public school system, in the end you will have nothing. You will have children in the public school system who cannot afford to flee. That is what you will be left with." Schwartz denied responsibility for the sorry state of public education, but PAC leader James Venema expressed the view of many residents of New Castle County. "Certainly school officials must shoulder some of the blame for the disastrous condition of our federal schools," he wrote. "But Judge Schwartz cannot wash the dirt off his hands. . . . His preordained decision was 'forced racial balancing' at any cost. He now arrogantly tells school officials to shape up because the schools are at a 'crossroads.' Wrong! The schools were there in 1978, and he turned his bus down the wrong road."[217]

The results of metropolitan desegregation in New Castle County are susceptible to different interpretations. William L. Taylor, a committed integrationist and one of the lawyers for the plaintiffs in *Evans v. Buchanan,* has hailed the experience in Delaware as "one of the success stories of busing." Senator Joseph R. Biden, on the other hand, more accurately characterized busing in New Castle County as a failure. "It is true that there has been no violence in Wilmington," Biden stated. "[But] this doesn't mean there haven't been other serious negative impacts on the community. Anyone who talks with parents, teachers, and students, both black and white, . . . will agree."[218]

The best results from desegregation came in student performance on the California Achievement Tests, where blacks and whites both scored impressive gains. Many people scoffed at the tests, however, and maintained that academic and disciplinary standards had declined. Rather than submit to judges who were intent upon substituting their sense of what is decent for the intention of the Fourteenth Amendment, many parents moved away from the desegregation area or sent their children to private schools. After five years of busing, most of those who wanted to leave had gone, and the public schools began to regain a measure of stability. The proportion of black students continued to increase, but at a much slower rate, and there remained the possibility that another wave of white flight would occur. Some whites who patronized the public schools did so enthusiastically, believing that integrated education was a marvelous learning experience that prepared youngsters for situations they would eventually have to face as adults. A greater number accepted the public schools because they could not afford the alternatives. Thirty years after *Brown* the prevailing mood in New Castle County was a combination of resentment, acquiescence, and apathy.[219]

The public schools in Delaware today face an uncertain future. The percentage decline in high school graduates is projected at a steeper rate than that of any state in the nation, and the University of Delaware predicts that to maintain the size of its entering class, two-thirds of the freshmen will have to be residents of other states. Governor du Pont has secured passage of legislation that may make Delaware a major center for banking and insurance, but it remains to be seen if middle-class managers and office workers will settle in an area where the public schools are no longer highly regarded. Assessing the situation candidly, Marilyn Harwick, the primary white initiator of the *Evans v. Buchanan* lawsuit, says that the public schools in New Castle County are

> at the stage where Wilmington was in the early 1960s. Many of my friends are teachers, and they say some classes are like a zoo. Our next door neighbor —a black woman from Trinidad—won't send her daughter to the public schools. I don't know what we'll do when it comes time to send our little granddaughter Rebecca to school. . . . We won the lawsuit, but we didn't want what has happened. All we wanted was the opportunity to send our children to good public schools. We would have been delighted with a voluntary transfer plan, but the lawyers and judges lost sight of our interests. Instead of pursuing free choice, they got caught up in the rationale of racial balance.[220]

PART FIVE

BACK IN TOPEKA

Immediately upon receipt of the Supreme Court's order to desegregate, officials in Topeka, Kansas came forward with a plan that satisfied the district court, and the *Brown* case then lay dormant for twenty-four years. Yet by 1979 the meaning of desegregation had changed, and black plaintiffs returned to court to demand that Topeka abandon neighborhood schools and achieve the sort of proportional mixing that *Brunson* and *Evans* had required in South Carolina and Delaware.

The black community in Topeka was relatively smaller than in the sister districts, with the proportion of blacks increasing from 8.3 percent in 1950 to 9.5 percent in 1980. Nor was the pattern of residential concentration as sharply etched in Topeka as in most American cities. Most blacks and many whites of middling circumstances lived on the east side of town, with the more well-to-do whites and a sprinkling of blacks settled in western Topeka. Yet there was nothing resembling the dense pockets of blacks found in many larger cities. "We don't have a concentrated black ghetto here," explained Don Oden, a black president of the local school board. "There aren't a great many blacks in the western part of the city, but we're not concentrated in one corner of town."[1]

Perhaps because the black population was comparatively small and relatively dispersed, desegregation fared better in Topeka than in Washington, Prince Edward, Summerton, or Wilmington. There were some problems, of course. Academic standards were buffeted, and racial relations became especially strained in the late 1960s and early 1970s. Yet, despite the difficulties, there was nothing like the massive white flight that occurred in the other districts. In Topeka, at least, desegregation was not an obvious failure.

I

Under Topeka's 1955 desegregation plan all children, regardless of race, were assigned to schools in the neighborhood of their residence. Since the residential districts were racially imbalanced, this did not lead to proportional mixing in each school. Yet in the mid-1950s *Brown* was not understood to require state officials to go beyond racial neutrality. "Desegregation does not mean that there must be intermingling of the races in all school districts," a unanimous U.S. district court wrote in accepting the Topeka plan. "It means only that they may not be prevented from intermingling or going to school together because of race."[2]

For more than a decade after *Brown,* blacks in Topeka did not complain about the lack of proportional mixing. Concern focused instead on protecting the jobs of black teachers. In 1953, when a Supreme Court decision on *Brown* was thought to be impending, the Topeka Board of Education had refused to reemploy six black teachers. It gave as its reason the belief that "the majority of people in Topeka will not want to employ Negro teachers next year for white children." The teachers were rehired when the Supreme Court postponed its decision, and the number of black teachers increased gradually, from about twenty-five at the time of *Brown* to forty in 1969 and seventy-five in 1974. These black teachers made up 7 percent of the overall faculty—only one-half the black percentage of the total student enrollment (14 percent)—but blacks were so well represented on the staff that by 1974 minorities made up 12.5 percent of the school district's combined faculty and staff.[3]

Topeka's first crisis after desegregation grew out of conditions at the city's integrated high schools. Unlike the elementary schools, which had been segregated in the years before *Brown,* the high schools had been desegregated for decades. Yet despite the long experience with biracial education, there had been discrimination in the high schools, and prior to 1955 some of it was not so subtle. Black and white students attended the same classes at Topeka High School, but whites were summoned to segregated assemblies by one set of bells while blacks responded to another chime—the so-called "nigger bell." Blacks and whites played together on the football team, but the school maintained two basketball teams, the white Trojans and the black Ramblers. In the fall the Homecoming queen was always white, but in basketball season there were both black and white winter queens. Author Richard Kluger observed that black girls were "urged to avoid taking typing and stenography since they were given to understand that few jobs requiring these skills would be waiting for them in the community." As late as 1969, the Human Relations Commission reported that black boys were steered into "courses that will lead to trade school rather than preparatory courses that will lead to college."[4]

Blatant discrimination was curtailed after *Brown,* but a 1970 survey by the NAACP indicated that three-fourths of the black high school students still felt victimized by neglect and outright prejudice. They said that as members of a minority they found it almost impossible to win election to the student government, the cheerleading squad, or the drill team. In the classrooms, they said, many teachers showed racial prejudice by making disparaging comments and by imposing harsher penalties on blacks who were guilty of minor offenses. They also alleged that some teachers assumed blacks were virtually ineducable and thus made no effort to assist students with special problems.[5]

Black discontent came to a head in the spring of 1970 when the principal of Highland Park High School in east Topeka refused to authorize a school assembly on the Thursday of Black Culture Week. Other black assemblies and presentations had been held earlier in the week, and principal Bob Jennings decided that by Thursday the students needed time to catch up on class work that had been interrupted.[6] Jennings did, however, authorize use of the auditorium that day for a meeting to promote charities favored by Cathy Menninger, the wife of one of the psychiatrists associated with the world-famous Menninger Foundation. Black students did not object to Menninger's project, which involved securing sponsors who would contribute to charity for each mile the students walked, but they resented the fact that a meeting was held on the day when they had been refused permission for an assembly. They also took exception to what they regarded as bowing to a white woman with an influential name. "Jennings just caved in to White Power," one member of the school board recalled. "The black students were incensed and decided to show some Black Power." Shortly after the meeting they set fire to the curtains in the auditorium.[7]

The damage from the fire came to $27,446, with the blaze destroying the 20-foot curtains, auditorium seats, the stage floor, a grand piano, and theatrical equipment. Several youths were later convicted in juvenile court, but in the meantime black high school students organized a city-wide black boycott of classes. Asserting that black students were "punished too severely for minor offenses," the black protesters called for an end to "harrassment" and the reinstatement of all blacks who had been expelled or suspended. They demanded the employment of more blacks "as cooks, secretaries, teachers, counselors and principals" and the dismissal of twenty allegedly prejudiced teachers and administrators, including the principals of two of the city's three high schools. The black students also demanded a general review of school rules and assurance that no disciplinary action would be taken against any student participating in the boycott.[8]

The school board was caught between two groups, with most whites demanding prosecution of the arsonists and calling for strict enforcement of the schools' rules against disruption and truancy. At an assembly of a thousand people at Eisenhower Junior High School, one father maintained, "There is no excuse for a bunch of troublemakers to be able to destroy property." Another father complained that "the halls at Highland Park High aren't safe to walk in . . . Negro boys walk arm-in-arm down the corridors, and the whites have to duck to get out of the way." A mother said there was talk of a vigilante committee where she worked. "We're tired of juvenile delinquents running around loose," the woman said. "This town is really going to rip loose if those responsible for all this aren't punished." "The silent majority wants the school board to know they don't condone violence, disruption, or threats by any element," another man declared. "Those responsible should be expelled and prosecuted, and authority given back to principals and administrators who have felt their hands are tied."[9]

White resentment had been building for years. During the 1960s complaints about theft, intimidation, and extortion by blacks had led teachers to demand that security guards be placed on duty in the high schools—a request that black attorney Charles S. Scott condemned as biased and "tantamount to . . . a condition of servitude." In 1968 school authorities also found it necessary for the first time to specify that verbal abuse of teachers and the use of vulgar language was in violation of the code of student conduct. Even Linda Brown Smith, the first-named plaintiff in Topeka's original desegregation suit, was concerned about the lack of discipline. Her younger sister, who taught sixth grade at mostly black Monroe Elementary School, reported that their discipline problem had gotten "out of hand. . . . The teacher tells the kids something to do and he [*sic*] just talks right back." Mrs. Smith observed similar problems at the schools her children attended. She thought it was because many parents had failed to instill proper attitudes in their homes. "We have so many broken homes now," she explained. "So many mothers are working."[10]

In February of 1970, before the fire at Highland Park, several white students had informed a group of county legislators of "fighting in the halls . . . and widespread use of profanity and obscenities at the schools." After the fire about fifty whites marched on the Board of Education with placards demanding "Law and Order in Our Schools." One of the boys said whites were forced to say "Black Is Beautiful" before they could leave a rest room. "I think [blacks] ought to be treated like white people," another said. "If we get up in class and say 'damn,' we'd be punished. Yet teachers and counselors are afraid to do anything when blacks scream obscenities in their faces." The white students said the enforcement of two sets of rules—one for whites and a more lenient standard for blacks—was hurting education and morale at the school.[11]

Some blacks sympathized with the call for uniformly enforcing a strict disciplinary policy. Student leader Lance Murphy, who has since become a policeman in Topeka, recalled, "My whole point during the protest was that we should have strict rules for everybody." He conceded that some white teachers allowed black youths to neglect their school work, misbehave, and defy the authorities. "They'd look the other way and say, 'Well, that's how they do. They're just niggers.' They thought we always wore our hats and that we played our 'ghetto blasters' [loud portable radios] even when we were at home. The brothers know better. At home I had to take off my hat and turn down the radio or my daddy would knock me down." Murphy characterized white acceptance of black boorishness as another indication of racial insensitivity and, more fundamentally, of a lack of white concern for blacks. He recalled that the black teachers at Washington Elementary School in his neighborhood never tolerated the abuse and misbehavior that white teachers routinely accepted at Topeka High. "Those black teachers at Washington really cared about students," Murphy recalled. "At least they cared about some of us."[12]

Although there were occasional criticisms of teachers who, through fear, indifference, or sympathy, allowed black students to pass through the grades without measuring up to academic standards, there were many more complaints about traditional classes that were said to be "not relevant." The boycotters wanted "classes [we] can relate to"—more courses on black studies and contemporary social problems. They wanted a committee of blacks to interview and hire prospective teachers who would use "new and innovative educational techniques" in classes where "self-expression and originality is optimum." They thought discipline should be used not as a punishment but as "an educational tool to rehabilitate students," and they wanted a student grievance committee to be consulted in disciplinary cases.[13]

To make the boycott effective, the student leaders enlisted the cooperation of the black clergymen in Topeka. This was no small accomplishment, for some of the black ministers initially saw no justification for the fire and boycott. "You have created a monster and something that is uncontrollable," one of them declared in a private meeting. Yet, because they saw the need to keep the boycotters out of trouble, the black ministers opened their churches as day centers. Thanks to the support of the clergy, the divisions within black Topeka were not apparent to most whites, and the morale of the boycotting students remained high. Between 17 April and 30 April 1970, approximately three-fourths of the black students stayed away from the schools.[14]

Fearing that Topeka might be subjected to the sort of trashing that had occurred in the nearby city of Lawrence, the city supplied police with riot gear and stationed them on rooftops downtown. But violence was averted, and sympathetic whites and black clergymen stepped in with a major effort at reconciliation and crisis management.[15] Among the whites, the most conspicuous role was played by Connie Menninger, the sister-in-law of the woman whose assembly for charity had touched off the blaze at Highland Park High and the wife of another member of the famous clan of psychiatrists. As a member of the Board of Education, Connie Menninger immediately perceived trouble ahead if truancy regulations were enforced and the boycotting seniors did not receive diplomas at the commencement in June. To get blacks "off the hook" and to reduce tensions, Menninger supported a plan whereby regular studies were suspended for seven school days. During this period attendance was made voluntary, and teachers were told to focus on human relations and on "understanding the problems facing the community and the schools."[16]

During this hiatus an ad hoc committee was set up to consider the students' grievances. Composed of representatives from the school administration, the school board, and the boycotting students, this group met daily. By the end of April its progress was such that the Reverend Edward Kirtdoll, the pastor at the black St. Luke Baptist Church and a man who enjoyed the confidence of the student leaders, urged that the boycott be ended.[17]

The blacks returned to class on May 4, and the seniors received their diplomas a month later (after marching into the assembly with fists clenched in the black power salute). The ad hoc committee continued to meet regularly and by the end of the summer had come up with recommendations that, when implemented in the fall of 1970, enabled the schools to operate with fewer disruptions. Blacks, whites, and Chicanos were guaranteed proportional representation on the cheerleading squad, drill team, and student government, and special efforts were made to supplement the curriculum with material on the cultural contributions of minority groups. No teachers were dismissed for racial prejudice, but the principal at Topeka High was reassigned and the dress code was changed to accommodate long hair and short skirts. The ban on smoking at the high schools was dropped, and students were allowed to leave school during lunch time. A new student bill of rights assured youngsters the right to a conference before a short-term suspension and a formal hearing before an extended suspension or expulsion.[18]

Some found it difficult to work under the new regime. Fourteen of the thirty-one teachers employed in two eastside schools actually resigned during the first four months of the 1970–71 school year. A special parents' advisory committee was then established to interview prospective teachers. Their job was to find employees "with sensitivity to modern life and the knowledge required to survive in culturally deprived areas." [19]

Some whites saw reform as the key to averting violence. Psychiatrist Walter Menninger, the husband of school board member Connie Menninger, advised his fellow citizens to "avoid the trap of the all-or-nothing stance." To protect the essentials of the society, Menninger thought Topeka would have to pay an "inevitable cost." It was necessary to give some ground in order "to control these people . . . whom society is not able to successfully train to live by the rules of society." The Reverend John J. Skelly similarly maintained that compromise and liberalized regulations were the keys to easing tensions and averting violence. [20]

Yet most whites and some blacks viewed the situation from a different perspective. Believing that the boycott eventually would have ended even if there had been no compromises, the faculty at Highland Park High School endorsed a statement condemning the school board for suspending regular classes. "We have really taken a beating . . . , and we all feel let down," one teacher said. "Most of us were upset when [the school board] made school attendance voluntary. . . . Many of us feel the absentees should make up the work they have missed . . . if they are to pass." [21] When the school board suspended classes, several parents filed a suit to protect their children's right to regular academic classes, and 1,840 citizens signed petitions calling for the enforcement of truancy regulations. District Judge George Templar indicated in comments from the bench that the school board had acted illegally, but the point was moot since normal classes had been resumed before a trial could be scheduled. Connie Menninger recalled that she was "really clobbered" when she ran for reelection to the school board. "Especially in the white residential districts there was a terrible ruckus. People complained about 'those liberals' and 'that Menninger woman.'" [22]

Even some blacks had reservations about the compromises that ended the boycott. In an interview in 1982, former student leader Lance Murphy expressed the belief that the reforms had harmed blacks by undermining discipline in the schools. "We wanted more controls, and they took the controls away," he said. "All we wanted was an end to racial discrimination and equal treatment for blacks and whites." Murphy thought powerful white liberals, always in control, used the black boycott and the threat of disruption as a pretext for making changes they had long favored. They thought their children would do better with more independent study, more elective courses, and fewer disciplinary rules. Murphy said he knew this approach would not work well with poor blacks. "But the liberals don't care about us. They think it's impossible to discipline lower-class blacks. They think we're going to fail anyway, so what's the use of trying to make us learn. Back in 1970 I thought I was doing the right thing. Now I know we were used."[23]

After the crisis of 1970 things quieted down but never returned to what had once been normal. So many electives were added to the curriculum that high school students in Topeka had more courses to choose from than students at many colleges. At Topeka High School examinations were no longer required as a matter of school policy but were left to the discretion of individual teachers. Stories in the student newspaper called attention to the availability of birth control devices and treatment for veneral disease, to the progressive educational theories of Charles E. Silberman, to Ralph Nader's criticisms of American business, and to the way the American system supposedly discouraged women. Editorials questioned the need for uniformed police in the school, called for teachers to be evaluated by their students, and maintained that standardized tests discriminated against blacks. Teachers were paid $30 a day to attend sensitivity workshops where they were instructed in the etiquette of race relations and techniques thought to be effective in controlling black students. Black counselors were employed to deal with incidents of racial discrimination and with black parents who, one of the counselors recalled, "would come to school at the drop of a hat . . . and expect me to coddle their kids and endorse them in every case."[24]

After 1970 the races generally congregated separately at Topeka High School, with blacks occupying the center of the main hall before classes while whites moved to the outlying spaces—a reversal from the situation up through the 1960s. At lunch period one could observe a striking contrast of cultures as black youths wearing pimp hats played loud music on portable radios just outside the school's central Gothic tower. Outside the classrooms and athletics, members of the races generally went separate ways. One black father thought this resulted from the students' "basic honesty." By the time the youngsters reached junior high school, he said, most students recognized that their parents associated with members of their own race whenever they could. Hence they saw "no good reason why they should have to put up with tensions and conflicts that most adults manage to avoid in their lives."[25]

With the passage of time racial tensions eased somewhat. Most students got along all right, and each year there was some interracial dating which almost always involved black males and white females, who were then ostracized by other white students. At football games there was not much racial mixing in the grandstand, but neither were the rooting sections conspicuously racial; rather than sitting in a block with all members of their race, blacks and whites sat in small, racially homogeneous groups that were interspersed with one another. Some whites complained that school authorities were so sensitive to black allegations of mistreatment that they had become oblivious to reverse discrimination against whites. And almost everyone conceded that in racially mixed schools like Topeka High (where the minority proportion increased to 33 percent in 1982), "things are always boiling just below the surface." "Anybody who doesn't realize that is a damn fool," Connie Menninger said. "Things are better now than in 1970. But there's still an undercurrent of racial tension and school administrators feel a real need to have police visible on the perimeter of the schools and to have security guards stationed in the halls. White kids who haven't had much experience with blacks come into a different world at Topeka High. They have to learn to keep their cool. The black kids can be very provocative."[26]

Despite the interracial difficulties, the Menningers sent their six children to Topeka High. "I wouldn't have had them go anywhere else," Mrs. Menninger stated. She and many other prominent Topekans wanted their children to have the experience of associating with diverse groups before they continued their education, as the Menninger children did, at more exclusive sanctuaries like Stanford, M.I.T., and the University of Kansas. There was no ability grouping in Topeka and only a skeletal enrichment program for gifted children (in contrast with a full array of special programs for slow learners). Nevertheless, academic standards remained high in the college preparatory courses, with a handful of students winning competitive merit scholarships and a larger number gaining admission to well-regarded colleges and universities. On the standardized Iowa Test of Basic Skills, Topeka's elementary students scored above the national norm throughout the 1970s. High school students did not do as well, but, except in 1977 and 1978 (when their average scores fell to the 36th and 25th percentiles), Topeka's teenagers hovered near the national average on the Sequential Tests of Academic Progress.[27]

Of course, many people did not want their children to have to deal with the problems that accompanied desegregation in Topeka. By 1970 the population of the city had grown to 115,000, including a substantial number of professional and managerial people — the sort of people who elsewhere had moved to homogeneous middle-class suburbs rather than confront problems of racial and cultural adjustment. In addition to functioning as the hub of an extensive agricultural hinterland, Topeka since the 1870s has been the headquarters of the Atchison, Topeka and Santa Fe Railroad. As the capital of Kansas it is also the home of a large number of middle-class civil servants. Yet Topeka is best known as a center of medical research and treatment. First and foremost there is the Menninger Foundation, known throughout the world for its work in psychiatry. But there are other hospitals as well: the Kansas State Hospital, a Veterans Administration Hospital, the Capper Foundation for Crippled Children, St. Francis Hospital, and Memorial Hospital. About 10,000 people are involved in Topeka's medical community.

Some of Topeka's professional people welcomed desegregation, but others who wanted a different ambience for their children patronized the local parochial schools or moved to one of the four predominantly white suburban school districts adjoining the city. Despite a declining white birth rate, enrollment in these systems remained at about 13,000 students throughout the 1970s—a period when Topeka's public school enrollment declined by more than 30 percent, from 22,753 to 15,572.[28] Migration to the suburbs probably would have assumed greater proportions if Topeka's neighborhood school policy had not made it possible for parents to ensure a middle-class socialization for their children on the west side of town. West Topeka was the major growth area of the city during the 1970s. It was an area of middle-class housing developments, an area so predominantly white that only 39 blacks could be counted among the 1,430 students enrolled at Topeka West High School in 1982.[29] As noted above, there was no well-defined black ghetto in heterogeneous eastern Topeka, but to the west the population was homogeneously middle class and overwhelmingly white. White flight was minimal in Topeka because well-fixed parents who were skeptical of liberal sociology did not have to flee the city; they simply moved to the west side of town.

II

With federal courts elsewhere insisting on proportional mixing in the name of desegregation, it was probably inevitable that attention in Topeka eventually would focus on racial imbalance in neighborhood schools. The confrontation was hastened by the presence in the community of white civil rights lawyer Fred W. Phelps. The father of thirteen children and the pastor of a small primitive Baptist church on the west side of town, Phelps was a graduate of Bob Jones University and of the law school at Washburn University in Topeka.

In 1964 he won acquittal of a group of black students who had been arrested for trespassing during a sit-in at the University of Kansas.[30] Phelps then achieved greater prominence as the scourge of an unethical business known as the Tom, Dick and Harry Furniture Store. One case involved Marlene Miller, a black woman who had paid cash for what she had been led to believe was a new television set. The set had been used previously as a rental unit—a fact that came to light when a repair man discovered a tell-tale sticker inside the set. Miller then sued and collected $12,000 in damages. Another of Phelps's cases concerned a white welfare recipient whose television had been repossessed. With the assistance of prominent Menninger Foundation psychiatrist Herbert Modlin, Phelps convinced a jury that Diana Carnegie and her children had suffered traumatic neuroses as a result of the repossession. The Kansas Supreme Court later disallowed the jury's award of $45,000 in damages, but the case reinforced Phelps's belief that unscrupulous business practices and unchristian racial discrimination could be ended if perpetrators were required to pay for the mental and emotional pain that accompanied victimization.[31]

With this belief Phelps in 1973 prepared a desegregation suit on behalf of Marlene Miller's ten-year-old niece and ward, Evelyn Rene Johnson. Young Rene lived on the east side of Topeka in an area that one longtime resident and neighbor described as "like a bad dream. . . . The neighborhood gets worse, the kids act and look worse every year, and the bad words are coming out of younger mouths every fall." The children from the neighborhood were assigned to the Parkdale Elementary School, a school whose enrollment was 87 percent black and Hispanic at a time when these minorities together made up only 18 percent of Topeka's total student population. Rene's suit alleged that she had been denied the advantages of "social intercourse and opportunity to study with, engage in discussions with and exchange ideas with white children who are providentially favored economically and socially." The suit also charged that Parkdale and other disproportionately minority schools on the east side of town were in disrepair and contained inferior equipment.[32]

The lawsuit took Topeka by surprise, for most people in the community thought their schools had long since been desegregated. At a Harvard law school seminar earlier in 1973, however, Phelps had been brought up to date on recent developments in desegregation law. After reviewing *Green* and its progeny, Phelps concluded that school districts that had been found guilty of legal segregation had an affirmative obligation to achieve substantially proportional racial mixing in each school. To create a unitary system, he thought, it was necessary to dismantle the last vestiges of the racial imbalance that had characterized the historic dual system of segregated schools. As Phelps explained to a newspaper reporter, "It's not just that blacks aren't getting their fair share of education funds. It's just that once a city has been found guilty of having laws permitting school segregation, it simply has to integrate its schools. . . ." Phelps's suit on behalf of Evelyn Rene Johnson sought a court order requiring an even dispersion of blacks throughout the public schools in all sections of Topeka.[33]

In this respect Phelps's petition did not differ from the pleadings in *Brunson* and *Evans* and other desegregation cases. Yet Phelps broke new ground when he joined a plea for monetary damages to the request for injunctive relief. As Phelps assessed the situation, Rene Johnson's education would have "a value to her . . . of at least $10,000 lower than that of white children . . . attending elementary and junior high schools in West Topeka." Moreover, Phelps calculated that Rene was only one of 10,000 minority children who had been similarly disadvantaged by attending disproportionately black schools in the years since *Brown*. Phelps then demanded that a like amount of punitive damages be assessed against the Topeka schools for failing to dismantle their racially imbalanced dual system. Phelps thus sought a total of $200 million in damages for Evelyn Rene Johnson and the class of 10,000 students she represented. If courts awarded damages of this order, Phelps said, segregation could be ended in less time than it takes to read even a paragraph in a sociological treatise.[34]

Like most civil rights lawyers of the early 1970s, Phelps assumed that race relations would improve and black students would develop a better self-image and do better academic work if they were dispersed as a minority in predominantly white schools. Of course Phelps also stood to profit if his clients collected large awards for damages, and he would merit at least a footnote in American history if he persuaded the federal judiciary to rely on monetary damages as a key to achieving balanced desegregation. Yet fame, fortune, and liberal sociology were not the only considerations. First and foremost, Phelps was a man of the cloth and a father of children who attended a nearby elementary school named in honor of the Reverend Charles M. Sheldon, a nineteenth-century Topeka Congregationalist who had once written a best-selling novel that challenged Americans to be guided in their actions by constant consideration of what Jesus would have done in the same situation. The Sheldon School was newer than Rene Johnson's Parkdale, and 295 of its 300 students were white (in contrast to only 35 whites among the 270 students at Parkdale). "It couldn't have been clearer to my mind that this was in violation of *Brown*," Phelps said. "That's why I sued the school board."[35]

The District Court denied class action status to the *Johnson* suit in 1975, and Phelps's subsequent appeals to the Tenth Circuit Court and the U.S. Supreme Court were to no avail. The case proceeded for a time as an individual action and finally was settled out of court. With beguiling courtroom manners and an ability to quote extemporaneously from the biblical prophets, Abraham Lincoln, Lord Mansfield, and Earl Warren, Phelps had been known to cast a spell over more than one jury. After a job discrimination case in which Phelps won $500,000 in damages for a black plaintiff, U.S. District Judge Patrick F. Kelly declared that the reverend barrister was "one of the finest trial lawyers . . . that I have ever known." The company that insured Topeka's public schools thought Phelps was unlikely to succeed with his unprecedented claims but calculated that a full defense would cost approximately $100,000. The company therefore concluded that this was an instance where discretion was the better part of valor. It settled out of court for $19,500.[36]

Since out-of-court settlements have no significance as legal precedent, Phelps failed to establish a new principle in the *Johnson* lawsuit. Yet the settlement did raise suspicions that he was making money through a sophisticated form of legal extortion. Noting that Phelps had filed more than one-half the class-action suits in Kansas, one federal judge summed up the feelings of many members of the bar when he reportedly asserted that Phelps was "making all the money in the world" by filing suits of little merit in the hope that defendants would offer a settlement rather than suffer the inconvenience and expense of litigation.[37]

The *Johnson* lawsuit prompted HEW to make an investigation of how desegregation was being implemented in Topeka. Corroborating the principal points in Phelps's complaint, HEW discovered that the racial enrollments in Topeka's fifty schools were widely skewed. In seven schools on the east side of town blacks and Hispanics made up more than 40 percent of the students, whereas enrollment in seven schools in western Topeka was more than 95 percent white. The HEW investigators also reported that a disproportionate percentage of minority teachers were employed in schools with larger-than-average enrollments of blacks and Hispanics, and that minority students were more likely to attend schools that were older and smaller than those attended by whites.[38]

The Topeka public schools maintained that racial imbalance resulted not from discrimination but from a color-blind policy of assigning students to schools in their neighborhoods. The schools on the east side were admittedly older and smaller than those to the west, but that was because east Topeka had been settled earlier. School administrators also noted that the eastern schools generally had superior libraries and a smaller average class size. They pointed out as well that the great majority of teachers in all sections were white and said that more blacks were employed on the east side because they had been teaching there for years and the district had not compelled them to move.[39]

HEW nevertheless cited Topeka for failing to comply with its guidelines for enforcing the 1964 Civil Rights Act. The director of the department's regional office in Kansas City explained that the "substantially disproportionate minority student compositions" in some schools were "clearly the result of a former dual pattern of operation." HEW also concluded that the older school buildings were "generally inferior" and that teachers had been assigned "in a manner which reinforced the racial identity of substantially disproportionate and one-race schools." HEW informed the school board that racial enrollments in individual schools should not vary by more than

20 percentage points from the proportion of minority students in the entire district. It then gave Topeka one month to make arrangements for reducing minority enrollments to less than 40 percent in each school. Otherwise, HEW indicated, it would take steps to cut off approximately $1.3 million in annual federal aid.[40]

In response, the Topeka school board hastily prepared a plan that would have satisfied HEW's guidelines by revising school attendance boundaries and by closing seven disproportionately minority schools. The proposal was withdrawn, however, when public hearings indicated that most people in Topeka considered the new plan an educational monstrosity. "Without regard to race, color, creed or national origin," the local newspaper reported, "voters, neighbors, parents and taxpayers lined up before microphones and television cameras to chastise the local board and berate Washington bureaucrats who are trying to force them to create a 'racial balance' in their schools." Partisans of neighborhood schools complained that many students would have to travel longer distances to school and cross busy highways, while integrationists noted that minority enrollments could still vary by as much as 39 percent. Parents on the east side of town were particularly upset because their children would have to travel longer distances past closed schools. "My girl's not gonna go to Highland Park," one mother said. "This is not upgrading the schools. It's just switchin'."[41]

The Topeka schools blocked HEW from cutting off federal funds by securing an injunction from the local district court. Because a final decree had never been entered to close the books on the *Brown v. Board of Education* lawsuit of the 1950s, the court ruled that it had retained exclusive jurisdiction to determine whether the Topeka schools were desegregated.[42] Then, after repulsing HEW's attempt to apply economic sanctions, the school board proceeded to develop a Long Range Facilities Plan that ultimately satisfied both HEW and most people in Topeka. Under the plan, eleven schools were closed between 1974 and 1979, and $13 million was spent for repairs and new schools. Attendance zones were also redrawn, with the director of demographic services conceding that the new boundaries were set up to promote more racial mixing (although a precise balance was impossible due to natural barriers like the Kansas River and the Shunganunga channel, manmade obstacles like the Santa Fe railroad tracks and some major highways, and the overwhelmingly white character of the population on the western side of town). In 1976, HEW dismissed its complaint against the Topeka schools and accepted the Long Range Plan, along with an affirmative action program and a citizens' advisory board, as substantial compliance with desegregation.[43]

Civil rights groups nevertheless charged that the new arrangements fell short of achieving the degree of racial mixing that HEW should have required. In 1974 the Topeka branch of the NAACP had released a twelve-page report urging busing for equal racial dispersion througout all the school districts in Shawnee County. In 1979 the U.S. Commission on Civil Rights urged the Department of Justice to investigate the situation in Topeka, and its local affiliate, the Kansas Advisory Committee, asked HEW to make another "thorough and comprehensive investigation of the extent to which Topeka's schools are in compliance with the requirements of the Constitution." After receiving a formal complaint from a white psychiatrist, HEW made a second investigation, which finally resulted in Topeka's being found in full compliance with the Constitution and the Civil Rights Act.[44]

This was not good enough for Fred W. Phelps. Even before the results of the second HEW investigation had been released, Phelps had filed another suit, this time on behalf of Marlene Miller's daughter, Carla Michelle. The suit noted that in 1979 blacks still made up as few as 3 percent and as many as 74 percent of the students in particular schools (as compared with a range of from 1 percent to 92 percent at the time of the *Johnson* lawsuit). Phelps conceded that the school board had changed attendance zones in an attempt to promote racial mixing but said that the Long Range Plan was "nothing but a cloak to cover continued segregation." Most black students remained in disproportionately black schools where, Phelps alleged, they inevitably suffered "feelings of inferiority as to their status in the community, thus affecting their hearts and minds in a way unlikely ever to be undone." Phelps requested injunctive relief, including cross-town busing to achieve racial balance throughout Topeka.[45]

Then Phelps filed a second class action along the lines of *Johnson,* alleging unconstitutional segregation and requesting monetary damages for a proposed class of 10,000. "Twenty years after *Brown,*" Phelps said, the Topeka school board was still "thrashing about resisting meaningful integration." He wanted compensation for the children who were pyschologically damaged by the policies of the school board. "If I can win it," Phelps observed, "that will be a lot of money."[46]

For a while it appeared that, as with *Johnson,* Phelps had upstaged Charles S. Scott, the local black attorney who had represented the Browns in the desegregation litigation of the 1950s. This time, however, the dean of Topeka's black legal community was not caught napping. On 22 August 1979, Scott trumped Phelps's lawsuit by returning to the district court in Topeka with an allegation that, because black students and teachers were unevenly dispersed, the school board had never truly desegregated its schools. To remedy this situation Scott requested that the *Brown* case be reopened and that the court issue whatever orders were necessary to bring Topeka into full compliance with all constitutional requirements.[47]

District judge Richard Rogers granted Scott's request, and although final disposition of the new litigation will not be made for several years, one effect became apparent immediately. With *Brown* reopened, Phelps's desegregation suits were dismissed on the grounds that separate actions could not be maintained. With *Brown* still alive, there was no need for additional litigation to determine whether the mandates of the Supreme Court had been implemented.[48]

Some whites in Topeka expressed skepticism about Scott's motives. They said the black attorney had been miffed in 1973 when Fred Phelps unexpectedly filed the *Johnson* suit and then was paid court by a phalanx of liberal newsmen. Scott reportedly was determined not to suffer a similar neglect when the media descended on Topeka in 1979 for the twenty-fifth anniversary of *Brown*.[49] Yet this may have been unfair to Scott. For a brief period around the time when *Johnson* was filed, Scott opposed dispersion and touted the advantages of black control of predominantly black neighborhood schools. "It's peculiar what twenty years of disillusionment can do to you," he said. Scott asserted that by making it difficult to maintain predominantly black institutions, dispersion actually undermined blacks' confidence and placed them at a psychological disadvantage.[50]

Most of the time, however, Scott tended to equate desegregation with dispersion. "If there's any meaning whatsoever to desegregation or racial balance," he told reporters in 1974, "there has to be some sort of program such as busing or a central educational complex where kids from all over the city come to school." To overcome housing patterns that inhibited interracial mixing, Scott thought, there had to be "some sort of artificial type of program such as busing. . . ."[51]

His opinion was echoed by two young black lawyers who are doing most of the work on the new *Brown* litigation, Charles S. Scott, Jr., and Richard E. Jones. Scott, the more outspoken of the two, said the quality of black education had actually declined in the years since *Brown*, whereas Jones conceded that before desegregation black teachers identified with their community and its schools and were more likely to go out of their way to assist black students. The two men nevertheless insisted on the importance of racial dispersion because, as Jones explained, "we need to learn how to get along with whites."[52]

The plaintiffs in the new *Brown* lawsuit maintained that Topeka had failed to satisfy its constitutional obligation to establish a unitary school system. Topeka's youngsters were no longer segregated, as they once had been, but Jones and the Scotts said substantial integration had been thwarted by the pattern of residential settlement. "The school board will argue that racially imbalanced neighborhoods are the result of personal choices," Jones predicted. "But that's not true. When the case comes to trial we will show that there is always some government policy that has aggravated the pattern of residential separation." Jones said the legal prerequisites for dispersion would be satisfied if the court was convinced, for example, that racial imbalance had been aggravated by a school board decision to build a new school in the midst of a white neighborhood instead of on the border with the minority community. Or the court might find fault with an open enrollment plan the school board had implemented in 1978.[53] From the outset the plan was monitored to make sure it did not promote racial imbalance. In fact it was modified in 1980, after HEW reported that minority enrollments in three disproportionately black schools would have been reduced by about 1 percent if there had been no open enrollment. Black students were then refused permission to leave predominantly white schools, and whites were allowed to transfer only to schools that had a greater enrollment of blacks. Nevertheless, despite the efforts to use open enrollment to promote racial mixing, between 1978 and 1980 the policy had contributed slightly to racial imbalance. In the eyes of an active judicial integrationist, this could prove to be the "constitutional violation" that would warrant compulsory cross-town busing for racial dispersion.[54]

The new *Brown* litigation concerns the meaning of "desegregation." People like Albert Carrington, a black parent who has been active in school affairs, support the lawsuit because "we haven't yet achieved what Oliver Brown set out to accomplish. He wanted to establish that regardless of where children live they should be placed in an integrated school." Others, like Harry Craig, a white former president of the school board, consider it ironic that "the Rev. Oliver Brown filed suit back in 1950 to persuade the Court that his daughter should be able to attend a neighborhood school as opposed to riding a bus to a 'colored' school twenty blocks away. Now [we are being asked], if you will, to identify minority students and to redistribute them to foreign schools by busing. Why, we've gone 360 degrees in twenty years."[55]

Given the confusion, perhaps it is appropriate that Linda Brown Smith, the original plaintiff in *Brown,* has been unsure of the need for dispersing blacks. Now a divorced mother of two children, she has worked as a keypunch operator at the local Goodyear plant and does not consider herself an activist or a spokeswoman for the black community. The closest she ever came to behaving like a black militant, Linda once said, was when the NAACP asked her to speak before a street rally in Harlem. Her father, who died in 1961, took care to shield Linda from unnecessary publicity, but she has repeatedly said she is proud of her involvement in the case. "Things are definitely better in Topeka now," she observed. "That decision was the basis for everything."[56]

Nevertheless, Linda Brown Smith was initially opposed to busing. "I am not for it at all," she declared in 1974. "To me this is a reversion to what we were getting into before *Brown*." She recalled that before her father went to court she had played with white youngsters in a mixed neighborhood on the southern side of the Kansas River. "I just couldn't understand why we could play with them all summer and then I couldn't go to school with them." It was for that reason, she said, that she was "opposed to busing just for the sake of integration. My kids would be playing with one group and going to school with another, and it'd start all over again. There's got to be a better way to do it." "I don't want my kids bused," Linda said on another occasion. "I know what that's like." "One of the reasons I went to court back in the 1950s was to escape busing and all the hassle it causes." "Kids like me were taken out of our neighborhoods and bused across town. I still feel kids should be able to attend schools in their own neighborhoods."[57]

Yet these statements were made at a time when Fred Phelps was petitioning for desegregation. Linda Brown Smith changed her mind five years later when her friend Charles Scott reopened the litigation that bears her name. More than that, she joined with seven other black parents in a motion to intervene as named plaintiffs in petitioning for an order commanding compliance with the Supreme Court's order in *Brown*. In granting this motion district judge Richard Rogers observed that if the school board was "found out of compliance with the *Brown* decision and if busing is found to be an efficient and efficacious remedy for the problem, we have no doubt that the intervening plaintiffs in *Brown* will request and this court will order such busing."[58]

The new *Brown* litigation promises to be long and drawn-out, with appeals eventually to the Tenth Circuit Court and the U.S. Supreme Court. Thus far the NAACP has declined to enter the case, but attorneys Jones and Scott, Jr., are employed by the city of Topeka and the Kansas Department of Transportation, respectively, and have had their expenses in *Brown* covered by funds from the American Civil Liberties Union.[59]

The school board, for its part, is not about to give in. Most members believe their schools were desegregated long ago when the board developed a color-blind policy for assigning all children to neighborhood schools. The Long Range Plan of 1974 went beyond desegregation and promoted integration by taking color into account when closing schools and drawing attendance boundaries. But this compromise was made in the hope that federal bureaucrats and courts would be placated and would allow Topeka to continue its system of neighborhood schools with only slight modifications. Blacks had admittedly not been dispersed evenly throughout all schools in the city, but members of the school board boggled at the allegation that Topeka and Highland Park high schools (with white enrollments of 67 and 64 percent, respectively) were racially identifiable black schools because only 3 percent of the students at Topeka West High School were members of a recognized minority group. In 1980 Superintendent James M. Gray predicted that the final cost of defending against the new *Brown* lawsuit would amount to hundreds of thousands of dollars. The school board had emerged unscathed from two previous HEW investigations, however, and would not be intimidated by lawyers who were thought to be reaping publicity and financial gain from what has been called "the case of the century." [60]

The verdict in the new *Brown* lawsuit is difficult to predict because, as one black parent observed, desegregation has come to resemble pornography. "No two people agree about what it means or what our goal should be." [61] Unlike the law of torts or contracts, where a consensus has emerged after centuries of experience, desegregation law has been shaped by divided appellate courts in a brief compass of time. There is no agreement as to whether "desegregation" requires color-conscious policies to ensure an even dispersion of blacks and whites. In this field the personalities and ideologies of the judges are more important than legal principles or precedents. It is ironic that a written Constitution that was intended to protect Americans against the vagaries of idiosyncratic rule has become the basis for government by judges. The fact remains: social policy with regard to balanced racial mixing depends on the personal philosophies of the judges who hear the cases. In Topeka, as elsewhere, there are legal grounds and precedents for deciding either way.

CONCLUSION

What can be said by way of final assessment? Despite the benefits that blacks and the nation have gained from the prohibition of official segregation, I believe it must be conceded that integration has been a failure in four of the five *Brown* school districts. My primary goal has been to write an interesting account of desegregation in these districts, not to prove a point or offer solutions to legal and educational problems. Yet one cannot study a failure of this magnitude without formulating opinions as to why things went wrong and what should be done.

I

In the early 1950s neither Congress nor the state legislatures were prepared to end the racial segregation that had become an anachronism that damaged America's reputation abroad and jeopardized domestic tranquility. Thanks to the Supreme Court's prohibition of segregation in *Brown,* America's standing in the international community was enhanced and convulsive domestic violence, as distinguished from sporadic racial rioting, was averted. Defenders of the Warren Court maintain that in the process no great damage was done to the Constitution, for the founding fathers had wisely included vague phrases like "equal protection" and "due process," which were intended to mean whatever the Supreme Court wanted them to mean.

Critics of *Brown,* on the other hand, insist that the framers and ratifiers of the equal protection clause did not intend to outlaw segregation. Believing that the original understanding of a constitutional provision is crucial to its proper interpretation, they conclude that as a matter of law the *Brown* opinion was shockingly bad. In the guise of interpreting the equal protection clause, the justices of the Warren Court usurped the power to amend the Constitution. To achieve a result they regarded as socially desirable, they ignored the established rule for constitutional construction and read their idea of proper social policy into the Constitution.

In terms of legal history, the critics of the Warren Court have the better argument. Advocates of judicial activism have not presented evidence to prove that the framers of the Fourteenth Amendment intentionally camouflaged an undisclosed purpose. Even if such evidence were discovered, it would not be conclusive. Constitutional amendments must be ratified by three-fourths of the states, and the doctrine of ratification presumes that the principals understand what they are ratifying. The fact that the Congress that submitted the Fourteenth Amendment also provided for segregated schools in the District of Columbia, and that several ratifying states continued to operate segregated schools, indicates that the equal protection clause was not originally understood to prohibit segregation.[1]

Of course an enduring Constitution must be modified periodically. The founding fathers provided for this in Article V, which sets forth procedures for amending the nation's basic charter. It has been difficult to amend the Constitution, but that is what the founders intended. They did not mean for the Supreme Court to serve as a standing constitutional convention.

II

Whether or not the Supreme Court acted with warrant, the ultimate verdict on *Brown* will depend on whether the decision is thought to have been correct. Despite the vehement objections of many people, most Americans accepted the principle that the government should not discriminate among citizens on the basis of race.[2] The prestige of the Supreme Court was never higher than in 1964, when Congress enacted a civil rights law that prohibited racial discrimination as a matter of national legislative policy. Yet government agencies had hardly ceased their race-conscious policies of the past when the Supreme Court, in its 1968 *Green* decision, required proportional mixing in the name of desegregation. When understood in light of its fundamental psychology, the *Brown* opinion was found to require that race be taken into account to undo the effects of segregation. An opinion that had previously been understood to forbid pupil assignment on the basis of race paradoxically became the rationale for requiring assignment on the grounds of race.

Although this book is essentially a description of what has happened in five school districts, it lends support to legal scholars who have criticized the Supreme Court. The justices say that when they render an opinion they are affirming the values our ancestors democratically adopted. In *Brown* and *Green,* however, the justices actually clothed in constitutional attire the social values of impatient men who happened to occupy seats on the Court.

An additional problem in *Brown* was ambiguity. Until 1968 the Court's opinion was generally understood to mean that race was prohibited as an inherently arbitrary classification; since *Green,* however, it has been held to mean that equality of educational opportunity cannot be obtained in schools that are disproportionately black.

When dealing with *Green* and its progeny, we must distinguish between what the courts said they were doing and what they actually did. Everything the courts have done since 1954 has been done in the name of enforcing *Brown.* Racial integration is not required as such, the courts have stated repeatedly; there is no constitutional right to attend racially balanced schools. All that is required is the undoing of the racial segregation that has resulted from intentional discrimination by state agencies, not the undoing of all racial separation whatever its cause. Assignments on the basis of race were required only to achieve as much mixing as there would have been except for the past practice of unconstitutional segregation.

In the *Brown* school districts, however, the federal courts have repeatedly prohibited educational policies that are neutral on their face. Tuition grants and freedom of choice were forbidden in Virginia and South Carolina, and in Washington ability grouping was disallowed because a disproportionate number of blacks were placed in the lower groups. In Delaware the judges assumed that the races would have been evenly dispersed in terms of residential settlement, if there had been no official discrimination before 1954. Then, to achieve racial balance in each school, the dispersion of students was ordered rather than the reservation of a portion of each block or neighborhood for minority residence (a requirement that is virtually unthinkable at this time).

Judicial activists say that their orders are designed only to correct segregation resulting from intentional actions by state officials, and that even after intentional discrimination has been found the relief must be tailored to match the scope of the legal wrong. Their stated goal is to achieve as much mixing as there would have been in the absence of intentional, official discrimination. But then the courts play fast and loose with their principles. In Northern Delaware, for example, the judges disregarded their own finding that there had been no intentional discrimination after *Brown* and then required more dispersion than anyone honestly believes would have occurred. It is hard to avoid the suspicion that in this instance the courts' acceptance of flawed evidence and dubious premises was influenced by an underlying conviction that racially imbalanced schools must be prohibited, regardless of how they came into existence.

The federal courts have also misinterpreted the Civil Rights Act of 1964. In that act, as North Carolina's Senator Sam Ervin has noted, "Congress decided to take no chances with the courts so it put in something that even a judge ought to be able to understand. It not only defined desegregation affirmatively but also defined what desegregation is not."[3] Desegregation meant "the assignment of students to public schools . . . without regard to their race," but "not . . . the assignment of students to public schools in order to overcome racial imbalance."[4] Yet in *Green* the Supreme Court incredibly cited the Civil Rights Act in support of its ruling that students could not be permitted an admittedly unencumbered freedom of choice unless that choice led to approximately proportional racial enrollments. Students were compelled to do what they were free to do already. One is reminded of what the historian Crane Brinton wrote about Robespierre: "If Frenchmen would not be free and virtuous voluntarily, then he would force them to be free and cram virtue down their throats."[5]

When the *Brown* litigation was before the Supreme Court, NAACP attorney Robert L. Carter told the justices that his organization had "one fundamental contention which we will seek to develop in the course of this argument, and that contention is that no state has any authority under the equal protection clause of the Fourteenth Amendment to use race as a factor in affording educational opportunities among its citizens."[6] Thurgood Marshall insisted that the Fourteenth Amendment deprived states of the power "to make any racial classification in any governmental field."[7]

Since the 1960s, however, the NAACP has departed from its historic insistence that the government should treat citizens as individuals, without regard to race, color, creed, or national origin. Instead it has put forward the idea that blacks as a group should receive preferential treatment as reparation for the racial discrimination of the past. Thurgood Marshall, after becoming a member of the Supreme Court, maintained that the constitutional guarantee of equal protection meant one thing when applied to blacks and something else when applied to a person of another color. It was "inconceivable that the Fourteenth Amendment was intended to prohibit all race-conscious relief measures," Marshall wrote. "To remedy the effects of the Nation's past treatment of Negroes," blacks were entitled to "special treatment" and "greater protection under the Fourteenth Amendment."[8] Commenting on the change in approach, the noted constitutional scholar Alexander M. Bickel observed, "Now . . . we are told that [racial discrimination] is not a matter of principle but only a matter of whose ox is gored.

Those for whom racial equality was demanded are to be more equal than others."[9]

In 1980, after the issue had been thoroughly discussed, only 10 percent of those responding to a Gallup Poll believed that race should determine decisions about employment or college entry.[10] By then, however, the question had already been decided, not by the people's elected representatives but by appointed officials and federal judges. Harold Howe II, the Commissioner of Education who played a leading role in developing HEW guidelines that disregarded the congressional definition of desegregation, characterized the race riots of the 1960s as "a revolution . . . brewing under our feet" and said that "it is largely up to the schools to determine whether the energies of that revolution can be converted into a new and vigorous source of American progress, or whether their explosion will rip this nation into two societies."[11] The Supreme Court was undoubtedly prompted by good motives when it ruled that both the Constitution and the Civil Rights Act required a shift from color blindness to color consciousness, from the rights of individuals to the concept of group rights. Martin Luther King had been assassinated the day after the Court heard the oral arguments in the crucial *Green* case, and the nation experienced its worst period of racial rioting during the weeks when the justices deliberated on the issue. Once again, they decided, the time had arrived for decisive judicial leadership. Yet good intentions can be pleaded for any abuse of authority and, as Daniel Webster once observed, "It is hardly too strong to say that the Constitution was made to guard the people against the dangers of good intentions."[12]

III

Congressional deference is the other side of judicial activism. The Court, after all, has no army to enforce its orders. And the Constitution—consistent with its underlying premises regarding checks and balances—has given the legislative branch the authority to curb an errant judiciary.

The most certain way to halt court-ordered racial balance would be to pass a constitutional amendment prohibiting government agencies from making distinctions on account of race, color, or national origin. Yet, due to strong opposition from the civil rights establishment, such proposals have been bottled up in congressional committees. As Senator Orrin G. Hatch of Utah has noted, "The idea of a society in which the law would take no account of an individual's skin color—the great goal of the civil rights movement of the 1950s and 1960s—is now regarded by many as, at best, an exceedingly naive sentiment and, at worst, as one reflecting a commitment to second class citizenship, even servitude, for this country's minorities." [13]

As a presidential candidate in 1980, Ronald Reagan criticized racial and ethnic quotas and said people should be judged on their merits as individuals rather than as members of a group. Reagan's platform contained a strong statement against court-ordered busing for racial balance, and he was generally thought to owe his political viability to the support of social conservatives—people who had voted Democratic in the past but switched to Reagan and other Republicans who criticized the imposition of new moral standards through judicial review.

Thus far, however, President Reagan has proceeded cautiously on civil rights. A proposed constitutional amendment prohibiting all sorts of racial discrimination has remained in the Democratically controlled House Judiciary Committee, as has an antibusing bill that passed the Republican-dominated Senate in 1982 by a vote of 57 to 37. The 218 signatures required to secure discharge from the committee could have been obtained if the president had placed either the amendment or the bill on his list of essential measures, but counselors in the White House apparently feared that the media would depict the president as a bigot if he pushed for redress before critics of reverse discrimination had proceeded further in modifying the intellectual climate of the country. In the meantime, social conservatives began to fret that they were being taken for granted or, worse yet, that for fear of jeopardizing its economic and foreign policies the Reagan administration would never do anything to antagonize the influential interests that are committed to racial proportionality.

Although a constitutional amendment is a possibility, critics of government by judiciary generally maintain that it is not necessary to amend the Constitution to make it mean what it was understood to mean before a majority of the Supreme Court received its latest revelation. Nor do they embrace the proposition that they should wait until more strict constructionists are appointed and then pray that the Court will reverse itself. Proportional representation may be scotched in this way eventually, but the critics fear that public education will never recover if it takes the Court as long to overrule *Green* as it did to repudiate *Plessy*.

These critics maintain that by a simple majority vote Congress may enact new laws that will shape the meaning of equal protection and will require the judiciary to respect the original understanding of the Civil Rights Act. They call attention to Section 5 of the Fourteenth Amendment, wherein Congress is explicitly granted "the power to enforce, by appropriate legislation, the provisions of this article." And they note that in the Constitution the relevant Article III provides that the Supreme Court shall have original jurisdiction in certain cases, but in all other cases it shall have appellate jurisdiction "with such exceptions, and under such regulations as Congress may make."

Some critics favor legislation that would require federal courts to order school districts that have been found guilty of intentional discrimination to provide transportation for any student who wishes to transfer from a school in which his race is in the majority to a school in which his race is in the minority. This qualified freedom-of-choice would not limit the jurisdiction of the courts, since it would still be up to the judges to determine if there had been unconstitutional racial discrimination. The legislation can even be defended from the perspective of freeing blacks from the disproportionate share of the transportation burden that minorities inevitably must bear in any mandatory plan of busing for racial balance. Middle-class blacks might make greater use of the transfers, thereby leaving their neighborhood schools relatively poor as well as black, but those who favor free transfers see no cause for alarm if the parents of non-transferring black students are satisfied with the education their children are receiving. They do not believe that disproportionately black schools are inherently inferior or that a history of racial discrimination has rendered the present generation of black parents incapable of choosing wisely for their children.[14]

Others maintain that Congress should curb the Supreme Court by removing its jurisdiction over certain classes of cases, a prerogative that the court itself has repeatedly conceded. The legal scholar C. Dickerman Williams has noted that since the judicial system was organized in 1789 Congress has occasionally made exceptions to the appellate jurisdiction of the Supreme Court, and the Court has "uniformly acquiesced in and upheld these exceptions to its appellate jurisdiction." "Congress has—in the plain language of the Constitution and in the construction which the Supreme Court has repeatedly given that language—the power to remove from the appellate jurisdiction of the Supreme Court such cases as it sees fit."[15] Even prominent advocates of reform by judiciary have conceded that courts would not be allowed to settle questions of social policy in a democracy unless Congress had the authority to modify or remove jurisdiction.[16]

One can only speculate about the reasons for the deference of Congress. One consideration is that many Members have come to question their authority to withdraw jurisdiction. As Grover Rees has noted, "Whenever a bill to withdraw jurisdiction seems to have even a remote chance of passage . . . the organized bar and the academic establishment descends on Washington . . . to pronounce constitutional anathemas. There is much talk of the Founders, of the Constitution, of the justices doing the best they can at their difficult task of interpreting a two-hundred-year-old document."[17]

Other legislators use the perception of unconstitutionality as a shield against their constituents. On the basis of personal experience, they have concluded that the legislative branch is inept, corrupt, and beset by the stasis of political pressures. Legislatures cannot protect vulnerable interests, they say, because elected representatives are beholden to well-organized pressure groups and lobbies.[18] In these circumstances they think it best for the Supreme Court to be, as Pennsylvania's Senator Arlen Specter put it, "the final decider of important national questions."[19] There is also a matter of psychology. Many legislators are lawyers who have yet to unlearn the pretensions of their profession; they think courts should proclaim moral values and make social policy as well as resolve the conflicts of individual litigants.[20]

When the Supreme Court held in *Brown* that Jim Crow segregation was at odds with the nation's best values, it expressed a view that was emerging as a moral consensus among Americans. Fourteen years later, when the *Green* Court ordered racial balance in the name of desegregation, it precipitated a furor of criticism. From the outset many people insisted that past racial discrimination against blacks should not be overcome by compensatory discrimination against whites. The criticism mounted as affirmative action plans spread to the North and West and to the economy as well as to schools.

The popular acceptance of *Brown* demonstrated that the Court can push the national consensus beyond where it is, if its decision is in keeping with the nation's best traditions and if the Court gives the populace time to consider and endorse the new morality. But the mounting criticism since 1968 indicates that the consensus can also turn against a Court that repudiates traditional principles and tries to remake the society according to its own vision. Despite congressional reluctance to curb the courts, it is hard to see how decisions that lack intellectual respectability and popular support can be maintained indefinitely.

I V

Integrationist sociology assumed that, as Judge Simon Sobeloff once explained, "the quality of a school depends largely on its 'class climate,' and that middle class schools are better." Since "white" was presumed to be synonymous with "middle class" and "black" the same as "lower class," the purpose of integration was to create schools with "enough middle class students to establish the class character of the school and . . . a substantial number of lower-class children to benefit from it."[21]

Ironically, while integrationists promoted racial balance as the best way to ensure that blacks were socialized properly, many progressive educational reformers insisted that the schools should place less emphasis on transmitting middle-class values. It was not consistent with *Brown*'s concern for equality and self-respect, they said, if weak students were disproportionately assigned to lower-level classes or made to study subjects for which they were poorly prepared. Thus, in the 1960s and 1970s, many schools repudiated curricula that emphasized well-defined bodies of knowledge and differentiated students on the basis of academic performance. Students with widely varying levels of achievement were assigned to the same classes, authoritative teachers were criticized for stifling the budding curiosity of their pupils, and teacher-dominated classrooms were replaced with informal groupings in which teachers and students treated one another as peers. There was more emphasis on creativity, less concern for mastering the fundamentals of reading, writing, and mathematics. There were more elective courses and fewer examinations. Progressive education enjoyed a renaissance as schools complied with egalitarian court orders that prohibited educational policies that had racially disproportionate results.

The new concern for uplifting blacks affected the course of American educational history. In the late-1950s and early-1960s, after the Soviet scientific triumph that Sputnik symbolized, American schools had emphasized academic courses that challenged their brightest students. After the race riots of the 1960s, however, identifying the gifted and stimulating high achievement seemed less important than reforming disruptive students. Civil rights leaders brought their demands to the schools and, as historian Diane Ravitch has noted, "before long the pursuit of excellence was overshadowed by concern about the needs of the disadvantaged. As the racial crisis and the urban crisis became the nation's most pressing problems, the Cold War competition with the Soviets moved to the back burner and lost its motivating power."[22]

By the 1980s there was a growing recognition that the public schools had suffered from many of the changes associated with desegregation. Instead of solving complex prolems that went beyond the schools, it seemed, the reformers had undermined the quality of academic instruction. "The liberal educational reformers had a running field as open as it ever gets in the public policy game," the *Wall Street Journal* observed, "and they blew it. They failed. The state of the schools and the drop in test scores are an unanswerable indictment."[23]

Some said the time had come to reemphasize the importance of academic subjects. A new pedagogy—sometimes called the "back to basics" approach—was similar to the philosophy of education that Carl F. Hansen had implemented in Washington and that Robert T. Redd and Edna F. Rowe had brought to their private academies in Prince Edward and Clarendon counties. It was also similar to a point of view that W.E.B. Du Bois expressed in a 1935 address to the National Education Association.

> Whenever a teachers' convention gets together and tries to find out how it can cure the ills of society there is simply one answer: the school has but one way to cure the ills of society and that is by making men intelligent. To make men intelligent, the school has again but one way, and that is, first and last, to teach them to read, write and count. And if the school fails to do that, and tries beyond that to do something for which a school is not adapted, it not only fails its own function, but it fails in all other attempted functions. Because no school as such can organize industry or settle the matter of wage and income, can found homes or furnish parents, can establish justice or make a civilized world.[24]

V

Blacks have trailed whites in average academic achievement for many years, but at the time of *Brown* most educators attributed this to poor schools. Although an approximation of separate-but-equal had been achieved by then in the *Brown* school districts, black children in other areas were still being educated in grossly inferior schools. With equalization and desegregation it was thought that blacks would shed the feelings of inferiority the Supreme Court had mentioned and then do better in schoolwork and in later life.

This assumption was paradoxically challenged *and* reinforced by the Coleman report of 1966, *Equality of Educational Opportunity.*[25] Instead of finding large deficiencies in predominantly black schools, the Coleman researchers discovered that by 1966 there was substantial equality in facilities and other measurable resources at majority-black and majority-white schools. The nation had come close to achieving the traditional notion of equality of educational opportunity.

The Coleman researchers also found very little difference in the average scores made by blacks who attended schools that were mostly black, mostly white, or mixed in various proportions. Yet the full impact of this finding was muted because the summary of the study emphasized that black children in majority-white schools scored slightly higher than other blacks. The principal author of the study, James S. Coleman, also filed depositions and gave interviews in which he touted the benefits that black children would receive if they were dispersed and educated in predominantly white classrooms.[26] It was partly on the basis of Coleman's testimony that judges such as J. Skelly Wright concluded, in *Hobson v. Hansen,* that "Negro students' educational achievement improves when they transfer into white or integrated educational institutions."[27] Because of Coleman's eminence as a sociologist and his frequent depositions in favor of dispersion, the professor became known as "The Scholar Who Inspired Busing."[28]

Coleman's defense of integration was timely because by the early 1960s the social science research the Supreme Court had cited in *Brown* had been widely discredited. Advocates of desegregation no longer believed that segregated schools had a belittling effect on the blacks' self-image. They shifted instead to Coleman's emphasis on the role of peer group culture in affecting individual attitudes toward academic accomplishment. As explained by Coleman, the theory was that "children who themselves may be undisciplined, coming into classrooms that are highly disciplined, would take on the characteristics of their classmates and be governed by the norms of the classrooms, so that the middle-class values would come to govern the integrated classrooms. In that situation both white and black children would learn."[29]

In the 1970s, however, Coleman conceded that it was mistaken to assume that integration automatically would improve the schoolwork of lower-class black children. Most of the blacks who integrated southern schools in the early 1960s and who had provided the basis for Coleman's earlier conclusions were well-motivated volunteers who enrolled under freedom-of-choice plans. They were superior students from families who considered education important. It was simply "wishful thinking," Coleman admitted, to believe that similar academic improvement would result from the massive integration of all blacks under mandatory court orders.[30]

What happened all too frequently, Coleman said, was that "characteristics of the lower-class black classroom, namely a high degree of disorder, came to take over and constitute the values and characteristics of the classroom in the integrated school." Many middle-class parents, blacks as well as whites, then fled to the refuge of private schools or to public schools in predominantly white areas—a phenomenon that Coleman considered "quite understandable" because so many integrated schools had "failed to control lower-class black children" and had to spend "90 percent of the time . . . not on instruction but on discipline."[31]

Coleman doubted that this flight could be stayed by the dispersion of blacks as smaller minorities in large metropolitan districts. The incidence of flight was so much greater in large districts than in medium or small ones that Coleman concluded there were two independent factors at work. One was the integration of lower-class blacks; "that is, the more blacks, the faster the white out-migration." But the statistical evidence suggested that whites were also fleeing from large and distant school districts where parents felt they had little influence over the education of their children. The parents were leaving school systems they saw as "too large, as unmanageable, as unresponsive." Consequently, Coleman predicted, "if the [school] system is made even larger, to cover the whole metropolitan area, many parents will find ways to escape it, either by moving even farther out or by the use of private schools." It would be only a matter of time before the departures "completely overcome the results of the integration, leading to a system that is more segregated than was the case before." "From now on," Coleman said, "we will see a general resegregation in all areas of the country. . . . School integration is just not stable where the proportion of blacks in the district is very large."[32]

In 1978 Coleman also renounced his earlier belief that educational benefits would flow to black children in integrated classrooms. His studies of the 1960s had suggested such gains, but no such conclusion emerged from a 1975 survey of 120 studies of the relation of school racial composition and the achievement of students. The most that could be said for large-scale integration was that academic scores usually did not decline. The worst, and a result Coleman conceded after reading some careful case studies, was that sometimes academic scores declined after integration. Thus, Coleman concluded, what once appeared to be fact—that integration would improve the achievement of lower-class black children—turned out to be fiction.[33]

This study of the *Brown* school districts supports Coleman's revised hypotheses. Contrary to the expectations of those who favored desegregation, the quality of public education available to blacks is generally no better than it was in 1954. The situation has improved in Prince Edward County and has stayed about the same in Summerton, but in Washington and Wilmington black education retrogressed during the 1960s and 1970s. There was also widespread white flight, with almost all the whites in Summerton, Washington, and Wilmington either moving elsewhere or transferring their children to private schools. It has been more difficult to flee from countywide school districts, but more than half the white students in Prince Edward County are enrolled in a private academy while the proportion of whites attending private schools in New Castle County has increased to one-third.

Some readers may be surprised by the evidence from the districts where desegregation began. They have been told, as in *Newsweek,* that "educationally, integration has been shown to be at worst harmless and often beneficial. Repeated studies have nearly always reached the same conclusion: black children profit from integration efforts, while white children do not suffer."[34] The *New Republic* has reassuringly reported that "research overwhelmingly indicates that blacks in a desegregated environment learn more than their segregated peers, and that white students do not suffer at all."[35]

The research on desegregation actually proves nothing of the sort. If there is one thing that characterizes the work of scholars in this area it is a lack of consensus. For every study that proves that desegregation is accompanied by academic gains, another proves the opposite. There is disagreement over the extent to which white flight is a result of desegregation. And for every instance in which mixing is said to have led to increased interracial friendship, there is another case of heightened racial tensions and chauvinism.

Of course the studies are not equally sound. Nor were they all undertaken for the same purposes. Many were financed by local school districts that are understandably interested in accentuating their positive accomplishments. Others were sponsored by government agencies that have made it clear they do not want balanced and objective assessments of desegregation. Top officials in the U.S. Commission on Civil Rights have told staff workers that the purpose of their research is to show that desegregation has worked well or can be made to do so.[36] The Department of Education has spent millions of dollars for research on desegregation, but scholars are clearly given to understand that "desegregation is essential" and that grants are intended only for studies that will "improve the education of students in multiracial and multilingual schools."[37] The committee that judges the research proposals is chaired by a political scientist who candidly equates desegregation and racial balance. It is not surprising, then, that much of the government-sponsored research indicates that "there are no losses for white children in the desegregation process . . . [and] substantial gains for minority children."[38] The surprise is that journalists who are usually suspicious of government propaganda have uncritically accepted the validity of studies that are, at best, briefs that bring together the evidence on one side of a controversial question.[39]

VI

Despite desegregation and billions of dollars spent for compensatory programs to assist disadvantaged students, the best studies indicate that on standardized examinations the average black student still scores about where he did in the 1950s—below 85 percent of the whites. Put differently, the average black first-grade student is about one year below the national average for his age group, and the deficiency increases to more than three years in high school.[40]

By documenting an already well-established correlation between social class and academic achievement, the Coleman report confirmed the belief that black underachievement is related to a disparity in socioeconomic status.[41] And here, as Theodore H. White has noted, "A writer must contend with an issue that, when raised, so embitters Negro leaders as almost to hush friendly dialogue: the rate of illegitimate births among Negroes."[42] In 1954 about 20 percent of all black children were growing up in homes with only one parent caring for them; by 1980 that figure had increased to more than 50 percent. In the 1930s black and white women bore children at equal rates in urban areas. By the 1970s, however, the black birth rate was almost 40 percent greater than the white, with the difference made up of children born out of wedlock.[43] A new pattern of mating and breeding had emerged, one that is at odds with traditional moral standards.

The change in black family life was clearly evident in the *Brown* districts, where the proportion of black babies born out of wedlock increased by 1980 to two-thirds in Delaware and the District of Columbia and to almost half in South Carolina and Virginia. Given the disadvantages that many of these children suffered in their home evironments, the surprise is not that the gap between the academic achievement of blacks and whites has persisted but that it has not increased.

Integrationists generally look askance at the notion that children fail because of deficiencies in their homes. This has been called "blaming the victim," a sophisticated way of reproaching blacks and absolving the schools of the responsibility to uplift disadvantaged youths through balanced integration. Yet it would be naïve not to recognize that widespread illegitimacy is only one of a tangle of problems that have militated against the effective education of many blacks: there are also near-epidemic rates of alcoholism, drug addiction, venereal disease, vandalism, violence, and crime. Blacks have admittedly faced special obstacles, but blaming racism for the disproportionate incidence of destructive behavior obscures the fact that there has been a breakdown in morality at a time of decreasing white prejudice and increasing economic opportunities for blacks.

By focusing so much attention on racial mixing, integrationists have obscured the importance of self-reliance and have drawn a veil over a crucial point that W.E.B. Du Bois recognized long ago: that "the Negro race has an appalling work of social reform before it." Du Bois insisted that whites were morally obliged to give blacks an equal chance to attain an education and earn a living. Until this was done, they had no right to complain if black youths lost interest in work and drifted into idleness and crime. But Du Bois also maintained that "the bulk of the work of raising the Negro must be done by the Negro himself, and the greatest help for him will be not to hinder and curtail and discourage his efforts."[44]

According to Du Bois, justice demanded "that talent should be rewarded, and aptness used in commerce and industry whether its owner be black or white; that the same incentive to good, honest effective work be placed before a black office boy as before a white one." Yet Du Bois conceded that justice did not require a wholesale exchange of whites for blacks "out of sympathy or philanthopy." Nor did it require that whites relinquish their insistence that blacks measure up to traditional standards. Du Bois knew that in the past blacks had been enslaved and barbarously mistreated, but this gave them "no right to demand that the civilization and morality of the land be seriously menaced for their benefit." The nation could "rightly demand, even of a people it has consciously and intentionally wronged . . . every effort and sacrifice possible on their part toward making themselves fit members of the community within a reasonable length of time: that thus they may early become a source of strength and help instead of a national burden."[45]

Du Bois's candid approach did not suit the temper of the 1960s and 1970s, when most writing on race relations was swept along by strong currents of sentiment for integration. As the nation emerges from the mood of collective guilt and self-denigration that characterized those decades, and as the disappointing results of integration become apparent, there may be a renewed appreciation of the importance of self-help and moral reform.

In the meantime, many people will continue to insist that the government should not shuffle children around without regard to the preferences of their parents. The autonomy of the family is at "the heart of the matter," Senator Jesse Helms of North Carolina has declared. "Just as the parent determines what he wants for his child, so do the multitude of parents, who group themselves together in neighborhoods and communities . . . have the right to determine what kind of culture will be the setting for the education of their children."[46] Iowa's Senator Charles E. Grassley similarly noted that many parents make "immense sacrifices to provide a particular learning environment for their children." For them, "the purpose of education goes far beyond intellectual development" and extends to "shap[ing] the character and values of the next generation."[47]

Because of differentials in mores and academic achievement, many middle-class parents continue to oppose proportional mixing. With rates of drug use, early pregnancy, and illegitimacy climbing in middle-class communities, many concerned parents wish above all to sequester their children from the pull of downward mobility. They understand the influence of the peer group and consider it an unwarranted intrusion if the state insists on exposing their children to the black underclass. Despite the reassurances of liberal sociologists, many parents are convinced that their children will not benefit from this sort of mixing. At bottom this attitude is doubtless influenced by age-old racial prejudices (although it appears to be as prevalent among middle-class blacks as anywhere). Whatever the basis, the attitudes are entrenched and will not yield unless the federal courts increase their efforts to prescribe the education of all children.

More compulsion. That is what integrationists will need if they are to shape the education of most middle-class children. Despite substantial middle-class flight to private schools, the determined use of federal power has led to increased racial mixing in southern public schools. In the Northeast, however, black students have become increasingly concentrated in predominantly black, urban school districts. The segregationists of yesteryear have had to mix with blacks or pay private tuition for their children, while their Yankee cousins fled to the refuge of free public schools in predominantly white suburbs. The two trends have neutralized one another, and as a result the percentage of black children attending substantially mixed schools is only slightly higher today than in 1968.[48]

The pattern of racial imbalance outside the South could be changed by imposing the sort of metropolitan dispersion the federal courts eventually fashioned for northern Delaware. Yet this sort of remedy cannot be compelled outside the South unless the Supreme Court revises its theory of desegregation. However much integrationists may find fault with racial imbalance, the Supreme Court has repeatedly said that there is no constitutional requirement for integration or racial mixing. All that is required is that the results of official discrimination be corrected.

Pursuant to *Green,* the litigation in New Castle County established that metropolitan dispersion is an appropriate remedy for a previously overt statewide policy of segregation. But the *Milliken* decision in Detroit established that outside the southern and border states dispersion must be limited to individual school districts whose officials have been found guilty of racial discrimination: thus busing has been required in Detroit, Boston, San Francisco, and other northern cities, but not between these cities and their suburbs. Unless the Supreme Court repudiates *Milliken,* the pattern of increasing racial separation will continue in the North and West. Unless it repudiates *Green,* Dixie will remain under a judicial bill of attainder and the equal protection clause will continue to have a different meaning in the South than in the rest of the nation.

Prudent social policy and a consistent application of the Constitution require that *Green* be repudiated and that Judge Parker's dictum in *Briggs* be revived as the correct interpretation of the equal protection clause. The ambiguous *Brown* opinion would then be understood to mean what most people thought it meant in 1954, and desegregation would mean what Congress certainly intended when it enacted the Civil Rights Act of 1964: the prohibition of official racial discrimination, not the prohibition of racially neutral policies that do not lead to a substantial amount of racial mixing. Management of the public schools would then be returned to local school boards and superintendents, and racial policies would be fashioned through the give-and-take of the democratic process. With every form of racial discrimination prohibited, local officials would almost certainly improve on the sorry record that disingenuous judges and naïve educational reformers have made in the *Brown* school districts.

NOTES

NOTES TO THE INTRODUCTION

1. *Brown v. Board of Education of Topeka,* 347 U.S. 483 (1954).
2. Speech, 3 May 1907, as quoted in William Lockhart, Yale Kamisar, and Jesse Choper, *Constitutional Law,* 3rd ed. (St. Paul, Minn., 1970), 7.
3. *Plessy v. Ferguson,* 163 U.S. 537 (1896).
4. Quoted in G.W. Foster, Jr., "The North and West Have Problems, Too," *Saturday Review* 46 (20 Apr. 1963): 72; *Landmark Briefs and Arguments of the Supreme Court,* ed. Philip B. Kurland (Arlington, Va.: University Publications of America, 1975), vols. 49–49A.
5. Leon Friedman, ed., *Argument: The Oral Argument Before the Supreme Court in Brown v. Board Education of Topeka, 1952–1955* (New York: Chelsea House, 1969), 47, 375, 402.
6. 347 U.S. 483 (1954) at 495, 494; emphasis added.
7. Quoted in Nathan Glazer, "Is Integration Possible in the New York Schools?" *Commentary* 30 (Sept. 1960): 186.
8. *Brown v. Board of Education of Topeka,* 349 U.S. 295 (1955) at 301, 298.
9. *Bolling v. Sharpe,* 347 U.S. 497 (1954) at 499, quoting from *Gibson v. Mississippi,* 162 U.S. 565 (1896).
10. *Briggs, v. Elliott,* 132 F. Supp. 776 (1955) at 777.
11. Public Law 88–352 (1964) 246.
12. *Green v. County School Board of New Kent County,* 391 U.S. 430 (1968).

NOTES TO PART ONE

1. *Bolling v. Sharpe,* 347 U.S. 497 (1954) at 500.
2. Erwin Knoll, "Washington: Showcase of Integration," Commentary 27 (Mar. 1959): 195–96; Mary A. Morton, "The Education of Negroes in the District of Columbia," *Journal of Negro Education* 16 (Summer 1947): 325–29; *Carr v. Corning,*

182 F. 2d 14 (1950); Carl F. Hansen, "The Scholastic Performance of Negro and White Pupils in the Integrated Public Schools of the District of Columbia," *Harvard Educational Review* 30 (Summer 1960): 221.

3. Morton, "Education of Negroes in the District." Carl F. Hansen, *Danger in Washington: The Story of My Twenty Years in the Public Schools in the Nation's Capital* (West Nyack, N.Y.: Parker, 1968), vi.

4. *Carr v. Corning,* 182 F. 2d 14 (1950).

5. Hansen, *Danger in Washington,* 10; Knoll, "Washington," 195; George D. Strayer, *The Report of a Survey of the Public Schools of the District of Columbia* (Washington, D.C., 1949).

6. *Carr v. Corning,* 182 F. 2d 14 (1950) at 22, 23; Richard Kluger, *Simple Justice* (New York: Vintage ed., Knopf, 1977), 513.

7. *Carr v. Corning,* 182 F. 2d 14 (1950) at 19, 22.

8. Ibid., 16.

9. Ibid., 32–33.

10. Kluger, *Simple Justice,* 521.

11. Hansen, *Danger in Washington,* 24–25; *Brown v. Board of Education,* 349 U.S. 294 (1955) at 298.

12. Hansen, *Danger in Washington,* 39–41; *Washington Post,* 12 May 1974.

13. *New York Times,* 19 Sept. 1956, p. 74; 21 Sept. 1956, p. 1; 3 Oct. 1956, p. 15; 29 Dec. 1956, p. 1.

14. *New Republic* 135 (8 Oct. 1956): 3–4.

15. *Investigation of Public School Conditions, Hearings before the Subcommittee of the Committee on the District of Columbia, House of Representatives,* 84th Cong., 2d sess., 1956, pp. 36–37, 131, 139 (cited hereafter as *1956 Investigation*).

16. Ibid., 36, 80, 271–72.

17. *Time* 69 (7 Jan. 1957): 49; *U.S. News* 43 (12 July 1957): 66–68 and 45 (12 Dec. 1958): 66.

18. *1956 Investigation,* 267, 73, 133, 179.

19. Ibid., pp. 95, 36.

20. Ibid., p. 38, 39, 66.

21. Ibid., pp. 230–31.

22. Ibid., pp. 344, 161; *Time* 69 (7 Jan. 1957): 49.

23. *U.S. News* 40 (3 Feb. 1956): 40.

24. Ibid.

25. *1956 Investigation,* pp. 124, 149, 97.

26. *New York Times,* 29 Dec. 1956, p. 1.

27. Joseph Alsop, "No More Nonsense About Ghetto Education!" *New Republic* 157 (22 July 1967): p. 19.

28. Kenneth J. Gergen, "The Significance of Skin Color in Human Relations," in John Hope Franklin, ed., *Race and Color* (Boston: Houghton Mifflin, 1968), 115.

29. Hansen, *Danger in Washington,* 65–68. During the first five years after desegregation, however, almost all the white flight was to suburban public schools. In 1959 some 19,000 Washington children were enrolled in nonpublic schools. As a percentage of total school population, this number had actually decreased since desegregation began in 1954.

30. Ibid., 16–17.
31. Ibid., 43–45; *1956 Investigation*, 340, 345, 356–58.
32. *1956 Investigation*, 365; Hansen, *Danger in Washington*, 47.
33. Carl F. Hansen, "Ability Grouping in the High School," *Atlantic Monthly* 206 (Nov. 1960): 123–27; James D. Koerner, "Carl F. Hansen," *Saturday Review* 44 (16 Dec. 1961): 49–51.
34. *1956 Investigation*, 360; *New York Times*, 13 Oct. 1960; trial transcript, Hobson v. Hansen, Civil Action 82–66, U.S. District Court, Washington, D.C., pp. 607–11.
35. Hansen, "Ability Grouping in the High Schools"; *Investigation of Schools and Poverty in the District of Columbia, Hearings before the Task Force on Anti-poverty, House of Representatives, Committee on Education and Labor*, 89th Cong., 1st and 2d sess., 1965–1966 (cited hereafter as *1966 Investigation*), pp. 219–226. Ability grouping was widely practiced throughout the nation, although most educators preferred to use euphemistic labels. Hansen's use of "basic," "general," and "honors" stemmed partly from a preference for straight talk but also from his deep conviction that "ability grouping is inevitable and desirable, and ought to be planned rather than left to chance." *1966 Investigation*, 207.
36. *Washington Evening Star*, 16 June 1959; *1966 Investigation*, 205, 220–22; Hansen, "Ability Grouping in the High Schools," 124.
37. Susanna McBee, "D.C. Schools' Basic Track Program Is In Trouble Again," *Washington Post* clipping, n.d., in scrapbooks of Washington Board of Education.
38. *Time* 75 (1 Feb. 1960): 64; *1966 Investigation*, 342; *New York Times*, 4 Apr. 1960, p. 1.
39. *Time* 75 (1 Feb. 1960): 64; 76 (31 Oct. 1960): 53; Koerner, "Carl F. Hansen," 51.
40. *Washington Post*, 17 Aug. 1960 and 27 Oct. 1963; *Washington Star*, 14 Dec. 1963.
41. Normand Poirier, "The Extraordinary Amidon School," *Saturday Evening Post* 237 (19 Dec. 1964): 22–23.
42. Ibid.; *New Republic* 145 (23 Oct. 1961): 6.
43. Koerner, "Carl F. Hansen," 51; Jencks was the author of two unsigned pieces in the *New Republic* 145 (23 Oct. 1961): 6 and 142 (4 Apr. 1960): 6.
44. Poirier, "Extraordinary Amidon," 22.
45. *1966 Investigation*, 157.
46. *Time* 86 (9 July 1965): 56.
47. *New Republic* 147 (15 Dec. 1962): 6–7; *U.S. News* 54 (21 Jan. 1963): 72–74.
48. *Washington Post*, 23 Nov. 1962.
49. *New York Times*, 28 Nov. 1962, p. 26.
50. The report was summarized in *U.S. News* 54 (21 Jan. 1963): 72–74.
51. *New York Times*, 14 Mar. 1962, p. 29; 21 Feb. 1963, p. 6; *U.S. News* 54 (18 Feb. 1963): 37–39; 54 (11 Mar. 1963): 62–68.
52. *New York Times*, 21 Feb. 1963, p. 6; *U.S. News* 54 (18 Feb. 1963): 37–39.
53. Commission Report, Board of Education files.
54. *America* 108 (30 Mar. 1963): 425; *Commonweal* 77 (14 Dec. 1962): 304–5.
55. Charles E. Silberman, *Crisis in the Classroom* (New York: Random, 1970); Silberman, *Crisis in Black and White* (New York: Random, 1964), 266; John Holt,

How Children Fail (New York: Pitman, 1964), 181; Holt, quoted by Arthur Pearl, "What's Wrong With the New Informalism in Education," *Social Policy* 1 (Mar.–Apr. 1971): 15–23.

56. Ray C. Rist, *The Urban School* (Cambridge: M.I.T. Univ. Press, 1973), 14. Also see Diane Ravitch, *The Revisionists Revised* (New York: Basic Books, 1978); Marvin Lazerson, "Revisionism and American Educational History," *Harvard Educational Review* 43 (May 1973): 269–83.

57. Colin Greer, "Much Ado About Joy," *Social Policy* 1 (Mar.–Apr. 1971): 64–65.

58. *U.S. News* 63 (24 July 1967): 40–46.

59. Ibid.; *1956 Investigation,* 347–48; *Hobson v. Hansen,* 269 F. Supp. 401 (1967) at 451–54.

60. *1966 Investigation,* 306.

61. Ibid., 609–11, 579–80.

62. Ibid., 204–6; Hansen, "No Retreat in the Drive for Excellence," 22 Apr. 1965 typescript in Board of Education files.

63. Hansen, "No Retreat in the Drive for Excellence."

64. *Washington Post,* 15 Oct. 1965; 23 Oct. 1962; *1966 Investigation,* 601.

65. *Washington Post,* 19 June 1959.

66. *U.S. News* 54 (18 Feb. 1963): 37–39; 54 (11 Mar. 1963): 62–68; 63 (24 July 1967): 40–46; *New York Times,* 21 Feb. 1963, p. 6.

67. *1966 Investigation,* 306–21, 282–85, 589–91.

68. Ibid., 574, 490, 485.

69. Doxey A. Wilkerson, "Compensatory Education and Powerlessness," in Dwight W. Allen and Jeffrey C. Hecht, eds., *Controversies in Education* (Philadelphia: Saunders, 1974), 510.

70. *Washington Post,* 24 Mar., 6 Apr. 1977; *New York Times,* 25 Mar. 1977, sec. IV, p. 14.

71. *1966 Investigation,* 235–36, 253–54; *1956 Investigation,* 57, 155; *Washington Post,* 24 Mar. 1977; Deposition of Julius Hobson, 18 June 1966, Civil Action 82–66, U.S. District Court, Washington, D.C.; *Hobson v. Hansen,* 269 F. Supp. 401 (1967) at 406, 433; Alsop, "No More Nonsense," 19.

72. *1966 Investigation,* 323, 832.

73. *U.S. News* 54 (11 Mar. 1963): 62–68; 63 (24 July 1967): 40–46; Defendants' Proposed Findings of Fact, 22 Dec. 1966, CA 82–66; Defendants' Brief, 3 Feb. 1967, CA 82–66; *Hobson v. Hansen,* 269 F. Supp. 401 (1967) at 414.

74. Julius Hobson, "Using the Legal Process for Change," in Allen and Hecht, *Controversies in Education,* 535; Deposition of Julius Hobson, 18 June 1966, CA 82–66; *Washington Post,* 24 Mar. 1967 and 2 Apr. 1967.

75. *1966 Investigation,* 237, 238, 241.

76. Ibid., 232, 243, 377.

77. *Washington Star,* 20 Nov. 1966.

78. Ibid., 1 May 1967; *1966 Investigation,* 251.

79. Hansen, *Danger in Washington,* 94.

80. *University of Virginia Law Review* 58 (Jan. 1962): 161–76; *Harvard Law Review* 85 (Mar. 1972): 1049–59.

81. Stephen R. Goldstein, "Interdistrict Inequalities in School Financing," *University of Pennsylvania Law Review* 120 (Jan. 1972): 504–44.

82. *San Antonio School District v. Rodriguez,* 411 U.S. 1 (1973).

83. Plaintiffs' Memorandum to the Court, 8 Dec. 1970, Civil Action 21–167, U.S. Court of Appeals, Washington, D.C.

84. *Hobson v. Hansen,* 265 F. Supp. 902 (1967).

85. J. Skelly Wright, "A Colleague's Tribute to Judge David L. Bazelon," University of Pennsylvania Law Review 123 (Dec. 1974): 250–53.

86. *New York Times,* 4 Apr. 1962, p. 1; J. Skelly Wright, "Public School Desegregation," *New York University Law Review* 40 (Apr. 1965): 285–309.

87. Wright, "Public School Desegregation," 293, 301–2.

88. Ibid., 295, 304–6. Also see J. Skelly Wright, "The Role of the Supreme Court in a Democratic Society," *Cornell Law Review* 54 (Nov. 1968): 1–28; and Wright, "Are the Courts Abandoning the Cities?" *Journal of Law and Education* 4 (Jan. 1975): 218–26.

89. Appellants' Brief, CA 21–167; *Richmond News Leader,* 19 Sept. 1966.

90. *New York Times,* 20 June 1967, p. 1; *Newsweek* 75(23 Feb. 1970):108; Hansen, *Danger in Washington,* 93.

91. Plaintiffs' Brief, CA 82–66; *Richmond News Leader,* 19 Sept. 1966.

92. *Hobson v. Hansen,* 269 F. Supp. 401 (1967) at 406.

93. Deposition of Robert Coles, 25 Aug. 1966, CA 82–66.

94. Deposition of Christopher Jencks, 14 July 1966, CA 82–66.

95. Deposition of James S. Coleman, 23 July 1966, CA 82–66; testimony of James S. Coleman, 5 Aug. 1966, ibid; James S. Coleman, et al., *Equality of Educational Opportunity* (Washington, D.C.: Department of Health, Education, and Welfare, 1966), 21; Christopher Jencks, et al., *Inequality* (New York: Basic Books, 1972), 81; Frederick Mosteller and Daniel Moynihan, *On Equality of Educational Opportunity* (New York: Vintage, 1972), 14–15.

96. *Hobson v. Hansen,* 269 F. Supp. 401 (1967) at 474, 484, 491, 513–515.

97. Ibid., 419, 504–5.

98. Ibid., 426, 503, 497.

99. Ibid., 415–18, 515–16.

100. Ibid., 515–16, 510–11.

101. *Newsweek* 70 (3 July 1967): 48–49; *New York Times,* 16 Nov. 1967, p. 1; 18 Aug. 1970, p. 24; 26 Sept. 1971, p. 42; *Washington Post,* 14 Oct. 1976.

102. *New York Times,* 30 June 1967, p. 1; 23 June 1967, p. 38; Hansen, *Danger in Washington,* 91.

103. *New York Times,* 18 July 1967, p. 15; Appellants Brief, CA 2–167; Hansen, *Danger in Washington,* 105, 229.

104. *Hobson v. Hansen,* 269 F. Supp. 401 (1967) at 407, 507–8, 517. With NAACP officials boasting that blacks controlled "the balance of power" in American politics and Congress regularly enacting legislation designed to assist the black minority, many found these contentions rather hollow. The noted constitutional scholar Alexander M. Bickel even characterized such assertions as sounding "for all the world like some banana republic justifying its takeover." Alexander M. Bickel, reply to Michael E. Tigar, *New Republic* 157 (5 Aug. 1967): 43.

105. *Smuck v. Hobson,* 408 F. 2d 175 (1969) at 185–87.

106. *Iowa Law Review* 53 (1967–1968): 1187–88.

107. *University of Pittsburgh Law Review* 29 (1967): 164–65.

108. *Harvard Law Review* 81 (1968): 1525; *Stanford Law Review* 20 (1968): 1249–1268; *Korematsu v. U.S.,* 323 U.S. 214 (1944); *Hirabayshi v. U.S.,* 320 U.S. 81 (1943).

109. Alsop, "No More Nonsense," 18–23; Alsop, "Ghetto Education," *New Republic* 157 (18 Nov. 1967): 18–23.

110. Alsop, "No More Nonsense," 18, 20.

111. Washington Post, 20 Nov. 1970; Larry Cuban, "Hobson v. Hansen," *Educational Administration Quarterly* 11 (Spring 1975): 15–37; George R. La Noue and Bruce L.R. Smith, *The Politics of School Decentralization* (Lexington, Mass.: Heath, 1973), ch. 6; Donald L. Horowitz, *The Courts and Social Policy* (Washington: Brookings, 1977), ch. 4.

112. *Washington Post,* 31 Mar. 1978.

113. Ibid., 2 Aug. 1968, 4 Mar. 1973, 7 Dec. 1976.

114. Plaintiffs' Memorandum, 8 Dec. 1970, CA 82–66; *Hobson v. Hansen,* 327 F. Supp. 844 (1971).

115. Defendants' Answer, CA 82–66; *Washington Post,* 21 Feb. 1971.

116. *Hobson v. Hansen,* 327 F. Supp. (1971) at 844, 846, 850, 851, 854, 855, 858, 859, 863.

117. *Washington Post,* 29 Aug. 1971; Louis Malone, "Comment on Compliance," *Bulletin Board* (of D.C. Citizens for Better Public Education), 1971 newsletter in files of Washington Board of Education.

118. Joan Baratz, "Court Decisions and Educational Change, *Journal of Law and Education* 4 (Jan. 1975): 75–76; Horowitz, *Courts and Social Policy,* 150–65.

119. Horowitz, *Courts and Social Policy,* 150; *Washington Post,* 9, 10 Feb. 1975.

120. *Washington Post,* 11 Mar. 1972; *Washington Star,* 21 Apr. 1972, 6 Jan. 1973.

121. *Washington Post,* 13 Sept. and 30 June 1977; *Hobson v. Hansen,* 269 F. Supp. 401 (1967) at 434, n. 33.

122. *San Antonio School District v. Rodriguez,* 411 U.S. 1 (1973): *Washington v. Davis,* 426 U.S. 229 (1976); *Arlington Heights v. Metropolitan Housing Corporation,* 429 U.S. 252 (1977).

123. *Washington Post,* 20 Apr. 1972; Cuban, "Hobson v. Hansen," p. 2.

124. Susan L. Jacoby, "National Monument to Failure," *Saturday Review* 50 (18 Nov. 1967): 71–73; *Washington Post,* 15 Sept. 1967.

125. Baratz, "Court Decisions," p. 71.

126. La Noue and Smith, *The Politics of School Decentralization,* 96–102; Paul Lauter, "The Short, Happy Life of the Adams-Morgan Community School Project," *Harvard Educational Review* 38 (Spring 1968): 238; *Washington Post,* 6 July 1971.

127. Lauter, "Short, Happy Life," 239–40.

128. *New York Times,* 9 Jan. 1969, p. 68; *Washington Post,* 6 July 1971.

129. Lauter, "Short, Happy Life," 242–43, 253, 245.

130. Ibid., 255–56.

131. *Washington Post,* 6 July 1971.

132. Jacoby, "National Monument to Failure," 90.

133. *Washington Post,* 6 July 1971.

134. Walter Goodman, "Kenneth Clark's Revolutionary Slogan: Teach Them To Read!" *New York Times Magazine,* 18 Mar. 1973, p. 14. For an extended discussion, see Helen Gouldner, *Teachers' Pets, Troublemakers, and Nobodies: Black Children in Elementary School* (Westport, Conn.: Greenwood, 1978).

135. Goodman, "Kenneth Clark's Revolutionary Slogan"; Nat Hentoff, "Profile," *New Yorker,* 23 Aug. 1982, pp. 37–73.

136. Kenneth B. Clark, "Social Policy, Power, and Social Science Research," *Harvard Educational Review* 43 (Feb. 1973): 113–121; *Washington Post,* 19 July and 28 Sept. 1970.

137. Clark's plan is in the files of the Washington Board of Education.

138. *Washington Post,* 7 Mar. 1978, 10 July 1970, 8 Aug. 1975.

139. *Washington Post,* 18 Aug. 1970.

140. *Washington Post,* 10 Sept. and 3 Apr. 1970.

141. Ibid., 19 July, 30 Aug., 27 Sept. 1970.

142. Ibid., 10 Sept., 10 July, 26 Sept. 1970.

143. Ibid., 24 Nov. 1970.

144. *Washington Star,* 18 Apr. 1971; *New York Times,* 22 Feb. 1978, p. 22.

145. *Washington Post,* 20 Nov., 10 Sept., 21 Nov., 20 Apr. 1970, 19 Feb. 1973; 1 July, 31 Aug. 1975; *Washington Teacher,* Oct. 1970; *Washington Star,* 10 Dec. 1970, 18 Mar. 1971.

146. *Washington Post,* 20 Nov. 1970; statement of Charles Cassell, *Hearings before Special Select Committee on the District of Columbia, House of Representatives,* 91st Cong., 2d sess., 1970, p. 321.

147. *Washington Post,* 6 Jan., 28 July 1973, 31 May 1971.

148. Ibid., 9 June, 1 Aug., 7 Aug., 1 Oct. 1973.

149. "Superintendent's 120 Day Report," Mar. 1974, Board of Education Files, 11, 12, 15, 17, 21, 29; *Washington Post,* 2 Sept. 1973.

150. *Washington Post,* 5 Sept. 1973.

151. Ibid., 23 Apr., 5 Apr., 16 Apr. 1975.

152. Ibid., 28 Aug. 1974.

153. Ibid., 15 Dec. 1974, May–Nov. 1975.

154. Ibid., 7 July 1974, 5, 16, 23 Apr. 1975; "120 Day Report," 10.

155. *Washington Post,* 23 Aug., 7 Sept., 9 May, 7 Nov. 1975.

156. Ibid., 11 Nov. 1975.

157. Ibid., 11 Oct. 1975, 10 Oct. 1979.

158. Barbara Sizemore to *Washington Post,* 1 Dec. 1976. Also see, Sizemore, *The Ruptured Diamond: The Politics of Decentralization of the District of Columbia Public Schools* (Washington, D.C.: Univ. Press of America, 1981), and Nancy Arnez, *The Beseiged School Superintendent* (Washington, D.C.: Univ. Press of America, 1981); *Washington Post,* 20 Mar. 1976, 3 Jan. 1977.

159. *Washington Post,* 3 Jan. 1977, 17 Nov. 1975.

160. Ibid., 3 Jan. 1977, 24 Sept. 1976.

161. Ibid., 3 Jan. 1977; "Competency Tests Set in City Schools," undated press clipping, Board of Education files.

162. *Washington Post,* 31 Aug., 7, 13 Sept. 1978.

163. Ibid., 11 May 1960, 14 Sept. 1978; Carl F. Hansen, "Review of the Track System," typescript in Board of Education files, 13 Jan. 1964. Each state was given a quota that amounted to a fraction of 1 percent of the high school seniors, and the awards were distributed on the basis of student scores on a standardized examination. Only the most gifted students bothered to compete, and the results, though hardly a good index to the overall quality of a school program, said something about the quality of students in the senior high school academic program. In the early 1960s, when Carl Hansen had been superintendent, Washington's public school students averaged better than twenty semifinalist awards each year, about two-thirds of the awards then granted to the District of Columbia. By 1978, however, the situation had turned around dramatically. Only one of the thirty-seven semifinalist awards apportioned to the District of Columbia was won by a public school student; private high school enrollment was less than a quarter that of the public schools.

164. *Washington Post,* 15 Aug. 1976, 23 May 1977, 5 Sept. 1976, 21 Aug. 1976, 2 May 1978.

165. Ibid., 24 Nov. 1978, 5 Sept. 1976.

166. Ibid., 21 Mar., 10 July 1976, 27 Jan. 1975. In 1981, after Reed resigned as superintendent to become an assistant secretary to the U.S. Department of Education, Banneker Senior High School was established as an academic school. *Newsweek* noted, "Although [Reed] denies any link, it was widely speculated that [he] resigned . . . largely out of frustration at the board's action." *Newsweek,* 21 Dec. 1981, p. 80.

167. Thomas Sowell, "Black Excellence—The Case of Dunbar High School," *Public Interest* 35 (Spring 1974): 13, 3–4, 5–6; Adelaide Cromwell Hill, "A Lesson From the Past," in Floyd B. Barbour, ed., *The Black Seventies* (Boston: Porter Sargent, 1970), 51–67; Mary Gibson Hundley, *The Dunbar Story* (New York: Vantage Press, 1965).

168. *Washington Post,* 27 Jan. 1975.

169. Sowell, "Black Excellence," 9; *Washington Post,* 28 Dec., 4 May 1977, 2 Apr. 1974, 15 Apr. 1979.

170. *Washington Post,* 28 Mar., 3 Jan. 1975.

171. "Competency Tests Set in Public Schools" *Washington Post,* 3 Jan. 1977.

172. Ibid., 14 Nov. 1968.

173. Ibid., 3 Jan. 1977, 14 Nov. 1978.

174. Ibid., 3, 12 Jan. 1977, 21 Nov. 1978.

175. Ibid., 24 Nov. 1978.

176. Ibid., 27 May 1973.

177. Walter Sanderson to *Washington Post,* 13 June 1973; Williams' articles on Eastern High School ran daily in the *Washington Post,* 30 Apr. 1978 through 4 May 1978.

178. Ibid., 30 Apr. 1978.

179. Ibid., 25, 30 July 1980.

180. Ibid., 18 Jan., 23 Mar. 1981, 17 May 1979.

181. Ibid., 9 May 1975. Beginning in 1979 the Washington public schools reported that elementary students were doing better on standardized examinations, while test scores in the high schools remained unchanged or continued to decline. See articles by Judith Valente in the *Washington Post,* 31 Jan., 11 June, 6 Dec. 1981. Lawrence Feinberg has noted that "school officials see the elementary school gains as vindication for the more structured, rigorous curriculums and stiffer promotion policies introduced as part of a national 'back to basics' trend. Some experts say it may also stem from applying research on effective schools, which stresses spending more time on important tasks, teaching step by step in orderly classrooms, and following a clear common plan rather than the flexibility and decentralization that were the watchwords of the reformist 1960s.

"Why achievement has continued to fall in high schools . . . is a subject of sharp debate. Proponents of the structured curriculum note that even the most recent groups of 11th and 12th graders attended elementary school before most of these programs were introduced in the last half of the 1970s. They foresee gains in the high schools over the next few years, though some say the senior highs themselves will have to make significant changes, systematically teaching analytical skills and cutting back on 'soft' electives. Critics contend that the structured programs— often marked by long checklists of skills and a plethora of short 'mastery' exams— may actually have caused a decline in the more complex reasoning and analytical abilities needed to do well on end-of-high school exams." *Washington Post,* 31 Aug. 1982.

182. *Hobson v. Hansen,* 269 F. Supp. 401 (1967) 508.

183. Ibid., 503, 517.

NOTES TO PART TWO

1. Bob Smith, *They Closed Their Schools: Prince Edward County, Virginia, 1951–1964* (Chapel Hill: Univ. of North Carolina Press, 1965), 3–4, 6.

2. W.E.B. Du Bois, *The Negroes of Farmville, Virginia: A Social Study,* Bulletin of the U.S. Department of labor, No. 14 (Jan. 1898), 34–35; Du Bois, *The Souls of Black Folk* (Kraus-Thompson, 1973 reprint of 1903 ed.), 193; Kluger, *Simple Justice,* 461.

3. Smith, *They Closed Their Schools,* 7–13 and passim.

4. Ibid.; L. Francis Griffin to *Farmville Herald,* 18 July 1969; *Richmond Times Dispatch,* 19 Jan. 1980.

5. Kluger, *Simple Justice,* 132–38; W.E.B. Du Bois, "The Ignorant Negro Child," *Crisis* 40 (Sept. 1933): 213.

6. Kluger, *Simple Justice,* 132.

7. *Southern School News,* Jan. 1956.

8. Doxey A. Wilkerson, "The Negro School Movement in Virginia: From 'Equalization' to 'Integration,'" *Journal of Negro Education* 29 (Winter 1960): 24, 19; Kluger, *Simple Justice,* 474.

9. Kluger, *Simple Justice,* 459; Smith, *They Closed Their Schools,* 15.

10. John Steck, *The Prince Edward County Story* (Farmville, Va.: Farmville Herald, 1960), 5; Smith, *They Closed Their Schools,* 3–26.

11. Smith, *They Closed Their Schools,* 22, 25, 103; Leon Friedman, ed., *Argument: The Oral Argument Before the Supreme Court in Brown v. Board of Education of Topeka, 1952–1955* (New York: Chelsea, 1969), 89.

12. Smith, *They Closed Their Schools,* 40, 37, 39.

13. Ibid., 63; Kluger, *Simple Justice,* 469; interview with T.J. McIlwaine, 15 May 1980.

14. W.E.B. Du Bois, "Segregation," *Crisis* 41 (Jan. 1934): 20.

15. Walter White, "Segregation," *Crisis* 41 (Mar. 1934): 80–81; Raymond Wolters, *Negroes and the Great Depression: The Problem of Economic Recovery* (Westport, Conn.: Greenwood, 1970), ch. 10; August Meier and Elliott Rudwick, "The Rise of the Black Secretariat in the NAACP, 1909–1935," in Meier and Rudwick, *Along the Color Line* (Urbana: Univ. of Illinois Press, 1976), 117–18 and passim.

16. Kluger, *Simple Justice,* 276.

17. *Sweatt v. Painter,* 339 U.S. 629 (1950) at 634.

18. *New York Times,* 3 Sept. 1950, p. 25.

19. Kluger, *Simple Justice,* 293–94; Minutes of the Board of Directors, 9 Oct. 1950, NAACP Papers, Ser. A, Box 13, Library of Congress.

20. Smith, *They Closed Their Schools,* 55; Steck, *The Prince Edward Story,* 6.

21. Smith, *They Closed Their Schools,* 69–70, 55, 58, 59.

22. Ibid., 54, 53.

23. Kluger, *Simple Justice,* 478; Edgar A. Schuler and Robert L. Green, "A Southern Educator and School Integration," *Phylon* 28 (Fall 1967): 32.

24. *Farmville Herald,* 26 June 1951.

25. Trial transcript, *Davis v. County School Board,* Supreme Court Library, 51.

26. Friedman, *Argument,* 76, 100.

27. Trial transcript, 206, 184–85, 175.

28. Ibid., 239, 289.

29. Friedman, *Argument,* 97, 85. The Virginians' argument has found impressive scholarly support in Howard N. Rabinowitz, *Race Relations in the Urban South, 1865–1890* (New York: Oxford Univ. Press, 1978), 127, 168, and passim. Segregated public education, Rabinowitz writes, "ironically often signified an improvement, for what it replaced was not integration but exclusion."

30. Friedman, *Argument,* 218.

31. Trial transcript, 51.

32. Friedman, *Argument,* 90–91.

33. Ibid., 81.

34. Trial transcript, 554–55.

35. Friedman, *Argument,* 92; Kluger, *Simple Justice,* 504.

36. Friedman, *Argument,* 94, 95–99, 224–26, 231–33.

37. Ibid., 86 and passim.

38. Kluger, *Simple Justice,* 487.

39. *Davis v. County School Board,* 103 F. Supp. 337 (1952) at 340, 339.

40. Ibid., 338–39.

41. Ibid., 339, 340, 341.

42. *Brown v. Board of Education of Topeka*, 347 U.S. 483 (1954) at 489, 493, 494, 495.

43. Ibid., 495.

44. Friedman, *Argument*, 424–36.

45. Ibid.; *Southern School News*, 4 May 1955.

46. Friedman, *Argument*, 424–36; *Southern School News*, 1 Dec. 1954.

47. Friedman, *Argument*, 436–39; Roy Wilkins to Robert Robertson, 23 Jan. 1959, NAACP papers, Group III, Ser. B, Box 201; Oliver Hill, text of speech for TV station WXES, 25 Jan. 1959, NAACP Papers, Group III, Ser. A, Box 154.

48. *Brown v. Board of Education*, 349 U.S. 294 (1955) at 298, 299, 300, 301.

49. *Davis v. County School Board*, 149 F. Supp. 431 (1957) at pp. 438, 439, 440 and passim. Also see Judge Hutcheson's opinion in *Allen v. County School Board*, 164 F. Supp. 786 (1958) at 786, 788 and passim.

50. *Davis v. County School Board*, 149 F. Supp. 431 (1957) at 436, 438, 439; *Allen v. County School Board*, 164 F. Supp. 786 (1958) at 792.

51. *Allen v. County School Board*, 239 F. 2d. 462 (1957) at 465.

52. *Davis v. County School Board*, 149 F. Supp. 431 (1957) at 436, 438, 439, 440; *Allen v. County School Board*, 164 F. Supp. 786 (1958) at 792, 786, 788.

53. *Allen v. County School Board*, 266 F. 2d 507 (1959).

54. *Richmond News Leader*, 1 June 1955; Steck, *The Prince Edward Story*, 9.

55. Steck, *The Prince Edward Story*, 11–12; Smith, *They Closed Their Schools*, 6–7.

56. Steck, *The Prince Edward Story*, 13.

57. Smith, *They Closed Their Schools*, 117.

58. *Richmond News Leader*, 8 June 1955; Smith, *They Closed Their Schools*, 117–22.

59. *Richmond Times Dispatch*, 8 June 1955; *Richmond News Leader*, 8 June 1955; *Farmville Herald*, 10 June, 18 July 1955.

60. Smith, *They Closed Their Schools*, 123.

61. Haldore Hanson, "No Surrender in Farmville," *New Republic* 133 (10 Oct. 1955); 14.

62. Irv Goodman, "Public Schools Died Here," *Saturday Evening Post* 234 (29 Apr. 1961): 87; Hanson, "No Surrender," 14; interview with Robert T. Taylor, 23 July 1979.

63. Interview with Robert T. Taylor.

64. James Rorty, "Virginia's Creeping Desegregation," *Commentary* 22 (July 1956): 47; *Farmville Herald*, 9 June 1959, 4 Nov. 1955; Hanson, "No Surrender," 14–15.

65. Henry E. Garrett, *How Classroom Desegregation Will Work* (1966 pamphlet); Garrett, *IQ and Racial Differentials* (1973 pamphlet).

66. Garrett, *IQ and Racial Differentials*, 13; *Farmville Herald*, 14 June 1963.

67. James J. Kilpatrick, *The Southern Case for School Segregation* (New York: Crowell-Collier, 1962), 43, 49–51.

68. Ibid., 52–54, 97; Robert Gaines Corley, "James Jackson Kilpatrick: The Evolution of a Southern Conservative, 1955–1965," M.A. thesis, Univ. of Virginia, 1971, p. 50.

69. Ibid., 52–53, 70–72.

70. James W. Ely, Jr., *The Crisis of Conservative Virginia: The Byrd Organization and the Politics of Massive Resistance* (Knoxville: Univ. of Tennessee Press, 1976), 114–15; Robbins L. Gates, *The Making of Massive Resistance: Virginia's Politics of Public School Desegregation* (Chapel Hill: Univ. of North Carolina Press, 1962), 172.

71. *Farmville Herald,* 25 June 1954; *Richmond News Leader,* 8 June 1954.

72. Roy Wilkins to Robert Whitehead, 26 Feb. 1959; Whitehead to Oliver Hill and Spottswood Robinson, 17 Feb. 1959; Wilkins to Robert D. Robertson, 18 Feb. 1959; Wilkins to David E. Longley, 4 Mar. 1959, all in NAACP Papers, Group III, Ser. B, Box 201.

73. *Richmond Times Dispatch,* 26 Mar. 1957; Ely, *Crisis of Conservative Virginia,* 97.

74. Gates, *Massive Resistance,* chs. 2–5; Ely, *Crisis of Conservative Virginia,* ch. 3.

75. *New York Times,* 26 Feb. 1956, p. 1.

76. Gates, *Massive Resistance,* ch. 11.

77. Kilpatrick, *Southern Case,* 105; *Richmond News Leader,* 1 June 1955.

78. *Richmond News Leader,* 21, 22, and 23 Nov. 1955; James J. Kilpatrick, *The Sovereign States; Notes of a Citizen of Virginia* (Chicago: Henry Regnery, 1957).

79. Virginia, Acts of the General Assembly, Regular Session, 1956; Ely, *Crisis of Conservative Virginia,* 61.

80. *Farmville Herald,* 17 Apr. 1956, 19 July 1955; Smith, *They Closed Their Schools,* 157.

81. *Farmville Herald,* 14 June 1962.

82. Ibid., 15 Sept. 1959.

83. *Richmond News Leader,* 1 June 1955.

84. *Richmond Times Dispatch,* 28 July 1956.

85. *Richmond News Leader,* 31 Oct. 1957; Benjamin Muse, *Virginia's Massive Resistance* (Bloomington: Indiana Univ. Press, 1961), 43.

86. Ely, *Crisis of Conservative Virginia,* 68–69.

87. *Harrison v. Day,* 200 Va. 439 (1959); *James v. Almond,* 170 F. Supp. 331 (1959) at 337, 338.

88. *Richmond Times Dispatch,* 21 Jan. 1959.

89. *Richmond News Leader,* 28 Jan. 1959; *Norfolk Virginia Pilot,* 9 June 1964.

90. Ely, *Crisis of Conservative Virginia,* 130–31; J. Harvie Wilkinson III, *Harry Byrd and the Changing Face of Virginia Politics* (Charlottesville: Univ. of Virginia Press, 1968), 147–49.

91. Ely, *Crisis of Conservative Virginia,* 132; *Richmond Times Dispatch,* 7 May 1959.

92. *Allen v. County School Board,* 266 F. 2d 507 (1959); Steck, *The Prince Edward Story,* 16.

93. *Farmville Herald,* 19, 9 June 1959.

94. *Wall Street Journal,* 1 Dec. 1959; *Newsday,* 21 Dec. 1960; Goodman, "Public Schools Died Here," 32ff.

95. *Richmond News Leader,* 12 Sept. 1959; *Farmville Herald,* 25 Aug. 1959; Smith, *They Closed Their Schools,* 165–166.

96. *Richmond Times Dispatch,* 11 Sept. 1959; *Newsday,* 21 Dec. 1960; interviews with Charles W. Glenn, W.T. "Tom" Joiner, and Robert T. Taylor, 23 July 1979.

97. *Farmville Herald,* quoted by Eva Newmark, "Freedom Teacher and Gentle Ladies," *Nation* 200 (22 Feb. 1965): 193. The Academy's regional reputation was even reflected in its football schedule, which included games with teams from other southern states. *Farmville Herald,* 24 Sept. 1971; *Prince Edward Reporter,* Winter 1972.

98. *Wall Street Journal,* 1 Dec. 1959; *Farmville Herald,* 19 Sept. 1961.

99. Interview with Robert T. Redd, 23 July 1979.

100. *Farmville Herald,* 17 Jan. 1961; "Excellence In Education" (1979 pamphlet in files, Prince Edward Academy); interview with Robert T. Redd.

101. *New Republic* 147 (1 Dec. 1962): 5–6; *Newsday,* 21 Dec. 1960; "Excellence in Education"; Robert T. Redd to author, 21 July 1982; *Prince Edward Reporter,* June 1982.

102. Interview with Robert T. Redd; interview with Doris Davis, 27 July 1979.

103. Interview with Robert T. Redd; *Lynchburg News,* 3 Nov. 1966.

104. Interview with Robert T. Redd.

105. Ibid; interview with James C. Melvin, 26 July 1979.

106. Interviews with Reeves Holman (27 July 1979), Anne Bennett Jefferson (26 July 1979), and Bo Prichard (24 July 1979).

107. John Egerton, "A Gentlemen's Fight," *American Heritage* 30 (Aug.–Sept. 1979): 62; *Lynchburg News,* 3 Nov. 1966; interviews with Robert T. Redd, Frances Hazelwood (26 July 1979), Doris Davis (27 July 1979), and Jennifer Halladay (26 July 1979).

108. *Farmville Herald,* 27 May 1960, 1 Sept. 1961.

109. Ibid., 1 July, 10 June 1970, 15 Nov. 1963; Mills E. Godwin, commencement address, 9 June 1978.

110. Interviews with Robert T. Redd (23 July 1979), Ellen Cox (26 July 1979), and Bonnie V. Smith (25 July 1979); *New York Times,* 13 May 1974, p. 24.

111. Interview with Nancy Holman (27 July 1979).

112. *Newsday,* 19 Dec. 1960; Smith, *They Closed Their Schools,* 176, 243.

113. Interview with J. Barrye Wall, 23 July 1979; Smith, *They Closed Their Schools,* 184; *Newsday,* 19 Dec. 1960; Goodman, "Public Schools Died Here," 89; *Christian Science Monitor,* 5, 14, 18 Apr. 1962.

114. Kennell Jackson, Jr., "Reducing the Kids to Dust," *Nation* 203 (14 Nov. 1966): 521–22; Goodman, "Public Schools Died Here," 89.

115. Schuler and Green, "A Southern Educator," 120; *Farmville Herald,* 26 June 1959.

116. Smith, *They Closed Their Schools; Newsday,* 23 Dec. 1960; Schuler and Green, "A Southern Educator," 39.

117. *Newsday,* 23 Dec. 1960; *New York Times,* 9 Sept. 1962, p. 66; Smith, *They Closed Their Schools,* 218; Goodman, "Public Schools Died Here," 89.

118. Smith, *They Closed Their Schools,* 217.

119. *Southern School News,* Feb. 1960, Mar. 1962.

120. *Newsday,* 19 Dec. 1960; *New York Times,* 30 Apr. 1961, p. 30; *Time* 82 (9 Aug. 1963): 56; Smith, *They Closed Their Schools,* 197; Roy Wilkins to Robert D.

Robertson, 19 Dec. 1958, NAACP Papers, Group III, Ser. B, Box 201; *New York Times,* 15 Aug. 1963, p. 28.

121. *Newsday,* 22 Dec. 1960.

122. Ibid.; *Farmville Herald,* 24 Mar. 1961; Goodman, "Public Schools Died Here," 86.

123. *Farmville Herald,* 10 Sept. 1959; *Southern School News,* Sept. 1962, Nov. 1962, June 1963; *New York Times,* 20 Oct. 1962, p. 26; Smith, *They Closed Their Schools,* 253, 170.

124. *Southern School News,* Aug. 1963.

125. *Congressional Record,* 87th Cong. 1st sess., 17 May 1961, p. A7526; *Southern School News,* Jan. 1960, Feb. 1960; *Farmville Herald,* 22 Dec. 1959.

126. *Richmond News Leader,* 12 Sept. 1959; Smith, *They Closed Their Schools,* 172.

127. *Farmville Herald,* 24 Mar., 16 June 1961; Steck, *the Prince Edward Story,* 4.

128. *Southern School News,* Jan., Feb. 1960; Smith, *They Closed Their Schools,* 198; Jackson, "Reducing the Kids to Dust," 522; *New York Times,* 21 May 1961, p. 77.

129. *Farmville Herald,* 19 June 1959; 16 Dec. 1960.

130. *Newsday,* 19 Dec. 1960; *Farmville Herald,* 24 Mar. 1961; *Farmville Herald,* as quoted in *Southern School News,* Jan. 1960 and Apr. 1962.

131. Smith, *They Closed Their Schools,* 249; *Southern School News,* Mar. 1963; Jackson, "Reducing the Kids to Dust."

132. Robert L. Green, et al., *The Educational Status of Children in a District Without Public Schools* (U.S. Department of Health, Education and Welfare, 1964); Green, et al., "Some Effects of Deprivation on Intelligence, Achievement, and Cognitive Growth," *Journal of Negro Education* 36 (Winter 1967): 5–14; Green and Robert F. Morgan, "The Effects of Resumed Schooling on the Measured Intelligence of Prince Edward County's Black Children," *Journal of Negro Education* 38 (Spring 1969): 147–55.

133. Smith, *They Closed Their Schools,* 237; *Southern School News,* May 1963.

134. Southern School News, May, Aug. 1963; Neil V. Sullivan, *Bound For Freedom: An Educator's Adventure in Prince Edward County, Virginia* (Boston: Little, Brown, 1965), 106–8.

135. Arthur M. Schlesinger, Jr., *Robert Kennedy and His Times* (Boston: Houghton Mifflin, 1978), 359; *New York Times,* 15 Aug. 1963, p. 18.

136. Sullivan, *Bound For Freedom,* 157–58, 38, 80.

137. Ibid., 30, 32.

138. Ibid., 27–28.

139. Ibid., 39.

140. Ibid., 139; *Southern School News,* Jan. 1964.

141. *New York Times,* 17 Sept. 1963, p. 26; Sullivan, *Bound For Freedom,* 23, 96–98, 63–66, 181–82.

142. Sullivan, *Bound for Freedom,* 127, 123–25.

143. Ibid., 183–91.

144. Interview with C.G. Gordon Moss, 13 May 1980.

145. Sullivan, *Bound for Freedom,* 131–39; Newmark, "Freedom Teacher and Gentle Ladies," 194; *Newsweek* 57 (8 May 1961): 25.

146. Steck, *The Prince Edward Story*, 24. Thomas D. Lipps, "Understanding Prince Edward County" (unpublished seminar paper, Harvard Law School, 1969), 29; Brief for Petitioners, Griffin v. Prince Edward County (1963), Supreme Court Library; *New York Times*, 31 Mar. 1964, p. 24; *Southern School News*, Feb. 1963.

147. Brief for Board of Supervisors, Griffin v. Prince Edward County (1963), Supreme Court Library.

148. *Newsday*, 31 Dec. 1960; *New York Times*, 26 July 1961, p. 31.

149. *Allen v. County School Board*, 198 F. Supp. 497 (1961).

150. Ibid.

151. *Southern School News*, Mar. 1962; *Griffin v. Board of Supervisors*, 126 S.E. 2d 22 (1962); *County School Board v. Griffin*, 133 S.E. 2d 565 (1963).

152. *Allen v. County School Board*, 207 F. Supp. 349 (1962) at 355, 351, 353.

153. *Griffin v. Board of Supervisors*, 322 F. 2d 332 (1963) at 336.

154. Ibid.

155. J. Segar Gravatt to John C. Steck, 8 Apr. 1964, in files of *Farmville Herald*; Peggy Bebie Thomson, "A Fresh Wind in Farmville," *Progressive* 28 (Apr. 1964): 27.

156. *Southern School News*, Apr. 1964.

157. *Griffin v. School Board*, 377 U.S. 218 (1964) at 231.

158. Ibid., 234.

159. *Washington Post*, 31 May 1964; *New York Times*, 27 May 1964, p. 38; *New Republic* 150 (6 June 1964): 5–6.

160. *Southern School News*, June 1964; *Richmond Times Dispatch*, quoted in *New York Times*, 31 May 1964, Sec. IV, p. 9.

161. *Southern School News*, June 1964.

162. *New York Times*, 27 May 1964, p. 38; *New Republic* 150 (6 June 1964): 5–6.

163. Briefs for Plaintiffs and Defendants, Griffin v. Board of Supervisors, case 9597, Fourth Circuit Court of Appeals, 1964, Library of Congress; *Southern School News*, Dec. 1964.

164. *Griffin v. Board of Supervisors*, 339 F. 2d 486 (1964) at 492, 493.

165. *Bradley v. School Board of Richmond*, 345 F. 2d 310 (1965) at 316.

166. *Prince Edward Reporter*, Mar. 1968, Nov. 1967.

167. *Griffin v. State Board of Education*, 239 F. Supp. 560 (1965) at 564; *Harvard Law Review* 79 (Feb. 1966): 841.

168. *Griffin v. State Board of Education*, 296 F. Supp. 1178 (1969); *Poindexter v. Louisiana Financial System Commission*, 275 F. Supp. 833 (1967); *Brown v. South Carolina State Board of Education*, 296 F. Supp. 199 (1968); 389 U.S. 571 (1968).

169. Reply of Board of Supervisors, *Griffin v. Board of Supervisors*, case 9597, Fourth Circuit Court of Appeals, 1964, Library of Congress; *New York Times*, 8 Sept. 1964, p. 35.

170. *Farmville Herald*, 14 Aug. 1968.

171. Ibid., 23 June 1972.

172. Ibid., 16 Apr. 1969, 21 June, 10 May 1972.

173. Interview with L. Francis Griffin, 25 July 1979. Rev. Griffin expressed similar views in a newspaper column that appeared regularly on the op-ed page of the *Richmond Afro-American*.

174. Interview with J. Samuel Williams, 14 May 1980.

175. Interview with James E. Ghee, 13 May 1980.
176. *Farmville Herald,* 14 July, 21, 23 June 1972.
177. Ibid., 17, 19 July 1972.
178. *The Edwardian,* Feb. 1980.
179. *Richmond Times Dispatch,* 13 May 1979.
180. Interviews with Vera Allen (26 July 1979), James M. Anderson (13 May 1980).
181. Interviews with Kate Young, (25 July 1979), Mrs. H.A. Simpson (25 July 1979), and L. Francis Griffin (25 July 1979).
182. *The Edwardian,* Mar. 1980; interview with James M. Anderson.
183. *Farmville Herald,* 31 Jan. 1979.
184. Interviews with Mrs. H.A. Simpson (25 July 1979) and Rita Lawhorne (26 July 1979); *Farmville Herald,* 8 Aug. 1979; *The Edwardian,* Oct. 1979.
185. *Washington Post,* 18 Jan., 4 Sept. 1979.
186. Interview with L. Francis Griffin.
187. Interview with Patton Lockwood, 24 July 1979.
188. Interviews with Mrs. C.G. Gordon Moss (13 May 1980), W.T. "Tom" Joiner (23 July 1979), and Patton Lockwood (24 July 1979).
189. Interviews with Kate Young (25 July 1979) and Mike Boykin (13 May 1980).
190. Interviews with Kate Young, Robin Lockwood (24 July 1979), Mrs. H.A. Simpson, Rita Lawhorne, and Jennifer Halladay.
191. Interview with Robin Lockwood; conversation with Kate Young, 14 May 1980.
192. Interviews with Bill Townes (14 May 1980), Jamantha and Psyche Williams (15 May 1980), and Nancy Fawcett (14 May 1980).
193. Interviews with L. Francis Griffin, Jennifer Halladay, and Kate Young.
194. Interviews with James M. Anderson, Thomas Mayfield (13 May 1980), and Jamantha and Psyche Williams; *Farmville Herald,* 12 Dec. 1979, 11 Apr. 1980.
195. Interviews with James E. Ghee, J. Samuel Williams, Amil Myshin (27 July 1980), and Leonard Brown (27 July 1980).
196. Interviews with Patton Lockwood and L. Francis Griffin.
197. *Farmville Herald,* 9 Nov. 1979, 11 Apr. 1980.
198. Interview with L. Francis Griffin; Egerton, "A Gentlemen's Fight," 57.
199. Green, *The Educational Status of Children in a District Without Public Schools; New York Times,* 6 Sept. 1976, p. 20; interview with James E. Ghee.
200. Alexander M. Bickel, "Desegregation: Where Do We Go From Here?" *New Republic* 162 (7 Feb. 1970): 20–22.
201. Ely, *Crisis of Conservative Virginia,* 102; interview with J. Barrye Wall; Egerton, "A Gentlemen's Fight," 57.
202. Interview with J. Barrye Wall; Egerton, "A Gentlemen's Fight," 62.

NOTES TO PART THREE

1. *Green v. County School Board of New Kent County,* 391 U.S. 430 (1968).
2. John Bartlow Martin, *The Deep South Says 'Never'* (New York: Ballantine, 1957), 55; Kluger, *Simple Justice,* 4–5.

3. *Census of Agriculture,* 1954 (pt. 16, p. 382) and 1974 (pt. 40, p. IV–85); interviews with Ralph Bell (22 Aug. 1980) and Henry Lawson (23 Aug. 1980).

4. Santee-Lynches Council for Governments, "Report on Distressed Areas," June 1980; interview with Billie S. Fleming, 25 Aug. 1980.

5. Kluger, *Simple Justice,* 8, 331–32, 350–51; Defendants' Answer, 5 Feb. 1951, Briggs v. Elliott, Civil Action 2657, U.S. District Court, Columbia; *New York Times,* 3 June 1951, sec. IV, p. 7; report of Matthew J. Whitehead, CA 2657.

6. Interview with Robert McC. Figg, 20 Aug. 1980; Defendants' Answer, CA 2657.

7. Kluger, *Simple Justice,* 8–13; Grace Jordan McFadden, TV interview with Mattie DeLaine, 1979, Univ. of South Carolina film files.

8. Kluger, *Simple Justice,* 15–17.

9. Ibid., 18.

10. Plaintiffs' Complaint, CA 2657.

11. Julian Scheer, "The White Folks Fight Back," *New Republic* 133 (31 Oct. 1955): 24; Martin, *The Deep South Says 'Never',* 67.

12. Interviews with Robert McC. Figg (20 Aug. 1980) and Billie S. Fleming (25 Aug. 1980); Kluger, *Simple Justice,* 295–305; *American Mercury* 70 (May 1950): 562–69.

13. Summons, CA 2657.

14. Trial transcript, CA 2657.

15. *Brown v. Board of Education,* 347 U.S. 483 (1954) at n. 11; trial transcript (especially the testimony of Kenneth B. Clark, David Krech, Harold McNally, Helen Trager, and Louis Kesselman), CA 2657; petition for appeal, CA 2657.

16. Kluger, *Simple Justice,* 355.

17. Ibid.; Edmond Cahn, "Jurisprudence," *New York University Law Review* 30 (1955): 163–64.

18. Ernest van den Haag, "Social Science Testimony in the Desegregation Cases—A Reply to Professor Kenneth Clark," *Villanova Law Review* 6 (Fall 1960): 69, 71.

19. Ibid., 77; William F. Buckley, Jr., "Footnote to Brown v. Board of Education," *National Review* 10, (11 Mar. 1960): 137.

20. Defendants' brief, CA 2657; *Gong Lum v. Rice,* 275 U.S. 78 (1927) at 86.

21. Defendants' brief, CA 2657.

22. James F. Byrnes, *All In One Lifetime* (New York: Harper, 1958), 407; *New York Times,* 27 May 1951, p. 40; *Southern School News,* 3 Sept. 1954.

23. *Southern School News,* 3 Sept. 1954.

24. *Charleston News and Courier,* 23 Dec. 1953; Martin, *The Deep South Says 'Never',* 55.

25. *Briggs v. Elliott,* 98 F. Supp. 529 (1951) at 537.

26. John W. Davis, "Brief for Appellees" (1952) and "Brief for Appellees on Reargument" (1953), Supreme Court Library.

27. *Ex parte Bain,* 121 U.S. 1 (1887) at 12; *Eisner v. Macomber,* 252 U.S. 189 (1920) at 220; Friedman, *Argument,* 55. Davis's view is in marked contrast to that of J. Skelly Wright, who at a testimonial dinner in 1962 observed, "The Supreme Court is more than a law court—it is a policy court, or, if you will a political court. It is an instrument of government, and while most judges have the habit, through

long years of precedent, of looking backward, the Supreme Court must look forward through a knowledge of life, of people, of sociology, of psychology. The Supreme Court is the final interpreter of the Constitution, a living document. It should not be interpreted with reference to the time in which it was written but rather in reference to the present, or, better still, the future." Quoted by Reed Sarratt, *The Ordeal of Desegregation* (New York: Harper and Row, 1966), 203.

28. Brief for Appellees on Reargument, Supreme Court Library; Friedman, *Argument*, 38, 45; Brief for Appellants, Supreme Court Library.

29. *Brown v. Board of Education*, 349 U.S. 294 (1955).

30. *Briggs v. Elliott*, 132 F. Supp. 776 (1955) at 777.

31. Robert L. Carter, "Equal Educational Opportunity for Negroes," in John H. McCord, ed., *With All Deliberate Speed* (Urbana: Univ. of Illinois Press, 1969), 59. Also see *U.S. News* 53 (17 Dec. 1962): 68–69; *Time* 96 (26 Oct. 1970): 55–56.

32. *Columbia State*, 2 June 1955; *Charleston News and Courier*, 1 June 1955; *Southern School News*, Jan. 1956.

33. *Greenville News*, 18 Mar. 1979.

34. Kluger, *Simple Justice*, 25; *Columbia State*, 10 Oct. 1955.

35. Ibid.; *Columbia State*, 10 Aug. 1955, 2 Feb. 1956, 27 May 1958; *Charleston News and Courier*, 11 Oct. 1955; *New York Times*, 26 Nov. 1955, p. 9; McFadden, interview with Mattie DeLaine; telephone conversation with Billie S. Fleming, 6 July 1982.

36. Harold R. Boulware, Spottswood W. Robinson, Robert L. Carter, and Thurgood Marshall, "Statement as to Jurisdiction," Briggs v. Elliott, Supreme Court Library; Friedman, *Argument*, 395, 399–400, 405.

37. CA 2657, transcript of testimony; Friedman, *Argument*, pp. 417–418, 410–414, 419; *Southern School News*, 4 May 1955; *St. Louis Post Dispatch*, 12 April 1955.

38. Martin, *The Deep South Says 'Never'*, 62; *U.S. News* 39 (19 Aug. 1955): 51–54; *Greenville Delta Democrat*, 2 July 1956; Howard H. Quint, *Profile in Black and White: A Frank Portrait of South Carolina* (Washington: Public Affairs Press, 1958), 25.

39. *Southern School News*, 8 June 1955, Aug. 1956; *Charleston News and Courier*, 18 May 1954.

40. Ibid.; *Charleston News and Courier*, 1 June 1955; Scheer, "White Folks Fight Back," 10.

41. Martin, *The Deep South Says 'Never'*, 62; *Columbia State*, 1 Sept. 1955.

42. *Southern School News*, 3 September 1954; *Columbia State*, 11 May 1964.

43. David Potenziani, "Striking Back: Richard B. Russell and Racial Relocation," *Georgia Historical Quarterly* 65 (Fall 1981): 263–77; *Charleston News and Courier*, 30 Jan. 1962; *Southern School News*, Oct. 1959.

44. *Southern School News*, July 1959; James F. Byrnes, "The Supreme Court Must Be Curbed," *U.S. News* 40 (18 May 1956): 50, 58.

45. Byrnes, "Supreme Court Must Be Curbed," 50, 58.

46. *Southern School News*, 3 Mar. 1955, Dec. 1958; *Columbia State*, 4 June 1955; *New York Times*, 17 July 1955, p. 37.

47. James F. Byrnes, "Guns and Bayonets Cannot Promote Education," *U.S. News* 41 (5 Oct. 1956): 104; Quint, *Profile in Black and White*, 31.

48. Byrnes, "Supreme Court Must Be Curbed," 56; Byrnes, speech at dedication of Municipal Auditorium, Spartanburg, 1 Dec. 1951.

49. Herbert Ravenal Sass, "Mixed Schools and Mixed Blood," *Atlantic Monthly* 198 (Nov. 1956): 45–49.

50. Thomas R. Waring, "The Southern Case Against Desegregation," *Harpers* 212 (Jan. 1956): 39–45; *Charleston News and Courier*, 13 Dec. 1959.

51. *Charleston News and Courier*, 25 Feb. 1956.

52. Martin, *The Deep South Says 'Never'*, 65; *Columbia State*, 11 July 1955; *Columbia Record*, 30 Aug. 1955; *Charleston News and Courier*, 31 Aug. 1955.

53. *Charlotte News*, 2 Sept. 1955; *Charleston News and Courier*, 4 Sept. 1958. Wilkins later said he was misquoted.

54. *Columbia State*, 21 Aug. 1955.

55. Friedman, *Argument*, 239.

56. Trial transcript, Brown v. School District No. 20, Civil Action 7747, U.S. District Court, Charleston; *Charlotte Observer*, 6 Aug. 1963; *Columbia State*, 6 Aug. 1963.

57. Trial transcript, CA 7747; Brief of Appellees, CA 7747; *Columbia State*, 6 Aug. 1963.

58. *Southern School News*, Nov. 1960; Trial transcript, CA 7747; *Charlotte Observer*, 6 Aug. 1963.

59. Motion to Invervene, CA 7747; Brief of Intervenors, CA 7747.

60. Brief of Appellees, CA 7747.

61. Ibid.

62. Ibid.

63. Friedman, *Argument*, 402.

64. Brief of Appellees, CA 7747.

65. *Brown v. School District No. 20, Charleston*, 226 F. Supp. 819 (1963); 328 F. 2d 618 (1964); *Allen v. Brown*, 379 U.S. 825 (1964).

66. William Bagwell, *School Desegregation in the Carolinas* (Columbia: Univ. of South Carolina Press, 1972), 69, 167; Sarratt, *Ordeal of Desegregation*, 285; *Southern School News*, Jan. 1963.

67. *Charleston News and Courier*, 5 May 1960; *Charlotte Observer*, 5 May 1960.

68. *Southern School News*, Feb., Apr., May, and June 1963.

69. Ibid., Apr. and Feb. 1963.

70. Ibid., Feb., Apr., May, June 1963; Jan. 1964.

71. Ibid., May 1963; *Charleston News and Courier*, 6 Apr. 1968, 21 July and 4 Dec. 1965; *Brown v. South Carolina State Board of Education*, 296 F. Supp. 199 (1968); *South Carolina State Board of Education v. Brown*, 393 U.S. 222 (1968).

72. *Columbia State*, 11 May 1964; *Southern School News*, May, Dec. 1964.

73. *Manning Times*, 9 Sept. 1965; Defendants' Memorandum, 2 June 1969, Brunson v. Board of Trustees, Civil Action 7210, U.S. District Court, Columbia, S.C.

74. Court order, 18 July 1969, CA 7210; Return of the School District, 18 Dec. 1968, CA 7210; interview with Marian Barksdale, 20 Aug. 1980.

75. 244 F. Supp. 859 (1965); 429 F. 2d 820 (1970).

76. Complaint, CA 7210; testimony of C.E. Buttes, Jr., 20 May 1965, CA 7210.

77. 244 F. Supp. 859 (1965).

78. Return of the School District, 18 Dec. 1968, CA 7210; Court Order, 18 July 1969, CA 7210; Plaintiffs' Motion to Vacate, 28 Aug. 1965, CA 7210.

79. Friedman, *Argument,* 47. Also see 38, 45, and 48–49. Justice Frankfurter said it was "important to know, before one starts, where he is going." If the Supreme Court decided the *Briggs* case for the NAACP, Frankfurter asked, would it entitle "every mother to have her child go to a nonsegregated school in Clarendon County?" "No, sir," Thurgood Marshall replied. It would merely require that students be assigned to school by "some other method," "a means other than race."

80. Terry Eastland and William J. Bennett, *Counting By Race* (Ithaca, N.Y.: Cornell Univ. Press, 1976), 48–52.

81. Appeal of U.S. Department of Justice, May 1966, CA 7210.

82. 110 *Congressional Record* 12715 (1964).

83. Ibid., 12715–16; Public Law 88–352 (1964), 246; Lino A. Graglia, *Disaster By Decree* (Ithaca, N.Y.: Cornell Univ. Press, 1976), 48–52.

84. Public Law 88–352 (1964), 252–53; Graglia, *Disaster By Decree,* 52–58; James R. Dunn, "Title VI, the Guidelines and School Desegregation in the South," *Virginia Law Review* 53 (1967): 42–88; "The Courts, HEW, and School Desegregation," *Yale Law Journal* 77 (Dec. 1967): 321–65.

85. Gary Orfield, *The Reconstruction of Southern Education* (New York: Wiley, 1969), xi and passim.

86. *Current Biography,* 1967, pp. 185–88; U.S. Office of Education, Revised Statement of Policies for School Desegregation Plans Under Title VI of the Civil Rights Act of 1964 (1966).

87. "Policies and Guidelines for School Desegregation," *Hearings before the Committee on Rules,* House of Representatives, 89th Cong., 2nd sess., 1966; *New York Times,* 7 Dec. 1966, p. 46.

88. *Bowman v. County School Board,* 382 F. 2d 326 (1967) at 327, 329.

89. *United States v. Jefferson County Board of Education,* 372 F. 2d 836 (1966), hereafter cited as *Jefferson I; United States v. Jefferson County Board of Education,* 380 F. 2d 385 (1967), hereafter cited as *Jefferson II.*

90. *Jefferson I* at 847; *Jefferson II* at 389.

91. Graglia, *Disaster By Decree,* 61; *Jefferson I,* at 848, 849, 878; Jack Bass, *Unlikely Heroes* (New York: Simon and Schuster, 1981), 305–6.

92. *Jefferson I,* at 848, 883, 910; Graglia, *Disaster By Decree,* 60.

93. *Green v. County School Board,* 391 U.S. 430 (1968).

94. Philip B. Kurland, ed., *Landmark Briefs and Arguments of the Supreme Court* (Arlington, Va.: University Publications of America, 1975), vol. 66, 1–298.

95. Ibid., 31, 225, 231–32, 259, 262; 382 F. 2d 338 (1967) at 32.

96. Kurland, *Landmark Briefs,* 25, 38; 382 F. 2d 326 (1967) at 334; 391 U.S. 430 (1968) at 440–41.

97. Kurland, *Landmark Briefs,* 223–25.

98. 391 U.S. 430 (1968) at 435, 439.

99. Graglia, *Disaster By Decree,* 73, 83.

100. *Henry v. Clarksdale Municipal Separate School District,* 409 F. 2d 682 (1969) at 687; *U.S. v. Indianola Municipal Separate School District,* 410 F. 2d 626 (1969)

at 631, quoting *Montgomery County Board of Education v. Carr,* 402 F. 2d 782 (1968) at 786; *Walker v. Brunswick County School Board,* 413 F. 2d 53 (1969) at 54.

101. *Memorandum Decisions,* 425 F. 2d (1970) at 1216, 1220.

102. Plaintiffs' Objection, 1 Dec. 1966, CA 7210.

103. *Brunson v. Board of Trustees,* 271 F. Supp. 586 (1967) at 587.

104. Motion for Further Relief, 19 June 1968, CA 7210.

105. Return of the School District, 13 Sept. 1968, CA 7210.

106. Plaintiffs' Memorandum, 20 Feb. 1969, CA 7210.

107. "Application of the Law to the Facts," CA 7210; interview with David W. Robinson, 20 Aug. 1980.

108. *Whittenberg v. Greenville County School District,* 298 F. Supp. 784 (1969) at 789, 791.

109. Return of the School Districts, 13 Sept. 1968, CA 7210; Court Order, 6 Mar. 1970, CA 7210.

110. Court Order, 18 July 1969, CA 7210.

111. Ibid.

112. Brunson v. Board of Trustees, 429 F. 2d 820 (1970).

113. Ibid., 820–23.

114. Ibid., 823–27.

115. *Bowman v. County School Board,* 382 F. 2d 326 (1967) at 330–38.

116. See Rowland Evans, Jr., and Robert D. Novak, *Nixon in the White House* (New York: Random, 1971), ch. 6; John Osborne, *The Second Year of the Nixon Watch* (New York: Liveright, 1971), chs. 4, 9, 10, and 23; Osborne, *The Third Year of the Nixon Watch* (New York: Liveright, 1972), chs. 3, 14, 16, 19, and 25.

117. Osborne, *Second Year,* 23; *Bowman v. County School Board,* 382 F. 2d 326 (1967).

118. Evans and Novak, *Nixon in the White House,* 159–64.

119. Ibid., 171–72.

120. Osborne, *Second Year,* 123–25.

121. John Egerton, "Report Card on Southern School Desegregation," *Saturday Review* 55 (1 Apr. 1972): 41–48; Osborne, *Third Year,* 11.

122. Osborne, *Second Year,* 129.

123. Evans and Novak, *Nixon in the White House,* 174; Osborne, *Second Year,* 21–24, 122–26; Osborne, *Third Year,* 11–14, 85–89, 95–98.

124. *National Review* 22 (22 Sept. 1970): 1016; ibid. (2 Sept. 1970): 986–88.

125. *Manning Times,* 24 Oct. 1968, 11 Dec. 1969.

126. Interview with Doris Holladay, 26 Aug. 1980.

127. Interview with local official who must stand for reelection and did not wish to be identified, 23 Aug. 1980; interview with Edna F. Rowe, 20 Aug. 1980.

128. Interviews with Ralph Bell (22 Aug. 1980) and Edna F. Rowe (20 Aug. 1980).

129. Interview with Mabel Hinson, 22 Aug. 1980.

130. Interviews with Ralph Bell and Edna F. Rowe.

131. Interview with Edna F. Rowe; Clarendon Hall Student Handbook, 1980–1981.

132. David Nevin and Robert E. Bills, *The Schools That Fear Built* (Washington, D.C.: Acropolis, 1976), 41.

133. Ibid., passim; *This Is Clarendon Hall (*1981 pamphlet).

134. Information provided by Fred E. Wagoner, executive secretary, South Carolina Independent School Association.

135. *Manning Times,* 8 Apr. 1965; interviews with Edna F. Rowe and Ann Darby (22 Aug. 1980).

136. Nevin and Bills, *The Schools That Fear Built,* passim.

137. Interview with Edna F. Rowe.

138. *Charleston News and Courier,* 20 June 1966.

139. *Rankings of the Counties and School Districts of South Carolina* (S.C. Department of Education, 1980), 60, 64; 1979–1980 Directory of South Carolina Schools, 78; SCISA (1979 pamphlet), 14, 17, 18.

140. American Friends Service Committee, *Financing Public Education in South Carolina* (research report, 1972), 82 and passim.

141. Ibid., 20, 29; Joel D. Sherman, *Underfunding of Majority-Black School Districts in South Carolina* (Washington, D.C.: Lawyers' Committee for Civil Rights, 1977), appendix C.

142. *Serrano v. Priest,* 5 Ca. 3d 584 (1971); *Rodriguez v. San Antonio Independent School District,* 337 F. Supp. 280 (1971). *San Antonio School District v. Rodriguez,* 411 U.S. 1 (1973).

143. Act 163, South Carolina General Assembly, 1977; Philip T. Kelly, "South Carolina's New School Finance Law," *Journal of Educational Finance* 3 (Spring 1978): 515–23; interview with Joel D. Sherman, 5 Mar. 1981.

144. *Manning Times,* 25 Jan., 14, 19 Mar., 4 Apr. 1979, 26 Mar. 1980; interview with Phyllis H. Womick, 25 Aug. 1980.

145. Interview, 23 Aug. 1980.

146. Interviews with Dorian Duren (21 Aug. 1980), Ondre Richbert (21 Aug. 1980), Alonzo P. Swinton (26 Aug. 1980), and Henry Lawson (23 Aug. 1980).

147. Interview with Henry Lawson.

148. Interviews with Marian Barksdale, Doris Holladay, and Ann Darby.

149. Interview with a teacher who does not wish to be identified, 22 Aug. 1980.

150. Interview with Doris Holladay; between 1970 and 1980 enrollment in Summerton's public schools declined from 2,300 to 1,800.

151. Interview with Billie Fleming.

152. *Greenville News,* 18 Mar. 1979.

153. Ibid.; interviews with Alonzo P. Swinton and Henry Lawson.

154. *Greenville News,* 18 Mar. 1979; *New York Times,* 18 May 1979, p. 14.

155. Telephone conversation with Joseph Lemons, 25 Aug. 1980.

NOTES TO PART FOUR

1. Carol E. Hoffecker, *Corporate Capital: Wilmington in the Twentieth Century* (Philadelphia: Temple Univ. Press, 1983).

2. John A. Munroe, *History of Delaware* (Newark: Univ. of Delaware Press, 1979), 225–227.

3. *Wilmington Morning News,* 16 June 1980; Kluger, *Simple Justice,* 434; Preston Eisenbrey to Fred Bulah, 10 Oct. 1950, Bulah v. Gebhart, Civil Action 258, Delaware Court of Chancery; George R. Miller to Fred Bulah, 18 Dec. 1950, CA 258; H. Albert Young, Answer to the Complaint, CA 258.

4. Kluger, *Simple Justice,* 435.

5. Trial transcript, 27–38, CA 258.

6. *Belton v. Gebhart,* 87 A. 2d 862 (1952) at 864, 865–66.

7. Trial transcript, 510–582, CA 258.

8. *Belton v. Gebhart,* 87 A. 2d 862 (1952) at 868; emphasis added.

9. The Delaware State Supreme Court did make this concession in the course of affirming Seitz's decision. *Gebhart v. Belton,* 91 A. 2d. 137 (1952).

10. Kluger, *Simple Justice,* 447.

11. *Belton v. Gebhart,* 87 A. 2d 862 (1952) at 869, 865; *Brown v. Board of Education,* 347 U.S. 483 (1954), n. 10.

12. *Wilmington Morning News,* 11 Dec. 1954; *Minneapolis Tribune,* 4 Dec. 1953.

13. *Minneapolis Tribune,* 1 Dec. 1953.

14. *Wilmington Morning News,* 16 June 1980; *Minneapolis Tribune,* 2 Dec. 1959.

15. *Minneapolis Tribune,* 2 Dec. 1959. "But a wise man changes," Kilson said. "They say this integration is working like a clock. And the school board says the children are doing better in mixed schools, so I suppose it has been an improvement. If I was to do any recommending today, I would tell my members to go on over to that white school."

16. *Minneapolis Tribune,* 2 Dec. 1959.

17. *Southern School News,* Nov. 1957, Apr. 1958; *Wilmington Journal Every Evening,* 21 Mar. 1958; *Wilmington Morning News,* 14 Sept. 1954, 6 Mar. 1963, 25 June 1958; Herbert Wey and John Corey, *Action Patterns in School Desegregation* (Indianapolis: Phi Delta Kappa, 1959), 57, 115–16; Wilmington *Staff Reporter,* 25 June 1958.

18. *Wilmington Morning News,* 14 Feb. 1956, 25 June 1958; *Wilmington Evening Journal,* 21 Sept. 1954; *Southern School News,* Mar. 1958; *New York Times,* 13 May 1957, p. 1.

19. *Wilmington Morning News,* 25 June 1958; *New York Times,* 13 May 1957, p. 1; *Wilmington Evening Journal,* 18 Mar. 1959.

20. *New York Times,* 13 May 1957, p. 1; *Wilmington Morning News,* 28 Mar. 1957, 29 Sept. 1969.

21. *Wilmington Morning News,* 29 Sept. 1955.

22. Hoffecker, *Corporate Capital,* 165.

23. Herbert R. Baringer, "Integration in Newark, Delaware," in Raymond W. Mack, ed., *Our Children's Burden* (New York: Random, 1968), 148, 149; *Wilmington Morning News,* 3 Jan. 1963.

24. 19 Aug. 1958.

25. *Staff Reporter,* Nov., Apr. 1956, Sept. 1958, Mar. 1961.

26. *Wilmington Morning News,* 16 Nov. 1959; Muriel Crosby, *An Adventure in Human Relations* (Chicago: Follett, 1965), 8–10; emphasis in original.

27. *Staff Reporter,* Feb. 1960, Feb. 1963.

28. *Wilmington Morning News,* 5 Oct. 1961, 15–18 Oct. 1962.

29. *Wilmington Morning News,* 15–18 Oct. 1962.

30. *Profile* (magazine published by Wilmington Public Schools), Apr. 1970, Jan. 1971; Annual Report of Wilmington Public Schools, 1971–1972; *News Journal* Clippings, 10 Aug. 1973, in *Wilmington News Journal* Library (hereafter cited as *News Journal* Clippings).

31. Annual Reports of the Wilmington Public Schools, 1968–1977.

32. Jeffrey A. Raffel, *The Challenge of Educational Change: An Evaluation of the Follow Through Program in the Wilmington Public Schools* (Univ. of Delaware Division of Urban Affairs, 1974), 2, 15, 22, 51, and passim.

33. National Association for Neighborhood Schools, *Newsletter,* 9 Feb. 1980; for a calculation based on data for 1974–75, see Jeffrey A. Raffel, *The Politics of School Desegregation: The Metropolitan Remedy in Delaware* (Philadelphia: Temple Univ. Press, 1980), 24–25.

34. Annual Report, Wilmington Superintendent of Schools, 1975–76.

35. Edward J. Butler, "The Role of the Change Agent in Community Development" (M.A. thesis, Univ. of Delaware, 1968), 55–56, 93.

36. Ibid., 75, 102, 109, 86, 94.

37. Ibid., 110–16, 104–6; *Wilmington Evening Journal,* 24 May 1966.

38. U.S. Senate, *Hearings before the Permanent Subcommittee on Investigations of the Committee on Government Operations,* 90th Cong., 2d sess., Oct. 1968, pp. 2783–85 (hereafter cited as *1968 Investigation*).

39. Ibid., 2885, 2898, 2894–2907; *Delmarva Dialog,* 23 June 1967.

40. *1968 Investigation,* 2784, 2907, 2822.

41. Ibid., 2914, 2828, 2908–28.

42. Ibid., 2829, 2798, 2882; *Wilmington Evening Journal,* 8, and 9 Apr. 1968.

43. *1968 Investigation,* p. 2831; Hoffecker, *Corporate Capital,* 201.

44. *Corporate Capital,* 198.

45. Telephone conversation with Peal Herlihy Daniels, 12 Oct. 1982; *1968 Investigation,* 2822.

46. *Evans v. Buchanan,* 207 F. Supp. 820 (1962) at 823–24.

47. Interview with Jeanette McDonnal, 4 Aug. 1981.

48. *News Journal* Clippings, 29 Sept. 1970, 7 Oct. 1967.

49. Ibid., 12 July, 8 Nov. 1968.

50. Ibid., 4 Jan. 1969, 15 June 1968, 6 Dec. 1968, 4 Feb. 1975, 4 Jan. 1969.

51. Ibid., 23 Apr. 1970, 1 Apr. 1975.

52. Statement of Russell F. Dineen, in Plaintiffs' Proposed Findings of Fact, Dec. 1977, docket 668, Evans v. Buchanan, Civil Action 1816, U.S. District Court, Wilmington.

53. Interview with Jeanette McDonnal.

54. Ibid.

55. Interview with Russell F. Dineen, 8 Aug. 1981.

56. *News Journal* Clippings, 29 Feb. 1964, 8 Apr. 1976, 24 Feb., 7 Oct. 1977, 30 Sept. 1969; *Profile,* Jan. 1971.

57. *News Journal* Clippings, 24, 26, and 30 Sept. 1969.

58. *Wilmington Evening Journal,* 1 May 1973; interview with Helen Bayliss, 28 July 1981.

59. *Southern School News,* May 1956, Aug. 1958; *Wilmington Morning News,* 28 June 1955.

60. *New York Times,* 24, 25 Sept. and 1, 12 Oct. 1954; *Wilmington Morning News,* 23, 24, 29 Sept. and 4, 20 Oct. 1954; *Wilmington Evening Journal,* 20 Sept., 1 Oct. 1954.

61. *Steiner v. Simmons,* 111 A. 2d 574 (1955) at 585; *Wilmington Evening Journal,* 1 Oct. 1954; *Laurel State Register,* quoted in *Wilmington Morning News,* 4 Oct. 1954.

62. *Wilmington Morning News,* 29 Sept. 1954.

63. *New York Times,* 18 Oct. 1954; *Wilmington Evening Journal,* 11 Oct. 1954.

64. *Wilmington Morning News,* 31 Aug. 1955, 27 Mar. 1956, 28 Dec. 1955.

65. *Southern School News,* 6 Jan. and Oct. 1955; testimony of Richard P. Gousha, 15 Jan. 1974, docket 258, CA 1816; *Wilmington Morning News,* 23, 28 Sept., 4 Oct. 1954, 8 Feb. 1956.

66. *Wilmington Morning News,* 4 Oct. 1954.

67. Ibid., 24 Sept. 1954; *New York Times,* 1 Oct. 1954.

68. *Steiner v. Simmons,* 111 A. 2d 574 (1955) at 579.

69. *Evans v. Buchanan,* 152 F. Supp. 886 (1957) at 888.

70. *Southern School News,* May 1957; *Wilmington Evening Journal,* 11 Jan. 1958.

71. *Southern School News,* May 1957; *Evans v. Members of State Board of Education,* 149 F. Supp. 376 (1957); *Evans v. Buchanan,* 152 F. Supp. 886 (1957); *Evans v. Buchanan,* 256 F. 2d 688 (1958),

72. Plaintiffs' reply brief, 16 Mar. 1959, CA 1816.

73. *Evans v. Buchanan,* 172 F. Supp. 508 (1959). *Southern School News,* Apr. 1959, summarizes state testimony supporting the approach.

74. *Evans v. Ennis,* 281 F. 2d 385 (1960).

75. *Sussex Countian,* 4 Oct. 1954.

76. *Evans. v. Buchanan,* 281 F. 2d 385 (1960); testimony of Richard P. Gousha, 15 Jan. 1974, docket 258, CA 1816.

77. Testimony of Gousha, ibid.; testimony of Howard E. Row, 10 and 11 Jan. 1974, dockets 255–56, CA 1916; minutes of State Board of Education, 9 Feb. 1965, p. 60.

78. Testimony of Gousha, 15 Jan. 1974, docket 258, CA 1816; *Evans v. Buchanan,* 393 F. Supp. 428 (1975) at 451.

79. Testimony of Gousha, 15 Jan. 1974, docket 258, CA 1816.

80. *Evans v. Buchanan,* 393 F. Supp. 428 (1975) at 451.

81. *Green v. County School Board,* 391 U.S. 430 (1968) at 435; *Keyes v. School District No. 1, Denver,* 433 U.S. 189 (1973) at 257–58.

82. Interview with Marilyn Harwick, 23 Dec. 1981; Julie Schmidt, "School Desegregation in Wilmington, Delaware" (M.A. thesis, Univ. of Delaware, 1979), 163.

83. Interview with Marilyn Harwick.

84. *1950 Census of Population,* 8: 11, 54; *1970 Census of Population,* 9: 11, 12, 23.

85. Interview with Marilyn Harwick; Schmidt, "School Desegregation in Wilmington," 164–68.

86. "A Study of School Plant and Program Requirements in Wilmington, Dela-

ware" (New York Univ. Center for Field Research and School Service, 1967), 31; *Wilmington Evening Journal,* 26 Apr. 1977.

87. Interview with Hicks Anderson, 23 Dec. 1981; *Wilmington Evening Journal,* 13 May 1975; undated *News Journal* editorial, in scrapbooks of Professor Jeffrey R. Raffel (hereafter cited as Raffel scrapbooks).

88. Schmidt, "School Desegregation in Wilmington," 170; *Wilmington Evening Journal,* 22 Oct. 1970; interview with Marilyn Harwick.

89. Interview with Janet Greenwell, 22 Dec. 1981; telephone conversation with Phyllis Ploener, 24 Jan. 1982.

90. Interview with Marilyn Harwick; interview with Irving Morris, 11 Dec. 1981.

91. Interview with Marilyn Harwick.

92. Telephone conversation with Jeanne Q. Lewis, 18 Dec. 1981; depositions of Jeanne and Clifton Lewis, 8 Sept. 1973, dockets 173, 174, CA 1816.

93. Depositions of Jeanne and Clifton Lewis, 8 Sept. 1973, dockets 173, 174, CA 1816.

94. Deposition of Lillian Richardson, 15 Sept. 1973, docket 176, CA 1816; deposition of Wilber Carr, 8 Sept. 1973, docket 175, CA 1816.

95. Petition for Supplemental Order, 27 July 1971, docket 118, CA 1816.

96. *Swann v. Charlotte-Mecklenburg Board of Education,* 402 U.S. 1 (1971); *Briggs v. Elliott,* 132 F. Supp. 776 (1965) at 777.

97. *Bradley v. School Board of Richmond,* 462 F. 2d 1058 (1972) at 1066.

98. Interview with Irving Morris; telephone conversation with James H. Sills, 22 Jan. 1982.

99. Interview with Victor F. Battaglia, 16 December 1981.

100. Raffel, *Politics of School Desegregation,* 191; interview with a member of the Haskell administration who asked to remain anonymous.

101. Schmidt, "Desegregation in Wilmington," 185, 184; interview with Janet Greenwell; Minutes of the Wilmington Board of Education, 19 June 1972; Motion to intervene as plaintiff, 14 Sept. 1972, docket 138,CA 1816; Memorandum opinion, 8 Dec. 1980, docket 966, CA 1816. In this opinion Judge Murray M. Schwartz approved an award to the plaintiffs' lawyers of an additional $1 million in legal fees paid by the State of Delaware.

102. Answer of intervening plaintiff, 14 Oct. 1973, docket 178, CA 1816; "Principles, Educational Components, and Pupil Reassignment Plans," 11 June 1975, docket 326, CA 1816; Annual Report of the Wilmington Public Schools, 1971–1972; *Profile,* Jan. 1976.

103. Amendment to Plaintiffs' Petition, 3 Feb. 1972, docket 132, CA 1816; *Evans v. Buchanan,* 393 F. Supp. 428 (1975) at 432–43.

104. Amicus Brief, National Conference of Christians and Jews, docket 266, CA 1816; Raffel, *The Politics of School Desegregation,* 46; Roger C. Mowrey, *Delaware School District Reorganization and Boundaries* (Dover: State Department of Public Instruction, 1974).

105. Petition for Supplemental Order, 27 July 1971, docket 118, CA 1816; Plaintiffs' Draft of a pretrial order, 30 Nov. 1973, docket 199, CA 1816.

106. Plaintiffs' Pre-Trial Memorandum, 12 Dec. 1979, docket 211, CA 1816.

107. Defendants' Opening Post-trial Brief, 2 Feb. 1976, docket 446, CA 1816.

108. Affidavit of Clarice U. Heckert, 17 Sept. 1971, docket 123, CA 1816; testimony of Clarice U. Heckert, 21 Dec. 1973, docket 251, CA 1816.

109. Testimony of Clarice Heckert, 21 Dec. 1973, docket 251, CA 1816.

110. *Evans v. Buchanan,* 393 F. Supp. 428 (1975) at 452.

111. *Evans v. Buchanan,* 393 F. Supp. 428 (1975) at 434, 436n., 438.

112. Ibid., 439.

113. *Wilmington Evening Journal,* 20 May 1976; interview with an attorney who does not wish to be identified.

114. *Wilmington Evening Journal,* 20 May 1976; *Evans v. Buchanan,* 393 F. Supp. 428 (1975) at 448, 449.

115. *Evans v. Buchanan,* 207 F. Supp. 820 (1962) at 823–24.

116. *Evans v. Buchanan,* 379 F. Supp. 1218 (1974).

117. Ibid., 1225–28.

118. *Evans v. Buchanan,* 393 F. Supp. 428 (1975); statement of Caleb Wright, hearing, 11 Oct. 1973, docket 189, CA 1816.

119. *Milliken v. Bradley,* 418 U.S. 717 (1974), at 740, 731, 756, 746.

120. *Evans v. Buchanan,* 393 F. Supp. 428 (1975) at 446, 453.

121. Ibid., 439; *Bradley v. Milliken,* 338 F. Supp. 582 (1971) at 592.

122. Statement of Philip B. Kurland, hearing, 15 Jan. 1975, docket 300, CA 1816; Brief of State Board of Education, 15 July 1977, docket 547, CA 1816.

123. *Washington v. Davis,* 426 U.S. 229 (1976) at 240.

124. *Evans v. Buchanan,* 379 F. Supp. 1218 (1974) at 1228; *Evans v. Buchanan,* 393 F. Supp. 428 (1975) at 440–43.

125. *Evans v. Buchanan,* 393 F. Supp. 428 (1975) at 441.

126. *San Antonio School District v. Rodriguez,* 411 U.S. 1 (1971).

127. *Dayton v. Brinkman,* 433 U.S. 406 (1977) at 420; emphasis added.

128. Post-hearing Memorandum of State Board of Education, 25 July 1977, docket 557, CA 1816; *Wilmington Morning News,* 11 Aug. 1977; *Green v. County School Board,* 391 U.S. 430 (1968) at 438; *Swann v. Charlotte-Mecklenburg,* 402 U.S. 1. (1971) at 26.

129. *Milliken v. Bradley,* 418 U.S. 717 (1974) at 761, 782, 808, 814.

130. *Evans v. Buchanan,* 416 F. Supp. 328 (1976) at 340; statement of Judge Gibbons, hearing, 15 Jan. 1975, docket 300, CA 1816.

131. Statement of Philip Kurland, hearing, 15 Jan. 1975, docket 300, CA 1816.

132. Interview with William Prickett, 11 Dec. 1981.

133. *Buchanan v. Evans,* 423 U.S. 963 (1975) at 964.

134. *Evans v. Buchanan,* 555 F. 2d 373 (1977) at 379.

135. Ibid. at 385, 390, 388–89.

136. 434 U.S. 880 (1977); 446 U.S. 923 (1980).

137. 446 U.S. 923 (1980) at 928; *Wilmington Morning News,* 29 Apr. 1980.

138. *Delaware State Board of Education v. Evans,* 446 U.S. 923 (1980) at 923.

139. *Wilmington Morning News,* 15 Nov. 1975.

140. Brief for Newark School District, Feb. 1976, docket 442, CA 1816.

141. Statement of individual plaintiffs, 16 Oct. 1975, docket 391, CA 1816; Position Paper of Mt. Pleasant School District, 2 Feb. 1976, docket 438, CA 1816.

142. *Evans v. Buchanan,* 416 F. Supp. 328 (1976) at 354–55.

143. *Evans v. Buchanan,* 447 F. Supp. 982 (1978) at 1001n.; 14 Del. C. 603(c) [1976].

144. Briefs and position papers in dockets 340–46, CA 1816. *Evans v. Buchanan,* 435 F. Supp. 832 (1977) at 838–41; *Evans v. Buchanan,* 416 F. Supp. 328 (1976) at 344–348.

145. *Evans v. Buchanan,* 447 F. Supp. 982 (1978) at 999, 1001.

146. Ibid., 1001; *Evans v. Buchanan,* 435 F. Supp. 832 (1977) at 838–41.

147. *Evans v. Buchanan,* 447 F. Supp. 982 (1978) at 990.

148. Nancy H. St. John, *School Desegregation: Outcomes for Children* (New York: Wiley, 1975).

149. Christopher Jencks, *Inequality* (New York: Basic Books, 1972), 97–106; for additional discussion of Coleman's recantation, see below pp. 282–84.

150. *Evans v. Buchanan,* 416 F. Supp. 328 (1976) at 365.

151. *With All Deliberate Speed,* Clearinghouse Publication 69 (Washington D.C.: 1981), 34.

152. *Wilmington Evening Journal,* 8 Mar. 1976, 11 July 1975; *News Journal,* 11 Apr. 1981; *Wilmington Morning News,* 12 June 1975.

153. Raffel, *Politics of School Desegregation,* 123; Helen K. Foss, "Getting Ready for Desegregation," in Dennis C. Carey, ed., *The Politics of Metropolitan School Reorganization* (typescript in Univ. of Delaware Library); *Philadelphia Inquirer,* 11 Apr. 1976.

154. Raffel, *Politics of School Desegregation,* 128–34; comments of Sen. Joseph R. Biden, "The Fourteenth Amendment and School Busing," *Hearings of Constitution Subcommittee of Senate Judiciary Committee,* 97th Cong., 1st sess. (1981), 242.

155. Pierre S. du Pont, "The Governor's Perspective," in Carey, *Metropolitan School Reorganization,* 1, 5.

156. *Evans v. Buchanan,* 447 F. Supp. 982 (1977) at 1014–17; Billy E. Ross, "Training: The Key to Successful School Desegregation," in Carey, ed., *Metropolitan School Reorganization;* Raffel, *Politics of School Desegregation,* 80.

157. Ross, "Training"; *Newark Weekly Post,* 15 Dec. 1976.

158. Quoted in Carroll W. Biggs, "Communications: Master Key to Peaceful Desegregation," in Carey, *Metropolitan School Reorganization,* 14.

159. Raffel, *Politics of School Desegregation,* 28–38.

160. Ibid., 28, 29, 30.

161. *Philadelphia Inquirer,* 13 June 1976; *Newark Weekly Post,* 21–28 Apr. 1976.

162. *Philadelphia Inquirer,* 4 Apr. 1976; *Wilmington Evening Journal,* 29 June 1977; *Wilmington Morning News,* 21 Dec. 1975.

163. *Sunday News Journal,* 24 June 1979, 17 Sept. 1978.

164. Raffel, *Politics of School Desegregation,* 163–72; *Newark Weekly Post,* 1, 22 June 1977.

165. Legislative hearing on desegregation, 15 Mar. 1975, pp. 11, 5.

166. *Newark Weekly Post,* 21–28 Apr. 1976; *Philadelphia Inquirer,* 12 Mar. 1978; NANS [National Association for Neighborhood Schools] Bulletin 15, Aug. 1979.

167. *Philadelphia Inquirer,* 13 July 1974; *Wilmington Evening Journal,* 5 June 1976.

168. *Bill Roth Reports,* 5 Feb. 1976; *Wilmington Evening Journal,* 28 June 1976; *Newark Weekly Post,* 16 Feb. 1977; PAC Bulletin 18, 21 Mar. 1977; *Wilmington Morning News,* 20 Mar. 1979.

169. *Philadelphia Inquirer,* 12 June 1977; *Washington Post,* 22 Sept. 1977; *Delaware Spectator,* 28 Nov. 1975; *Wilmington Morning News,* 28 Sept. 1977.

170. *Wilmington Evening Journal,* 16 June 1977; *Sunday News Journal,* 10 Aug. 1980.

171. *St. Louis Post Dispatch,* 9 Oct. 1977; telephone conversation with William D. D'Onofrio, 7 Apr. 1982.

172. NANS Bulletin 19, Apr. 1980.

173. *Wilmington Morning News,* 13 May 1980; *Sunday News Journal,* 11 May 1980.

174. *Sunday News Journal,* 12 Aug. 1979; *Wilmington Morning News,* 2 Aug. 1979.

175. *Sunday News Journal,* 17 Aug. 1980, 30 Aug. 1981.

176. Robert L. Green, "Metropolitan School Desegregation in New Castle County" (paper presented at Rockefeller Foundation Conference, Oct. 1981), 17, 12, 18, 68; *News Journal,* 10 Oct. 1981.

177. *Wilmington Morning News,* 22 Oct. 1982; *Sunday News Journal,* 7 Nov. 1982; William D. D'Onofrio, "An Analysis of White Flight and Test Scores" (1982 manuscript). Robert L. Green reported that "At the elementary level at the beginning of desegregation the gap between the black and white students was 1.7 years. Even though the black students made greater than expected gains, the gap in achievement between blacks and whites steadily increased to 3.3 years at the end of the third year. This was due to the very large gains in achievement made by white students at this level." *Metropolitan School Desegregation in New Castle County, Delaware* (final report to the Rockfeller Foundation, Oct. 1982), 338.

178. Green, "Metropolitan School Desegregation," 70, 36, 38, 49, 61, 44.

179. Jeffrey R. Raffel, "One Year Later: Parent Attitudes Toward Schools in New Castle County," in "School Desegregation," *Hearings before Subcommittee on Civil and Constitutional Rights, House Judiciary Committee,* 97th Cong., 1st sess. (1981), 454–509; *Sunday News Journal,* 3 Sept. 1979.

180. *Time* 118 (13 July 1981), 56.

181. *Sunday News Journal,* 30 Aug. 1981.

182. *Newark Weekly Post,* Dec. 27–Jan. 2, 1978–79; *Wilmington Morning News,* 12 May 1980.

183. Morris, James Hitchens and Williams, "Memorandum on Racial Imbalance in Certain Classes," 12 Jan. 1979, supplied by Dennis Carey, from files of New Castle County School District; *Wilmington Morning News,* 23 Feb. 1979.

184. Interview with Gladys Sharnoff, 17 Mar. 1982; Guidelines of 26 Feb. 1980, quoted in Charles M. Achilles, et al., "A Study of Issues Related to Discipline, Grouping and Tracking, and Special Education in New Castle County" (Mar. 1982), 2: 7. These percentages did not apply to "elective and advanced levels of skilled courses, such as calculus and foreign languages." Robert L. Green has reported that "district educators [also] employed a student team learning approach in their classrooms. This concept grouped heterogeneous teams of high and low performers, boys and

girls, of different racial and ethnic backgrounds. District educators were hopeful that this teaching method would increase the achievement performance of all students, especially minority students, and foster a positive environment for racial integration on a social level. . . ." *Metropolitan School Desegregation,* 49.

185. *Wilmington Evening Journal,* 23 Aug. 1977; *Newark Weekly Post,* 9 Feb. 1977.

186. 2 Aug. 1979.

187. *Sunday News Journal,* 6 May 1979.

188. Interviews with Bruce Laird (4 Mar. 1982), Jennifer Reynolds (16 Feb. 1982), and Lenora Cobb (15 Mar. 1982).

189. *Wilmington Morning News,* 12 May 1980; *Sunday News Journal,* 24 June 1979; 10 June 1979.

190. *Wilmington Morning News,* 27, 30 Apr. 1979.

191. Interview with Jea P. Street, 7 Mar. 1982; Lozelle de Luz, "The Nature and Level of Black Parent Participation: Prior to and After Metropolitan Desegregation" (Ph.D. diss., Univ. of Delaware, 1982).

192. *Philadelphia Sunday Bulletin,* 12 Feb. 1978; *Sunday News Journal,* 26 Dec. 1976.

193. PAC Bulletin 24, Oct. 1978; *Wilmington Evening Journal,* 28 Sept. 1977, 10 Jan. 1979; interviews with police Sergeant Alex Von Koch, 23 Feb. 1982, and Major John Lingo, 3 Mar. 1982; *Sunday News Journal,* 4 Feb. 1979; *University of Delaware Review,* 27 Apr. 1979.

The statistics on discipline have been analyzed in two lengthy scholarly studies that are in the files of the New Castle County public schools: Charles M. Achilles, et al., "A Study of Issues Related to Discipline . . ." and Gloria Grantham, et al., "An Interim Report of the Special Student Concerns Project." Also see *Sunday News Journal,* 6 May and 26 Aug. 1979, 20 Jan. 1980, 13 Dec. 1981, and *Wilmington Morning News,* 26 Jan. 1982.

194. Interviews with Alex Von Koch and John Lingo; *Wilmington Morning News,* 14 Nov. 1979.

195. Gary Govert, "Mr. Peepers Doesn't Teach Here Anymore," *Delaware Today,* May 1981, pp. 33–39, 61; interview with Dorothy Munroe, 10 Mar. 1982; *Newark Weekly Post,* 14–20 Feb. 1979.

196. Interview with Alex Von Koch; Govert, "Mr. Peepers," 35.

197. Govert, "Mr. Peepers," 35; conversation with Dan Defoe, 2 Feb. 1982; interview with Gladys Sharnoff.

198. *Wilmington Evening Journal,* 6 Mar. 1979.

199. *Sunday News Journal,* 14 Dec. 1980; *Wilmington Morning News,* 28 Jan., 11 Feb., 11 Mar. 1982.

200. *Sunday News Journal,* 13 Feb. 1977; Govert, "Mr. Peepers," 36.

201. Achilles, "Issues Related to Discipline," 1: 6–20, 26–28, 72–84, and passim; Grantham, "An Interim Report," 187–88 and passim.

202. Achilles, "Issues Related to Discipline," 27, 72, 77; *Wilmington Morning News,* 19 Mar. 1982.

203. Interviews with Bruce Laird (4 Mar. 1982) and Lisa Bullock (5 Mar. 1982); *Sunday News Journal,* 11 June 1978.

204. Interview with Gloria Grantham, 5 Mar. 1982; *Wilmington Morning News,* 9 Aug. 1979.

205. Interview with Lisa Bullock.

206. *Sunday News Journal,* 10 Aug. 1980.

207. Statement of Joseph R. Biden, "The Fourteenth Amendment and School Busing," 303.

208. Raffel, *The Politics of School Desegregation,* pp. 175–187.

209. *Wilmington Morning News,* 15 Sept. 1979.

210. *Philadelphia Inquirer,* 18 July 1976, 27 Aug. 1978; *Philadelphia Bulletin,* 7 Sept. 1975; conversation with Tai Liu, 4 Nov. 1980; *Sunday News Journal,* 6 May 1979.

211. *Philadelphia Inquirer,* 27 Aug. 1978; *Sunday News Journal,* 15 June 1980; *Wilmington Evening Journal,* 15 Feb. 1978; *Philadelphia Bulletin,* 6 Nov. 1977.

212. *Sunday News Journal,* 28 Sept. 1980; *Wilmington Morning News,* 1 Mar. 1979.

213. *Wilmington Morning News,* 23 Oct. 1980.

214. *Sunday News Journal,* 19 Oct. 1980, 13 Dec. 1981.

215. *Washington Post,* 19 Nov. 1978; *Sunday News Journal,* 12 Nov. 1978; James H. Sills, "Equalizing Teacher Salaries: Racial and Policy Implications in a New Metropolitan Public School District," *Urban Education* 17 (Oct. 1982): 351–74.

216. *Wilmington Morning News,* 28 Mar. 1980.

217. *Wilmington Morning News,* 25 Oct. 1980, 8, 21 July 1981.

218. Ibid., 16 May 1981.

219. Public confidence increased in 1981 after the district court approved the conversion of the single New Castle County school district into four smaller, racially balanced school districts. For a balanced but generally optimistic recent assessment, see Denise Antonelli, "Desegregation After Five Years: A Lesson for the Schools," *Delaware Today,* Sept. 1983, 43–46, 63–67.

220. Western Interstate Commission for Higher Education, "High School Graduates: Projections for the Fifty States" (Nov. 1979); Carol Pemberton, Univ. of Delaware Institutional Research Studies 80–4 (21 Jan. 1980) and 82–19 (4 May 1982); interview with Marilyn Harwick, 23 Dec. 1981. Contemporaneous with the flight of middle-class whites, a smaller number of aesthetically inclined professional people purchased and refurbished homes in Wilmington — a process sometimes called "gentrification." Property values soared in some neighborhoods that became fashionable once again, and integrationists claimed some of the credit for the "return flight." With the city and county schools combined, they said, there was no longer an advantage for couples with children to live in the suburbs. The public schools in Wilmington were just as good — or bad — as those elsewhere.

It should be noted, however, that gentrification was a national phenomenon that occurred in many cities that did not experience busing for metropolitan dispersion. With the rising cost of energy, some commuters moved to smaller houses closer to their offices, but this affected only certain parts of Wilmington, whose overall white population declined by 30 percent in the 1970s. By 1980 blacks made up 51 percent of the city's population, a majority for the first time. The professional people who returned to the city were few in number and apparently had small families or sent their children to private schools. Between 1978 and 1980 the number of white public school students residing in the city increased by only 100.

Meanwhile, property values in most suburbs in New Castle County increased at less than the rate of inflation, and builders reported a rush of Delaware buyers after they ran advertisements for new developments located "right over the state line" in Pennsylvania and Maryland. An executive at I.C.I., Inc., a large chemical manufacturer, estimated that one-third of the company's new professional employees had settled across the state line, and an official at Du Pont said many of the Company's employees were "genuinely concerned about the quality of education available for their children in New Castle County. They're also worried that white flight may precipitate a depression in suburban real estate values."

Some observers said there would have been even more white flight if building costs and mortgage rates had not increased sharply in the late-1970s. By the end of the decade new single family houses in nearby Maryland and Pennsylvania were selling for about 20 percent more than comparable houses in New Castle County. The situation was further complicated because the neighboring counties had very few houses priced below $70,000, while Delaware possessed an abundant supply of World War II-vintage tracts and row houses that sold for less than $50,000. In these circumstances, and with second jobs for spouses more readily available in populous New Castle County than in rural Maryland and Pennsylvania, many middle class Delaware families calculated that it cost more to move than to send their children to private schools.

See Peter Mucha, "Return Flight," *Delaware Today,* (July 1983), pp. 46, 54; Vivian Z. Klaff, "Metropolitan School Desegregation: Impact on Racial Integration of Neighborhoods in the United States" (unpublished paper, Department of Sociology, University of Delaware, 1981); *Wilmington Evening Journal,* 12 May 1977; *Sunday News Journal,* 20 November 1977; *Philadelphia Inquirer,* 18 July 1976; 27 August 1978, 27 August 1978.

NOTES TO PART FIVE

1. *U.S. Census of Population,* 1950, 16: 85; *U.S. Census of Population,* 1980, 18: 9; *Topeka Capital,* 2 Apr. 1975.

2. *Brown v. Board of Education,* 139 F. Supp. 468 (1955) at 470.

3. *Minneapolis Tribune,* 30 Nov. 1953; John L. Eberhardt, "Racial Concentration in Kansas Schools," 1956 pamphlet in Kansas Historical Society, Topeka; *Topeka Capital,* 29 Jan. 1956; *Wichita Eagle and Beacon,* 8 Dec. 1962; Bruce R. Powell, "Segregation, An Unresolved Controversy in the Public Schools of Topeka, Kansas," (honors thesis, Univ. of Kansas, 1975), 97.

4. *Topeka Capital Journal* clippings, 16 Mar. 1979; Kluger, *Simple Justice,* 382; "Community Insight," 1969 pamphlet in Kansas Historical Society.

5. *Topeka Daily Capital,* 17 Apr. 1970; interviews with Albert Carrington, 22 Oct. 1982; Rev. Augustus Pearson, 22 Oct. 1982; and Lance Murphy, 23 Oct. 1982.

6. *Topeka State Journal,* 16 Apr. 1970; Robert Jennings, Memorandum to Owen Henson, 19 Dec. 1982, copy to author.

7. *Topeka State Journal,* 16 Apr. 1970; interview with Connie Menninger, 21 Oct. 1982.

8. *Topeka State Journal,* 7 July, 14, 22 Apr., 1970; *Topeka Daily Capital,* 24 June, 1, 2, 7 July, 18, 22, 23 Apr. 1970; interview with Lance Murphy.

9. *Topeka Daily Capital,* 21 Apr. 1970.

10. *Topeka Capital,* 8 Oct. 1968; *Topeka Journal,* 26 Sept. 1968; *Washington Post,* 12 May 1974.

11. *Topeka Capital,* 12 Feb. 1970; *Topeka Journal,* 20 Apr. 1970.

12. Interview with Lance Murphy.

13. *Topeka Daily Capital,* 21 Apr., 6 May 1970; *Topeka Capital Journal,* 27 May 1970.

14. John J. Skelly, "The Role of the Pastor as Reconciler" (typescript in possession of Connie Menninger), 7; *Topeka State Journal,* 21, 22, 24 Apr. 1970; *Topeka Daily Capital,* 22, 27 Apr. 1970.

15. *Topeka Daily Capital,* 25 Apr. 1970; Skelly, "The Role of the Pastor"; interview with Augustus Pearson.

16. Interview with Connie Menninger; *Topeka State Journal,* 24, 23 Apr. 1970, 2 May 1970; *Topeka Daily Capital,* 24 Apr. 1970.

17. *Topeka State Journal,* 1 May, 29 Apr. 1970; *Topeka Daily Capital,* 30 Apr. 1970; interview with Augustus Pearson.

18. *Topeka Daily Capital,* 20 June, 7 July, 4 Sept. 1970.

19. Interview with Albert Carrington; *Topeka Daily Capital,* 6 May 1970.

20. *Topeka State Journal,* 23 Apr. 1970; Skelly, "The Role of the Pastor."

21. *Topeka Daily Capital,* 30 Apr. 1970.

22. Ibid., 28, 29 Apr. 1970; *Topeka State Journal,* 2, 4 May 1970; *Topeka Capital Journal,* 5 May 1970; interview with Connie Menninger.

23. Interview with Lance Murphy. Connie Menninger commented: "I think that's Lance's imagination. I never felt I was using the blacks."

24. *Topeka High School World,* 29 Jan., 5 Mar., 8, 15 Jan., 12 Mar. 1971, 2 Oct. 18 Sept. 1970, 30 Apr. 1971, 11 Dec. 1970; *Topeka Capital Journal* clippings, 13 Aug. 1977; interview with Augustus Pearson.

25. *Topeka Capital Journal,* 7 May 1972; author's personal observation, 22 Oct. 1982; interview with Albert Carrington.

26. *Topeka High School World,* 2 Apr. 1971; interviews with Albert Carrington, Connie Menninger, Lance Murphy, and Sharon McCubbin, 20 Oct. 1982.

27. Interview with Connie Menninger; Topeka Public Schools, *Six Year Report* (1981), 21. The Topeka Public Schools do not have a racial breakdown on test scores.

28. "Summary of Student Enrollment Changes, Shawnee County, Kansas, 1972–1981," provided by Gerald A. Miller, director of Demographic Services, Topeka Public Schools.

29. *Topeka Capital Journal,* 17 Oct. 1982.

30. Fred W. Phelps to author, 20 Nov. 1982; *State v. Sayers,* in District Court of Douglas County, Kansas.

31. *Miller v. Tom, Dick & Harry Furniture,* Case No. 123, 108, District Court, Shawnee County; *Carnegie v. Gage Furniture, Inc.* 217 Kan 564 (1975).

32. *Wall Street Journal,* 2 May 1974; complaint, 19 Sept. 1973, *Johnson v. Whittier,* T 5430, U.S. District Court, Topeka.

33. *Washington Post,* 12 May 1974; *New York Times,* 23 Oct. 1973, p. 24.

34. Complaint, 10 Sept. 1973, T. 5430; interview with Fred W. Phelps, 19 Oct. 1982.

35. Interview with Fred W. Phelps. The novelist was Charles M. Sheldon whose *In His Steps* was published by Thompson and Thomas, 1897.

36. Petitioner's Reply Brief, *Phelps v. Kansas Supreme Court,* Case No. 81–1411, U.S. Supreme Court, 1981; *Kansas City Star,* 15 Apr. 1979; *Topeka Daily Capital,* 16 Apr. 1979.

37. Judge Richard Rogers, quoted in affidavits of LeRoy Chambers, 8 Apr. 1981, and Emery Goad, 3 Oct. 1982, in possession of Fred W. Phelps. Also see *Wichita Eagle Beacon,* 13 Feb. 1983.

38. *Topeka Capital Journal,* 18 Jan., 17 Feb. 1974; *Topeka State Journal,* 30 Jan. 1974; *Topeka Daily Capital,* 7 May 1974.

39. *Topeka Capital Journal,* 18 Jan., 17 Feb. 1974; *Topeka State Journal,* 30 Jan. 1974; *Topeka Daily Capital,* 7 May 1974.

40. *Topeka Capital Journal,* 18 Jan., 17 Feb., 12 May 1974; *Topeka State Journal,* 30 Jan. 1974; *Topeka Daily Capital,* 7 May 1974.

41. *Topeka Capital Journal,* 12 May 1974; *Topeka Daily Capital,* 7 May 1974.

42. USD 501 v. Weinberger, summarized in *Brown v. Board of Education,* 84 F.R.D. 383 (1979) at 390–91; *Topeka Daily Capital,* 14 May 1974; *Topeka Capital Journal,* 27 Aug. 1974, 24 Apr. 1979; *National Observer,* 18 May 1974; Powell, "An Unresolved Controversy."

43. *Topeka Daily Capital,* 6 Dec. 1974; *Topeka State Journal,* 21 Nov. 1974; *Topeka Capital Journal* clippings, 22 May, 29 June, 23 Aug. 1979.

44. *Topeka Capital,* 10 July 1974; *Topeka Capital Journal* clippings, 29, 30 June 1979, 15 May 1979; *Topeka State Journal,* 6 Sept., 31 Aug. 1979; *Topeka Daily Capital,* 20 Apr. 1979.

45. Complaint, Miller v. Board of Education, Case No. 79–1408, U.S. District Court, Topeka; *Wichita Eagle Beacon,* 17 Aug., 8 Sept. 1979; *Topeka Capital Journal* clippings, 17 Aug. 1979.

46. *Chapman v. Board of Education,* Case No. 79–1473, U.S. District Court, Topeka; *Kansas City Star,* 7 Sept. 1979; *Wichita Eagle Beacon,* 8 Sept. 1979.

47. *Brown v. Board of Education,* 84 F.R.D. 383 (1979); *Topeka State Journal,* 22 Aug. 1979; *Washington Post,* 30 Nov. 1979.

48. *Topeka Capital Journal* clippings, 29 Nov. 1979, 18 Jan. 1980.

49. Interview with Barbara Kudlacek, 22 Oct. 1982.

50. *Washington Post,* 12 May 1974.

51. *Wichita Beacon,* 9 May 1974; *Topeka Capital Journal,* 12 May 1974.

52. *Washington Post,* 30 Nov. 1979; interview with Richard E. Jones, 20 Oct. 1982.

53. Interview with Richard E. Jones.

54. Jesse L. High to James M. Gray, 31 Aug. 1980, files of Topeka Public Schools; *Topeka Capital Journal* clippings, 25 Mar. 1979, 16 July 1980.

55. Interview with Albert Carrington; *National Observer,* 18 May 1974.

56. *Topeka Capital Journal,* 12 May 1974; *Kansas City Star,* 21 Oct. 1973.
57. *Washington Post,* 12 May 1974; *Topeka Capital Journal,* 12 May 1974; *Wall Street Journal,* 2 May 1974; *New York Times,* 23 Oct. 1974, p. 24; *National Observer,* 18 May 1974.
58. *Brown v. Board of Education,* 84 F.R.D 383 (1979).
59. Interview with Richard E. Jones; *Topeka Capital Journal* clippings, 5 Dec. 1979; *Kansas City Star,* 17 Aug. 1979; *Washington Post,* 30 Nov. 1979.
60. *Topeka State Journal,* 21 Nov. 1974; *Topeka Capital Journal* clippings, 16 July 1980; *Brown v. Board of Education,* 84 F.R.D. 383 (1979) at 386.
61. Interview with Albert Carrington.

NOTES TO THE CONCLUSION

1. On this point see Raoul Berger, *Government By Judiciary: The Transformation of the Fourteenth Amendment* (Cambridge, Mass.: Harvard Univ. Press, 1977), ch. 6.
2. See polls done by the National Opinion Research Center, summarized in *Scientific American* 195 (Dec. 1956): 35–39; 211 (July 1964): 16–23; 225 (Dec. 1971): 13–19.
3. Quoted in "Court-Ordered School Busing," *Hearings before the Subcommittee on Separation of Powers,* Senate Judiciary Committee, 97th Cong. 1st sess. (1981), 356.
4. Public Law 88–352 (1964), 246.
5. Crane Brinton, *A History of Civilization* (New York: Prentice Hall, 1955), 2: 115.
6. Leon Friedman, *Argument* (New York: Chelsea House Publishers, 1969), 14.
7. Ibid., 202.
8. *University of California Regents v. Bakke,* 438 U.S. 265 (1978) at 397, 398, 401.
9. Alexander M. Bickel, *The Morality of Consent* (New Haven, Conn.: Yale Univ. Press, 1975), 133.
10. Diane Ravitch, *The Troubled Crusade: American Education, 1945–1980.* (New York: Basic Books, 1983), 292.
11. Harold Howe II, "The Time is Now," *Saturday Review* 49 (16 July 1966): 57.
12. Quoted by Sam J. Ervin, Jr., "Judicial Verbicide," in Patrick B. McGuigan and Randall R. Rader, eds., *A Blueprint for Judicial Reform* (Washington, D.C.: Free Congress Research Foundation, 1981), 8.
13. Orrin G. Hatch, "The Son of Separate But Equal," in McGuigan and Rader, *Blueprint,* 63.
14. Dennis L. Cuddy, "Blacks and Education," *Tony Brown's Journal* (July/September 1983): 7; *Denver Post* 23 May 1983; *Detroit Free Press,* 24 May 1983; William Raspberry, "Is This the Way to Racial Balance?" *Washington Post,* 5 Nov. 1982.
15. C. Dickerman Williams, "Congress and the Supreme Court," *National Review* 34 (Feb. 1982): 109–111, 126.
16. Michael J. Perry, *The Constitution, the Courts, and Human Rights* (New Haven, Conn.: Yale Univ. Press, 1982), 128–138.

17. Grover Rees, "Prophets Without Portfolio," *National Review* 25 (2 September 1983): 1080.

18. Former congresswoman Elizabeth Holtzman, quoted and paraphrased, *University of Delaware Review,* 8 Apr. 1983.

19. McNeil-Lehrer Report, 17 Aug. 1982, Transcript 1797, p. 3.

20. See Perry, *The Constitution, the Courts, and Human Rights,* and John Hart Ely, *Democracy and Distrust* (Cambridge Mass.: Harvard Univ. Press, 1980).

21. *Brunson v. School Board No. 1, Clarendon County,* 429 F. 2d 820 (1970) at 824.

22. Ravitch, *Troubled Crusade,* 233–234.

23. *Wall Street Journal,* 28 Apr. 1983.

24. Diane Ravitch, "A Bifurcated Vision of Urban Education," in Jane Newitt, ed., *Future Trends in Educational Policy* (Lexington, Mass.: Lexington Books, 1979), 80.

25. James S. Coleman, et al., *Equality of Educational Opportunity* (Washington, D.C.: U.S. Department of Health, Education, and Welfare, 1966).

26. *New York Times,* 9 March 1970, p. 1.

27. *Hobson v. Hansen,* 269 F. Supp. 401 (1967) at 420.

28. *National Observer,* 7 June 1975.

29. Ibid.

30. Ibid.

31. Ibid.

32. Ibid.

33. Ibid.; Nancy H. St. John, *Desegregation: Outcomes for Children* (New York: Wiley, 1975); James S. Coleman, "School Desegregation and City-Suburban Relations," 1978 paper reprinted in "Court-Ordered School Busing," 454–459.

34. *Newsweek* 96 (15 Sept. 1980): 101–102.

35. *New Republic* 186 (24 Feb. 1982): 5–7.

36. *Time* 108 (29 Nov. 1976): 51.

37. *Grants for Research on Desegregation* (Washington, D.C.: U.S. Department of Education, 1981), 2.

38. Testimony of Gary Orfield, "School Desegregation," *Hearings before Subcommittee on Civil and Constitutional Rights,* 97th Cong., 1st sess. (1981) 147.

39. For an example of gullible journalism, see Lee A. Daniels, "In Defense of Busing," *New York Times Magazine,* 17 Apr. 1983. For a witty but accurate summary of fifteen years of scholarly research on the effects of desegregation, see the testimony of Herbert J. Walberg, "Court-Ordered School Busing," 152–153.

40. Christopher Jencks, et al., *Inequality* (New York: Basic Books, 1972), 81; James S. Coleman, et al., *Equality of Educational Opportunity,* 21; Frederick Mosteller and Daniel Moynihan, *On Equality of Educational Opportunity* (New York: Vintage Books, 1972), 14–15.

41. This is not the whole story, however, for even middle-class black children are not doing as well as one would hope. Sociologist Eleanor P. Wolf, the author of an excellent book on the use of social science material in school desegregation cases, has noted "the troubling and perhaps not widely known finding" that black and white differences persist even when students of similar socioeconomic levels

are compared. The U.S. Commission on Civil Rights has reported that when the verbal achievement of high school seniors was compared, whites in the lowest social class grouping did better than blacks in the highest. Sociologist David Goslin has called attention to the fact that "rural Southern whites, who have the lowest average scores of any white group, outscore midwest urban Negroes, who have the highest average scores of any Negro group, on every single test given from grade one to grade twelve."

Given the present uncertainty concerning the relative importance of heredity and environment, the racist explanation for persistent black retardation is inconclusive. A plausible alternative explanation revolves around the constellation of values and attitudes that make up a culture. The distinctive values that the various immigrant groups brought to America appear to have caused different rates of social mobility among white ethnics. It may be, then, that black progress has also been influenced by deeply held values that served a purpose in the past but function today as an impediment to taking advantage of opportunities that are available now.

See Eleanor P. Wolf, *Trial and Error: The Detroit Desegregation Case* (Detroit: Wayne State Univ. Press, 1981), 88, 94, 96, 97; *Racial Isolation in the Public Schools* (Washington, D.C.: U.S. Commission on Civil Rights, 1967), 80; David A. Goslin, "The School in a Changing Society," *American Journal of Orthopsychiatry* 37 (Oct. 1967): 851.

42. Theodore H. White, *The Making of the President, 1964* (New York: Atheneum, 1965), 239.

43. Robert L. Heuser (Chief, Natality Statistics Branch, National Center for Health Statistics) to author, 14 June 1983. Also see Raymond Pearl, "Fertility and Contraception in Urban Whites and Negroes," *Science* 83 (22 May 1936): 503–506; Clyde V. Kiser, *Group Differences in Urban Fertility* (Baltimore: Williams and Wilkins, 1942), ch. 2; Kiser, "Fertility Trends and Differentials Among Nonwhites in the United States," *Milbank Memorial Fund Quarterly* 36 (Apr. 1958): 149–197.

44. W.E.B. Du Bois, *The Philadelphia Negro* (Philadelphia: Univ. of Pennsylvania Press, 1899), 389–390.

45. Ibid., 389–395.

46. "Court-Ordered School Busing," 453.

47. Charles E. Grassley, "Academic Freedom Needs Tuition Tax Credit's Help," *Human Events* 42 (18 Sept. 1982): 13.

48. Gary Orfield, *Desegregation of Black and Hispanic Students from 1968 to 1980* (Washington, D.C.: Joint Committee for Political Studies, 1982), 11.

BIBLIOGRAPHICAL NOTE

The notes indicate the extent of my indebtedness to various sources of information. Instead of listing these sources in a lengthy bibliography, I should like to conclude by calling attention to a few items that are especially important.

The Burden of Brown was initially conceived as a sequel to Richard Kluger's compelling narrative account of the *Brown* lawsuit, *Simple Justice* (New York: Knopf, 1975). From the outset I thought the story of desegregation was not as simple as Kluger's morality tale and that I could make a contribution by giving a balanced account that focused on the events that have transpired since *Brown*. Yet my initial revisionism was purely literary, for when I began this study I had no reservations about the prevailing liberal orthodoxy.

Three legal analyses were especially influential in shaping my thought. First and foremost there was Lino A. Graglia's book, *Disaster By Decree* (Ithaca, N.Y.: Cornell Univ. Press, 1976)—a devastating critique of the Supreme Court's decisions on race and public education. Then there was Raoul Berger's monograph on the transformation of the Fourteenth Amendment, *Government By Judiciary* (Cambridge, Mass.: Harvard Univ. Press, 1977). Finally, there was an especially able law review article by Frank I. Goodman, "De Facto Segregation," *California Law Review* 60 (Mar. 1972): 275–437. *From Brown to Bakke* (New York: Oxford Univ. Press, 1979), by J. Harvie Wilkinson III, is less trenchant but nevertheless perceptive. For the conventional liberal wisdom see Jack Bass, *Unlikely Heroes: The Dramatic Story of the Southern Judges of the Fifth Circuit Who Translated the Supreme Court's Brown Decision into a Revolution for Equality* (New York: Simon and Schuster, 1981).

The voluminous literature on the educational consequences of desegregation has been reviewed impartially by Nancy H. St. John, *Desegrega-*

tion: Outcomes for Children (New York: Wiley, 1975). Eleanor P. Wolf has critically assessed the use of social science evidence in desegregation litigation, *Trial and Error: The Detroit School Segregation Case.* (Detroit: Wayne State Univ. Press, 1981). And David Nevin and Robert E. Bills have written an unsympathetic but interesting assessment of private segregation academies, *The Schools That Fear Built* (Washington, D.C.: Acropolis Books, 1976). Diane Ravitch has written the best general account of American education since 1945, *The Troubled Crusade* (New York: Basic Books, 1983).

The work of several journalists was helpful. On the situation in Washington, I benefited especially from reading accounts by three writers for the *Washington Post:* Lawrence Feinberg, Erwin Knoll, and William Raspberry. J. Barrye Wall, John C. Steck, and Bo Prichard of the *Farmville Herald* gave detailed attention to events in Prince Edward County, while James J. Kilpatrick of the *Richmond News Leader* commented perceptively on the theoretical aspects of massive resistance. The *News Journal* papers covered the story in New Castle County; during the 1950s and 1960s the work of Bill Frank and Philip M. Boffey was particularly good, while Larry Nagengast, Steve Goldberg, and Nathan Gorenstein focused on busing in the 1970s and 1980s. Clarendon County did not receive as much coverage in the press, but helpful articles appeared occasionally in the *Charleston News and Courier,* the *Columbia State,* and the *Manning Times.* The *Topeka Capital Journal* papers carried many helpful articles on the situation in Kansas.

Throughout this study I have used an extensive collection of approximately 200 reels of microfilmed press clippings collected by the Southern Education Reporting Service. The Board of Education in Washington allowed me the use of their clippings, and University of Delaware professor Jeffrey A. Raffel and Mrs. Connie Menninger of Topeka loaned me their scrapbooks of clippings dealing with desegregation in Delaware and Kansas. The *Farmville Herald, Manning Times, Topeka Capital Journal,* and *Wilmington News Journal* generously gave access to their files of clippings.

A few books deserve special mention. James W. Ely, Jr., combined a knowledge of legal issues with a mastery of historical research and writing to produce a model monograph, *The Crisis of Conservative Virginia* (Knoxville: Univ. of Tennessee Press, 1976). Other good studies of desegregation in Virginia are: Bob Smith, *They Closed Their Schools* (Chapel Hill: Univ. of North Carolina Press, 1965); Benjamin Muse, *Virginia's Massive Resistance* (Bloomington: Indiana Univ. Press, 1961); Robbins L. Gates, *The Making of Massive Resistance* (Chapel Hill: Univ. of North Carolina Press, 1962); and J. Harvie Wilkinson III, *Harry Byrd and the Changing Face of Virginia Politics, 1945–1966* (Charlottesville: Univ. Press of Virginia, 1968).

Corporate Capital: Wilmington in the Twentieth Century (Philadelphia:

Temple Univ. Press, 1983), by Carol E. Hoffecker, contains a good discussion of urban renewal and youth gangs, while Jeffrey A. Raffel focused on the implementation of busing, *The Politics of School Desegregation: The Metropolitan Remedy in Delaware* (Philadelphia: Temple Univ. Press, 1980). The background to desegregation in South Carolina is discussed by Howard H. Quint, *Profile in Black and White: A Frank Portrait of South Carolina* (Washington, D.C.: Public Affairs Press, 1958); and by Jack Bass and Walter De Vries, *The Transformation of Southern Politics* (New York: Basic Books, 1976). For the situation in the District of Columbia, see Carl F. Hansen, *Danger in Washington: The Story of My Twenty Years in the Public Schools in the Nation's Capital* (West Nyack, N.Y.: Parker Publishing, 1968).

As indicated in my footnotes, most of the essential legal documents are on file in the United States district courts in Delaware, South Carolina, Virginia, and the District of Columbia; some are available at the Library of Congress and at the Supreme Court Library. My work was made easier by Leon Friedman, ed., *Argument: The Oral Argument Before the Supreme Court in Brown v. Board of Education of Topeka, 1952–1955* (New York: Chelsea House, 1969). The legal briefs for the *Brown* and *Green* cases are conveniently available in *Landmark Briefs and Arguments of the Supreme Court* (Arlington, Va.: University Publications of America, 1975), Philip B. Kurland, ed., volumes 49, 49A, and 66.

Congressional investigations were another important source of information, with the following Hearings being especially relevant to my work: (1) *Investigation of Public School Conditions, Hearings before the Subcommittee of the Committee on the District of Columbia, House of Representatives,* 84th Congress, 2nd session (1956); (2) *Investigation of Schools and Poverty in the District of Columbia, Hearings before the Task Force on Antipoverty, Committee on Education and Labor, House of Representatives,* 89th Congress, 1 and 2nd sessions (1965–1966); (3) *Riots, Civil and Criminal Disorder (Part 14: Wilmington), Hearings before the Permanent Subcommittee on Investigations of the Committee on Government Operations,* U.S. Senate, 90th Congress, 2nd session (1968); (4) *Equal Educational Opportunity, 1971, Hearings before the Select Committee, U.S. Senate,* 92nd Congress, 1st session (1971); (5) *School Busing: Hearings before Subcommittee 5, Committee on the Judiciary, House of Representatives,* 92nd Congress, 2nd session (1972); (6) *Busing of Schoolchildren, Hearings of the Committee on the Judiciary, U.S. Senate,* 93rd Congress, 2nd session (1974); (7) *School Desegregation, Hearings before the Subcommittee on Civil and Constitutional Rights, Committee on the Judiciary, House of Representatives,* 97th Congress, 1st session (1981); (8) *Court-Ordered School Busing, Hearings before the Subcommittee on Separation of Powers, Committee on the*

Judiciary, U.S. Senate, 97th Congress, 1st session (1981); and (9) *The Fourteenth Amendment and School Busing, Hearings before the Subcommittee on the Constitution, Committee on the Judiciary, U.S. Senate,* 97th Congress, 1st session (1981).

Readers may also wish to consult books that are written from different perspectives. For segregationist views see W.D. Workman, Jr., *The Case for the South* (New York: Devin-Adair, 1960); Carleton Putnam, *Race and Reason* (Washington, D.C.: Public Affairs Press, 1961), and *Race and Reality* (Washington, D.C.: Public Affairs Press, 1967); and two books by James J. Kilpatrick, *The Sovereign States* (Chicago: Henry Regnery, 1957) and *The Southern Case for School Segregation* (New York: Crowell-Collier, 1962). The case for mandatory racially balanced integration has been argued explicitly by Gary Orfield, *Must We Bus?* (Washington, D.C.: Brookings Institution, 1978), and less directly by the U.S. Commission on Civil Rights, *Racial Isolation in Public Schools* (Washington, D.C.: Government Printing Office, 1967). Other books that implicitly endorse the optimal-mix theory are Ray C. Rist, *The Invisible Children: School Integration in American Society* (Cambridge, Mass.: Harvard Univ. Press, 1978), and David L. Kirp, *Just Schools: The Idea of Racial Equality in American Education* (Berkeley: Univ. of California Press, 1981). The most substantial assessment of education and desegregation by radical writers is that of Christopher Jencks, et al., *Inequality: A Reassessment of the Effect of Family and Schooling in America* (New York: Basic Books, 1972).

ACKNOWLEDGMENTS

I am especially indebted to the University of Delaware, which has generously supported my scholarly work ever since I joined the faculty as an Instructor in 1965. The research for this book was begun during a sabbatical leave, and the writing was completed when I was released from teaching duties for a year's appointment at the university's Center for Advanced Study.

Several scholars and friends read portions of the manuscript and made valuable suggestions for its improvement: Garin Burbank, Carol E. Hoffecker, J. A. Leo Lemay, Ronald L. Lewis, Ralph E. Luker, and James M. McPherson. I also benefited from perceptive critical readings by several people who either participated in the events or observed them at first hand: James M. Anderson, Jr., Ann Darby, William D. D'Onofrio, Lawrence Feinberg, Robert McC. Figg, Carl F. Hansen, Charles N. Henson, Owen M. Henson, T. H. McIlwaine, Connie Menninger, Fred W. Phelps, James W. Porter, Robert T. Redd, David W. Robinson, Howard E. Row, Edna F. Rowe, Mason E. Turner, Jr., and J. Barrye Wall.

At the University of Tennessee Press, Mavis Bryant, Carol Orr, and Barbara B. Reitt prepared the way for publication and helped to make this book better and shorter than it otherwise would have been.

INDEX

Abbitt, Watkins M., 114
Abernathy, Brenda, 109
Abernathy, George, 109
ability grouping, in Washington, 19, 20–22, 25, 27–28, 32–33, 36, 39, 45, 46, 49, 54, 62; in Prince Edward County, 97, 108, 119–20, 124; in Clarendon County, 167; in Wilmington and New Castle County, 183–84, 186, 195, 238–39; in Topeka, 261, 275, 293 n.35
Achilles, Charles M., 244
activity centers, in Prince Edward County, 102–03, 104
Adams, John, 89
Adams-Morgan Community Council, 46–47
Addie, Bob, 23
affirmative action, 7, 139, 152, 154–55, 156–58, 202–203, 204, 212, 213, 216, 217, 230, 233, 263, 266, 280; *also see* color consciousness; preferential treatment; reparations
Aldisert, Ruggiero, 222
Alien and Sedition Acts, 89
Allen, Anita, 41–42, 51–52
Allen, Vera, 119–20
Almond, J. Lindsay, 74, 75, 78, 79, 87, 91, 92, 93
Alsop, Joseph, 17, 41
America, 25
American Civil Liberties Union, 207, 270
American Federation of Labor, 163

American Friends Service Committee, 104, 119
Americans for Democratic Action, 13
Amidon School, 20–22
Anacostia, 43
Anacostia High School, 12, 13
Anderson, James M., Jr., 119, 120, 121, 122, 124
Anderson, Julia, 103
Anderson, Leon V., 179
Anderson, William "Hicks," 206
Andrews, Lester, 127
Anti-Defamation League, 18
Antioch College, 47–48
Appoquinimink School District, 225
Arlington, Va., 93
Armstrong High School, 15
Armstrong, Samuel Chapman, 153
Associated Community Teams (ACT), 30
Atchison, Topeka & Santa Fe Railroad, 261
Atlas Chemical Company, 176
Avins, Alfred, 218–19

Babiarz, John E., 190
back-to-basics, 281, 299 n.181
Baker, Helen, 103
Bank Street College, 186
Banks, W. Lester, 72
Banneker Senior High School, 298 n.166
Bannockburn, Md., 38
Barksdale, Marian, 150
Barnard Elementary School, 14, 15

335

Barry, Marion, 55
Bash, James, 182
Battaglia, Victor F., 210
Battle, John F., 69
Baylliss, Helen, 197
Bazelon, David L., 33, 39
Bell, J. Spencer, 112
Bell, Ralph, 130–31
Bell and Howell, 108
Belton, Ethel, 177
Benn, Herman T., 55
Bethune, Thelma, 133
Bickel, Alexander M., 276, 295 n.104
Biden, Joseph R., 234, 246, 250
Biggs, Carroll W., 239, 243
"B. J.'s Corner," 189, 190
black belt, 65–66
Black Culture Week, 255
Black, Hugo, 113, 114
Blake, Elias, 27
Board of Supervisors (Prince Edward County), 81, 90, 91, 94, 113, 116, 117
Boggs, J. Caleb, 199, 200, 201
Bolling, Spottswood W., 11, 12, 61
Bolling v. Sharpe, 6, 9, 11–12, 16
Booker, Simeon, 24
Boothe, Armistead, 86
Boston, Mass., 288
Bowles, Bryant, 198–99
Boyce, Charles E., 199
Brandeis, Louis D., 137
Brandywine High School, 240, 242
Brennan, William J., Jr., 157, 204
Briggs, Harry, 139, 140, 173
Briggs, Liza, 133, 139
Briggs v. Elliott, 6, 7, 133, 134, 136, 137, 138, 140, 145, 147, 150, 154, 158, 162, 167, 209, 213, 288
Brinton, Crane, 276
Broadax, William, 61
Bronx School of Science, 58
Brooke, Edward W., 59
Brooks, John Julian,
Brown, Charles A., 146
Brown, George N., 188, 189
Brown, Leonard, 124
Brown, Linda. *See* Linda Brown Smith
Brown, Oliver, 267, 269
Brown, Robert, 48–49
Brown v. Topeka Board of Education (Brown I), opinion of the Supreme

Brown v. Topeka Board of Ed. (cont.)
Court, 3–5, 78, 138; assessments and interpretations of the opinion, 6, 7, 82, 86, 88, 89, 90, 92, 125–26, 135, 139, 143, 145, 148, 152, 154, 157, 158, 161, 191, 200, 204, 213, 216, 264, 269, 274, 275, 281, 288, 289; mentioned on, 9, 39, 62, 65, 79, 100, 111, 113, 115, 126, 127, 130, 133, 142, 149, 151, 153, 156, 175, 183, 197, 201, 207, 208, 214, 215, 218, 220, 221, 222, 224, 250, 253, 254, 255, 266, 268, 270, 271, 273, 276, 280, 282, 283, 284, 286
Brown v. Topeka Board of Education (Brown II), 79, 80, 81, 139, 157, 204, 216
Browne Junior High School, 10
Brunson, Bobby, 150, 151
Brunson v. Board of Trustees, 150–51, 158–59, 253, 263
Bryan, Alvert V., 116, 161
Buck, John Nelson, 77
Buckley, William F., 164
Bulah, Fred, 176, 180
Bulah, Sarah, 176, 177, 179, 180
Bulah, Shirley, 176, 179, 180
Bullock, Lisa, 245, 246
Bunche, Ralph J., 110
Burger, Warren E., 40, 222, 223
Burnett Middle School, 197
Bush League, 100–101
busing, in Washington, 37, 38, 40, 42, 87; in Clarendon County, 131, 132; in New Castle County, 176–77; *also see* metropolitan dispersion
Butler, Edward J., 187–89, 191
Butzner, John D., Jr., 116
Byrd, Harry F., 88, 89, 93, 201
Byrd, Harry F., Jr., 90
Byrd, Robert, 152
Byrnes, James F., 136, 142–44, 201

Cahn, Edmond, 135
Calhoun, John C., 89
Calvary Baptist Church, 166
Cardozo High School, 15
Carnegie, Diana, 263
Carr, Marguerite, 10
Carr v. Corning, 10–11
Carr, Wilber C., 208
Carrere, Thomas A., 146
Carrington, Albert, 269

Carswell, G. Harold, 163
Carter, Robert L., 139, 276
Casimir Pulaski Elementary School, 240
Cassell, Charles, 52
Casson, Lloyd, 211
Central Middle School, 241
Charleston News and Courier, 139, 142
Charleston, S.C., 145–48, 149–50
Charlottesville, Va., 91–92
Chein, Isador, 74, 75, 76
"Cherry Island Incident," 190
Chesapeake and Delaware Canal, 197, 218
Chippey African Union Methodist Church, 179
Christiana High School, 242, 243
Civil Rights Law, 1964, 7, 152, 153–55, 156, 183, 202, 265, 267, 274, 276, 277, 288
Clarendon County, S.C., 129–74, 183, 282
Clarendon Hall, 166, 167, 168, 173
Clark, Kenneth B., 5, 28–29, 36, 49–52, 75, 134–35, 147
Clark, Tom, 113
"classics," 187
Claymont, Del., 177, 178, 179
Claymont High School, 177, 178, 179, 240
Cleveland, Ohio, 238
Cline, Marvin, 30
Colbert, Vader, 124
Coleman, James S., 35, 36, 37, 40, 41, 63, 208, 211, 227, 282–84, 285; *also see* Equality of Educational Opportunity
Coles, Robert, 35, 37
Collins, John Paul, 13, 14
"color blind," 4, 7, 8, 38, 265, 270, 277
"color conscious," 7, 8, 37, 39, 40, 43, 270, 277; *also see* affirmative action
Columbia State, 139, 148
Commonweal, 25
compensatory education, 41, 285; *also see* Follow Through, Head Start
Competency Based Curriculum (CBC), 60–61, 299 n.181
Concord High School, 244
Congress of Racial Equality (CORE), 29, 30

Coolidge High School, 15
Corning, Hobart M., 12, 19
Cox, W. Harold, 155
Craig, Harry, 269
Craven, J. Braxton, 161
Crawford, Robert B., 84
Crisis in the Classroom, by Charles E. Silberman, 25
Croner, Dorothy, 102
Crosby, Muriel, 184, 185

Dalton, Ted, 86, 91
Darden, Colgate W., 108
Dark Ghetto, by Kenneth B. Clark, 49
Darley Road Elementary School, 246
Davis, Benjamin O., 59
Davis, James C., 15
Davis, John W., 137, 138
Davis, Ruth, 15
Davis, W.B., 141
Dayton v. Brinkman, 220–21, 222, 223, 234
Deal Junior High School, 42
Defenders of State Sovereignty and Individual Liberty, 87–88
Defoe, Dan, 243
DeLaine, J.A., 132, 133, 140
DeLaine, Mattie, 132
Delaware State Supreme Court, 200
Delaware Technical and Community College, 202
Delmarva Ecumenical Agency, 229
Dellums, Eric, 42
Dellums, Mrs. Ronald, 42
Denny, Collins, 111, 113
Denton, Dorothy, 14, 15
Detroit, Mich., 217–18, 288
Dickenson County, Va., 86
Dickenson High School, 240
Dimond, Paul, 239
discipline problems, in Washington, 13–15, 23–25, 28, 61, 62; at Prince Edward Academy, 98; in Summerton, 172, 173; in New Castle County, 187–91, 191–95, 195–96, 205, 241–46; in Topeka, 256–59, 261, 283, 287
Disraeli, Benjamin, 144
District of Columbia Teachers College, 15
doll tests, 134–35
D'Onofrio, William D., 234, 235, 248
Douglas, William O., 221

337

Dover, Del., 200, 203
Downs, Pat, 242
Drew, Charles, 59
Du Bois, W.E.B., 66, 70, 71, 282, 286–87
Dunbar High School, 15, 58–59
Du Pont Company, 176, 186, 229
du Pont, Pierre S., IV, 229, 249, 250
Dusenbury, Richard G., 148

East Williston, New York, 108
Eastern High School, 12, 13, 14, 23, 61–63
Easterner, 13
Edgerton, Henry, 11
Edison, Thomas A., 21
Education Finance Act (South Carolina), 170
Educational Advancement Act (Delaware), 212–17
Eggleston, John W., 92
Einstein, Albert, 21
Eisenhower, Dwight D., 24
Eisenhower Junior High School, 256
Eliot Junior High School, 10
Elliott, David, 232
Ely, James W., Jr., 91
Emery School, 15
Equality of Educational Opportunity, by James S. Coleman, 211, 282
equalization of school expenditures, 32, 40, 43, 44, 45, 169–70; *also see* Fourteenth Amendment
equalization of school facilities, NAACP lawsuits, 67; in Washington, 9–10; in Virginia, 68–72; in South Carolina, 136–37; in Delaware, 177–79
Ervin, Sam J., Jr., 276
Evans, Rowland, 164
Evans, Tom, 233, 234
Evans v. Buchanan, 200, 202, 207, 215, 216, 222–23, 236, 241, 246, 251, 263
expenditure per pupil, by race in 1930, 67; in Washington, 9, 32, 40, 43, 44, 45, 55; in Prince Edward County, 97, 109, 116–17, 125; in Charleston, 146; in Summerton, 131, 158, 169, 170; in New Castle County, 187, 224
Experimental Project on Schools in Changing Neighborhoods, 185

Farmville, Va., 66, 107
Farmville High School, 69, 75, 82
Farmville Herald, 73, 87, 94, 96, 99, 105, 106
Farmville Presbyterian Church, 94
Fauntroy, Walter, 27
Fawcett, Nancy, 123
Federal Mogul, 130
Feinberg, Lawrence, 60, 299 n.181
Field Foundation, 108
Fifth Amendment, due process clause, 6, 9
Fifth Circuit Court of Appeals, 154, 155, 158
Figg, Robert McCormick, 134, 135, 141
Fine, Benjamin, 180, 181
First Baptist Church (Farmville), 66, 67, 103
Fleming, Billie, 131, 140, 172
Flemming, Arthur S., 102
Follow Through Program, 86
Ford Foundation, 108
Fortas, Abe, 162
Fourteenth Amendment, original understanding of equal protection clause, 76–77, 90, 137–38, 273, 278; allows classifications that are not arbitrary, 40, 138, 145; applies to states, not to federal government, 6, 9; and equalization of expenditures for education, 169–70; as interpreted in *Plessy v. Ferguson*, 4; as interpreted in *Brown v. Topeka Board of Education*, 3–5, 78, 138; *also see Brown v. Topeka Board of Education*
Fourth Circuit Court of Appeals, 80, 81, 94, 112, 113, 115, 129, 149, 154, 155, 157, 158, 161, 162, 209
Fowler, Katherine, 14
Frank, Bill, 181, 196, 198, 199
Frankfurter, Felix, 310 n.79
Free Schools of Prince Edward County, 107–10, 113, 117
freedom of choice, 151, 154, 156, 157, 162, 163, 164, 165, 202–203, 251, 275, 276, 279; *also see* local option, optional transfers, tuition grants, voluntary desegregation
Freedom Rides, 24
Friends School, 206
Fund for the Advancement of Education, 9

Gallup Poll, 277
Garland Fund, 67
Garrett, Henry E., 76, 84–85, 98, 146–47
Garrett, Hermania, 211
Gaston, J.W., 149
Geisert, Gene A., 186, 206
General Electric Company, 108
gentrification, 321 n.220
George, Wesley Critz, 147
George W. Watkins School, 156
Georgetown, Del., 200
Ghee, James E., 118, 124, 126
Gibbons, John, 215, 216, 217, 218, 219, 220, 222, 223, 224, 225, 226, 227
Glancy, David, 27
Glenn, Terrell L., 152
Godwin, Mills E., 99
Goett, Edward J., 190
Goldberg, Steve, 240
Golden Rule, 67
Gordon High School, 58
Goslin, David, 327 n.41
Gousha, Richard P., 202–203
Govert, Gary, 243
Graglia, Lino A., 155, 157
Graham, Gerald, 122
Grantham, Gloria, 245–46
Grassley, Charles E., 287
Gravatt, J. Segar, 111, 113
Gray, Frederick T., 156
Green, Robert L., 106, 236, 237, 319 n.177, 319–20 n.184
Green v. New Kent County, 7, 129, 155, 156, 157, 158, 159, 160, 162, 202, 204, 207, 208, 209, 213, 216, 218, 221, 263, 274, 275, 276, 278, 280, 288
Greenberg, Jack, 156, 177, 210
Greenville News, 173
Greenwell, Janet, 206–207, 211
Greenwood, S.C., 169
Gresham, Foster B., 82
Gressette, L. Marion, 142, 148, 149
Griffin, Eric, 124
Griffin, L. Francis, 66–67, 69, 70, 72, 101, 102, 107, 111, 117, 118, 119, 120, 122, 125
Griffin v. Prince Edward County, 113, 114, 116, 126
guidelines for interpreting the Civil Rights Law, 153, 154, 155, 159, 160,

guidelines for interpreting the Civil Rights Law (*cont.*), 162, 265, 266; *also see* Civil Rights Law, 1964, U.S. Department of Health, Education, and Welfare (HEW)
Guines, James T., 62

Hager, Robert, 230
Hager, Walter E., 15
Hampden-Sydney College, 100, 122
Hanbury, B. Blanton, 83, 95
Hansen, Carl F., 17, 18, 19, 20, 21, 22, 23, 24, 25, 26, 27, 28, 30, 31, 34, 37, 38, 39, 53, 63, 97–98, 99, 281
Hargrove, Roy B., 104–105
Harlan Elementary School, 205
Harlan, John Marshall, 113
Harper, Bryant R., 117
Harrison, Albertis S., 114
Harrison v. Day, 92
Harvard University Center for Law and Education, 33
Harwick, Marilyn, 205, 206, 207, 210, 211, 251
Harwick, R.D., 205, 206
Haskell, Harry, 205, 210, 211
Haskins, Kenneth, 48
Hastie, William H., 59
Hatch, Orrin G., 277–78
Haynes, Euphemia, 21
Haynesworth, Clement F., 112, 154, 161, 162, 163
Head Start, 41
Heckert, Clarice, 213–14
Helms, Jesse, 99, 287
Henley, Benjamin, 51, 53
Herblock, 113–14
Hercules, Inc., 176
Herlihy, Pearl G., 191
Herlihy, Thomas, 191
HEW. *See* U.S. Department of Health, Education, and Welfare
Highland Park High School, 255, 256, 258, 259, 266, 270
Hill, Oliver W., 72, 79, 105
Himmler, David L., 240
Hitler, Adolph, 84
Hobson, Julius W., 29–45
Hobson v. Hansen, 29–45, 120, 220
Hockessin, Del., 176–80
Hockessin School No. 29, 177, 178, 179

Hockessin School No. 107, 176
Hoffecker, Carol E., 190
Hoffman, Walter E., 116
Holiday Inn, 130
Holloway, Herman M., 193, 196
Holman, Nancy, 99–100
Holman, Nathan, 99
Holmes, Oliver W., 137
Holt, John, 24–25
House Judiciary Committee, 278
Howard Career Center, 186
Howard High School, 177, 178, 179, 186, 191, 193, 235
Howe, Arthur, 153
Howe, Harold, 47, 153, 154, 277
Hoyle, Dennis C., 195
Hughes, Charles Evans, 3
Human Relations Commission, 254
Human Rights Advisory Council, 240
Humphrey, Hubert H., 152, 164
Huntley, Chet, 106
Hutcheson, Sterling, 80, 81
Hypps, Irene C., 15

illegitimacy, 13, 14, 79, 184, 185, 286, 287
incremental segregative effect, 209, 220, 221, 223, 234
inferiority complex, 4–5, 27, 28–29, 30–31, 32, 34, 35, 74–75, 76, 77, 78, 80, 117, 118–19, 134, 138, 178, 267, 283; *also see* doll tests
Ingrick, Helen, 15
intelligence quotient (IQ), 19, 21, 58, 106–107, 168, 181
intentional discrimination, 45, 209, 214, 215, 217, 219, 220, 223, 233, 234, 275, 279
Interfaith Task Force, 229
interposition, 89, 90, 149, 197, 232; *also see* James J. Kilpatrick

Jackson, Earl C., 186
Jackson, Kennell, Jr., 101, 106
Jefferson Junior High School, 56
Jefferson, Thomas, 89
Jencks, Christopher, 22, 35, 47, 227
Jenkins, Michael, 181
Jennings, Bob, 255
Jesus, 67, 264
Johns, Barbara, 70, 72
Johnson, Derek, 193
Johnson, Evelyn Rene, 263, 264

Johnson, George L., 189
Johnson v. Whittier, 263–65, 267, 268
Johnston, Olin D., 143
Jones, M. Boyd, 70
Jones, Richard E., 268, 269, 270
Jonkiert, Casimer, 196
jurisdiction of federal courts, 143, 233, 234, 235, 278–79

Kandler, Gerald, 207
Kansas Supreme Court, 263
Keene, William B., 236
Keller, B.J., 189
Kelly, Patrick F., 264
Kelly, William H., 76
Kennedy, John F., 107
Kennedy, Robert F., 107
Kent County, Del., 197–204, 207, 228, 247
Kilpatrick, James J., 81, 85, 86, 88–89, 93
Kilson, Martin Luther, 180, 313 n.15
King, Martin Luther, Jr., 105, 107, 190, 277
Kirtdoll, Edward, 259
Kittrell College, 104
Kluger, Richard, 73, 77, 134–35, 254
Knox, Ellis O., 29
Koerner, James, 20
Kunstler, William, 33
Kurland, Philip B., 219, 222, 223, 224

Laird, Bruce, 245
Lancaster, Dabney S., 82
Large, Maurice, 82
Laurel State Register, 198
Lauter, Paul, 47
Lawson, Henry, 131, 171, 173
Layton, Caleb R., 201, 215–18
Leahy, Paul, 200–201
Lemons, Joseph, 173
Leonard, George S., 145, 146
Lewis, Clifton, 207–208
Lewis, Jeanne Q., 207–208
Lewis, Oren, 111–12, 114
Lewis, Tony, 208
Lewis, Mr. and Mrs. Walter C., 109
Lilly, Donna J., 246
Lincoln, Abraham, 264
Lingo, John, 242
local option, 85, 86, 87, 91, 93, 94, 126, 148; *also see* freedom of

local option (*cont.*)
  choice, optional transfers, tuition
  grants
Lockridge, Calvin, 61
Lockwood, Patton, 125, 133
Lockwood, Robin, 123
Long Range Facilities Plan (Topeka),
  266, 267, 270
Longwood College, 82, 100, 101, 102,
  122
Lucas, Louis, 202, 209–210

Madden, C. Ware, 166
Madison, James, 89
mainstreaming, 186; *also see* ability
  grouping, progressive education
Malone, Thomas B., 199
Maloney, Tom, 233
Manning, S.C., 132, 169, 170, 172, 173
Manning Times, 164–65, 168
Manning, William, 51, 53
Mansfield, Lord, 264
Marshall, Thurgood, 71, 132, 133,
  134, 138, 140, 145, 147, 151, 152,
  157, 221, 223, 276, 310 n.79
Martin, J. Robert, 148
massive resistance, 65–127, especially
  87–93; 100, 148, 149
matriarchy, 24, 245
McCarthy, Shane, 24–25
McCluney, Amos, 196
McCord, L.B., 141
McDonald, John, 133
McDonald, Rita, 150
McDonnal, Jeanette, 191
McFarland High School, 13
McIlwaine, T.J., 83, 84
McKinley High School, 12, 14
McKissick, Floyd, 41
Meeting Individual Needs Daily
  (MIND), 46
Menninger, Cathy, 255
Menninger, Connie, 258, 259, 261, 323
  n.23
Menninger Foundation, 255, 261
Menninger, Walter, 259
Merit Scholarships, 57, 97, 261, 298
  n.163
metropolitan dispersion, 34–35, 38,
  40, 108, 175, 206, 209, 210, 211,
  214, 216, 217, 218, 223, 228, 231,
  232–50, 263, 267, 268, 269, 275,
  283, 288

Michelson, Stephen, 33
Milford, Del., 198–200
Milford High School, 198
Miller, Carla Michelle, 267
Miller, Charles (Chezzie), 189
Miller, Marlene, 262, 263, 267
Miller, Ward I., 180, 181, 183, 184,
  185, 186
Milliken v. Bradley, 217–18, 221, 222,
  223, 288
Minter, Thomas K., 206, 211
Miracle of Social Adjustment, by Carl F.
  Hansen, 18
miscegenation, 84–85, 123–24, 143–
  44, 150, 179, 181, 199, 260
Mitchell, Robert, 211
Modlin, Herbert, 263
Monroe Elementary School, 256
Moore, James, 186
Moore, T. Justin, 74–75
Morgan School, 46–49
Morris, Irving, 207, 208, 209, 210
Morris, Virginia, 55
Moss, C.G. Gordon, 73, 101–102,
  106, 110
Moss, Dickie, 109
Moton High School, 68–69, 70, 72,
  75, 78
Moton, Robert R., 68
Mount Pleasant High School, 205
Mountain Dew Gang, 188, 189
Mulrooney, Thomas W., 184
Murphy, Lance, 257, 259, 260
Myshin, Amil, 124

Nabrit, James M., 11, 62
Nader, Ralph, 260
National Association for Neighborhood Schools (NANS), 234, 235
National Association for the Advancement of Colored People (NAACP),
  oral argument in *Brown*, 4, 276,
  310 n.79; interpretation of Supreme
  Court's opinion in *Brown*, 5, 139;
  on *Brown II*, 79; and Julius W.
  Hobson, 29, 30, 31; equalization
  litigation, 67–68, 71; changes legal
  strategy—from equalization to desegregation, 71, 72; and Prince Edward County, 67, 70, 73, 74–76,
  78, 102–103, 105–106, 107; opposes token desegregation, 86, 87; opposes tuition grants, 111, 114, 115,

National Association for the Advancement of Colored People (*cont.*) 116, 149; and desegregation in Clarendon County, 132, 133, 134, 135, 144–45; and desegregation in Charleston, 145; opposes freedom of choice, 156, 157; and desegregation in Delaware, 177, 180, 199, 202, 210; denounces Senator Biden, 234; and desegregation in Topeka, 255, 267; departs from historic opposition to racial discrimination and demands preferential treatment for blacks, 276; *also see* 14, 77, 91, 101, 165, 223, 269, 295 n.104

National Association for the Advancement of White People, 198

National Conference of Christians and Jews, 180, 185, 229

National Conference of Negro Women, 102

National Education Association (NEA), 28, 228

National Review, 164

National Teacher Examination, 146, 172

Nelson, Marjory, 14

Newark, Del., 224, 225

Newark High School, 242

New Castle County, Del., 175–251, 288

New Kent County, Va., 156, 157; *also see Green v. New Kent County*

New Kent School, 156

New Republic, 13, 22, 23, 114, 115, 164, 284

New York Times, 38, 47, 72, 102, 103, 109, 114, 115, 117, 154, 180

Newsweek, 284, 298 n.166

Nixon, Richard M., 161, 162–65, 219, 226

Norfolk, Va., 91–92, 93

Novak, Robert D., 164

Oden, Don, 253, 257

Office of Civil Rights, 202; *also see* U.S. Department of Justice

Office of Education, 152–53, 155, 160, 165; *also see* U.S. Department of Health, Education, and Welfare (HEW)

Omaha Technical High School, 17

optimum mix theory, 161–62, 227, 235, 280, 283, 287; *also see* socio-

optimum mix theory (*cont.*) logical rationale for dispersion, James S. Coleman

optional transfer plans, in Washington, 37, 39, 42; in Wilmington and New Castle County, 180, 191, 216, 225–226; in Topeka, 269

Osborne, John, 164

Owen, Anna Hayes, 243

Padua Academy, 195

Panetta, Leon, 162

Parkdale Elementary School, 263, 264

Parker, John J., 6, 137, 138, 139, 154, 288

Parmenter, John, 22

Patrons (of Prince Edward Academy), 95

Peace Corps, 47, 108

Pearson, Levi, 132

Pearson, Roy, 95

peer group culture, 283; *also see* James S. Coleman, optimum mix theory, sociological rationale for dispersion

Penn, Clarence, 99

Perrow Commission, 93

Perrow, Mosby G., Jr., 93

Perry, Matthew, 159

Perry, Ronald J., 117–18, 119

Pervall, J.B., 72, 73

Peterson, Russell, 219

Phelps, Fred W., 262, 263, 264, 265, 267, 268, 269, 270

piedmont, S.C., 148, 149

Plessy v. Ferguson, 4, 5, 78, 278

Ploener, Phyllis, 207

Plowden, Charles N., 141, 145, 149

Poirier, Normand, 22

Positive Action Committee (PAC), 231–32, 233, 234

Powell, Lewis F., 93, 222, 223

prayer in school, 165–66

preferential treatment, 276; *also see* color consciousness, reparations

Presbyterian Synod (in Delaware), 189

Prettyman, E. Barrett, 11

Prichard, Bo, 98

Prickett, William, 219

Prince, Richard E., 61

Prince Edward Academy, 94–100, 101,

Prince Edward Academy (*cont.*)
105, 111, 113, 116–17, 118, 120,
121–22, 125, 127, 303 n.97
Prince Edward County High School,
120, 123–24
Prince Edward County, Va., 65–127,
129, 183, 253, 281, 284
Prince Edward School Foundation,
82–83, 94
progressive education, 25–26, 281;
in Washington, 46–49, 50, 52–
54, 60; in Prince Edward County,
108–10, 122; in Wilmington and
New Castle County, 185–87, 230,
245–46, 319–20 n.184; in Topeka,
258–60
Project E.S.O., 186
Project Expansion, 186
Project Open-Out, 186
P.S. du Pont High School, 181, 191–
95, 205, 206, 235, 240
Pucinski, Roman, 31

Rabinowitz, Howard N., 300 n.29
race riots, in Washington, 23–24, 48;
in Wilmington, 189–90, 196, 205
Racial Isolation in the Public Schools,
by U.S. Commission on Civil
Rights, 41
Raffel, Jeffrey A., 231
Ragin, William, 133
Raskin, Barbara, 48
Raskin, Marcus, 47
Raspberry, William, 54, 59, 60
Ravitch, Diane, 281
Reagan, Ronald, 278
Redd, Robert T., 96, 97–98, 281
Redd, Willie, 72, 73
Redding, Louis L., 177, 180, 200,
207, 208, 209, 210, 216
redefinition of desegregation, 3, 154–
58, 175, 204, 274; *also see Green v.
New Kent County,* U.S. Supreme
Court
Reed, Vincent, 38, 56–61, 62, 298 n.166
Rees, Grover, 279
Rehnquist, William H., 204, 222,
223, 224
Reid, Herbert O., 56
Reid, Katherine, 14
reparations, 276; *also see* affirmative
action, color consciousness, prefer-
ential treatment

Richardson, Lillian, 208, 241
Richmond News Leader, 88
Richmond Times-Dispatch, 87, 114
Riddick, Charles, 60
Rispoli, Marcello, 196
Robertson, A.G., 78–79
Robespierre, Maximilien, 276
Robinson, David W., 160
Robinson, Mr. and Mrs. Jackie, 110
Robinson, Spottswood W., 72
Rock Creek Park, 30, 37, 41, 43
Rockefeller Foundation, 236
*Rodriguez v. San Antonio Indepen-
dent School District,* 170
Rogers, Richard, 267, 270
Rogers, S. Emory, 133, 134, 136,
141–42, 145, 148–49, 167
Roosevelt, Franklin D., 136
Rorty, James, 84
Rosemond, Patricia Saltonstall, 32
Rosenthal, Joseph, 207
Ross, Billy E., 230
Roth, William V., 233, 234
Rowe, Edna F., 167, 281
Ruggiero, William, 195
Russell, Richard B., 142

St. John, Nancy H., 227
St. John's High School, 23
St. Paul's Elementary School, 160
Salesianum School, 195
*San Antonio School District v. Rodri-
guez,* 220, 221, 222, 223
SANE, 229
San Francisco, Cal., 288
Sass, Herbert Ravenall, 144
SAT scores, 20, 57–58, 97
Saturday Evening Post, 102
Saturday Review, 20
Schwartz, Murray M., 226–27, 230,
232, 239, 244, 248, 249–50, 316
n.101
Scott, Charles S., 256, 267, 268, 270
Scott, Charles S., Jr., 268, 270
Scott, Hugh, 51, 52, 53, 62
Scotts Branch School, 131, 132, 136,
160, 170
Seitz, Collins, 177, 178, 179
self-fulfilling prophecy, 36, 49, 117;
also see Kenneth B. Clark
separation of powers, 82, 90, 112,
113–14, 126, 143–44, 233
Shadd Elementary School, 45

343

Sharnoff, Gladys, 243
Shaw University, 67
Sheldon, Charles M., 264
Sheldon Elementary School, 264
Silberman, Charles E., 25, 260
Silver, S.C., 132
Simmons, Charles E., 151, 159,
    160–61, 165
Simons, William, 50–51
Sinclair, John P., 225
Sizemore, Barbara, 49, 53–54, 55, 56,
    60
Skelly, John J., 259
Smith, Bob, 66, 73
Smith, Harris P., 149
Smith, Hugh Stewart, 14
Smith, Linda Brown, 256, 257,
    269–70
Smith, M. Brewster, 74
Smith, Sally, 172–73
"soapboxing," 189
Sobeloff, Simon E., 115, 161, 162
social conservatives, 278
sociological rationale for dispersion,
    235; *also see* James S. Coleman,
    optimum mix theory
Solomon, Maisie, 133
Solon, 81
South Carolina Independent Schools
    Association, 168
Southern School News, 114
Southside, 65
Southside Schools, 104–105, 107
Sowell, Thomas, 59
Specter, Arlen, 280
Spingarn High School, 12, 15
Sputnik, 28, 281
Staff Reporter (Wilmington), 183
Stahl, Harvey E., 179
Stanley, Thomas B., 88
State School Committee (South Caro-
    lina), 142, 148
states' rights, 90; *also see* separation
    of powers
Steck, John, 105
Stevens, John Paul, 223
Stevenson, Adlai E., 108
Stewart, Potter, 223
Stiles, Lindley, 76
Stockard, James, 38
Stokes, John, 72
Stone, Chuck, 24
Stone, Harlan F., 137

Storey, Arthur, 13
Strayer, George D., 10
Street, Jea P., 241
strict construction, 163, 219
strict scrutiny, as applied by J. Skelly
    Wright, 40–41; as applied by Caleb M.
    Wright, 219–20; as applied by the
    Supreme Court, 40, 45, 220; *also
    see* Fourteenth Amendment, inten-
    tional discrimination
student boycotts, in Prince Edward
    County, 70–72; in Topeka, 255–59
Student Special Concerns Project,
    245–46
Sullivan, Neil V., 108–10
Summerton, S.C., 129–30, 131, 136,
    137, 139, 141, 145, 150, 151, 152,
    158, 159, 160, 165, 166, 167, 169,
    170, 171, 172, 173, 174, 253, 284
Summerton Elementary and High
    School, 131, 150, 160, 165, 173
Sunday News Journal, 236
Sussex County, Del., 197–204, 207,
    228, 247
Swaim, Martha, 55
*Swann v. Charlotte-Mecklenburg
    Board of Education,* 209, 221
Sweatt, Herman M., 71
Sweatt v. Painter, 71–72
Swinton, Alonzo P., 171, 173

Tatnall School, 207
tax referenda, for desegregated public
    schools, 125, 170, 248–49
Taylor, Robert, 83–84
Taylor, William L., 250
Tenth Circuit Court of Appeals, 264,
    270
Terry, Charles L., 190
test scores, in Washington, 14–15, 18,
    20, 28, 36, 54, 57, 59, 299 n.181; in
    Prince Edward County, 83, 84, 97,
    106, 119, 120–21; in Summerton,
    168, 171; in Wilmington and New
    Castle County, 187, 188, 197, 235,
    236–37, 238, 250; in Topeka, 261,
    323 n.27; *also see* 145–46, 282, 285,
    286
Theodore Roosevelt High School, 13
Third Circuit Court of Appeals, 201,
    222, 223
Thurmond, Strom, 142–43, 201
Till, Emmett, 24

Time Magazine, 20, 22–23, 102
Timmerman, George Bell, 137, 138
Tobriner, Walter N., 21
Tom, Dick and Harry Furniture
    Store, 262
Topeka High School, 254, 260, 261,
    270
Topeka, Kansas, 3, 253–71
Topeka West High School, 262, 271
Townes, Bill, 123
"trumpcats," 187
Tuck, William M., 99
tuition grants, 87, 88, 93, 100, 105,
    111, 114, 115, 116, 149
Turbeville, S.C., 169, 172
Turner, Mason E., Jr., 219
Tyler School, 14

U.S. Commission on Civil Rights, 41,
    228, 285, 327 n.41
U.S. Court of Appeals for the District
    of Columbia, 10–11, 39–40
U.S. Department of Education, 285
U.S. Department of Health, Educa-
    tion, and Welfare, 152, 161, 163,
    202, 204, 265, 266, 267, 269, 271;
    also see guidelines for interpreting
    the Civil Rights Law, Office of
    Education
U.S. Department of Justice, 149, 152,
    162, 202
U.S. Senate, 162, 278
U.S. Supreme Court, *Plessy v. Fergu-
    son,* 4, 67, 73, 77; *Sweatt v. Painter,*
    71–72; *Brown v. Topeka Board of
    Education* (Brown I), 3, 4, 5, 78,
    80, 82, 134, 138, 283; *Brown v. To-
    peka Board of Education* (Brown
    II), 12, 79, 80, 139, 141, 198; *Boll-
    ing v. Sharpe,* 6, 9, 11–12; *Griffin
    v. Prince Edward County,* 113;
    Green v. New Kent County, 7, 8,
    155–59, 277; *Milliken v. Bradley,*
    217–18, 221; *Washington v. Davis,*
    219; *Dayton v. Brinkman,* 220–21;
    on strict scrutiny, 40, 45, 170; on
    tuition grants, 116, 149; jurisdiction
    of, 143, 233, 279; *passim*
*U.S. v. Jefferson County Board of
    Education,* 154–55, 157, 158
University of Delaware, 230, 237,
    242, 250
University of Kansas, 262

University of Texas, 71
Ursuline Academy, 195

van den Haag, Ernest, 135, 147
vanden Heuvel, William J., 107
Venema, James A., 231–32, 234, 249–
    50
venereal disease, 13, 79
Vinson, Fred, 71
Violent Schools, Safe Schools, 98
Virginia and Kentucky Resolves, 89
Virginia Commission on Public Edu-
    cation, 87, 93
Virginia Council on Human Rela-
    tions, 101
Virginia Legal Aid Society, 124
Virginia Supreme Court of Appeals,
    92, 112, 113
Virginia Teachers Association, 104
voluntary desegregation, 225–26
Von Koch, Alex, 242

Wagner, Robert F., 110
Wagstaff, Roy, 211
Wall, J. Barrye, 82, 84, 86, 90, 127
Wall, J. Barrye, Jr., 104
Wall Street Journal, 281
Wannamaker, T. Elliott, 168–69
Ward, Thomas, 195
Waring, J. Waties, 133, 137, 138
Waring, Thomas R., 144
Warren County, Va., 91–92
Warren Court, 5, 221, 273, 274
Warren, Earl, 5, 78, 113, 134, 157,
    191, 264
Washington, D.C., 3, 9–63, 65, 183,
    253, 281, 284
Washington Elementary School, 257
Washington, Exie Mae, 42
Washington Post, 18, 23, 28, 42, 45,
    55, 68, 113–14, 121
Washington Teachers Union, 50–51,
    52
Washington v. Davis, 219, 220, 222,
    223, 234
Waskow, Arthur, 47
Weaver, Robert C., 59
Weber, F. David, 229
Webster, Daniel, 277
Wells, Eva, 13
West, Olivia E., 245
Western High School, 15, 42
White, Byron, 219

white flight, 16–17, 34, 42–43, 96, 158, 160, 161, 169, 175, 181, 182, 183, 193–94, 196, 203, 205, 209, 225, 228, 238–39, 246–48, 249, 253, 262, 284, 285, 287–88, 292, 322 n.220
White, Theodore H., 285
White, Walter, 71
Wilkerson, Doxey A., 29, 68
Wilkins, Roy, 79, 86, 105, 144, 145, 309 n.53
William C. Jason High School, 202
William Penn High School, 241
Williams, C. Dickerman, 279
Williams, John J., 201
Williams, J. Samuel, 118, 124
Williams, Juan, 61–62
Wilmer E. Shue Middle School, 240
Wilmington, Del., 175, 176, 177, 178, 180–97, 205–214, 216, 217, 224, 225, 226, 227, 228, 229, 230, 231, 235, 237, 238, 239, 242, 248, 251, 253, 284
Wilmington Evening Journal, 188

Wilmington High School, 191, 195–97, 240, 241, 244
Wilmington Morning News, 183, 236, 238, 239
Wilmington News Journal, 195, 228
Wilmington Youth Emergency Action Council (WYEAC), 187–91, 246
Wilson High School, 15
Winter, Harrison L., 161
Wisdom, John Minor, 154–55
Wolf, Eleanor P., 326–27 n.41
Worsham High School, 69
Worsham, Va., 94
Worthy, Dorothy, 192
Wright, Caleb M., 191, 215–16, 217, 218, 219–20, 221, 222, 223, 224, 225, 226, 227
Wright, J. Skelly, 33–46, 62–63, 220, 307–308 n.27
Wynne Campus School, 122

Young, H. Albert, 177, 198
Young, Kate, 123

The Burden of Brown has been composed on a Compugraphic digital photo-typesetter in ten point Sabon with two points of spacing between the lines. The book was designed by Jim Billingsley, typeset by Metricomp, Inc., printed offset by Thomson-Shore, Inc., and bound by John H. Dekker & Sons. The paper on which the book is printed is S.D. Warren's Olde Style Wove carrying acid-free characteristics for an effective shelf life of at least three hundred years.

THE UNIVERSITY OF TENNESSEE PRESS : KNOXVILLE